ROUTLEDGE LIBRARY EDITIONS: THE GERMAN ECONOMY

Volume 3

T0313315

ECONOMIC PLANNING AND POLICIES IN BRITAIN, FRANCE AND GERMANY

ECONOMIC PLANNING AND POLICIES IN BRITAIN, FRANCE AND GERMANY

GEOFFREY DENTON, MURRAY FORSYTH AND
MALCOLM MACLENNAN

Routledge
Taylor & Francis Group

LONDON AND NEW YORK

First published in 1968 by PEP
First published in 1969 by George Allen & Unwin Ltd

This edition first published in 2018
by Routledge
2 Park Square, Milton Park, Abingdon, Oxon OX14 4RN

and by Routledge
711 Third Avenue, New York, NY 10017

Routledge is an imprint of the Taylor & Francis Group, an informa business

British Library Cataloguing in Publication Data
A catalogue record for this book is available from the British Library

ISBN: 978-1-138-29360-1 (Set)
ISBN: 978-1-315-18656-6 (Set) (ebk)
ISBN: 978-0-415-78598-3 (Volume 3) (hbk)
ISBN: 978-0-415-78599-0 (Volume 3) (pbk)
ISBN: 978-1-315-22805-1 (Volume 3) (ebk)

Publisher's Note
The publisher has gone to great lengths to ensure the quality of this reprint but
points out that some imperfections in the original copies may be apparent.

Disclaimer
The publisher has made every effort to trace copyright holders and would welcome
correspondence from those they have been unable to trace.

ECONOMIC PLANNING AND POLICIES IN BRITAIN, FRANCE AND GERMANY

GEOFFREY DENTON
MURRAY FORSYTH
MALCOLM MACLENNAN

PEP

12 Upper Belgrave Street

London

GEORGE ALLEN & UNWIN LTD

RUSKIN HOUSE · MUSEUM STREET

PRINTED IN GREAT BRITAIN
in 11 on 12 point Ehrhardt
BY SIMSON SHAND LTD
LONDON, HERTFORD AND HARLOW

PREFACE

Two lines of study have occupied much of PEP's attention during recent years. The first concerns the problem of growth in the British economy. The second concerns the European Community and its relations with Britain, and PEP is indebted to the Ford Foundation for a grant that has made possible this programme of European studies. This book has built upon PEP's work in both these fields.

Few attempts have been made at a comparative analysis of economic policies in the three major economies of Western Europe. The reason may be that this is a bigger task than appears at first sight, because it is necessary for specialists on each of the three countries to pool their ideas and knowledge and to compare and analyse them together. This has been made possible, in this book, by the collaboration of its three authors: Geoffrey Denton, Reader in Economics at the University of Reading and formerly on the staff of PEP; Murray Forsyth, Lecturer in International Politics at the University of Leicester and likewise formerly on the staff of PEP; and Malcolm MacLennan, Lecturer in Applied Economics, Department of Social and Economic Research, University of Glasgow.

The authors wish to acknowledge the indispensable contribution to this book made by John Pinder, OBE, Director of Political and Economic Planning (PEP). John, who died in 2015 aged 90, not only initiated the concept of the book, selected the authors and persuaded them to collaborate; he also invited them on numerous weekends, both Saturdays and Sundays, to work with him at his home, examining and discussing their drafts, thereby stimulating their individual labours, and ensuring coherence in the policy comparisons. John's wife, Pauline, who had earlier worked with him at the Economist Intelligence Unit, tolerated this invasion of their privacy, and provided lunch each day. John's modesty typically allowed no recognition of their role to appear in the published volume, and this omission should be corrected.

CONTENTS

ANALYTICAL TABLE OF CONTENTS

CHAPTER 1

INTRODUCTION: PLANNING AND THE MARKET

For the major economies of Western Europe the past two decades have been a period of unprecedented prosperity. Certain scientific, technological and economic trends have contributed to this material progress and to the great alleviation of the major social ills of the first half of the century: mass poverty, unemployment, and inequality of opportunity. But these trends have also raised new problems, both for maintaining and increasing the advance in living standards, and for other social values. This book sets out to describe the new problems as they have appeared in Britain, France and the Federal Republic of Germany, and to examine the various solutions that have been attempted or proposed; and this introductory chapter begins by defining the economic trends, outlining the problems and classifying the solutions.

The main trends in Western economies have been characterized by a number of writers[1] as a decisive change in the nature of capitalist societies. A description which would be widely accepted as valid runs as follows. The prime stimulus to economic progress in advanced Western economies has been the pace of technological progress. Technological progress requires in most industries large concentrations of finance and of scientific manpower, so that it must be predominantly financed either by very large firms or by the State. The products of modern science-based industry are subject to keen international competition, which has been increased deliberately by trade-liberalization policies, and the consequences of falling behind in the technological race are severe, both for any national industry and for the economy in which it plays an important part.

[1] See especially A. Shonfield, *Modern Capitalism*, Oxford University Press, 1965; and J. K. Galbraith, *The New Industrial State*, Hamish Hamilton, 1967.

Governments have therefore been increasingly impelled to adopt a set of policies for the promotion of scientific research and training, and of invention and innovation in industry, and for the embodiment of the results in new industrial investment. But success in thus generating an adequately competitive rate of technological advance raises further difficulties. Structural change in industry is accelerated as new methods, products and industries oust the old. In many industries, if not in all, the size of firms and the degree of concentration are increased, partly on account of the technological economies of scale, partly because it is necessary to pool financial resources in order to cope with major investments. The proportion of fixed to variable cost increases, thus further encouraging the development of monopoly or oligopoly, and the formation of cartels. Over large sections of Western economies prices are no longer determined competitively in the market but are administered: output rather than price is changed in response to changes in demand, and competition is carried on primarily in terms of sales promotion or product development.

More important even than the changing structure of private industry is the alteration in the balance of economic power between private industry as a whole and the State. The role of the State is increased, not only because of the part it plays in promoting technological progress, but also because it intervenes to correct the consequences of that progress, especially to ease the adaptation of industrial structures in response to the rapidly changing patterns of production and trade, and to offset the regional imbalance which the changing location of economic activity produces. The importance of the State in economic life has been further enhanced by two activities which, though they arise from different motives, have vital influence on the trends so far described: defence spending has been decisive in the development of a number of the most advanced technologies, such as nuclear power, aircraft, electronics and computers; education, the most rapidly expanding area of public expenditure in recent years, provides the literate and numerate manpower on which scientific and technological progress is based. The numerous responsibilities that governments have accepted for social insurance, pensions, health services and other aspects of welfare, though they are not so directly associated with the industrial changes, form part of the social apparatus which is both an essential basis for, and a response to, the new economic structure. It is, moreover, not only in the sphere of public expenditure and the finance of technological development that State intervention increases. The priority given in economic policy to full employment, together with the growth of monopoly power on both sides of industry, has caused endemic pressure on the levels of prices and incomes, a depreciation in the value of currencies, and balance-of-payments problems. These difficulties have in turn given rise to further interventions, most notably in the determination of prices and incomes.

The question of how far these trends in the organization and control of Western economies may be said to constitute problems is controversial, since this depends on whether they are regarded as leading to a more desirable economic and social structure than that which they are destroying. But before we attempt to classify the different attitudes towards these changes and the solutions that are based on them, it may be helpful to outline, however briefly, the problems that most economists and politicians would be able to agree exist, even though their proposed solutions may differ radically. There appear to be three broad issues. First, the change in the relative power of the State and private organizations and individuals would be widely admitted to give rise to a need for the redefinition of the respective roles of government, private firms, workers and consumers. At present there is a degree of confusion: as the State takes over new tasks, owners and managers of private firms are required to accept much broader responsibilities than the profit maximization of traditional economic theory; workers and their official and unofficial representatives are urged to look beyond the immediate realization of maximum return for the minimum effort; and consumers are mobilized to play an active part in moderating the behaviour of other parts of the economy, rather than their usual passive reaction to the production and pricing decisions of manufacturers. Second, it is essential to achieve in the new conditions an economic mechanism that can maintain and renew the incentives and sanctions that any society needs for initiative and enterprise. The change in the economic structure, and the broadening of responsibilities and blurring of objectives to which it has contributed, imply the decay of many of the incentives of the earlier form of capitalist society, which must therefore be replaced or renewed. Third, the new forms of economic management have to solve the problem of the reconciliation of micro-economic decisions, whether by private or public agencies, with the macro-economic requirements. Here again, the mechanisms that supposedly once achieved an automatic reconciliation have been rendered more and more ineffective by the concentration of economic decisions into fewer and fewer units. To state the issues in such broad terms may be to indulge in unhelpful generalization; it is intended only as a reminder that the various schools of thought are concerned with the same problems and are, indeed, often pursuing similar objectives, even if their proposed solutions may range from full reliance on a competitive system to a highly centralized form of *dirigisme*.

Can the problems be solved by a thorough application of the principles of the competitive market system, or do they inevitably lead to the progressive replacement of the market mechanism by central direction? Or can new planning methods be grafted on to a system which remains largely a market economy? In this book, French, German and British innovations in economic policy which attempt to deal with these problems are examined. All three countries have rejected both what we may term the paleo-liberal approach of complete *laissez faire*, and the paleo-collectivist command economy. But this by no means implies that there are no choices left. There are two broad schools of thought in these, as in other Western countries, which hold what may be termed neo-collectivist and neo-liberal views. The neo-collectivist view is commonly associated with France, and the neo-liberal with Germany, though, as we shall see, the division of opinion by no means coincides with national boundaries, and there have been important changes of official thinking in both countries in recent years, which have softened the distinction between the two approaches. Britain, for its part, seems to have been seeking a compromise between the two forms of economic policy; and so, at the international level, has the European Community, in its formulation of a Medium-term Economic Policy Programme, in which both the French and the Germans have, together with the other four member States, defined a fairly wide area of agreement about the use of longer-term economic policies.

The neo-collectivist belief, which has been held especially strongly in France, is that technological progress has rendered most market mechanisms out of date, and necessitated their replacement by State administration. The financing of research by firms in competition with each other is impossible: the task must be handed over to monopolistic or at least oligopolistic units, or to the State. The pressure of economies of scale towards the monopolization of many industries is so great that an anti-trust policy cannot hope to succeed. The solution therefore is some form of central supervision of such industries, in order to ensure that their policies correspond to the public interest. One has either to accept an economy dominated by monopolistic private interests or move towards extensive State direction. As regards the volume of public expenditure, it is held that the more important private needs of the consumers have been satisfied, and that market mechanisms now tend to provoke new and artificial individual wants at the expense of urgent and real collective needs. So far as problems of regional balance are concerned, it is thought that market forces cannot be relied upon to prevent the continuing concentration of industry in certain areas and the corresponding depopulation and poverty of others. Finally, the neo-collectivists hold that the pressure on the general level of prices and incomes cannot be resisted by the use of general fiscal, monetary and competition policies, without an unacceptable level of unemployment. Limits have to be imposed on the growth of prices and incomes.

The neo-liberals on the other hand hold that, despite all the new problems, the plans of individual producers and consumers are still best co-ordinated by market mechanisms, though these must be consistently developed and adjusted to meet the new problems as they arise. The main and overriding goal of the State's economic policy, as well as the central point around which its social policy should be framed, must therefore be the preservation and positive stimulation of market mechanisms. Great emphasis is placed on securing price stability, primarily through the operation of monetary policy; excessive concentrations of economic power can be prevented by anti-trust action and by the encouragement of small and medium-sized firms; State subsidies, if they are necessary, must be temporary and degressive; the interests of the community as a whole can still be secured by the stimulation of individual initiative through individual self-interest. These are the main priorities of neo-liberal economic policy.

These differences in economic philosophy are certainly fundamental. But it is essential to know whether they really tend towards the establishment of a different kind of economic order, or whether the similar problems facing the three countries in fact evoke similar solutions. Thus it is necessary to examine not only the differences between the views that have been held on economic policy in France and in Germany, but also the actual policies, and their practical effects, if one is to understand the nature of the distinction between the neo-liberal and neo-collectivist economic methods. In this book we examine not only what these two schools have said, but also what they have done.

British practice has in recent years combined features of both these systems. If the distinction between neo-liberalism and neo-collectivism is mainly a matter of economic mythology, this pragmatic approach may be correct; and one of the objects of the study is to find out whether or not this is so.

PLANNING AND GROWTH: THE THEORY

This book is about planning and policies for growth rather than about growth itself.[1] However, it is necessary to understand the reasons for particular governmental interventions, and these must rest on some more or less explicit theory of how growth can be influenced. This section therefore reviews those theories of growth that have been influential with economic planners and are used to justify their interventions in the economic process. The purpose is only to outline the main variants as a guide to later chapters, where the relevant theories are discussed in relation to particular countries or particular problems, for example in relation to Germany in Chapter 2, to the significance of national programmes in Chapter 5, and to the balance of payments in Chapter 11.

The theory of growth starts from the simple notion that output is determined by the quantity of inputs. The chief inputs are normally classified as the traditional factors, capital and labour, and a simple macro-production function states that the gross national product is a function of capital and labour. Since labour supply is determined largely by the size and growth of population, and by social pressures which decide what proportion of the total population is active in the labour force, the length of the working week, etc., the attention of economists has tended to concentrate on the input of capital. A further reason for this preference is, of course, that labour is a consumer as well as a producer of output and that the final object of

---

[1] The most valuable recent works on growth performance in the countries covered in this book are: E. F. Denison, *Why Growth Rates Differ*, The Brookings Institution, Washington, 1967, and A. Maddison, *Economic Growth in the West*, Allen and Unwin, 1964. See also J. Knapp and K. Lomax, Britain's Growth Performance: the Enigma of the 1950s, *Lloyds Bank Review*, October 1964; and A. Maddison, How Fast can Britain Grow? *Lloyds Bank Review*, January 1966.

a growth policy is to maximize the rate of growth of output per head rather than of total product. National plans in Eastern Europe and in France have been very largely plans for increasing the total of net investment, and for raising the proportion of the gross national product devoted to it. In Britain in the late 1950s, the relatively poor growth performance was associated with a relatively low proportion of net investment to GNP in the famous 'league tables'.[1] Yet the application of a crude capital-output ratio was clearly unsatisfactory: the quality as well as the quantity of capital was extremely relevant to growth. Attention was therefore devoted to the allocation of investment to different industries and to different purposes. In particular, a distinction was drawn between investment aimed at 'widening' the capital stock and that for 'deepening' it; for in a period when the labour force was growing only very slowly, the widening investment would add to the pressure on labour supply, while the deepening investment was more relevant to the real problem, the raising of labour productivity. A distinction was also drawn, for similar reasons, between 'productive' and 'non-productive' investment, with particular emphasis on the amount of net investment in manufacturing industry. The limitations of reliance on the sheer quantity of capital diverted attention not only to the question of increasing its effectiveness, but also to that of increasing both the quantity and the efficiency of labour. The attraction of more women into industry and the use of the reserves of unemployed or underemployed labour in the less prosperous regions could enhance the growth of output per head for the whole community. The quality of the labour force could also be raised by more attention to education and training, including management education, while its efficiency could be improved by removing restrictive practices, generally reforming working methods, and speeding the process of redeployment into more productive jobs.

So far as planning and policies for growth are concerned the implications of this focusing upon factors on the supply side are by no means clear. The theory leads to no easy decision as between the neo-liberal and the neo-collectivist methods. It is possible to argue that the quantity and quality of labour and capital inputs are improved by a positive policy for enhancing competition, or alternatively, that this will be achieved by the initiative of the State as buyer

[1] The debates on this subject were examined by PEP in *Growth in the British Economy*, 1960.

of one-third of the national output, or by its operation of selective policies designed to affect the particular decisions of individual industries and firms, within or without a quantitative national programme for growth. Only a detailed assessment of particular supply problems can determine, in each case, whether the competitive model or the collectivist is the more appropriate.

There is, however, an alternative theory of growth which has been more relevant to the choice between the neo-liberal and the neo-collectivist models. This is based on the proposition that it is the expected level of demand and not shortage of factors that is the effective constraint on growth in many advanced countries. Neither the availability of finance for capital investments nor the factors affecting the supply of labour are regarded as the significant limits on growth, but rather the state of business expectations as to the future level of demand. The reduction of uncertainty, and increasing business confidence that growth will be faster in the future, become the key to a faster growth rate. Quantitative programming, it is held, can contribute to the solution of this problem by co-ordinating the market forecasts of individual firms and industries and injecting a degree of optimism into them. This view need not necessarily lead to the conviction that the government should force firms to adopt investment policies that will cause the targets to be met. It is quite conceivable that the government should try to alter expectations by means of an ambitious forecast without interfering in any way with market mechanisms, and this does not seem to be different in principle from the policies of exhortation in which neo-liberal statesmen have sometimes indulged. Nor, indeed, was the role of the targets themselves in the British National Plan much more than that of a general encouragement to industry: interventionist policies were hardly at all directed so as to force firms to make specified investments with a view to helping their industries to hit the targets. But support for quantitative programmes has in the past been generally associated with support for an extensive policy of specific government interventions, as was undertaken by French planners in the 1950s. Programmes have, therefore, tended to be a part of the policies of neo-collectivists, who held that the market, though much more flexible than any planning system in the short run, is not capable of reducing uncertainty *ex ante* so much as of bringing about an *ex post* adjustment to changing conditions by the decline and bankruptcy of some firms and the expansion of others. They felt that, while this type of adjustment may be appropriate under conditions of a multiplicity of firms, relatively slow technological change, and short gestation periods for investment, it is much harder to justify under conditions such as those described earlier: rapid technological innovation, monopoly and oligopoly as the dominant forms of industrial structure, and the need for long periods to design, construct and run in new capital investments. The theoretical advantages of quantitative planning under modern conditions, following the demand expectations theory of growth, would not, however, be a sufficient justification for the adoption of such methods; it has to be shown that national programmes implemented with the help of government intervention can in practice deal with the problems of uncertainty, especially technological uncertainty, better than firms acting autonomously in the market, even if it is an oligopolistic market.

Special problems are also raised for this theory of the relevance of quantitative planning to growth by the existence of international trading relations. The three countries we are here concerned with are all open economies, with substantial foreign trade. The reduction of uncertainty about the level of demand at home may serve little purpose if the balance-of-payments situation remains uncertain, especially if the foreign currency reserves are so low that the level of exports becomes the leading supply constraint on the rate of growth. The key factor in growth then becomes the achievement of buoyant and competitive exports in world markets, providing the assurance to home business that growth of home demand will not be curtailed by the exigencies of the balance of payments. The theory is therefore transmuted from 'demand expectations' to 'export-led growth'.

Whether the competitive model or an interventionist programming model is accepted, whether the supply factors or the level of demand are stressed in the theory of how growth is caused, a virtuous or a vicious circle is a crucial element in the situation facing these countries. According to the theory of demand expectations, a high level of current demand will increase the rate of growth by giving rise to sanguine expectations about the future level of demand: that is, it is growth that causes growth, unless expectations of future growth can be stimulated by means of persuasion rather than past performance. According to the theory that rests on the supply constraints, the achievement of a breakthrough in the proportion of investment, the level of productivity, or the competitiveness of exports (and these may well amount to the same thing) will enable further such improvements to continue, with further cumulative effects, and a continuation of high growth rates.

The popular theories of growth have therefore given rise to three main variants of economic policy. First, the theory of demand expectations has given theoretical support to those who believe in the efficacy of quantitative targets, and who often combine this with a belief in the desirability of interventionist policies to ensure that industry meets these targets. This school of thought may be called 'demand-side collectivist'. This theory is most likely to be held by those who wish to accelerate growth in an economy that has previously been growing only slowly and where it may be important to raise rates of investment, an objective which may be achieved, at least in part, by raising expectations. If it is a question of maintaining a rate of growth that has already come to be accepted as 'normal', however, action on the demand side is less likely to be relevant, although the reduction of uncertainty that is claimed for medium-term quantitative programmes can in theory be relevant in both these cases, through its effect in maintaining a more stable level of investment. Therefore, there is a second theory that stresses the supply side, and gives support to those we may call 'supply-side collectivists', who believe in selective interventions to overcome 'obstacles to growth'. Thirdly, the supply-side theory is also consistent with the neo-liberal view that such obstacles to growth are best removed by the operation of general market sanctions and incentives. After examining the detail in the intervening chapters, we shall attempt in the 'Conclusions' to make a more general assessment of the systems of policy based on these three variants.

PLANNING AND POLICIES FOR GROWTH

The word 'planning' is often used to describe a group of these policy innovations, usually associated with the neo-collectivist school of thought; and the term 'planned economy' is used where such 'planning' takes place. This terminology has, however, been used so loosely and in so many different senses that it has tended to confuse rather than clarify. The terms are often employed as if the difference between a 'planned' and 'non-planned' economy was something that could readily be known by the application of some simple criteria. The existence of a quantitative programme for the growth of the main industries and economic aggregates over a medium-term period (4–7 years) is held generally to be a necessary and a central criterion, and sometimes indeed to be sufficient by itself to justify the use of the term 'planning'. But the term is also associated with the use of policies in order to attain defined objectives. The mere existence of a quantitative programme could not, therefore, be a sufficient indication that 'planning' also exists: the use of policy instruments that help more or less effectively to secure achievement of the objectives of the 'plan' would also be necessary. These objectives are commonly thought to be the numerical targets of the quantitative programme. It is, however, not at all easy, in the present state of econometrics, to know how far given policy measures are likely to contribute to the achievement of quantitative objectives, in relation to all the other factors that will influence the result. In these circumstances there is a tendency among sophisticated 'planners', for example in France, to emphasize the achievement of qualitative objectives such as structural reorganization in industry or the stimulation of research and development or of exports, and to lay less emphasis on the numerical targets. This leads one to ask whether the quantitative programme need be so central to the definition of planning (or even necessary to it). This is not to cast doubt on the value of a quantitative programme as a tool of analysis for policy-makers; it is merely to stress that, if the term 'planning' is to be defined in such a way as to be useful in discussions of economic policy, too much emphasis should not be laid on the quantitative targets.

Any useful definition of 'planning' must, then, take account of the extent to which economic policies are effectively employed to achieve the objectives of the 'plan'. This requires an assessment of the extent to which policies are so employed in each main sector of policy. Even with respect to each of these sectors, it would be preferable to say that an economy was 'more planned' or 'less planned' rather than 'planned' or 'not planned'. Since a given economy might well be 'more planned' in some sectors of policy and 'less planned' in others, it will be seen that a proper definition of the term 'planned economy' is a complex matter.

So much confusion and ill-informed controversy have in fact surrounded the use of the terms 'planning' and 'planned economy' that we thought it better to employ them only sparingly except where their meaning is specific and is made quite clear by the context, e.g. the Fifth French Plan, the French planners, and the British National Plan. The following analysis of the policy innovations with which this book is concerned will, however, also show to which aspects of them the word planning tends to be attached, and may at the same time point the way towards a definition that would make the word more useful in economic discussion in the future.

The objectives of policy

Most Western governments now recognize a wide range of objectives of economic policy. Many policy innovations have resulted from new emphasis on objectives such as faster growth or a fairer distribution of income. Although different governments have pursued particular objectives with different degrees of persistence, in different orders of priority and, most important, with varying readiness to sacrifice related objectives, there has been widespread agreement that at least some weight should be attached to the following:

> price stability
> a satisfactory balance of external payments
> full employment
> fairer distribution of income or wealth
> adequate provision of social goods
> a substantial rate of growth of GNP
> balanced development of the country's regions
> restriction of the growth of money incomes to that of productivity
> sufficient competition between firms and equal competitive conditions.

The adoption of some of these objectives, such as price stability and a satisfactory balance of payments, has come to be regarded as virtually obligatory on any government worthy of the name, although they have both been stressed particularly strongly by the German neo-liberals, who have contended that other desirable things, for example full employment and growth, will in the long run follow if these objectives are steadfastly pursued. Full employment and redistribution have come to be accepted as normal in both Britain and France since the war, and the provision of social goods was indeed a major element in the strategy of the French Fifth Plan. Redistribution and social welfare expenditure are also accepted by German neo-liberals as objectives in their own right, but with the emphasis on the wider distribution of wealth in order to place the diffusion of economic power and the wider distribution of income on a more permanent footing, and on the provision of social goods in such a way as to minimize interference with market mechanisms.

It is, however, the attainment of a substantial rate of growth that has been central to the establishment of the institutions of the French Plan and to the emergence of the 'planning movement' in Britain. If the German neo-liberals have denied that rapid growth was one of their main objectives, it nevertheless appears that their policies have usually been well adapted to encourage it and most successful in doing so. The acceptance of rapid growth as a major criterion of the success of economic policy is, indeed, the most important postwar development in relation to economic objectives, and policies for growth are consequently the central theme of this book.

Balanced regional development is an objective that also has been closely connected with planning innovations in Britain and France. The same applies to the restriction of the growth of money incomes to that of productivity, if for different reasons. This is in fact merely another way of stating the stability of prices. But it has been found desirable to restate the objective in this way because in conditions of full employment monetary and fiscal policy have, by themselves, proved inadequate to prevent inflation caused by cost push which results from the prevalence of monopolies and oligopolies among both firms and trade unions. Institutions and policies are therefore being developed to supplement monetary and fiscal policy by acting directly on prices and incomes, and particularly in order to keep the growth of incomes within the growth of real productivity.

Sufficient competition between firms is similarly a means to other objectives rather than a final objective, at least in economic terms, although it can also be regarded as an expression, in the economic field, of the political objective of freedom. Under current usage competition is often held to have little to do with planning, or indeed to be its antithesis. But if competition can reasonably be supposed to make a major contribution to the achievement of the objectives of price stability, a balance on external payments and a fast rate of growth, any consideration of growth policy or prices and incomes policy will be seriously inadequate if it does not take competition policy into account; and if, as the neo-liberals contend, competition policy should comprise both long-term structural elements and a practice of active State intervention it begins to appear doubtful whether this element of policy should be excluded from the scope of a proper definition of planning.

Associated with the objective of sufficient competition between firms, which may be furthered by such means as policies to prevent restrictive practices or the creation of monopolies, is that of ensuring that firms compete under equal conditions. Theoretically, economic activity is 'optimized' if economic agents (consumers, entrepreneurs) can choose what to buy and sell at prices that are undistorted by forces other than those that operate in a perfectly competitive market. Government policies are 'neutral' if they introduce no new distortions, or counter distortions that already exist, and the neo-liberal aim is that policies should be as neutral as possible, and that any distortions introduced or allowed by the government to achieve specific objectives should be both temporary and degressive.

Even if a rapid rate of growth has, first in France then in Britain, become an essential and at times the predominant objective of economic policy, it does not seem wise to tie the definition of planning too exclusively to the adoption of this objective. Growth takes its place among the other objectives that have been discussed; it has already been pointed out that the provision of more social goods is a major objective of the French Fifth Plan, which is to some extent in conflict with the possibilities of faster growth of GNP. The making of a reasoned choice among various possible combinations of objectives is a better basis for a definition of planning than the adoption of any single objective such as a rapid rate of growth; and quantitative programmes are more likely to be relevant in making it possible to choose one's combination of objectives in a rational manner than in providing a precise numerical target for the growth of GNP as a single objective that overrides all others.

The institutions of economic policy
The policy innovations that are considered in this book have been closely associated with changes in the institutions for forming economic policy, or for directly influencing the economy. Changes designed to improve the process of arriving at governmental decisions, to take account of the adoption of the growth objective, have taken two forms. The first has been the reorganization of existing government departments, especially finance ministries, setting up special divisions concerned with medium- and long-term growth

policy, and seeking to establish procedures to give these new divisions adequate influence *vis-à-vis* those concerned with short-term problems. The second method, which may well follow an unsatisfactory experience of the first, has been to set up new departments with separate political heads, implying that the final reconciliation of growth with other objectives is passed to cabinet level rather than being determined within a single department that is also concerned with short-term financial and economic management.

In addition to changes within the machinery of government, the adoption of growth as a major objective has also led in some countries, but notably not in Germany, to the formation of new tripartite institutions, intended to associate business and the trade unions closely with the government in the management of the economy. These tripartite bodies at the national level have been placed in a special position, being neither within nor entirely separate from the machinery of government. They have been intended both to associate the two interest groups with the government in determining national economic policy, and to influence directly the policies of industry and the trade unions in directions consistent with the government's objectives. They are seen as contributing to a much closer co-operation and involvement of the two sides of industry with the government in the attainment of national economic objectives, especially growth.

This new close association of industry and trade unions with the government has, in Britain and France, been extended to the level of the individual industry. These tripartite industrial committees, feeding information back to the national institutions, are intended to ensure that the association of the three policy-making groups in economic policy is not restricted to generalizations, but has practical content and relevance to industrial problems.

New regional institutions have also been established and have been linked with the national institutions set up to plan for growth. New institutions have likewise been established to relate prices and incomes policy to growth and productivity and these have, naturally, stressed the tripartite approach.

It is probably not wise to be precise about the institutional criteria in any definition of planning; the institutions depend so much on the political and social circumstances of the country concerned. But it is fair to say that one element of planning should be the adaptation of institutions so that all the objectives adopted, including growth, are taken properly into account in the formation of policy, and so that adequate attention is paid by the policy-makers to quantitative assessments and forecasts. It can also be said that the existence of tripartite industrial committees is associated with a degree of detailed industrial planning.

The instruments of economic policy

New thinking about economic objectives, and in particular the adoption of a growth objective, has been accompanied by considerable changes in the use of instruments of economic policy. These have taken several forms: the adaptation of traditional policy instruments, such as monetary policy and fiscal policy, to the requirements of a new objective; the development of virtually new forms of policy, of which the prices and incomes policy is an outstanding example; and the relating of policy instruments to the framework of a national programme.

Traditional policies can be adapted to a bewildering degree of variety. A few only of the major adaptations, especially those that have a bearing on growth policy, are discussed in Chapters 2, 4, 6, 7 and 8. A broad distinction may be drawn between the removal of 'obstacles to growth', and the more positive biasing of the economy in ways favourable to growth, though the line between them is not easy to draw in practice. Chapter 2 describes the systematic and theoretically based adaptation of the German economy, while Chapter 4 devotes some attention to the more pragmatic changes in British policy in recent years. The further distinction may be made, although again it is not in practice clear cut, between a neutral policy and a selective policy which discriminates in its impact on individual decision-taking units. This distinction is discussed especially in Chapter 7.

An incomes policy, that is a direct institutional intervention in the formation of prices and incomes, is an example of a policy innovation that has been related to the growth objective. Although incomes policy can arise also through concern about price stability or the balance of payments, even in the absence of a growth objective, the adoption of a growth objective and the use of national programmes have greatly stimulated attempts to find a way of securing a satisfactory relationship between the growth of incomes and that of productivity. Policies on prices and incomes in the three countries are considered in Chapter 9.

A national programme may also be regarded as a policy innovation, as well as a series of growth objectives. It can aim, like the incomes policy, at a direct involvement of private collective organizations such as trade unions and employers' associations in order to influence the decisions of independent units in the economy. It can also influence public attitudes in such a way as to make other policy changes more effective. An indicative programme may do no more than provide a background against which the policies of government departments and individual firms are formed; or such policies may be closely integrated into a detailed and more imperative programme. In the latter case one would expect official policies to be biased toward more interventionist and selective measures.

Quantitative programmes
A quantitative programme can, then, take various forms, which have differing implications for economic policy. Individual State enterprises normally formulate their own investment programmes, just as large private firms do, and the government may co-ordinate the programmes of State enterprises and of government departments in such a way as to present a co-ordinated investment programme for the public sector. This may be organized in order to guide the economy along a particular path, using not only control over the investments of State enterprises and departments, but also their indirect influence, as suppliers and customers, on the private sector.

The programme may be extended to cover the private sector as well. Broad macro-economic forecasts can be made, or targets set, for the whole economy with respect to output, investment, savings, manpower, exports, imports, etc. Forecasts or targets can also be provided for individual industries, as has been done in the French Plans and the British National Plan. Finally, targets may be further disaggregated to the individual firm, either, as in orthodox Soviet planning, as a deliberate and essential part of the system, or as a practical consequence of setting industry-level targets, when investment decisions in oligopolistic industries are influenced by the planners in order to hit the targets.

It could be said that an economy was 'more-planned' the more the forecasts in its programme reach down to the level of the individual industry or the individual firm. But the relevance of the forecasts and the degree to which they constitute 'planning' is not determined only by how detailed and specific they are. It is necessary

also to pay attention to the varying degrees and methods of implementation of the forecasts, that is, the extent to which they are
regarded as targets. At one extreme the programme, having been
published, may be left to stand or fall according to its own, mainly
psychological, impact. The greater the degree of detail in the
programme, the greater this impact probably will be because of the
greater involvement of interest groups in its preparation. Nevertheless, the most detailed programme, without supporting measures,
may be less effective than the most general programme which is
supported by policy changes. At the other extreme, the national
programme may be backed up by very specific policy measures
that are closely integrated into its structure, so that it becomes a
framework for incentives and sanctions that are intended to ensure
its implementation by individual firms. Thus a national programme
may be little more than a statistical and public relations exercise; it
may be used in a serious way as a framework for the formation of
general economic policy; it may be the basis for a flexible 'indicative
plan' whereby incentives and sanctions are to a certain degree used
selectively to guide industries or firms towards targets in an
economy that is based predominantly on the free enterprise system;
or it may be the basis for a rigid 'imperative plan' in a command
economy where each enterprise receives instructions from the
State about its production, investment and prices.

It is useful also to distinguish the various quantitative programmes according to their time horizon. This may vary from short-
term programmes of one year, as used extensively in the Netherlands, through medium-term programmes of four, five or six
years, to long-term plans of ten, twenty or more years. The medium-
term programmes tend to be most closely associated with the
adoption of a growth objective; for short-term plans are too much
at the mercy of cyclical fluctuations, and too short for effective
planning of investment, to have a decisive impact on growth;
while the long-term plans, though important in providing a perspective within which to set plans for shorter periods, are too
remote from immediate decisions, and too much affected by uncertainty, especially in respect of technological developments.

The degree of State intervention
In each of the three countries under study, the new policies have
been associated with a substantial degree of State intervention.

The point hardly needs making with regard to Britain and France. This is partly, but only partly, a function of the size of the public sector and of the extent of public ownership of industry, which gives the State a ready opportunity to exercise direct control over investment, pricing and other decisions in the public enterprises. The larger the public sector, the larger *ceteris paribus* is likely to be the degree of government intervention. But it is control rather than ownership that is relevant, and public ownership does not always increase effective State control in an individual enterprise or industry. Nor does State ownership necessarily imply co-ordination between one State-owned industry and another. Public ownership is therefore conducive to a greater degree of intervention and of more co-ordination of individual enterprises, but whether this actually happens will depend on the administration of individual nationalized firms or industries, and the extent to which their development is integrated.

It is well known that German economic policy too has in fact been in many ways interventionist in the postwar years. But it is less widely realized that German neo-liberal doctrine recognizes the need for an active policy of State intervention to ensure that market mechanisms work as efficiently as possible, and that the social market economy implies extensive State activity for social reasons (see Chapter 2).

The word 'planning' is sometimes used in such a way as to imply that the greater the degree of State intervention in the economic process, the 'more planned' the economy. But, just as it seems misguided to call an economy 'planned' solely because a set of quantitative targets have been formulated, and regardless of the measures that may be taken to bring them about, so it seems unwise to call an economy 'planned' just because there is a lot of State intervention, and regardless of the extent to which it is directed coherently and effectively towards the achievement of explicit objectives.

B

CHAPTER 2

GERMANY: THE COMPETITIVE ORDER

The remarkable performance of West Germany's economy since the 1948 Currency Reform is well known. In terms of growth without inflation, the country's record has been one of the best in the non-Communist world. Less well known are the principles which have guided Germany's economic policy during this period and the extent to which they have been put into practice. The ideas expressed by Dr Erhard, the man who, until 1966, was chiefly responsible for German economic policy, have sometimes been regarded as a mere sophistry to mask action which has differed in no essential from that taken in other countries, and sometimes as an economic theory which has been implemented in every detail. Sometimes German policy is considered as a resuscitated *laissez faire* and sometimes as a kind of ingenious *dirigisme*. This chapter first examines the principles on which German economic policy during the period is claimed to be based, and then considers how far practice has followed theory. The reader who is already familiar with the theoretical aspects of German policy may wish to turn straight to page 50, where the section on practice begins.

THE THEORY

The guiding concept which the framers of German economic policy claim to have followed since 1948 is that of the 'social market economy'. The phrase was first given currency in 1946 by Professor Müller-Armack, who has not only written extensively on economics, but has also been one of Dr Erhard's closest advisers. Professor Müller-Armack has defined the concept in this way: 'The idea of the social market economy, if we look at its spiritual roots, has its origin in neo-liberal economic ideas, or in that revival of economic science which stressed the vital function of the principle of competition and at the same time sought to establish, in contrast to old-fashioned liberalism, a competitive order in accordance with the ideas of Walter Eucken and Franz Böhm.'[1]

To understand the principles of German economic policy, then, it is essential to begin by looking at German neo-liberalism, and in particular at the ideas of the so-called 'Freiburg School', which was founded in 1932-3 and whose leading members were Walter Eucken and Franz Böhm. Although during the course of the Third Reich many of its members left the country, the School's dominant figure, Walter Eucken, remained at Freiburg throughout this period. He was a member of the Goerdeler resistance 'circle' and was arrested by the Gestapo after the July 1944 bomb plot, but fortunately his release was secured. After the war he became a prominent figure in the discussions on future German economic policy; indeed, he stood in relation to German economic policy in very much the same relationship as Keynes did to British policy. Like Keynes, he did not live to see how far his ideas were implemented, as he died in 1950.

It is unnecessary here to enter into every facet of Eucken's economic theory and analysis. The two main elements which are relevant to this study are first, his methodology, in particular his concept of the economic 'order', and secondly, his proposals for the future, and in particular his advocacy of the 'competitive order'. Both these elements are expounded fully in Eucken's *Die Grundlagen der Nationalökonomie* (1940) and in *Grundsätze der Wirtschaftspolitik*, published posthumously in 1952.[2]

Eucken stressed repeatedly that his method, his approach to economics, was of greater importance than any particular result which it produced. The starting point of economic enquiry was the economic plan of the individual economic unit: firm, household, farm or whatever it might be. The main problem to be solved was

[1] A. Müller-Armack, *Studien zur Sozialen Marktwirtschaft*, Institut für Wirtschaftspolitik an der Universität zu Köln, Cologne, 1960, p. 10. This article, together with the article Wirtschaftslenkung und Marktwirtschaft (1946) in which Professor Müller-Armack first used the phrase 'social market economy', can both be found in A. Müller-Armack, *Wirtschafts-Ordnung und Wirtschaftspolitik*, Freiburg am Breisgau, Verlag Rombach, 1966.

[2] W. Eucken, *Die Grundlagen der Nationalökonomie*, Godesberg, Küpper (5th ed.), 1947 (this has been translated into English by T. W. Hutchison: *The Foundations of Economics*, Edinburgh, Hodge, 1950); *Grundsätze der Wirtschaftspolitik*, Tübingen, J. C. B. Mohr (Paul Siebeck), 1952.

that of the effective co-ordination of the many economic plans which went to make up the economic process in any given society. The first task was to discover how many forms of co-ordination were *possible*. To do this, Eucken elaborated, like Weber, before him, a number of 'pure forms' or 'ideal types'. Strongly influenced by Kant, Eucken believed that such concepts were essential in order to make analysis meaningful, 'or to reveal necessary relationships and unity where the naïve thinker sees only chance and arbitrariness'.[1]

In Eucken's view two basic forms or types were distinguishable in history: the centrally directed economy, and the exchange economy. The former was a system of subordination under one planning body, the latter a system of co-ordination in which individual plans were linked together by means of price or exchange values. Each of these two basic forms was capable of subdivision. The centrally directed economy could either be a small one, capable of being overseen by one man, in which case Eucken called it an 'independent economy', or it could embrace the economic process of a whole people, in which case he termed it 'the centrally administered economy'. The 'pure form' of the exchange economy was also capable of subdivision, depending on the 'market forms'. There were twenty-five such market forms in Eucken's morphology ranging from complete competition on the side of both supply and demand to monopoly on both sides. Each side of each market could further be 'open' (i.e. open to foreign competition) or 'closed'. An exchange economy could thus either be dominated by monopolies (single or collective) in which case it was co-ordinated by 'groups', or it could be composed of competitive markets in which case it was co-ordinated by competition. As a final instrument for classifying the exchange economy Eucken distinguished the various possible monetary systems.[2]

---

[1] W. Eucken, *Foundations*, op. cit., p. 300.

[2] cf. W. Eucken, *Grundsätze*, op. cit., p. 21 ff. In contrast to Weber, Eucken stressed that his 'pure forms' were not totally abstract, but derived from economic reality itself. His insistence can be understood if it is realized that Eucken was attempting to bridge the cleavage between economists of the 'historical school', who were immersed in the detail of reality, and those of the 'theoretical school', who tended to ignore reality in favour of models. For a critique of Eucken's methodology, see F. Machlup, Idealtypus, Wirklichkeit und Konstruktion, *Ordo*, Vol. 12, Düsseldorf and Munich, Küpper, 1961, p. 21. For a suggested modification of his typology see N. Kloten, Zur Typenheit der Wirtschafts- und Gesellschaftsordnungen, *Ordo*, Vol. 7, 1955, p. 123.

The basic pure forms, the market forms, and the montary systems were the constituent elements of Eucken's morphological system for classifying all possible forms of economic co-ordination. They were, in F. W. Meyer's words, equivalent to an 'alphabet of individual letters, combinations of which can without difficulty be made as needed for concrete problems'.[1] Or as Eucken himself wrote: 'Just as a huge variety of words of different composition can be formed out of two dozen letters, similarly an almost unlimited variety of actual economic systems can be made up out of a limited number of basic pure forms.'[2] We are now in a position to understand Eucken's central concept of the economic 'order', for this was no more and no less than the 'totality of realized forms within which, at any given time, firms and households are linked together, or in other words within which the economic process conducts itself *in concreto*'.[3] It was within this *total* framework that all particular economic problems in all periods of history had to be examined. What Eucken called 'pointilliste' economics—looking at a particular problem in isolation from the economic order which conditioned it —could only be misleading.

It is worth stressing that Eucken did not see all existing economic systems as being either totally 'centrally administered', or completely dominated by groups, or completely co-ordinated by competition. Most existing orders combined mixed forms. In Germany immediately before the 1948 Currency Reform, for example, the economic order was a bizarre mixture of the centrally administered economy, the exchange economy, and the independent economy (that is, family units producing solely for their own consumption). But when one or another form began to *dominate* an economy, then all particular actions or measures changed their nature. Thus within two economic orders in which different forms dominated, identical actions could mean quite different things. For example, in an economy in which central administration dominated, an anti-cartel law would mean virtually nothing; whereas in an exchange economy it would be highly important. The restriction of self-financing by firms in two such economies would also mean quite different things: in one it would make firms more dependent on the plans of the central authorities; in the other it could be a means of

[1] Quoted in W. Eucken, *Foundations*, op. cit., p. 300.
[2] Ibid., p. 109.
[3] W. Eucken, *Grundsätze*, op. cit., p. 372.

stimulating the capital market and preventing the concentration of economic power.

The concept of the economic order is clarified by contrasting it with the ideas to which it was opposed. At the most obvious level Eucken's terminology provided an alternative to the contentious and imprecise phrases 'capitalism' and 'socialism' which had so long clouded economic discussions. Instead of slogans left over from the battles of the nineteenth century Eucken's 'pure forms' and his concept of the economic order provided a vocabulary for describing economic structures which was 'value-free'. That economic discussion in Germany is now largely unencumbered by disputes over 'capitalism' may be attributed partly to the influence of Eucken's concepts. Similarly the concept of the economic order ran counter to many of the determinist myths. Eucken recognized the existence of certain historical trends, notably that towards monopoly, and indeed he stressed that in attempting to establish a particular economic order careful attention should be paid to the historical circumstances. He strenuously opposed, however, the idea that 'history' was moving society in the direction of one particular order or another. In his view history showed that certain types of economic order appeared and reappeared continuously. In Germany, for example, the monopolistic exchange economy of Weimar had given way to the central administration of the Third Reich, which had in turn collapsed into the most primitive form of exchange economy, barter, in 1945, which in turn had been transformed into an economy where central administration and exchange mechanisms jostled uneasily, and which finally in 1948 began to move decisively in the direction of a competitive exchange economy. The sensible approach was not to identify oneself with some inevitable historical movement, whether 'late' capitalism, or 'early' socialism, but to assess the effectiveness and humanity of different kinds of order, to choose the best, and then work actively to establish it.

If Eucken's methodology had certain clear advantages, it also had one disadvantage. This was a tendency to make people think of economic structures too rigidly in terms of black and white. This showed itself particularly in Germany after the Currency Reform, when the economic policy makers tended to dismiss anything that was even remotely connected with a centrally administered economy, such as medium-term forecasts for the economy as a whole, as incompatible with their own market economy. But this rigid approach has recently been softening. It now seems to be recognized that not all that goes by the name of 'planning' necessarily leads to a centrally administered economy.

In Eucken's view the most efficient and at the same time the most humane economic order was an exchange economy in which the market form of 'complete competition' prevailed. This was what he termed the 'competitive order'. The competitive order was certainly not anti-interventionist. What was important was for intervention to be moulded in the right way. As Eucken remarked in a striking phrase: 'more or less State activity—this kind of question misses the point. It is not a quantitative but a qualitative problem.'[1]—and, in more detail: 'The basic principle does not simply require that certain measures of economic policy should be avoided, e.g. State subsidies, the establishment of State monopolies, the freezing of prices, import restrictions, etc. It is also insufficient to forbid cartels. The principle is not primarily negative. Far more essential is a positive policy which aims at bringing the market form of complete competition into being, and which thereby fulfils the basic principle. It is here that the policy of the competitive order differs completely from the policy of *laissez faire* which, according to its own basic principles, did not recognize the need for a positive economic policy.'[2]

Certain principles were laid down as a guide to intervention in the competitive order, divided into 'constituent' and 'regulating' principles. The most important constituent principle was 'the primacy of monetary policy': 'All attempts to establish a competitive order will be in vain if a certain stability of the currency is not ensured. Monetary policy is therefore of primary importance for the competitive order. Only when one has succeeded in building a currency stabilizer into the monetary system can we hope that the tendencies immanent in a competitive order will work towards equilibrium, instead of transforming themselves, as they have done in the past because of the faulty construction of the monetary system, into an everlasting cyclical movement from inflation to deflation.'[3] Eucken was, indeed, remarkably optimistic regarding cyclical fluctuations. Once the basic principles of the competitive order had been implemented and the monetary system properly constructed on the lines he suggested, then he considered that 'special' anti-cyclical measures,

[1] W. Eucken, *Grundsätze*, op. cit., p. 336.
[2] Ibid., p. 254.
[3] Ibid., pp. 256–7.

in the form of tax changes or changes in public expenditure, would be necessary only on rare occasions. To ensure that monetary policy was not side-tracked from its main objective of maintaining stability, whether by political pressures, interest groups, theories of full employment or other influences, he recommended that it should be so arranged, as far as possible, to work automatically.

It was also essential for the competitive order to have 'open markets'. By this Eucken meant not only the removal of protective tariffs and of State controls on private industry, but the reduction to a minimum of quasi-monopolistic privileges granted by the State, the banning of restrictive practices, the introduction of maximum freedom in choosing one's trade or profession, the adaptation of patent legislation to encourage rather than restrict competition, and so on.

The remaining 'constituent' principles may be briefly summarized. Private ownership of the means of production and freedom to dispose of one's property were essential in the competitive order, just as the other elements of the order were essential to ensure that private property was not misused to the detriment of the common good. Freedom of contract was essential, but again only to the extent that contracts were not used to restrict competition. Company liability would have to be limited in a competitive order only to the extent strictly necessary, and such limitations as were imposed should certainly not encourage unnecessary industrial concentration. Economic policy should be kept as constant as possible to provide a steady basis for firms' planning and investment decisions. Finally, it was essential that all the principles were implemented together: it would be fruitless to select only one or two and ignore the rest.

Of the 'regulating' principles which were necessary to prevent possible distortions, perhaps the most important was the need to fight the trend towards monopoly. A progressive income tax could serve to correct distortions in the distribution of incomes within the competitive order, though there would have to be limits to the degree of progression so as to prevent it from relaxing or slackening the propensity to invest. In the labour market, where supply was 'anomalous', i.e. it could increase as wages went down, the fixing of minimum wages might be necessary. There would be instances when the plans of the individual firm would clearly run counter to the common interest; for example, the excessive destruction of natural resources, the pollution of water by chemical factories and the use of child labour. In such cases limitation of a firm's freedom of action was clearly necessary. But Eucken did not see the problem of social costs as something which threw the whole competitive process out of gear, or rendered market mechanisms out of date; rather there were certain clearly definable situations where corrective action would have to be taken. Regarding social policy, all the elements of the competitive order could be considered as being 'social' in that they helped to preserve the freedom of the individual and increase the supply of goods. The emphasis of social policy itself should be as far as possible on insurance and self-help, and welfare expenditure should be reserved for those who truly needed it.

This summary of the main elements of Eucken's competitive order has illustrated the comprehensiveness of his approach to the problems of economic policy. It is this comprehensiveness which is one of the key distinguishing marks of German neo-liberalism. Many of the specific recommendations or policy proposals made in neo-liberal circles have indeed been made elsewhere; but it is rare that one finds outside Germany such a positive attempt to mould all the elements of economic policy according to a single concept. It is also clear that the theoretical model for German economic policy after the 1948 Currency Reform was not one of *laissez faire*, even if in the prevailing circumstances the drift of government policy was, during the 1950s, in the direction of decontrol rather than of intervention by the State. There remain certain key points in Eucken's theory which require further development and analysis if this account of the theory behind German economic policy is to be in any sense complete. The first is the concept of 'complete competition'; the second is that of the correct limits of State intervention in a competitive order; the third is the place of anti-cyclical measures in such an order; and the fourth, though not the least important, is the ethical and political aspects of neo-liberal teaching.

Eucken argued, as has been indicated, that the competitive order required the establishment and maintenance of the market form of complete competition throughout the economy. Frequently he elaborated on this and called it 'complete productive competition'. Since this phrase is part of general neo-liberal usage it is important to make its meaning clear. Eucken stressed time and again that complete competition was not the 'perfect' or 'pure' competition defined by Anglo-Saxon economists such as J. Robinson and E. H. Chamberlin. The assumption that true competition only exists when there are an immense number of market participants of approximately the same strength, all offering identical products, was for Eucken an over-abstract one which excluded from the start any possibility of describing competition as it existed in the real world. Where he agreed with the 'perfect competition' school was in rejecting at the same time the assumption that the 'ruinous' or 'cut-throat' activity described by Marx provided the hall-mark of competition. This was, in Eucken's view, merely the 'struggle for monopoly'. True or 'complete competition' was a 'parallel race' to improve performance. It existed as a given process rather than as an abstract hypothesis, and its presence could be tested by a number of indicators, of which the size of the market was only one. The main objective should be to maximize its existence. 'What matters is not the degree to which the conditions for perfect competition are fulfilled, but the opportunity for the free and untrammelled exercise of all competitive energies which, in fact, exist. Every addition to competition is a gain, every diminution is a loss. . . . The extent to which competitive energies can be mobilized in any given country, and the degree to which the conditions for effective competition can be improved in a given market, is not a question for theoretical discussion or historical speculation; it can only be answered by political experiment.'[1] The neo-liberal definition is susceptible to attack from those who consider that competition is essentially aggressive, that each firm must seek to expand at the expense of others, and that industry must have a monopolistic element if it is to progress, and who therefore feel that the view of competition as essentially a parallel race to improve performance is either idealistic or hypocritical. To this accusation the neo-liberal can answer that there is indeed a streak of idealism in his definition, but that it is an idealism that is capable of producing practical and beneficial results.

One further comment may be made about Eucken's views on competition, and this concerns his attitude towards concentration. It has been noted that Eucken recognized a 'trend towards monopoly' which required active counter-measures in a competitive order. He strenuously opposed the notion, however, that technological development necessarily or inevitably caused the growth of vast industrial

[1] F. Böhm, in *Monopoly and Competition and their Regulation*, E. H. Chamberlin (ed.), Macmillan, 1954, pp. 157–8.

combines. Although such progress undoubtedly meant that the physical units of production increased in size, it did not necessarily mean that the legal units of production had constantly to merge, combine or concentrate. Any impetus which technological progress did give to such concentration was balanced by the impetus which it concomitantly gave to competition, by improving and cheapening transport and thus linking together hitherto isolated markets, by speeding up the process of substitution, and by making machinery easily adaptable to new and different kinds of production.[1]

The second feature of Eucken's theories requiring further analysis is the criteria for State intervention in a competitive order. It has been shown that this order is not anti-interventionist by nature, and he attempted to provide guidelines for intervention in such an economy. In his view the art of intervention was to avoid 'particular' (*punktuelle*) interventions in the economic process itself and to act only on and through what he called the '*gesamtwirtschaftlichen Daten*', the data which affected the economy as a whole. There were six such data: the needs of the people, the natural resources, the usable labour force, the stocks of goods already produced, the level of technical knowledge, and the legal and social order. For Eucken it was this sixth datum which provided the main scope for State action to influence the economy. Correct moulding of the legal and social order would obviate the need for particular interventions.

The attempt to provide general criteria for State intervention may be seen as the starting point for a long and still unfinished debate, peculiar to Germany, on the issue of *Marktkonformität*, the conformability or compatibility of interventions with market mechanisms. Eucken's definition of permissible interventions has been sharpened considerably by various other neo-liberal writers.[2] While most of them would probably agree that preference should be given in a market economy to general rather than particular interventions, most of them would equally agree that particular interventions are sometimes inevitable and that they too should follow certain criteria. H. von Stackelberg, for example, maintained that interventions could be said to be in conformity with a market economy when they

---

[1] W. Eucken, *Grundsätze*, op. cit., p. 225 ff.

[2] The following analysis is based largely on the summary made by J. Heinz Müller of the considerable literature on the subject in Grenzen der Raumpolitik im Rahmen einer Marktwirtschaft, *Ordo*, Vol. 12, Düsseldorf and Munich, Küpper, 1961, p. 147 ff.

did not disturb or destroy the prime purpose of the price mechanism which was to provide an 'automatic calculating machine'[1] of scarcity within the economy. But he also argued that in attempting to establish a competitive order non-conformable interventions might be unavoidable, and that in such cases preference should be given to those interventions which were best adapted to making themselves superfluous in the future. Similarly Röpke agreed with Eucken that in general the State should work on the framework of the economy rather than intervene directly in the operation of the market, but he also believed that market mechanisms often produce difficulties in adaptation which require more specific interventions. In his view those interventions which aid the movement towards a new equilibrium position are legitimate, those which merely preserve the *status quo* are not. Other writers have used the 'as if' formula: particular interventions in the economic process may well be necessary: the important point is that these interventions should try and create a situation 'as if' a competitive market existed. J. Heinz Müller has provided a not unrepresentative statement of the justification for particular measures of intervention: 'In attempting to ascertain what measures may be taken in a concrete situation which are in conformity with a market economy . . . the first criterion must be to ask whether the measure in question implies its own removal or not. Only those measures are allowed in a market economy which are in a position to render themselves superfluous. Of the interventions which satisfy this requirement preference must be given to those which have no major side-effects, those which take the shortest time to achieve their economic objective, and finally those which have a stimulating effect on productivity. Not all measures which are in conformity with a market economy are of the same value; it is on the contrary essential, after making a thorough investigation of the interconnecting factors, to establish a scale corresponding to the three subsidiary conditions mentioned above, and to select the measures on the basis of this.'[2] In assessing the interventions of the State in Germany since the Currency Reform one should bear in mind not only Eucken's general criteria for intervention, but the more precise criteria which these other neo-liberal writers have developed.

[1] H. von Stackelberg, Möglichkeiten und Grenzen der Wirtschaftslenkung, *Ordo*, Vol. 2, Düsseldorf and Munich, Küpper, 1949, p. 200.
[2] J. H. Müller, op. cit., pp. 175–6.

The third feature of Eucken's doctrine which needs further elucidation is the role which he assigned to anti-cyclical policy. It is a common criticism levelled at neo-liberal theory that it ignores or rejects the Keynesian revolution in economic thinking and continues to advocate old-fashioned remedies for cyclical movements. To this criticism is now added the comment that neo-liberals are gradually coming to realize the best of Keynesian teaching and are abandoning their earlier dogma.

As we have already seen, Eucken believed optimistically that the implementation of the basic principles he had enunciated would all but obviate the need for any special anti-cyclical measures, for example the active manipulation of taxes or public expenditure. He was not against this kind of measure *per se*, for in the very particular circumstances of the interwar years he had in fact recommended them. But he held that if steps were taken to establish competition as widely as possible, if economic policy was held constant, and monetary policy conducted vigorously and automatically on the principle of price stability, then fluctuations would almost completely disappear. Eucken based his optimism first on a belief that the faulty calculations of particular investors in an exchange economy were one of the main reasons for booms and slumps, and that an efficiently working price mechanism and a constant economic policy would eliminate these. Secondly, he believed that tight control over the quantity of money in circulation was an effective way of countering cyclical movements.

How far are these ideas representative of German neo-liberalism today? It is extremely difficult to generalize but it would probably be true to say that Eucken's general emphasis is still maintained, but some of his more particular recommendations are not. Thus neo-liberals would probably still agree that the most important long-term method of curing cyclical movements is to ensure that the basic *structure* of the economy is sound. Secondly, most neo-liberals would agree that in a market economy anti-cyclical measures, whether monetary or not, should be directed primarily at maintaining price stability, since this is the essential pre-condition of such an economy. Full employment is an important objective of policy, but should only in very special circumstances be given priority over price stability. Thirdly, most neo-liberals would agree that in a market economy each cyclical movement has its own *particular* causes, and so will require its own particular treatment.

Although there are some economists in Germany who still advocate that anti-cyclical policy should be based strictly on 'objective criteria' and thus work automatically, they are a minority. Most would accept that Eucken's proposals reflect too mechanistic an approach to the problem and do too little justice to the psychological causes of cyclical movements. Schmölders, for example, takes this view and Hahn, another neo-liberal writer, has long stressed the psychological roots of cyclical movements.[1] As long as the overall objectives are maintained, a certain flexibility of monetary and other anti-cyclical policies is now considered not only permissible but desirable. Eucken's exclusive reliance on monetary policy, so widely supported in the years immediately following the Currency Reform, has also been abandoned. Nowadays few neo-liberal writers would disagree with the proposition that so long as the main objective of price stability is maintained, non-monetary measures are a useful supplement to the anti-cyclical armoury, though they would probably agree with Lutz that, despite its weaknesses, monetary policy can never be entirely replaced by budgetary policy.[2]

Finally, there are the ethical and political aspects of neo-liberalism. Eucken wished to establish an economic order that was both efficient and humane, and he considered that the competitive order fulfilled not one but both of these criteria. Yet it is a criticism frequently levelled at neo-liberalism that it sanctions mere egoism and is incapable of generating any sense of the common good; that it believes purely in freedom for the individual from external restraint and has no positive values to offer; that it sacrifices society to the fetish of market forces.

Undoubtedly there are two sides to neo-liberal ethics, one negative and one positive. Neo-liberalism, as Röpke stated, fights a war on two fronts and as a result suffers from a certain internal tension.[3] To take the negative aspects first, neo-liberal writers firmly reject what Röpke calls *Moralismus*, or the attempt to subordinate economic realities to absolute ethical postulates, whether Catholic, Communist or Socialist. According to the neo-liberal view ignorance of economics

[1] Cf. G. Schmölders, *Geldpolitik*, Tübingen, J. C. B. Mohr (Paul Siebeck), 1962, p. 191 ff, and A. Hahn, Die Grundirrtümer in Lord Keynes' General Theory of Employment, Interest and Money, *Ordo*, Vol. 2, p. 170 ff.

[2] F. A. Lutz, *International Payments and Monetary Policy in the World Today*, Stockholm, Almqvist and Wiksell, 1961, p. 141.

[3] W. Röpke, Der Markt im Dienste der Gesellschaft, *Frankfurter Allgemeine Zeitung*, March 14, 1964.

can lead the supporters of such ethical programmes into the kind of society they would probably be the first to condemn. Thus Marx urged the overthrow of capitalism but made no analysis of the benefits or drawbacks of the centrally administered economy. The Catholic Church believes that class conflicts can be overcome by organizing the economy on the basis of groups or corporations, but again, according to neo-liberal critics, has made too little analysis of what a 'group economy' would really entail. The modern non-Communist Socialists try to find a middle way by means of the 'mixed economy' but fail to analyse the contradictions which this blanket concept implies for the co-ordination of the modern interdependent economic process. To this extent the neo-liberals can be said to reject the infusion of morality into economics. Again most neo-liberals would support the competitive order largely because it starts from the assumption that men work and do business in their own interest, and that this is a surer foundation on which to build an economic order than that of absolute ethical rules. They would also endorse the competitive order for the reason that it protects the individual from the arbitrary domination of others. Thus competition has the merit of breaking up concentrations of economic power, and preserving for the individual an area of 'negative' freedom. The State is certainly expected to intervene in the competitive order, but there are precise limits to the kind of intervention that it can make. The only force to which the individual is constantly subject is the impersonal 'objective' one of competition itself.

The positive side of neo-liberalism is reflected in Eucken's repeated emphasis that the whole economic process is interdependent and that the overall framework or economic 'order' is more important than any single part. It is a logical consequence of this that each individual in a competitive order must not simply pursue his own interests, but must also become aware of the interlocking of his own actions with those of everyone else, understand that each man's freedom depends on the right ordering of the whole economy, and that the increasing specialization of the modern age must be balanced through education, exhortation and example, by an increasing emphasis on seeing things in their totality. To this extent neo-liberalism, although it may start from the premise of self-interest, goes on to recommend what Böhm has called the 'responsible society' in which each member is acutely aware of his position within a larger unit. This larger unit may lack the spiritual significance with which some Catholics and Socialists endow society, but it is certainly not disregarded as a mere by-product of individual actions, as some critics of neo-liberalism have implied.[1] Similarly, while neo-liberals endorse competition partly as a means of atomizing power groupings within society, they do not make it a fetish to which society is subordinate; the emphasis of Eucken and the neo-liberals is precisely on ordering competition and market forces to ensure that they serve rather than dominate society. Nor do neo-liberals condemn social action by the State, rather they advocate that social action shall be carefully modelled so as not to destroy market mechanisms, and to stimulate as far as possible individual self-development. Professor Müller-Armack has repeatedly urged that social policy should include not only social insurance measures and State assistance to those in need, but also a vigorous 'environment policy' to enable the individual to develop his full potentialities. Such a policy would include, *inter alia*, increased public expenditure on educational and cultural facilities, and increased attention to the appearance and facilities of factories, industrial estates, towns and countryside.[2]

There is undoubtedly in neo-liberal political theory a strong trace of the traditional German belief in the neutral State, standing over and above the clash of particular interests, and working independently for the good of the whole. In the early neo-liberal writers, Eucken and Böhm, this belief in a sharp dividing line between the State and society was particularly strong. It would probably be fair to say that this view has now become more moderate. Most neo-liberals would still stress that it is the function of the State to express and maintain the common good, which is different from the particular interests of society, or any mere balance of these particular interests. They would also recognize, however, that in finding and defining the common good the particular interests of society must inevitably play a part. Political parties, in particular, must act as the transformers of the special interests of society into the common good of the whole. They are the continuous linking mechanism between society and the State. Pressure groups are still distrusted.

Eucken maintained that the competitive order should be anchored in the constitution of the country that wished to establish it, and

---

[1] For a fierce critique of neo-liberal social philosophy from the Catholic side, see E. E. Nawroth, *Die Sozial- und Wirtschaftsphilosophie des Neoliberalismus*, Heidelberg, F. H. Kerle Verlag, 1962.

[2] A. Müller-Armack, *Studien zur Sozialen Marktwirtschaft*, op. cit., p. 23 ff.

should also be reflected in the administrative structure. Here it is worth noting that even if the present constitution of Germany (the Basic Law of 1949) does not unequivocally sanction the 'social market economy', it certainly establishes, as some have argued, a *Rechtsstaat*, which for Eucken was the political counterpart of the competitive order.[1] The main elements of this system may be briefly adumbrated. First, the legislature, executive and judiciary are bound by a written constitution. That this constitution is more than merely a *règle de jeu*, as the French constitution has been described, and provides the basic foundation for the State, is shown by the powers given to the Federal Constitutional Court to pronounce upon the constitutionality of the legislature's activities. Secondly, the constitution enunciates certain fundamental human rights which the legislature, executive and judiciary must observe. (Just as the 'social' market economy differs from early liberalism, so the modern 'social' *Rechtsstaat* differs from the nineteenth-century *Rechtsstaat*, in that it obliges the State not only to observe and protect these human rights, but also to 'ensure that each person has the possibility of making use of them'.[2]) Thirdly, the constitution explicitly recognizes the existence of an unwritten moral law standing over and above the law as it is expressed *in concreto*, thus breaking entirely with the positivist tradition in German jurisprudence. And lastly, one of the oldest features of this German concept of the *Rechtsstaat*, the State is endowed with a system of administrative justice, that is to say a separate hierarchy of courts is provided for, which is specifically empowered to deal with cases concerning the acts of the administration. These four elements may reasonably be taken as showing the essential features of the modern German *Rechtsstaat*, and thus as indicating the extent to which the neo-liberal economic system is reflected in the political system.

From the foregoing account of neo-liberalism, it can be seen that it is not merely a technique for promoting faster growth or more exports, but an ambitious attempt to restate liberalism in a form suitable for modern society. Its outstanding characteristics would seem to be these. First, its comprehensive approach: that is its emphasis on taking an overall rather than a piecemeal view of economic and political problems, and in particular its stress that economic

---

[1] See *Grundsätze*, op. cit., p. 331 ff.

[2] H. J. Wolff, cited in T. Ellwein, *Das Regierungssystem der Bundesrepublik Deutschland*, Cologne and Opladen, Westdeutscher Verlag, 1963, p. 7.

policy must be 'all of one piece', and not a mere agglomeration of *ad hoc* measures. Second, its acceptance of State intervention: that is its concentration not on the problem of intervention versus non-intervention, but on the proper form and objectives of intervention. Third, its non-determinist approach to economic problems: that is its acceptance of the fact that the industrial revolution has made economic co-ordination a thousand times more complicated, but its rejection of the idea that either 'technological progress' or 'capitalism' is moving society inexorably towards a centrally directed economy. According to neo-liberal theory man is still free to choose amongst the underlying forms of co-ordination. Finally, mention must be made of the neo-liberal re-definition of competition. Neo-liberalism attempts to free competition and market forces from the stigma of either immorality or impossibility. Markets are not a product of 'capitalism' but a perennial form of human behaviour; competition is not an immoral or illusory activity, but one which is productive, fair, and capable of implementation.

While neo-liberalism is not merely a technique for growth, it may be said that neo-liberal economic policy is implicitly growth orientated. More specifically it is 'supply' or 'production' orientated. The prime objective of an economic system is to overcome scarcity; the neo-liberals believe that, by holding prices stable and encouraging productive competition, this objective will be achieved. Distribution, welfare, the regulation of demand, are not unimportant, but are secondary to this main task.

THE PRACTICE

The postwar situation and the Currency Reform
Eucken's competitive order was intended as a guiding principle; it was something to be worked for patiently and continuously, rather than a policy which could be implemented overnight. In 1948, however, when control over economic policy began to be restored to the Germans themselves, the position was hardly auspicious for even a start towards such an ideal. Western Germany was but a fragment of the former German Reich. It had been separated from those areas, particularly beyond the Oder-Neisse line, which traditionally supplied it with food. It was the destination of a stream of refugees from the east who required both food and housing; much of its industrial capacity had been destroyed or

dismantled; raw materials were scarce; the transport system had been dislocated. The economy was subject to a system of controls over prices, production and imports which was the antithesis of the competitive order. Financial order and rational economic activity were made almost impossible by the vast excess of money within the economy. There was full employment, but almost complete economic stagnation.

The picture was not, of course, entirely a black one. Germany also possessed certain advantages which were to be of considerable assistance to its economic development after 1948. Thus the refugees from the east, of whom the great bulk arrived in the years between 1944 and 1950, but who continued to arrive in considerable numbers until the building of the Berlin Wall in 1961, were both a burden and an advantage to the economy. They had to be provided with houses, food and social assistance, and thus absorbed a large amount of scarce capital, kept taxes higher than they might otherwise have been and probably had an adverse effect on the balance of payments. On the other hand, they provided an enterprising, skilled and mobile addition to the labour force, which helped to keep wages down during the critical early years of reconstruction and stimulated entrepreneurial competition. On balance it may be said that the refugees' advantages outweighed their disadvantages, and that they contributed positively to Germany's revival.

A second advantage was that defeat had left the economy unburdened by heavy defence expenditure. Up to 1950 the absence of a defence burden was balanced by the occupation costs the country had to bear; after 1950, however, the gradual expansion of Germany's own defence forces was offset by the reduction of these occupation costs, so that in real terms defence expenditure of both types remained at the 1950 level. Thus, as the national product rose in the 1950s, the proportion going to defence fell from 5.0 per cent in 1950 to only 2·7 per cent in 1958. The British figure for the latter year was 6.7 per cent. By 1965 the two figures had come much closer together, 6.7 per cent for Britain and 4.0 per cent for Germany, and they will probably continue to converge. Throughout the 1950s, however, Germany benefited considerably in this respect in comparison with other countries. A particular aspect of this German advantage was the absence of overseas military commitments, which constituted such a drain on foreign exchange for Britain.

Thirdly, the degree of damage done to German industry by the war and its aftermath should not be exaggerated. The remarkably high level of industrial investment sustained both before and during the war served to offset much of the damage and dismantling. Roskamp estimates that 'all told, West German industry actually had, in 1946, a greater industrial capacity than in 1936'.[1] Although much of the investment carried out during the Third Reich was naturally war-orientated it could be, and was, converted to civil production at no great expense.

A fourth factor which helped the economy was the direction which new investment took. It flowed largely into those sectors where rapid increases in productivity were possible and the export potential enormous. Cars, chemicals, machinery, electrical engineering: it was these sectors, the major growth industries of the world economy in the 1950s, which tended to benefit most. Germany thus possessed an advantage over countries, like Britain, where the industrial and export structure was slower in adapting to changed circumstances. The rapid increases in productivity also enabled wage increases to be absorbed more easily.

A fifth factor which must be mentioned was American aid at the end of the war. This aid, despite the offsetting factor of reparations, was crucial in its timing and objectives.[2]

The flow of refugees, the comparatively small defence burden, the high rate of industrial expansion sustained before and during the war, the favourable direction of new investment, American assistance: these are five main factors which helped to offset Germany's disadvantages in 1948 and later. Two other subsidiary factors, often cited, should be mentioned for the sake of completeness: the 'weakness' of the German trade unions and the hardworking character of the German people. The former is largely an illusion in that it fails to explain the ability of the unions to wrest a large measure of co-determination from an unwilling government as early as 1951. It is probably more accurate to say that, with some exceptions, the German trade unions, under the leadership of such exceptional men

[1] K. W. Roskamp, *Capital Formation in West Germany*, Detroit, Wayne State University Press, 1965, p. 36.

[2] H. C. Wallich, *Mainsprings of the German Revival*, New Haven, Yale University Press, p. 363. It has been estimated that West Germany received aid totalling $3,550 million from the USA between the end of the war and 1952. Of this, $1,280 million represented Marshall Aid. For comparison, Britain received $3,180 million in Marshall Aid, and France $2,700 million. *Frankfurter Allgemeine Zeitung*, June 3, 1967.

as Herr Böckler, devoted their energies in the period of reconstruction not to the disruption or dislocation of the market or capitalist system as such, but to deriving as much advantage as they reasonably could from within such a system. To this extent, it may be said, Germany benefited from the attitude of its unions. Finally, the hard-working character of the German people is indeed 'no myth', but for much of the period after the war 'it has not . . . been something altogether exceptional either in German experience or on the contemporary European scene'.[1]

In sum, then, there were factors which made the move towards a competitive order more difficult, and there were factors which were able to give the German economy a competitive advantage if and when the right policies were implemented. Both sets of factors should be remembered in the following account of the development of German economic policy. In considering this, one must inevitably start with the Currency Reform of 1948, which was desired by both the Allies and the Germans, and marks the beginning of the transfer of responsibility for economic policy.

The Reform removed the enormous surplus of money within the economy, by replacing the Reichsmark by the Deutsche Mark at a conversion rate which, when all the special provisions are taken into account, was equivalent to 100:6·5. This rate applied to firms' and individuals' cash and bank deposits, the latter being taken to include not only demand and time deposits but also savings deposits, a fact which caused considerable hardship to small savers. Public authorities' funds were completely cancelled, and lump-sum payments were made to individuals, firms and public authorities to help them over the transitional period. Apart from this the debt structure of the country was reorganized, all debts were devalued at a ratio of 10:1. Measures were taken to prevent profiteering and also to enable the banks to cover their liabilities.

The Currency Reform was accompanied by some tax reductions and concessions, and the removal of some controls. That it was a tough reform no one has questioned; it was unaccompanied by any general system of compensation for those who had suffered by it or by the war: not until 1952 when the Equalization of Burdens Law was passed did such a system emerge. Nevertheless, the reform cured at one stroke the fundamental cause of the economic disorder in the

[1] H. C. Wallich, op. cit., p. 363. See also p. 279, where German trade union attitudes are discussed further.

country. By removing the surplus of money it enabled many prices once again to perform their normal function, and rational economic activity to be resumed. Inflationary pressures and black markets began to disappear and the foundation for an economic policy based on neo-liberal principles was laid.

The following sections will examine how far neo-liberal principles have been applied in practice in certain fields since 1948. The discussion will, however, omit those subjects which will be examined in detail in later chapters, such as the very important question of monetary policy (Chapter 6), tax reform (Chapter 7) and balance-of-payments policies (Chapter 11).

The opening of markets

'Open markets' are a constituent principle of the competitive order that is second only to monetary stability in order of neo-liberal priority. The German Government has pursued a vigorous policy both of removing controls from the internal market and of liberalizing trade and payments.

The movement towards free trade is particularly well defined. Although the German Government did not recover complete control over foreign trade until 1952, it had taken the initiative in pressing for liberalization well before this. One year after the Currency Reform Germany joined the OEEC and by February 1954 had liberalized 91·4 per cent of its imports from other member countries. Not only did Germany pursue a policy of multilateral liberalization: it also, in 1956 and 1957 (and again in 1964 towards the other EEC countries), cut tariffs unilaterally. These unilateral measures have few parallels in Western Europe or North America. After the second, Germany entered the circle of 'low tariff countries' and as a result had to raise tariffs on many finished goods when the common external tariff of the EEC began to be set up.

The liberalization of services and capital movements accompanied that of goods, though capital liberalization took place rather more slowly. The decisive event in the latter process was the London Debt Agreement of 1953, which finally regulated Germany's pre-war and postwar debts, and returned to the German Government complete responsibility for exchange control. After this date the removal of restrictions on capital movements was very rapid, and Germany largely set the pace for the rest of Europe. By the end of the 1950s capital movements in and out of the country were almost completely freed. It is ironic that in recent years certain restrictions have had to be reimposed—for example, the tax on capital earnings on foreign holdings of German fixed-interest securities introduced in 1964—but this has been the result not of a revival of protectionism, but of an *embarras de richesse*.

The removal of State price-fixing and production controls also proceeded rapidly after 1948, though not until the end of the balance-of-payments crisis of 1950-1, caused by the Korean War, was the path a smooth one. The Currency Reform itself was accompanied by an ordinance freeing certain farm products, as well as nearly all capital and consumer goods, from price control. State direction of the iron and steel industries was terminated at the end of 1949, though certain restrictions on production remained, and prices were still fixed. The prices of most non-ferrous metals were freed in 1950, those of crude oil and certain fuels at the beginning of 1951. The 1950-1 crisis halted this move towards decontrol, and even caused some new restrictions to be imposed. The most extreme move was the Law for Economic Security of 1951, which gave the Government full powers to allocate raw materials, though in fact only limited use was made of it. But as early as the summer of 1951 the move towards decontrol had started again. Certain restrictions on energy production were loosened at this time and the ban on aluminium production lifted. During 1952 iron, steel and timber prices were freed, the last major restrictions on steel production removed, and greater flexibility given to energy prices; in 1953 State direction of the electricity and gas markets was terminated; and by the end of 1954 the market for precious metals had been decontrolled, and Ruhr coal prices were also freed.

These dates indicate the general tempo of decontrol. There were certain exceptions. Water and gas prices were not completely freed until early in 1959. It is also worth noting that the Price Law according to which prices were fixed in the early years is still in existence in Germany, though the Federal Constitutional Court laid down in 1958 that it is a 'transitional law' and that decisions to fix prices under it must aim at the eventual restoration of normal price relationships.

This general account of the reopening of markets has parallels in other countries, not least in Britain. And, like other countries, Germany has its exceptions in sectors such as agriculture, transport and energy, where special problems have prevented the application of neo-liberal principles. There is not space here for a detailed account of each of these sectors. But one sector in which the pursuance of social market ideas has clearly made a distinct difference to German, as compared with British or French policy, is housing, and this will therefore be treated more fully as an example of the application of neo-liberalism in a difficult sector.[1]

There was in Germany after the war an enormous demand for housing and an exiguous supply. The market was so unbalanced that intervention was essential. As well as controlling rents the Government acted to increase supply and, as the market righted itself, controls and interventions were systematically removed. Stress was placed at a very early stage on private construction and private ownership of houses, and a conscious effort was made to separate social objectives and social policy from market policy, so as to prevent them from distorting each other. In all these ways neo-liberal doctrines were reflected.

The development of housing policy can be traced through three main housing laws since the Currency Reform: the first Building of Dwellings Law of 1950 (amended in 1953), the second Building of Dwellings Law of 1956, and the Removal of Control Law of 1960. The first of these set the pattern for the rest by making a distinction between publicly encouraged social housing, tax-favoured housing, and 'free finance' housing. Social housing was entitled to direct public subsidies, in the form of low-interest or interest-free loans, as well as tax concessions. Dwellings in this category were subject to size, rent and occupancy controls, and certain conditions regarding income were laid down for applicants. But so long as their projects conformed with the regulations, private as well as public building promoters were equally entitled by the law to receive public money for the construction of these dwellings. Income tax and land tax concessions were the main stimuli for the second category of dwellings and special premia were also introduced for building investment in 1952. Tax-favoured dwellings were subject to certain overall size and rent controls but, again in order to create incentives, these were not nearly as rigid as those for the first category. In particular 'cost rents' or rents necessary to cover current expenditure were permitted within certain limits. Applicants in this category naturally could not receive public loans. Finally, the incentive for 'free finance', or

[1] The following historical account owes much to PEP, *Housing in Britain, France and West Germany*, Planning No. 490, 1965.

completely non-subsidized building, was that dwellings within this category were free of all controls, whether of rent, size or occupancy.

Under the first law the public authorities set themselves the target of constructing 1·8 million social dwellings over the following six years. In 1953 this was increased to 2 million and by the end of 1956 a total of 3,750,000 new dwellings had been built since 1949, as compared with Britain's 2,600,000 since 1945. The second Building of Dwellings Law of 1956 set a target of 1·8 million dwellings for the years up to 1962; it maintained the housing categories established by the first law, but gave a new and significant priority in the allocation of public funds to the construction of owner-occupied dwellings. It also relaxed the restrictions on the size of dwellings within the social housing category, allowed 'cost rents' to be introduced generally in this category, and introduced special measures of assistance for those with low incomes, thus applying neo-liberal principles to a further aspect of housing policy.

Finally in 1960, when nearly 6 million dwellings had been built and completions were running at nearly 600,000 per annum, the Removal of Control Law was passed. This major piece of legislation was aimed at bringing the housing sector completely within the framework of the competitive order, by progressively removing the remaining controls over occupancy and rents. The Law removed certain limited categories of dwellings from occupancy control, and provided that the Land authorities (regional governments) could remove all such controls in those urban and rural districts where demand exceeded supply by no more than 3 per cent. The Law also provided for the simultaneous removal of rent controls, once the Housing Assistance Law of 1963 had been passed. This Law provided for direct payments of those owner-occupiers and tenants of dwellings where control had been removed who could show that their total rent or outgoings exceeded a certain percentage of their income. This assistance, which is a legal right, is given only to those with incomes below a certain maximum, and the percentage is adjusted in accordance with the size of the family.

Those areas where all controls have been removed became known as 'white', and those where they remain as 'black'. Originally all controls were intended to have been removed by the end of 1966, but the final date was later extended to the end of 1967. At the start of 1967 only thirty-two out of a total of 564 areas were still 'black'— though this remainder included some of West Germany's largest towns, for which the final time limit may well be extended beyond 1967. According to the Ministry of Housing decontrol has not been accompanied by any sudden or excessive increase in rents, or by social tensions. (From the beginning of 1966 'black' area rents were allowed to go up by 25 per cent.) Finally, in 1965 the aims of the social housing programme were also restated. Even more than in the past the emphasis will be on priority dwellings for those who really need them: large families, young married couples and old people, and once again on encouraging owner-occupation. Of the 600,000 house completions in 1966, about 220,000 were in this social housing category. The total number of new houses built in Germany since 1949 stood at the end of 1966 at about $9 \cdot 5$ million, or half the houses in the country.

When compared with housing policy in Britain or France, the development of German housing policy is a good example of State intervention moulded on neo-liberal principles, even if many Germans are not inclined to regard it as having been entirely sound from this point of view. The restoration of market forces has been deliberately and systematically encouraged, though controls were maintained as long as the market was structurally out of balance; and social intervention has been such as to prevent those with low incomes from suffering, but carefully adapted so as to distort the market as little as possible.

*The enforcement of competition: anti-monopoly and
restrictive practices policy*
Apart from price stability and open markets, Eucken had called for the enforcement of complete productive competition through the banning of restrictive business practices; the establishment of a monopoly office designed to bring the holders of economic power into a relationship, 'as if complete competition existed'; and positive encouragement of competition by means of the other instruments of economic policy. In fact the attempt made by Dr Erhard and his colleagues to develop a restrictive practices policy in West Germany ran into stubborn opposition from industry and was the subject of acrimonious political debate. A draft government law appeared as early as 1952, but it was not until 1957 that the final legislation emerged in the form of a compromise. The Government could certainly claim that the basic principle of its original draft had been preserved in that the Law against Restraints of Competition

stated explicitly that horizontal and vertical restrictive agreements were prohibited *a priori*, thus marking a radical change in the traditional attitude of German law towards cartels. On the other hand Dr Erhard, in spite of the support which a section of his own party and the whole of the SPD gave to the principle of prohibition, was unable to prevent a number of highly important exceptions to this principle being written into the Law. Thus, if they fulfil certain conditions, several types of horizontal agreement are exempted from prohibition by the 1957 Law: agreements concerning general delivery terms or conditions; agreements concerning rebates, or the uniform application of standards and types; export and import agreements (including export agreements which involve restrictions on the internal market); rationalization agreements; agreements necessitated by a structural crisis in a particular sector; and agreements necessitated in exceptional circumstances for the good of the economy as a whole and the public welfare. Some of these agreements are subject to control only if the firms abuse their position. Not all these exceptions are of the same importance, but some undoubtedly weaken the Law considerably. The prohibition of vertical agreements is similarly attenuated by exceptions. The most important is that for resale price maintenance of branded goods which, so long as the products concerned are open to price competition, is wholly excepted and indeed legally protected. The only obligation is that details of the agreements must be filed with the Cartel Office. Exclusive dealing or sole-agency agreements are also exempt and can be invalidated by the Cartel Office only if they unfairly restrict the freedom of economic action of one party or of other enterprises, or substantially restrict competition in the markets concerned. In relation to restrictive agreements the 1957 Law was thus a compromise which permitted both those who supported prohibition and their opponents legitimately to claim certain victories.

A further striking feature of the Law was its mildness in relation to mergers and dominant firms. The Law provides for the notification of mergers if they enable the enterprises concerned to obtain a share of 20 per cent or more of the market for a specific type of goods or commercial services or if such a share was held by one of the firms before the merger. The Cartel Office, however, has no powers to act against those mergers; it can only summon the participants to an oral hearing or invite them to provide a written statement concerning the consolidation if it seems that the move will either lead to a market-dominating position or strengthen an already existing one. Dominant enterprises themselves are subject to control by the Cartel Office if they abuse their position in certain specified ways. They are defined in the law as enterprises which have no competition or are not exposed to any substantial competition with regard to a particular category of goods or commercial services. Oligopolies are defined and treated in a similar way.

The Law was amended in 1965 after considerable controversy about its operation, but the amendments were not radical. The most important of the Government's original proposals, the abolition of resale price maintenance, was not carried through, since the Government was unable to overcome the resistance within its own party. Instead a public register giving full details has been established, which it is hoped will lessen the number of undesirable resale price agreements. Apart from this most of the original proposals were passed. The procedure for agreement concerning types and standards has been simplified, and recommendations in this field are no longer prohibited. The procedure for permitting rationalization agreements, the object of which is specialization, has also been made easier. Such specialization agreements must leave substantial competition in the market but they can, if it is essential, include price and distribution agreements. These reforms for type, standard and specialization agreements are intended to help small and medium-sized firms in particular. It has also been made easier for the Cartel Office to take action against sole-agency agreements which unduly restrict entry to the market, and a new general clause gives the Office a freer hand in dealing with the misuse of power by a dominant firm. Thus the Office is now empowered to take action against a market-dominating enterprise whenever it abuses its position not only on its own but on other markets as well. In addition a much more precise definition has been provided of the kind of mergers which have to be registered with the Cartel Office. By the new rules, all mergers in which the participating firms together employed 10,000 people or over at any time during the previous year, or had a turnover of 500 million marks or over, or had a balance of 1,000 million marks or over in the last completed business year, must henceforth register. Finally, certain administrative reforms have been made: in particular the Cartel Office can now impose fines directly instead of having to request the Land Courts to impose them. The 1965 amendments thus modified but did not fundamentally alter the 1957 law.

On the whole the German Law is less tough than the British, which abolished resale price maintenance in 1964 and under which mergers can be prevented; it does however mark a radical change in the traditional German attitude towards cartels. The Cartel Office has been particularly vocal in calling for the strengthening of the Law in relation to mergers, and it has been supported by the Scientific Advisory Council of the Economics Ministry. What has been noticeable has been the softening of the Government's attitude. In 1961 it promised 'to hinder the emergence of economically harmful dominant enterprises'. But in its commentary on the 1964 report on concentration (see page 68), and in justifying its amendments to the Cartel Law, it took a rather more lenient view. This leniency found concrete expression in the fact that the limits (regarding turn-over, employment, etc.) above which mergers would have to be notified was considerably higher in the Government's 1964 proposals than in the earlier proposals of 1962. The argument which the Government has repeatedly put forward to justify this relaxation of attitude to anti-monopoly policy is that Germany's entry into the Common Market throws the problem of concentration into a new light and makes the more severe approach of former times un-tenable: monopolization of the output of a product in Germany need certainly not be regarded so seriously if, within the larger market of the EEC, several producers are going to remain in compe-tition. Indeed, to prevent concentration in such a situation may be to preclude the economies of scale that are one of the chief advantages of the formation of the EEC.

That membership of EEC has to some extent diverted the neo-liberal drive for a strong monopoly office is unquestionable. Even the Cartel Office, in another context, has changed its outlook in view of this development: in its 1962 and 1963 reports it stated that hence-forth account would have to be taken of the need to protect German firms against restrictive practices abroad and in particular in the other countries of the EEC. Economic integration thus creates an impetus not only for national programming but also for anti-monopoly policies to be transposed from the national to the international level. It would be disadvantageous unilaterally to control mergers and concentrations as well as restrictive practices, if elsewhere in the same economic area governments are actively encouraging them.

This fact helps to explain the very strong interest which Germany has taken in the development of the cartel and monopoly provisions of the EEC Treaty, and its efforts to ensure that they are moulded in a neo-liberal direction.[1]

It need only be added that the new Coalition Government seems rather more determined than its predecessor to tighten up the 1957 Law.

The encouragement of competition: middle-estate policy,
company law reform, denationalization, property ownership
'It is not sufficient,' Eucken had written, 'to prohibit a few cartels.' The negative approach to restrictive practices embodied in the Cartel Law has accordingly been balanced by a positive encouragement to the small and medium-sized firm. The *Mittelstandspolitik*, literally 'middle estate policy', was formally inaugurated as a political programme in 1957, when the Government declared that 'for political and cultural reasons it is absolutely necessary that we have a sound middle stratum. We do not want the people to be divided into a small class of economic overlords and a vast mass of dependants through the ever-increasing concentration of the economy into large firms. We require independent medium and small units in the crafts, trade, business, and in agriculture.'[2] What is notable here is the mixture of motives. *Mittelstandspolitik* is required not only as part of the battle against monopoly, but also because it is politically and culturally desirable. This combination of purposes gives the policy added strength, but it is also possible that the assistance to the middle stratum may be taken to a point at which it conflicts with the basic principles of the competitive order, becoming not merely a useful bulwark against monopoly, but an undue discrimination in favour of one group in the economy. One senses in the policy an attempt to steer a careful course, to further the middle stratum, but not to foster it too much. The Government has, for example, rejected the idea that there should be a special 'plan' for the middle stratum, rather like the 'Green Plans' for agriculture, because this would make the policy too rigid and discriminatory.

[1] See D. Swann and D. L. McLachlan, *Concentration or Competition: a European Dilemma?* Chatham House/PEP, European Series No. 1, January 1967.
[2] H. H. Götz, *Weil alle besser leben wollen: Porträt der deutschen Wirtschaftspolitik*, Düsseldorf, Econ-Verlag, 1963, p. 143.

The Government has refrained from making a precise definition of the term 'middle estate'. In practice it may be taken to signify the middle stratum of society in general and the small and medium-sized firm in particular. The handicrafts are invariably included, the hotel and catering business usually, and the professions sometimes. The policy itself is defined as one of constantly examining past, present and future legislation in order to ensure that any unnecessary harmful consequences for the small and medium-sized firm can be prevented, removed or modified. If this is impossible, 'the federal government intervenes in favour of small and medium-sized firms, and restores the balance through special measures of assistance'.[1]

Large sums of money have in fact been provided for this purpose. In 1966, for example, the Federal Government and the Länder provided credits and grants worth 666 million marks for the 'middle estate', and a further 310 million marks in guarantees. The grants provided by the federal authorities are directed at a number of different objectives. Some of them are used to subsidize research and development by small and medium-sized firms and the handicrafts. Others are used to provide economic advisory services for the same sectors, as well as for the catering, wholesale and retail trades. A substantial proportion is used to finance vocational training. The credits are provided in particular to help in the establishment of new independent businesses, and to help in the adaptation of sectors facing severe international competition.

Apart from direct financial assistance, mention should also be made of the deliberate attempt to give preference in the placing of public contracts with small and medium-sized firms, a policy which finds formal expression in the circular sent out by the Minister of Economics in October 1961 to all the federal ministries, the Länder and the communes. Between 1956 and 1964, of the defence contracts which could by their nature be placed with smaller firms, 46 per cent were placed with firms employing fewer than fifty persons. Similarly over 40 per cent of the total value of building contracts placed by the Federal Treasury in recent years has been given to the handicraft sector.

Another aspect of *Mittelstandspolitik* is the special adaptation of legislation to help the middle stratum. As far as taxation is con-

[1] *Die Mittelstandspolitik der Bundesregierung*, Bonn, Press and Information Office of the Federal Government (undated), pp. 6–7.

cerned the three most important measures have been the amendment to the turnover tax of 1961, which increased the free allowance for medium-sized firms and raised the level of turnover at which tax began; the raising of the free allowance for the transaction tax in the same year, which brought considerable benefit to smaller firms; and the smoothing out of the curve of progression of the income tax in 1964 to ensure that it did not weigh disproportionately on middle-income groups. Some of the changes brought about in the Cartel Law of 1965 were designed to help the smaller firm, and the publication of a 'co-operation handbook' in 1963 was specially intended for this purpose. The second law for promoting property formation by employees, passed in 1965, also gave special terms to smaller firms.

Another important element usually included as part of *Mittelstandspolitik*, though it was passed as early as 1953, is the Law laying down the principles on which the handicraft sector is to be organized. This *Handwerksordnung* set out the obligatory training and qualifications for those wishing to establish themselves in this sector, and reaffirmed the traditional role of the handicraft trade associations in ensuring that these standards are maintained. The Law in fact stands on the border line between *Mittelstandspolitik* and the kind of corporative ordering of the economy which the social market economy was deliberately attempting to avoid, and an amendment passed in 1964 loosened some of its more restrictive elements.

These seem to be the main concrete measures taken so far in implementing the *Mittelstandspolitik*. Institutionally the policy finds expression in the special *Mittelstand* committee of the Bundestag, a *Mittelstand* department in the Ministry of Economics, and the Institute for *Mittelstand* research attached to the Universities of Bonn and Cologne. The policy finds a remarkable echo in the business world in the 'Charter of industrial self-discipline and moderation with regard to concentration' issued by the Federation of German Industries (BDI) in 1959, in which members of the Federation were urged not to engage unnecessarily in taking over independent firms or moving out of their own field of production, in the interest of the economic system as a whole.

Two further aspects of policy, which, though they are not part of the *Mittelstandspolitik*, tend similarly to promote positively the diffusion of economic power, as a counterpart to the negative struggle against monopoly, are company law reform and the denationalization of State-owned enterprises.

The main purpose of the 1965 Company Law was to strengthen the influence of shareholders, particularly smaller shareholders, in the operation and the profit distribution of German companies. One of its most important provisions was to end the practice of forming undisclosed reserves, which severely distorted the annual balance of German companies and made it almost impossible for an outsider to get an accurate picture of the capital position and profitability of such companies, and correspondingly easy for 'insiders', particularly banks and credit institutions, to buy up blocks of shares from ignorant shareholders. The Law also placed limitations on the amount of reserves which a company could form. Henceforth companies will not be allowed to transfer more than half their profits to the published reserve fund, and reserves will not be allowed to be increased if they exceed half the share capital. Together with this spur to the greater distribution of profits, shareholding minorities are given greater control over the extent to which reserves may be increased and dividends reduced, and how far reserves will be transformed into share capital.

Banks and credit institutions which have exercised voting rights on behalf of shareholders (*Depotstimmrecht*) now have to inform each shareholder in good time of the agenda for company meetings, indicate how they intend to vote on each item, and ask for voting instructions. Only if the shareholder ignores this are the banks able to go ahead and vote at their own discretion. The Law also lays down that in future one person will not be allowed to sit on the supervisory board (*Aufsichtsrat*) of more than ten companies, though up to five seats on the boards of companies which form part of a larger combine may be discounted. Finally, it is now forbidden for a representative of one company to sit on another company's supervisory board if a member of the latter company's management sits on the former's supervisory board; that is, the practice of 'mutual supervision' is restricted, though not entirely removed. The Law entered into force on January 1, 1966, and it is still too early to judge its effects. However, it is a concrete example of the German Government's oft-expressed determination not to resign itself to the process of concentration but to take up arms against it.

Another important way in which the Government has promoted the wider distribution of property has been through denationalization. Three major steps have so far been taken in this direction. The

C

first, in 1959, was the partial denationalization of Preussag, the Prussian Mining and Smelting Company. By this operation Preussag shares to a value of 81·5 million marks were offered at a special 'social' discount to those whose taxable income did not exceed 16,000 marks per annum, with a further condition that no subscriber could buy more than five units. The move was a great success: demand for the shares outstripped supply by a huge margin, and in the end some 216,000 new small shareholders were created, though many of these sold out soon after. Those who held on did well; Preussag shares successfully weathered the 1962–3 slump in the German stock market and subsequently rose considerably.

The second step was the denationalization of Volkswagen in 1961, when 60 per cent of the share capital, worth 360 million marks, was acquired by about 1,500,000 shareholders. Shares were offered at a graduated 'social' discount: those with incomes lower than 16,000 marks per annum who pledged themselves not to sell out for a period of five years qualified for a further concession of 20 per cent under the Savings Premium Law. Shares could be paid for in instalments, and each applicant was finally limited to two or three shares. Once again demand was enormous; the shares rose on the day they were introduced on the exchange from 350 marks to 700 marks and later to 1,000 marks. They fell back again from this peak but remained comfortably above the issue price.

Finally, in 1965 came the partial denationalization of the enormous State-owned holding company VEBA, the United Electricity and Mining Company. This time 3,750,000 shares at 100 marks each were offered at a graduated 'social' discount to those with incomes under 14,000 marks, no one being allowed to buy more than five. This created 2,250,000 new shareholders. The issue proved, however, less of a success than the previous two, as the shares fell below their opening price soon after they were issued.

Denationalization policy has been accompanied by several other measures aimed at spreading property ownership. In 1959 the Savings Premium Act was passed which provides for a premium to be paid on any sum which an individual pledges himself to invest for five years. Savings accounts and certain securities, such as people's shares, new shares, securities paying a fixed rate of interest, investment certificates, etc., all qualify for this premium. In contrast to most of the earlier measures, however, a ceiling is fixed for the annual amount qualifying the holder for the premium, thus aiming the incentive specifically at the lower and middle income groups. Older people and people with large families are offered particularly favourable terms.

Apart from this important measure to promote savings, several steps have been taken in recent years to promote capital formation by employees. The 'small' Company Law Reform of 1959 made it possible for the management of a company to acquire shares in order to sell them at privileged prices to personnel. The number of people buying shares in the company they work for has increased in recent years. In 1962 the Bayer Dye Works, for example, had 20,000 shareholders amongst their employees—representing about 32 per cent of their employees working in Germany and 10 per cent of the total number of shareholders.

Another step in the same direction was the 1961 Law for the 'Promotion of capital formation by employed persons'. This law provides that bonus payments up to 312 marks a year will be exempt from taxation and social insurance provided that the employee invests them in some suitable way or uses them to buy or build a house. Although the number of firms making use of this concession gradually increased, the 1961 Law was not as successful as was hoped. Up to the end of 1964 only about 2 per cent of all employees were benefiting from the scheme. The main reason for this low response was that the Law covered agreements between individual firms and their employees only. In 1965 therefore an amendment was passed which permitted the amount of the bonuses (again up to 312 marks a year) to be negotiated through collective bargaining by trade unions. The response to this seems likely to be far more positive. Soon after the amendment was passed the construction workers negotiated an agreement of this sort which provided that, from January 1, 1966, building firms would contribute 9 pfennigs per hour to the savings account of every worker, while each worker would himself contribute 2 pfennigs per hour to the same fund. It has been estimated that through this agreement the average skilled building worker will be able to set aside some 20,000 marks or £2,100 (including payment of compound interest) after 40 years.

The Savings Premium Law, the measures taken to encourage employee investment, and denationalization are perhaps the most striking and original elements of the German Government's property policy. They are not the only ones. Special measures have also been taken to encourage house ownership and building investment. Tax relief is also given to insurance premia and to those investing in unit trusts. Taken as a whole the measures are impressive.

IS THE ECONOMY PLANNED BY THE BANKS?

The German Government has made substantial efforts to create a competitive order. But how far are these efforts thwarted because German business is financially interlocked? How far do banks and credit institutions exert an influence on trade and industry which renders the attack on restrictive practices nugatory and State planning of the private sector superfluous? The 1964 enquiry into concentration is particularly lucid and detailed on this subject.[1] As the findings of the enquiry have recently been taken to support the view that Germany really has a 'collective economic policy' in which 'co-ordination by banker' takes the place of co-ordination by the State,[2] it is worth looking at the report in some detail. One of the findings is discussed later on pp. 175-8, namely, the structural change in German banking during the post-1948 period, the breakdown of old specializations, and the increased competition in deposit and credit business which has resulted in a decline in the share of the big banks in this field. This increased competition between banks should not be forgotten when examining the extent of their participation in the non-banking sector; but it is the participation that is the main point at issue here.

The 1964 report began its study of the relationship between banks and industry and commerce by looking at the actual ownership by banks of other companies. In 1960 the share ownership of all credit institutions amounted to 3·2 per cent of the nominal capital of all joint-stock companies, or 4·9 per cent of those quoted on the exchanges. In 138 companies, most of them quoted, the banks had a minority holding capable of blocking decisions, i.e. a holding above 25 per cent, and a majority holding in a further 58. Two-thirds of the total value of shares owned by the banks was held by the big three, and the report noted that these three had obtained large quantities of shares through block-buying outside the exchanges. Ownership by the credit institutions was spread over all sectors of the economy, but was concentrated particularly in the wholesale and retail trade,

---

[1] *Bericht über das Ergebnis einer Untersuchung der Konzentration in der Wirtschaft*, Bonn, Deutscher Bundestag, Drucksache IV/2320, 1964.

[2] A. Shonfield, *Modern Capitalism*, Oxford University Press, 1965, pp. 246-55,

where it amounted to 27 per cent of the nominal capital of all joint stock companies, and the brewing industry, where it amounted to 19 per cent.

Apart from direct ownership, German banks also exert an influence on the non-banking sector through the proxy votes they wield at company meetings on behalf of their customers. Up to 1965, the 'deposit voting right' of the banks took the following form. Customers could give a blanket authorization to the banks at which they deposited their stocks and shares, to exercise their voting rights at general meetings, valid for 15 months at a time, and enabling banks to transfer the proxy votes, if they so wished, to third persons, including other banks. Customers could decide to issue their own voting instructions to their banks during the fifteen-month period, but the banks were not required to ask for instructions. To assess the effect of the *Depotstimmrecht* the 1964 concentration enquiry took a sample of 425 quoted joint-stock companies, representing about 75 per cent of the capital of all quoted companies of this type. The report estimated that voting power with respect to 70 per cent of the capital of this sample was held by the banks, of which 1,200 million marks was owned by the banks themselves, and about 8,000 million marks by customers. Of this 70 per cent the banks represented 42 per cent at company meetings, the remaining 28 per cent being represented in the main by the shareholders themselves. In some cases the banks did not bother to take up their voting rights. If, as the report estimated, some 70–80 per cent of voting capital was represented at the average German company meeting then the banks as a whole represented on average over 50 per cent of the capital present: 9 per cent actually owned by themselves and 41 per cent in the form of proxies renewable every 15 months. The report further calculated that in twenty-three general meetings a single bank was able, solely through proxies which it held, or which had been 'lent' to it by others, to represent over 50 per cent of the capital present. In a further eighteen general meetings a single bank was able to achieve this through a combination of its own holdings and proxies.

A third way in which German banks interlock with other companies is through the seats held by bankers on supervisory boards. The concentration enquiry, looking at 391 of the companies mentioned earlier, found that in 1960, seventy-three of them had no bankers on their supervisory boards. Of the 1,722 non-employee representatives on the supervisory boards of the remaining 318 companies, 573, or about one third, were from banks. Three-quarters of these banking representatives came from only eleven credit institutions, and in 150 companies a banking representative was chairman of the board.

Looking specifically at the boards of the big three banks, the report found that trade and industry were well represented there and particularly the larger firms. The big three themselves were represented on thirty-seven of the forty-seven joint stock companies with members on their own boards. On the other hand the report stressed that none of the big three was dominated by any single large shareholder and that they were active in guarding against this. The executive board (*Vorstand*) of each bank preserved a large measure of independence, and former members of the management tended to occupy the key positions on each bank's supervisory board.

Finally, the report looked at the consortia organized for subscribing to issues by the private sector over the last few years. Between 1954 and 1961 it estimated that 1,354 consortia had subscribed to 160 issues, but that these 1,354 had been formed of only seventy-three banks, of which nineteen had played a dominant role. The main point was that the composition of the consortia had tended to become 'frozen' over the years and that there had been hardly any opportunity for outsiders to join them.

Credit institutions clearly wield a very considerable influence within the economy, and at certain points this influence would seem to contradict the principles on which German economic policy is based. The two most vital issues are the questions of the enhancement of the economic power of large firms, and the degree to which the economy may be said to be effectively centrally directed by a closely inter-linked group of banker-industrialists.

On the first question, it is well known that German banks, in making loans, tend to favour larger, well-established firms with a broad spread of activities as against new, small and highly specialized firms. Large firms offer greater financial security, if less spectacular growth and profitability, as well as more prestige. Similarly, the banks tend to be positively interested in promoting mergers, which are good business for banks, since they provide many services in the process of amalgamation, quite apart from any profitable share dealings a merger may facilitate. But before we condemn 'planning by banks' in Germany on this score, it would be as well to note that in the more competitive British capital market banks also play a large part in handling mergers; that the investing institutions as well as the shareholding public show a strong preference for blue chip shares; and that State planners in France similarly prefer to deal with large firms (see p. 150). Moreover, these aspects of banking undoubtedly reflect to a considerable extent the economic advantages of scale both to the firms concerned and to the economy as a whole. But, this emphasis on the large firm may not invariably promote the requirements of an efficient market economy, and this is one of the reasons why the German Government has developed the *Mittelstandspolitik* described earlier.

The thesis that an oligopolistic banking structure, closely linked to and providing finance for the leading firms in the economy, operates effectively to plan the economy in much the same way as the French State planners is based on two assumptions: that the bankers are so similar in their outlook and objectives that they act according to a common policy; and that their aims are similar in practice to those of State planners. The question whether the bankers really have sufficient control over industry may be allowed to cancel out with the similar point that the French planners also are not in a position entirely to dictate policy to firms; both have the same weapon for exercising a substantial influence, namely, control over important sources of finance. The German bankers have in addition their voting power on the boards of firms. As regards the second assumption, it is time that a banker seeking secure and profitable investments must take into account the expected future demand for a firm's products; this in turn requires a view about the overall development of the economy similar to the perspective provided by a national plan. The banker is, of course, more likely to stress profitability as a criterion, and thus to arrive at a slightly different result from the planner, who is liable, at the present stage of the art, to think more in terms of quantities. The 1964 report, examining the reasons why German banks acquire shares in firms, concluded that they are interested first in possessing a safety reserve of long-term capital, and second in preserving and extending their business contacts. But it is not entirely clear how much can be made of this point, since forecasts both of profit rates and of future levels of demand for several years ahead are uncertain, and since the French planners have recently been laying stress on factors that affect the competitiveness and hence the profitability of firms. Moreover, we have already noted that the German bankers tend to favour the large firm, so there is no great difference from this point of view either.

With respect to the assumption that there may be an identity of outlook and objectives among German bankers, the picture is again not entirely clear. State planners, in so far as they control or influence major sources of finance, act as a monopoly. Different branches of the planning agencies will operate with different objectives and according to different criteria, but their decisions will be subject to overall guidance from the central planning body. The study of relationships between German banks and industry and commerce, although it reveals an oligopolistic structure, and although the bankers may work according to similar criteria, has not given support to the view that the banks act in concert to control credit and co-ordinate the economy. Competition between the banks is clear and vigorous in the short-term money market (see p. 175), and it seems likely that it exists in the field of longer-term credit and investments also.

A major difference between the French planners and the German bankers, however, about which there is no ambiguity, is in their relationship with the Governments. In France the planners, though they have to struggle to maintain their influence, can rely on some degree of support from the Government. In Germany, since central co-ordination of the economy is contrary to the principles of the social market economy, the policy of the State is directed against the hold of the banks over German industry. If government policy were reversed, then the structure of the banks is well adapted to provide the 'teeth' of a planning system. But in the face of official hostility to central co-ordination by plans, the German economy remains financially oligopolistic rather than collectively directed.

IS THE ECONOMY PLANNED BY THE STATE?

If discrimination must be used in assessing how far the banks 'plan' the German economy, it must also be used in assessing how far the State 'plans' it. While Dr Erhard steered the German economy—the most recent period will be discussed later—plans, programmes, and targets were not unknown in the German public sector. The Bundesbahn established medium-term investment plans; 'Green Plans' were prepared annually for agriculture; the State established a road-building programme; there were successive targets set for house-building; and there were annual European Recovery Programme (ERP) plans. An expert committee was established in 1964 to forecast the country's economic development, and a start was made towards medium-term budgetary planning. These measures, however, whether they are taken separately or as a whole, were not the equivalent of a French national plan. There was never any overall growth target toward which the planners attempted to guide the economy as a whole by means of specific interventions.

Two of the specific examples given in the previous paragraph will be discussed here to illustrate the differences: the ERP plans, and the expert committee established in 1963. Another of them, German housing policy, has been described above, and the trend towards budgetary planning is considered in Chapter 8.

The grants and loans which flow from the ERP Fund are the most significant instrument the German State possesses for guiding private investment. The Fund has its origins in the Marshall Plan, from which Germany received about $1,300 million. By the London Debt Agreement of 1953, only $1,000 million of this assistance had to be repaid, and the Federal Government undertook the task of repayment, leaving the ERP Fund to go on growing.

By the end of 1966 the Fund amounted to about 8,800 million marks. Since 1950 the total Fund has turned over about three times in the form of credits; some 20,000 million marks have been in-injected into the economy in both credits and grants, of which 6,400 million have gone to Berlin. Loans from the Fund are administered by the Minister for Federal Property through the Kreditanstalt für Wiederaufbau, the Lastenausgleichsbank, and, in Berlin, the Berliner Industriebank; grants are provided either directly by the Fund or by the ministries to which money has been allocated. Each year a plan is drawn up to decide how funds are to be distributed. But these ERP 'plans' are clearly not comparable to French plans. The ERP Fund stands not at the centre of German economic policy but rather to one side; it is a kind of emergency reserve which can be used to inject funds rapidly and flexibly into certain key points in the economy when structural difficulties have arisen, or social problems have emerged. The Germans call it *Schwerpunkt* planning, and the *Schwerpünkte* at which funds have been concentrated have changed over the years. In the early period of reconstruction, when Germany was suffering from an acute shortage of capital, ERP grants and credits were provided mainly to help the basic industries, mining, energy and transport. With the end of the critical periods, the funds were switched decisively to the aid of medium and small-sized firms. To begin with, this aid was earmarked for smaller firms unable to get access to the capital market. As the effectiveness of the capital market increased, that is from 1959 onwards, the funds provided for small firms became directed more and more at fulfilling regional and social objectives—firms established in economically backward areas were given greater assistance, as were those established by refugees and expellees. In recent years two other objectives have grown in importance, first, the granting of aid to developing countries and secondly, the prevention of water and air pollution.

Apart from this general trend in the Fund's objectives there have been various special purposes for which it has been used—such as aid for the Saar, aid for the Berlin economy, particularly after the building of the wall in 1961, aid to those areas which suffered from the North Sea floods, and finally aid in recent years for the shipbuilding industry, and for the modernization of German docks. The 1967 ERP Plan amounted to 1,600 million marks, of which 720 million was earmarked for development aid, 487 million for the economy, and 326 million for Berlin.

ERP plans may thus be defined as a means for curing tensions in a market economy as they arise, rather than as a means of guiding the economy towards a national medium-term target. They are, in neo-liberal terminology, 'marktkonform'.

The second of the 'planning bodies' mentioned above, the 'expert committee for the observation of overall economic development' (*Sachverständigenrat*), is composed of five independent experts, drawn from either the universities or from the many economic and social institutes. The Law of 1963 establishing the committee, expressly forbids those in government service or those who work for employer or employee organizations from being appointed.

The task of the committee is to provide an annual report in which it examines the overall economic situation at the time and in the foreseeable future. In doing so, the committee is charged with investigating how 'within the framework of a market economy, price stability, a high level of employment and external equilibrium can be simultaneously maintained, together with steady and reasonable growth'. The report must also take account of the formation and distribution of income and property, and draw attention to any actual or possible tensions between aggregate supply and demand which might endanger the objectives mentioned above. The committee has to make its prognoses on the basis of different assumptions; it must also pick out dangerous trends and indicate the various possibilities for countering them; it cannot, however, recommend specific measures of economic policy. (The exact power of the committee to make proposals is the vaguest of the Law's stipulations.) The Government must make known to the legislature its opinion on the report at least eight weeks after it has been published. An amendment to the Law, passed in November 1966, enables the committee to present additional reports, if developments occur in specific areas which look like endangering the overall objectives; the Government can also ask the committee to present further reports.

So far the committee has been extremely cautious in making predictions about the future. In none of its first three reports does it attempt a quantitative forecast of the economy's development for more than a year ahead, and it has always presented alternative projections for even this short period. A certain pattern is recognizable in the committee's policy proposals. On the one hand it has insisted that measures be taken to secure Germany from the danger of imported inflation. In its first report (1964) it recommended the adoption of flexible exchange rates, a move which the Government rejected, and in its third report (1966) it made further, more moderate, recommendations to the same end—and in particular it proposed that the exchange rate should be raised gradually over a fixed period to counterbalance rises in the international price level. The committee has also consistently advocated the adoption of a productivity-orientated wage policy, another recommendation which the Government, while Dr Erhard was in power, did not adopt.

Broadly speaking, the committee established in 1964 can be said to reflect two trends: first, a tendency on the part of the German Government to look more scientifically at future economic developments; secondly a tendency for it to stress 'growth' as an objective alongside the traditional ones; and thirdly a responsiveness to the pressures for medium-term planning emanating from the EEC.

CONCLUSIONS

This chapter has looked at some of the ways in which Dr Erhard and his colleagues implemented the idea of the 'social market economy'. Late in 1966, however, Dr Erhard left office, the 'Grand Coalition' Government took power, and, for the first time since 1949, a Social Democrat, Professor Schiller, became Minister of Economics. Does this mean that German economic policy is now moving in a different direction?

To answer this question it is worth looking briefly into the recent history of the Social Democrat Party (the SPD). A remarkable re-orientation of the SPD's views on economic policy took place during the Adenauer-Erhard regime. In the early years after the last war the SPD was strongly in favour of a centrally directed economy, and in the Frankfurt Economic Council its representatives made it clear that they regarded a market economy as a catastrophe. From the 1954 party congress onwards, however, a transformation began to take place. In that year Professor Schiller enunciated the principle of 'as much competition as possible, as much planning as necessary'. This principle was to be given formal recognition in the Party's famous Godesberger Programme of 1959, which stated *inter alia* that the SPD 'supports the free market, where real competition is always present'. Subsequently the word 'socialization' was struck from the official Party handbook.

It could be predicted, therefore, that when the 'Grand Coalition' was formed there would not be a radical change in the direction of economic policy. Soon after taking office Professor Schiller explicitly stated that the Government intended to achieve a synthesis between the neo-liberal imperative of competition and the Keynesian idea of managing aggregate demand. In fact the new Government has in some ways been more energetic than its predecessor in fulfilling neo-liberal principles. It has totally freed interest rates in the banking sector from official regulation; it has finally passed the law introducing an added-value turnover tax; it has established a special working group on competition in the Economics Ministry, which will study ways and means of improving legislation in this field; it has announced its intention to cut back unnecessary subsidies in the agricultural and social spheres; and it has put forward a comprehensive plan for adapting the German coal industry to new competitive conditions. Only in the transport sector has it made proposals which may increase controls.

The new Government's use of the budget as an anti-cyclical weapon in 1967, and the important legislation which it passed in June of that year enabling it to vary tax rates, establish an anti-cyclical reserve fund, and initiate a system of medium-term budgetary planning (see pp. 227–9), may also be seen, not so much as a break but as a continuation of policies started by Dr Erhard. Where the new Government does go beyond its predecessor is in the greater importance it attaches to growth targets. The estimates on which budgetary planning is to be based—that is, a 4 per cent annual increase in the real gross national product between 1968 and 1971, with price rises limited to about 1 per cent per annum—have been stated by Professor Schiller to be not merely projections, but a political programme, and are being used as the basis for what he calls 'concerted action'. The latter takes the form of regular meetings between the Government and both sides of industry to work out a productivity-orientated and equitable incomes policy. The provision which the new Government inserted in the legislation of June 1967, obliging the Government henceforth to make an annual economic report in which it makes a quantitative statement of its economic and financial objectives, may also be taken as an indication of this new emphasis. It remains to be seen whether this increased accent on growth and quantitative objectives will come into conflict with the Coalition Government's simultaneous desire to preserve and intensify neo-liberal policies.

A few conclusions regarding the questions raised at the beginning of this chapter may now be stated. First, it is misleading to categorize the principles which guided German economic policy after 1948 as those of either 'laissez faire' or 'dirigisme'. They amounted rather to a policy of positive, co-ordinated State intervention carefully moulded to achieve specific and limited objectives.

The extent to which these principles have been implemented has varied in the different economic sectors. There are certainly many areas in which little has been done to achieve a 'social market economy'. Possibly the most important deficiencies are the high level of protection accorded to agriculture; the oligopolistic capital market; the slowness with which steps were taken to free interest rates in the money market; the unco-ordinated and often protective measures taken with regard to the energy market; the preservation of several tax privileges long after they had outlived their original purpose; the long delay in changing the form of the turnover tax; the slowness in developing an anticyclical budgetary policy; the development of social policy in the direction of 'blanket' payments; and the failure to ban resale price maintenance or to control mergers.

But there are an impressive number of actions which stand to the credit of the social market economy. Prominent amongst these are the priority continuously accorded to monetary stability, and the special measures taken to help the Bundesbank achieve this; the positive policy towards removing barriers on international trade and payments; the careful modelling and gradual reduction of intervention in the housing market; the radical change in the traditional policy towards cartels; the positive measures taken to help smaller firms and to prevent excessive financial interlocking; the reform of the income and corporation taxes; and the broad range of measures taken to encourage widespread property ownership. On the whole, it can be said that German economic policy-makers have exerted considerable effort to put principles into practice during the period under discussion.

The following is a selection of works on German economic policy:

Patrick Boarman, *Germany's Economic Dilemma: inflation and the balance of payments*, New Haven-London, Yale University Press, 1964.

L. Erhard, *Prosperity through Competition*, Thames and Hudson, London, 1958.

W. Eucken, *Die Grundlagen der Nationalökonomie*, Godesberg, Küpper (5th ed.), 1947

W. Eucken, *Grundsätze der Wirtschaftspolitik*, Tübingen, J. C. B. Mohr (Paul Siebeck), 1952.

Hans Herbert Götz, *Weil alle besser leben wollen: Porträt der deutschen Wirtschaftspolitik*, Düsseldorf, Econ-Verlag, 1963.

G. Gutmann, H. J. Hochstrate and R. Schlüter, *Die Wirtschaftsverfassung der Bundesrepublik Deutschland: Entwicklung und ordnungspolitische Grundlagen*, Stuttgart, Gustav Fischer Verlag, 1964.

Albert Hunold (ed.), *Wirtschaft ohne Wunder: Volkswirtschaftliche Studien*, Erlenbach-Zürich, Eugen Rentsch Verlag, 1953.

Carlo Mötteli, *Licht und Schatten der sozialen Marktwirtschaft*, Zürich, Eugen Rentsch Verlag, 1961.

A. Müller-Armack, *Wirtschafts ordnung- und Wirtschaftspolitik*, Freiburg am Breisgau, Verlag Rombach, 1966.

A. Plitzko (ed.), *Planung ohne Planwirtschaft*, Basle, Kyklos-Verlag, 1964.

Frederick G. Reuss, *Fiscal Policy for Growth without Inflation: the German Experiment*, Baltimore, Johns Hopkins Press, 1963.

Karl W. Roskamp, *Capital Formation in West Germany*, Detroit, Wayne State University Press, 1965.

Sachverständigenrat zur Begutachtung der gesamtwirtshaftlichen

Entwicklung: *Jahresgutachten* 1964, 1965, 1966, Deutscher Bundestag, Drucksache IV/2890, V/123, V/1160, Bonn.

G. Stolper, K. Hauser, K. Borchardt, *Deutsche Wirtschaft seit 1870*, Tübingen, J. C. B. Mohr (Paul Siebeck), 1966.

Henry C. Wallich, *Mainsprings of the German Revival*, New Haven, Yale University Press, 1955.

CHAPTER 3

FRANCE: A NATIONAL PROGRAMME

The account of indicative planning in France given in this chapter has deliberately been kept brief, and concentrates on the most important developments in the techniques and practices of planning which have been introduced in the Fourth and Fifth Plans. This approach has been chosen for two reasons. There are already general studies of French planning available to the English reader and the considerable interest in French planning methods which grew up in Britain around 1960 has made the English reader much more familiar with economic problems and policies in France than in Germany.[1] Most of the studies of French planning have, however, tended to devote more attention to the earlier plans and to a general description of the planning process than to the many important changes which have been made with each new plan. This chapter seeks to fill this gap by analysing in some detail the important innovations of the Fourth and Fifth Plans and the substantial modifications in the planners' position and influence in economic policy-making circles which have occurred in the last few years. At a time when the purpose and usefulness of indicative planning are being severely re-examined in Britain it is particularly interesting to examine the changes which the French planners have felt compelled to make in their system.

THE FIRST THREE PLANS, 1946–61

Although the French economy has been guided by national programmes throughout the postwar period, it was not until the Fourth Plan (1962–5) that a reasonably sophisticated programme was introduced and its contribution to economic policy-making fully discussed. The First Plan (1946–52) illustrates the very pragmatic

[1] See the selected references on pp. 106–7.

origins of French planning. It was not the result of theoretical or ideological debates but a response to the problems and pressures of the immediate postwar situation. The American authorities were anxious that Marshall Aid funds should be rationally employed, and insisted that some kind of plan be drawn up to ensure this. The task of reconstruction obviously required large-scale intervention by the State, and this created a favourable environment for the development of some kind of national planning. But it was by no means inevitable that the model chosen should contain the features which are now characteristic of French planning. The development of planning along these lines was due in large measure to the ideas and personality of M. Jean Monnet, who was appointed as the first Commissaire Général du Plan in 1946. M. Monnet looked beyond the immediate task of postwar reconstruction. The performance of the French economy in the interwar years had given rise to a considerable body of opinion which attributed France's low rate of economic growth to the excessively cautious, restrictive attitude of industrialists, summed up in the term *Malthusianisme économique*. Monnet conceived the process of planning not in authoritarian or centralist terms, but as a dialogue between the Commissariat du Plan at the centre and Modernization Commissions representing the interests of particular industries and sectors in the economy, from which would emerge a thorough analysis of the possibilities of expansion. The development of improved statistical and econometric techniques and the refinement of forecasting methods in the later plans have not influenced the planners to dispense with this process of consultation and exchange of information. The most sophisticated quantitative forecasts still have to be supplemented by analyses of the particular problems and prospects of different sectors of the economy. This can be done only through extensive discussions with industrialists, trade unionists and others who are involved in the day-to-day running of industry. Monnet argued that it was necessary to raise the expectations of businessmen and remove some of the uncertainty which resulted in both business and private savings being diverted into channels that were relatively safe and reasonably profitable in the short term at the expense of more productive but longer-term and riskier investment. His solution was to supplement the typical French industrialist's short-term view of the market with a national programme indicating the feasibility of a given rate of expansion over a longer period. This thinking did not rely solely on the idea that faster growth could be attained simply by setting a global target and trusting that this would have a stimulating effect on businessmen, although there was something of this in it. Much more central was the belief that a coherent programme setting out the possibilities of expansion for each sector of the economy would provide every industry with the assurance that it would be able to secure the supplies and outlets necessary to justify the forecast rate of expansion. It was to carry this concept into practice that the system of indicative planning at both the central and the industry level was adopted.

The First Plan, however, was a special case. The exigencies of reconstruction demanded that the resources of the economy be concentrated on the basic industries. As a result the First Plan was centred round the heavy industries and transport, most of which were publicly owned; and private industry, especially the consumer goods industries, was accorded a very low priority. The effect of the Plan on business expectations and attitudes in the private sector is thus very hard to estimate. The restricted scope of the Plan was significant in other ways. There was virtually no problem of allocation: the objectives of reconstruction and development of the basic industries were almost self-selecting. The question of the extent to which the Plan's forecasts should replace the traditional criteria of the market was thus postponed. Another important point was the planners' acceptance of inflation as a consequence of heavy investment programmes and restrictions on consumer goods without adequate control of incomes. It is arguable whether this was a sound policy; but the planners circumvented the balance-of-payments consequences by means of import and exchange controls, and eventually devaluation, on the grounds that without an expansion of productive capacity and the removal of bottlenecks on the supply side neither growth nor stability would be achieved.

The objectives of the Second Plan (1954-7) followed fairly logically from the strategy adopted in the First. In place of the basic sector programmes the Second Plan concentrated on a series of 'basic actions' aimed at increasing productivity. The manufacturing sector, in particular, was given a much higher priority than in the First Plan, and tentative targets for industries were drawn up. But the really important aspect of the Plan was its insistence on the need to remove restrictive practices and to concentrate and rationalize the highly protected, small-scale manufacturing sector.

Most of the Plan targets were considerably overfulfilled. (The machine-tool industry was a notable exception.) Output increased more rapidly than it has done in any other five-year period since the war and investment easily surpassed the targets set. Public expenditure, both civil and military, rose sharply and social investment grew much faster than planned. This rapid expansion was quickly reflected in rising prices and an increasing deficit on the balance of payments but the Government sought to deal with these problems by methods other than the reduction of domestic demand.

The planners' responsibility for the success and failure of the Second Plan is not easy to estimate. In one sense they were very powerful. It was during this period that their control over sources of finance was at its most extensive and they had at their disposal a wide range of financial and fiscal incentives available to firms carrying out projects compatible with the Plan targets. Although the planners had very limited control over the growth of public expenditure there is little evidence that they considered that the rapid rise in prices could or should be halted by a restriction on any form of domestic demand. They were, therefore, responsible for urging that the growth of output should have priority over stable prices and, in consequence, for encouraging French businessmen to press ahead with expansion schemes in the knowledge that deflationary policies were unlikely. On the other hand, although the planners were a powerful expansionary force, the role of the actual forecasts and targets in the Plan is less clear cut. They were, despite some doubts during their formulation, not unambitious and it could well have been that they had a sizeable influence on events through their impact on expectations. But because in the event the targets were very considerably over-fulfilled, the planners must have found them only of limited use as criteria for their controls and incentives, and by the later years of the plan this must have been true also for industrialists. In these circumstances it is reasonable to conclude that it was not the internal coherence of the Plan which persuaded businessmen that a high rate of growth was possible but the stimulus of an inflationary economy and the willingness of the planners to promote incoherent expansion. The use of import controls and devaluation reduced the impact of rising prices on the balance of payments but the absence of control over internal demand allowed the consumer goods industries to expand much faster than the planners had forecast, at the expense of the capital goods industries where modernization was urgently required. The structural changes which the planners hoped to bring about in these industries were not achieved as the high level of domestic demand allowed inefficient firms to survive and removed any incentive to rationalize or amalgamate. The Second Plan was not, therefore, proof of the value of an indicative programme. It did illustrate what a powerful 'growth lobby' with resources at its disposal could achieve, but the growth that took place was not closely in accordance with the planners' priorities and was made possible by the very special and temporary circumstances of the French economy.

The Third Plan (1957–61) was the first attempt at a thoroughly integrated and coherent national programme. Techniques of forecasting and the available data were by this time greatly improved, and for the first time an input-output matrix, based on the year 1954, was used to give greater formality to the various industry targets. The targets for the different sectors were much more seriously calculated, and a series of production and investment objectives were set out for all major industries. There was also a more positive strategy than in the Second Plan. Large and continuing foreign trade deficits, and the impact of the newly-established European Economic Community, made a balance on external payments in the face of increased foreign competition a necessary condition for the Plan's success. The investment targets reflected this concern, and in the allocation of resources strong preference was shown for projects that would save imports and promote exports. During this period an Intermediate Plan (1960–1) also had to be prepared to stimulate expansion after the severe deflationary measures that accompanied the devaluation of 1958. This illustrated the important and awkward problem of harmonizing a medium-term plan for growth with shorter-term policy aimed at maintaining stability and a balance on external payments.

THE FOURTH AND FIFTH PLANS

The Fourth Plan (1962–5) occurred against a background of resurgent interest in planning, and introduced several important innovations in the methods of preparation and implementation of the Plan. General de Gaulle himself commended the Fourth Plan to the attention of the nation, and the Minister of Finance, M. Giscard d'Estaing, indicated that the annual budget would be worked out in the context of the Plan, and that economic policy generally would be formulated with reference to its objectives. The scope of the planning process was also significantly widened. It was no longer concerned simply with promoting the growth of production, but also took into account the allocation of the increment. This was made explicit in the measures taken to integrate a policy for prices and incomes into the Plan for the first time, the priority given to social investment, and the co-ordination of regional development policy with the national objectives of the Plan. There were also a number of refinements in forecasting techniques, and the Fourth Plan provided the most complete working example of a consistent and detailed programme for growth. It is this particular exercise that has been taken as the model of an indicative planning system by those countries, notably Britain, that began around 1961 to show keen interest in the French Plans.

This last point is of some significance, since it raises the question of the desirability of the refinement of detail in such programmes. During the period of the First and Second Plans, which were only partial attempts at national programmes, economic growth was no less fast, and in one or two years actually faster, than during the period since 1958 when more refined programming methods were introduced. But the price of this earlier growth was rapid inflation and cumulatively serious balance-of-payments crises, which would not now be tolerated. It is therefore possible to argue that it was the refusal of the authorities to enforce the constraints on the growth of the economy which allowed this rapid expansion by encouraging industrialists to believe that serious deflationary policies were not likely to be applied. The contribution of the quantitative forecasts of the Plans may still have been important in organizing this optimism but the peculiar situation of the French economy at this time was probably a more powerful factor. Stability of prices and a balance —in the case of the Fourth Plan a surplus—on external payments are now firmly established as necessary conditions for a sustained high rate of growth, and it is no longer possible, deliberately or otherwise, to mortgage price stability to the achievement of more rapid expansion or more specific gains such as an increase in social welfare expenditure. In these circumstances it is legitimate to ask whether a more refined forecasting system can help to stimulate and promote growth with stability. Experience of the working of a sophisticated indicative programme is still relatively slight, and in considering what returns may accrue from reorganizing economic management around such a programme it is necessary to pay a great deal of attention to the experience of the Fourth Plan, together with the modifications that have been introduced in the Fifth Plan. This does not, however, unduly limit the applicability of the analysis, for in other countries where indicative planning has been or is being adopted, methods similar to the French are being followed. We now proceed, therefore, to examine in more detail the methods used in the preparation of the Fourth and Fifth Plans.

The first stage of the work on the Fourth Plan began in 1959 when the Commissariat du Plan, in collaboration with the Service des Etudes Economiques et Financières (SEEF) of the Ministry of Finance, produced a projection of the economy up to 1975. The aim of this fairly general preliminary study was to investigate the long-term trends of population, productivity, consumption patterns and technical developments, before formulating more detailed medium-term estimates for the four-year period to 1965. The projection was based on three possible average annual rates of growth: 3 per cent, 4·5 per cent and 6 per cent, chosen in a fairly arbitrary fashion. The 3 per cent variant represented a falling off in the rate of growth registered in the 1950s, while 6 per cent constituted a higher rate of growth than had previously been achieved for any length of time. The planners attached considerable importance to this experiment in analysing the consequences and problems of different rates of expansion, since it allowed a more accurate assessment of the maximum rate of growth given the available human and material resources, technological developments, stability of prices and a balance of external payments. The analysis of the variants further served as a check on the adoption of incompatible policies by the Government; for example, an option for increased investment expenditure on social welfare projects could be shown to be attainable only at the expense of private consumption, if a lower variant were chosen; a high variant might permit such projects, but the pressure of the overall demand on resources would then cause inflation.

In the spring of 1960 the initial study for the Fourth Plan was submitted to the Conseil Economique et Social, a kind of official economic parliament, on which all the main interest groups in the economy are represented. The Investment and Planning Section of the Council discussed the draft forecasts with the planners and recommended that a rate of growth as close as possible to the 6 per cent variant should be chosen, and that certain priorities be established, particularly a large increase in social investment. On the basis of these recommendations the Government issued an outline of the broad general objectives of the Plan. These objectives were essentially political choices about the rate of growth of output, the desired balance of external payments, and the allocation of resources between consumption and investment and between productive and social welfare expenditure.

The third stage is the preparation by the Commissariat du Plan of a detailed and coherent forecast for the terminal year of the Plan, tracing out the implications of the general objectives. The basic technique involves projecting in base-year prices the resources of the economy and the various uses to which they will be directed.[1] The assumption of a target rate of growth gives an estimate of gross domestic product. To obtain a figure for the total supply of resources the volume of imports likely to be required in the terminal year of the Plan must be added. This kind of calculation is extremely difficult, but by projecting the previously recorded ratio of imports to gross domestic product, and correcting it to take account of reasonably foreseeable factors likely to increase or decrease dependence on foreign goods and services, an estimate can be obtained. The uses to which these total resources will be put are then calculated. Some demand variables are more or less fixed by the objectives already published, public investment, especially social investment, being an example in the Fourth Plan and military expenditure in the Fifth Plan. The achievement of the given rate of growth of output requires an increase in productive investment, which is estimated by extrapolation, using the incremental capital–output ratios registered in past periods. This initial figure is later discussed in the Modernization Commissions and corrections are made to take account of technical developments and the probable increases in labour productivity in different sectors. In the Fourth Plan the incremental capital–output ratio was set surprisingly low at 3·3, on account of optimistic assumptions about the contribution to increased productivity of technical and organizational improvements despite a virtually static labour force. The investment needs of the Fifth Plan were on the other hand revised upwards. Another key

[1] For a detailed exposition of how the Fourth Plan was prepared see E. Betout-Mossé, Comptabilité Nationale et le IVe Plan, *Etudes et Conjoncture*, April–May 1962, INSEE, Paris.

variable is exports, which are even more difficult to forecast than imports. The method used in the Fourth Plan was essentially to set a figure that could balance the required imports, to discuss its feasibility with industrialists, and to produce a final estimate which reflected both the expected and the desired increase. Consumption is finally determined as a residual, and the programme then appears as a coherent physical balance between resources and uses in the terminal year of the Plan.

When the initial outline of the Plan is complete it forms the basis for consultations with the Modernization Commissions, which are responsible for breaking down the global targets. Each Commission, which includes industrialists, trade unionists, civil servants and independent experts, is responsible for a particular branch or sector of the economy, and is required to submit a report indicating, where possible in quantitative form, the implications of the Plan for its sector, the problems it is likely to encounter and the measures which will be needed to ensure that the sector fulfils its role in the plan. In the Fourth Plan the Commissions were asked to pay particular attention to the volume and pattern of imports and exports in their sectors, and the degree to which firms in their sectors could play a part in the policy for regional development. The Commissions are also asked to check and modify the calculations of the national planners, and to provide information on matters such as technical innovations, structural changes, and institutional developments which the planners might have overlooked or misinterpreted. One of the most valuable functions of the Commissions is to check on the technical relationships, for example the capital–output ratio, the imports—GDP ratio and the pattern of inter-industry transactions, by drawing on their practical experience in particular industries. As a guide for the Commissions' work the planners produced an input-output table of sixty-four columns, and the Centre des Recherches et de la Documentation sur la Consommation (CREDOC) made projections of the pattern and structure of final demand by groups of products. By these methods the plan is disaggregated to the level of individual branches. The work of the Commissions, and the discussions they provoke at the Commissariat du Plan, are considered extremely valuable, and in the Fifth Plan they have continued to play an important role.

The extent to which indicative planning is worth while as an aid to policies aimed at removing obstacles to growth on the side of supply is largely dependent on the quality of the information supplied by the Modernization Commissions. Inevitably this varies. The report on the energy sector in the Fourth Plan was of the high quality to be expected from sophisticated and dynamic nationalized enterprises. Those produced by some of the more modern industries were much less informative than might have been hoped. In other sectors such as the varied, predominantly small-scale engineering industry, the reports reflect the difficulties involved in making target planning effective and useful in such circumstances. The Fifth Plan places much less stress than its predecessors on detailed branch or industry targets. But its major concern, to reshape French manufacturing industry into a more competitive structure, requires even greater cooperation from industry particularly in the provision of detailed industrial statistics. A system of industry planning is probably the most effective way in which reasonably reliable and comprehensive data of this kind can be collected.

When the Commissions have completed their work, their reports are married with the draft programme originally prepared by the planners, and a final synthesis is established after much consultation, both formal and informal, between the planners and the Commissions, which forms the basis of the final draft of the plan. The task of preparing the synthesis is entrusted to five 'horizontal' Commissions: general economy and finance, manpower, research, productivity and regional development. Each of these Commissions has the job of ensuring that the aggregation of the data supplied by the 'vertical' Commissions is compatible with the global parameters of the plan. Important alterations can be and have been made at this stage, and it is in this dialogue with the various Commissions that the Commissariat du Plan, as a centre of communications and clearing house of information, frequently plays its most important role.

The two most important 'horizontal' Commissions are those dealing with manpower and the general economy. The Manpower Commission prepares a forecast of the manpower resources and requirements taking account of productivity trends. In the Fourth Plan it recommended that the target rate of growth be increased from the Government's choice of 5 per cent to 5.5 per cent since productivity estimates emerging from the reports of the 'vertical' Commissions were estimated to result in too high a level of unemployment if production were to grow at only 5 per cent annually. The General Economy and Finance Commission, the most important

Commission, is concerned with the relationship between the financial equilibrium of the economy and the programme prepared in volume terms. Financial disequilibrium could of course distort the targets mapped out in volume terms by altering the balance between consumption and investment thus blocking necessary investments through a lack or a misdirection of savings, and creating a deficit on external payments. In the Fourth Plan the financial balances drawn up by the Commission were in no sense even 'indicative targets' but they carry much greater weight in the Fifth Plan, as will be described later.

After the final synthesis is drawn up it is submitted to the Conseil Supérieur du Plan, the planning council, whose chairman is the Prime Minister and which includes representatives from the main interest groups. Its task is to follow the execution of the plan and recommend changes or corrections if the original objectives seem unlikely to be achieved. The plan is then submitted once more to the Conseil Economique et Social, and in this forum some of the most informed debates take place. The report on the Fourth Plan was approved by the Council, but with 15 votes against and 42 abstentions out of 101 members—a reflection largely of the dissatisfaction of the trade union movement. The criticism of the Fifth Plan was much wider and much more vehement and the report to the Council was approved only after substantial amendments which reflected the many disagreements raised. Much of the argument was about the possibility of financing the Plan without inflation or a reduction in some of the items of social expenditure in order to provide more funds for productive investment and increased spending on defence. The representatives of the trade union movement again opposed the Plan almost unanimously but there were also many other critics who opposed various of the basic choices of the Plan as undesirable or not feasible. These debates emphasize the difficulties involved in operating a system of medium-term planning in an open economy liable to inflation, and should dispel any remaining notion that national planning is a panacea for economic problems.[1]

The very last step is the submission of the Plan to Parliament. Until the reforms of the Fifth Plan this offered much less opportunity for a genuine democratic debate than a bald description suggests. The Plan was presented to the Assembly in the form of a

[1] See Avis et Rapports du Conseil Economique et Social sur le Projet du Ve Plan, quoted in *Le Monde*, September 29–30, 1965, and October 2, 1965.

two-clause Bill, as a 'framework for investment programmes and an instrument of orientation of economic expansion and social progress'. It is difficult to imagine any deputy being so disaffected by every detail of the Plan that he would oppose the Bill in its entirety. On the other hand it is equally implausible that every detail should prove satisfactory. The outcome of this situation was a rambling debate in which the particular interests of members were raised, with very few speeches treating the broad options on which the Plan was based. It must be admitted, however, that the circumstances were hardly favourable to such a debate. For by the time the Plan appeared before Parliament it had been polished into a coherent, rounded entity which could not be substantially changed without immense and impracticable difficulties. It was in fact as massive, detailed and technical a document as the annual Finance Bill but could not reasonably, or indeed logically, be discussed clause by clause.

The Fifth Plan (1966–70) was a broadly similar exercise to the Fourth Plan, but there were important changes. In August 1962 the Government asked the Commissariat du Plan to prepare a preliminary report on the general orientation of the economy on the basis of an *'esquisse centrale'*: an outline showing the rate of growth to be chosen for the Plan, the broad balance between investment and consumption, the pattern of consumption, and the general lines of social and regional development policy. A working party, the 'Groupe de Travail 1985', was appointed to carry out this study.[1] It was not simply an exercise in long-term economic forecasting but a much broader 'brainstorming' effort to analyse the major technical, demographic and social changes likely to occur in France over the next generation, and their economic implications. These very long-term studies, though inevitably academic and hypothetical, are considered to have an important role in setting the medium-term plans in perspective and providing a link between each plan and its successor.

The analysis of the variants was much fuller than that employed in the preparation of the Fourth Plan.[2] They were divided into two categories. First, two basic projections, the higher involving an average annual rate of growth of GNP of 4·7 per cent and the lower

[1] *Réflexions pour* 1985, La Documentation Française, Paris, 1964.
[2] Préparation du Ve Plan, Rapport sur les Principales Options, *Journal Officiel*, December 23, 1964.

a rate of 3·7 per cent, were tried out for investment and man-power implications. A second series of variants were concerned with the distribution of the increased output. This was a natural extension of the Fourth Plan, which had for the first time attempted to indicate a pattern as well as a rate of growth. The specific variants discussed were:

a reduction of weekly hours worked by 10 per cent;
the general introduction of a fifth week of annual holidays with pay;
a reduction from 65 to 60 in the age when a State retirement pension is awarded, and an increase in that pension from 20 to 40 per cent of earnings;
an increase in the rate of growth of private consumption from 3·5 to 3·75 per cent a year;
an increase in social investment;
an increase in social security benefits such as sickness benefit, housing allowances and family allowances.

Each of these hypotheses clearly had significant implications for the rate of growth chosen as the basis for the plan, as well as for social policy. Possibly the most important issue in the French economy is the choice between an increase in personal consumption and a reduction in working hours which must, owing to the general shortage of labour, result in a reduction in the rate of growth unless productivity could be sufficiently improved by investment in new techniques. To examine this problem more fully the planners used a simple linear programming model to work out the effect of variations in the inputs and the cost of labour and in the techniques used in production, on productivity and on the rate of growth.[1]

More generally, the study of variants represented the desire of the Government, in response to considerable pressure, to make the planning process more democratic by setting out as thoroughly as possible the implications of different policy aims. Instead of submitting the draft plan to a special committee such as the Conseil Economique et Social in fully worked-out form, the planners produced a document which was the basis of a parliamentary debate in December 1964, on the *esquisse centrale* of the Fifth Plan. This was the first time the French Assembly had been introduced at this

[1] The results of this study are set out in an appendix of Préparation du Ve Plan, op. cit.

stage of the planning timetable, and therefore the first time it had been given the opportunity of debating the plan before it had become a finalized document which it was practically impossible to alter. It must be added, however, that the debate revolved around the central variant already chosen by the planners, and Parliament was not in practice able to insist that it be replaced by a significantly different alternative.

VALUE PLANNING

Apart from the study of variants, the most interesting aspects of the Fifth Plan are its attempts to reconcile the physical plan with financial flows, and to integrate medium-term programmes with short-term economic policy aimed at preventing fluctuations in the economy. A programme formulated for the terminal year of a four- or five-year period, and expressed in terms of a physical balance between resources and uses (that is, a balance formulated in constant prices) presupposes price stability and a steady rate of growth, and offers little help to short-term economic policy aimed at correcting disequilibria during the period of the plan. The work of the General Economy and Finance Commission on the Fourth Plan was an attempt to parallel the physical forecast with estimates of the movement of different categories of incomes compatible with it, and with an analysis of the problems of guiding public and private savings into the channels required by the investment projects of the plan. But it was a very tentative exercise, and did not pretend to set any financial targets. The inflationary developments which led to the interruption of the Fourth Plan by the Stabilization Plan of 1963, and the general accumulation of inflationary pressures in the French economy since then, have compelled the planners to pay much more attention to the problems of maintaining stability, and to indicate in some detail the ways in which stabilization measures can be integrated into a medium-term programme. The increasing emphasis on social policy in the plans is another factor requiring some kind of incomes planning, since it involves the redistribution of income in favour of certain sectors of the community, such as farmers and retired people. It also introduces an additional source of inflationary pressure into the plan, by increasing the amount of resources to be devoted to uses that are, at least on a short-term view, unproductive.

In response to these pressures the planners have developed a system of 'value-planning' (*programmation en valeur*). This was first suggested by M. Massé after a conference on incomes policy held in 1963. 'The function of value planning would be to set out guidelines for the growth of the main categories of income, wages and salaries, social security benefits, farm incomes and profits. It would also indicate the conditions for an equilibrium of savings and investment and public expenditure and receipts.'[1] One of the features of indicative planning in volume terms is that it leaves private consumption virtually unplanned. The growth of consumption would, of course, be limited by the targets set for investment, particularly public investment. But since consumption depends on incomes which are the outcome of 'unplanned' bargaining and negotiations, too rapid a growth of consumption could reduce the funds available for the planned investment programmes or cause them to be obtained only at the cost of inflation. Similarly, policies aimed at restraining consumption may, if continued too long or pressed too severely, reduce investment opportunities. An indicative programme in value terms would sketch out for different categories of incomes the rates of growth compatible with the growth of productivity forecast in the Plan.

This is done in some detail in the Fifth Plan. The first financial 'target' set is the estimated tolerable increase in the general price level. This is compounded out of a series of estimated increases for different products and sectors. The overall figure adopted in the Plan is an annual average increase of 1·5 per cent, although the General Economy and Finance Commission base their calculations on the slightly less optimistic forecast of a 1·9 per cent increase. It is calculated that the annual average increase (in real terms) of wage and salary incomes, net of tax, in the non-agricultural sectors should be 3·3 per cent; this is a significantly lower rate of growth than in any other period since 1954. The increase for undistributed profits is on the other hand higher than the level for any past period since that date; the annual growth rate in the Fifth Plan is 6·4 per cent. The planners consider this figure as the minimum necessary to allow the planned investment growth to be financed. It reflects a deliberate attempt to relieve the pressure on profit margins imposed by the price controls of the Stabilization Plan, the increase

[1] P. Massé, Rapport sur la Politique des Revenus, La Documentation Française, *Recueils et Monographies*, No. 47, 1964, p. 26.

in labour costs and the impact of foreign competition.[1] Although the above figures are only guidelines for policy the planners do consider them as serious measurements of the constraints on the economy which must be respected if the Plan is to remain feasible. They enable 'further information to be obtained about the problem of the limits of growth. These limits stem less from a shortage of physical resources in the economy than from the need to maintain stability by anticipating the phenomenon of overheating.'[2]

The setting of income guidelines is of course no substitute for an incomes policy.[3] It presupposes such a policy but it does not solve the problem of how to implement it at various levels. Indeed the planners admit that 'the Government considers that for the present it is not possible to think in terms of a contractual incomes policy'.[4] The norms in the Fifth Plan are also highly aggregated; there is no attempt to set norms for individual industries. The sections on incomes policy in the Fifth Plan recognize this difficulty and the interim solution proposed is to refer cases where the norm seems particularly inapplicable to a 'Collège d'Etude et d'Appréciation des Revenus'. This body was to be modelled on the National Incomes Commission in the United Kingdom, staffed by independent experts and empowered only to make recommendations, which would not be binding, but would be published at the Government's discretion. Particular care would be taken not to publish when the case concerns firms that are readily identifiable. In his report on the Incomes Conference M. Massé suggested that the guidelines should be altered according to the productivity performances of different industries. Other factors such as the pressure on profit margins in export industries should also be taken into account. The contribution that indicative planning can make to the working out of an incomes policy along those lines must be to provide detailed information about the conditions and prospects in different sectors and thus increase the amount of information upon which specific decisions about increases in incomes can be based. But in the present

---

[1] Ve Plan de Développement Economique et Social (1966–70), Tome I, Paris, Imprimerie Nationale, November 1965, p. 147 ff. The most detailed discussion of the financial targets is to be found in the *Rapport de la Commission de l'Economie Générale et du Financement* for the Fifth Plan, Commissariat du Plan, Summer 1966.

[2] Préparation du Ve Plan, op. cit., p. 54.

[3] For a fuller discussion see Chapter 9.

[4] Préparation du Ve Plan, op. cit., p. 23.

circumstances an effective incomes policy which lessens the need for general restrictions remains a necessary condition for the Plan's success which has yet to be fulfilled.

The introduction of value planning has also led to a much more detailed study of how the investment outlined in the Plan is financed in both the public and private sectors. This is a considerable innovation, for the earlier plans were marked by a general lack of consideration of financial flows. The Stabilization Plan of 1963 produced a flurry of effort in this field. Two main aims underlay this. The first was to manage public expenditure so that eventually, wherever possible, a balanced budget would be achieved, and a source of inflationary pressure removed. The second concerned the arrangements for financing the Treasury 'découvert', i.e. the amount of government expenditure not covered by tax receipts. The standard practice in France has been to finance the découvert by the issue of short-term Treasury bonds redeemable after three or five years. These bonds are not put out to competitive tender; they are sold directly to the public and the banks are required to maintain a certain minimum holding. They have proved extremely popular since, in addition to the liquidity and security which they offer, their effective yield is increased by the provisions for relieving the interest obtained from personal income tax.

The Government has for some time been concerned about the growth of this form of saving. Its expansion has further reduced the already limited attractiveness of longer-term securities and has made it more difficult and more costly for firms to raise money on the capital market. As the squeeze on profit margins reduced the possibilities of self-financing this became a threat to the investment foreseen by the Plans. The preference for highly liquid assets has also increased the liquidity of the banking system and the possibilities of an excessive expansion of credit. Finally, the reluctance of savers to hold longer-term securities has compelled the Treasury to 'transform' the short-term funds into long-term credits required to finance investment in both the private and public sectors through the media of the specialized financial institutions such as the Caisse des Dépôts et des Consignations, the Crédit Foncier and the Crédit National. This process of transformation is to be progressively replaced. The Treasury will meet its 'uncovered' requirements by direct long-term borrowing and the issue of short-term bonds will be reduced. Together with the suppression of the budget deficit this will release some private savings which, it is hoped, will expand and develop the supply of funds on the capital market and help to lower the cost of raising capital. Medium-term bank credit is also expected to expand considerably as an alternative to Treasury bonds, and investment trusts, hitherto unknown in France, have been established to allow firms and investors easier and cheaper access to the capital market.

Much of this reorganization stems from the recommendations of a group of experts, known as the Lorain Report.[1] But the report stressed that the task of removing the ingrained preference of French investors for short-term assets must necessarily take time. There is, therefore, a danger that the private savings released by the reduction of the *découvert* and the restricted role of the Treasury will not go immediately into productive investment. If this were to happen the effect of the new policy, at least initially, would be deflationary and prevent the plan forecasts from being achieved.

The increasing attention paid to the problems and methods of financing the medium-term plans has important implications for the French planning system. First, the insistence on a return to more balanced budgets and a closer scrutiny of public expenditure could degenerate into a crude anti-Keynesian approach such as has always struck a responsive cord among certain French economic policy-makers and is showing signs of a revival. It is indeed the case that during the mid-1950s the priority given to expansion allowed public expenditure to grow excessively, and the planners acquired the reputation of being over-tolerant of the instability which accompanied growth and excessively concerned with assuring the continuity of public spending. The planners are now moving towards a flexible policy which will allow them to indicate to the Ministry of Finance the consequences of any restrictive measures that have to be taken and to urge that cuts in public expenditure should be made as selectively as possible. A dialogue of this kind would at the very least ensure that neither growth nor stabilization would become too dominant as an aim of economic policy. It is certainly important, with the French economy working under much tighter constraints

[1] Rapport du Comité chargé d'étudier le Financement des Investissements (Lorain Report), published in *Statistiques et Etudes Financières*, No. 179 (supplement), Ministère des Finances, Paris, November 1963. A critical, detailed account of the policy changes is given in the *Rapport de la Commission de l'Economie Générale et du Financement* for the Fifth Plan.

D

than at any period since the war, that the planners should continue to act as flexible and realistic but determined advocates of expansion and a planned distribution of its benefits.

Secondly, the inflationary developments which led to the Stabilization Plan were not wholly the result of the pressure of excess demand and a tight labour market. Apart from accidental factors such as the severe winter of 1963 which caused agricultural prices to rise there was a considerable increase in labour costs due to increased social security payments and the general adoption of a fourth week of paid holidays. The particularly sharp rise in food prices reflected another familiar source of price increases: the inefficient and unnecessarily complex distributive system. It was not only, therefore, excessive emphasis on expansion which lay at the root of the problem. Several measures have been taken to deal with these cost pressures, notably an extension of the value-added tax to the distributive trades which will remove one disincentive to modernization in this sector. And the need for an incomes policy in some form has now been accepted at least officially. The planners, particularly through their consultations with the Modernization Commissions, could make many significant, if undramatic, contributions by exposing the structural defects, institutional weaknesses, and restrictive practices which push up costs and prices throughout the economy and limit the rate of growth of output. With the mass of contacts and information at their disposal the planners are well suited to participate in these longer-term solutions to the problem of rising prices which, if successful, would reduce the need for disruptive cuts in demand.

Finally, the proposed lessening of the Treasury's role as an investment agency reduces the ability of the Government to ensure the success of the Plan by controlling an important sector of the long-term credit market and using it to promote development in selected industries. The authorities can still intervene in the capital market and ration the supply of funds, but they have increasingly moved away from this kind of direct interference. The attainment of the Plan's investment programmes in the private sector is now much more dependent on firms and investors utilizing the capital market to a greater extent than has been usual in France, and on firms' willingness to adhere to the Plan targets. The renewed importance of medium-term credit from the banking system may well mark a further weakening of the planners' influence; for they have never, even in their most interventionist period, succeeded in fully controlling the volume and direction of bank loans and advances. All this is not to say that the Plan need become less important as a guide to economic policy. The planners can, as has been argued above, retain their influence by participating as growth advocates on all policy-making agencies, and, if necessary, be in a position to argue with the Ministry of Finance and the Bank of France. Present trends seem to indicate, however, that the medium-term Plan is becoming more closely linked with short-term economic policy and the influence of the planners more subtle and indirect.

INDICATORS OF ALERT

The first three Plans were aimed basically at stimulating the growth of output and capacity. The Fourth and Fifth Plans have the more delicate objective of sketching out the conditions for a high rate of growth and the pursuance of certain social policies, consistent with reasonably stable prices. To carry out this function the planners have outlined for the Fifth Plan a series of 'indicators of alert' (or *clignotants*) as a means of detecting in advance areas of potential disequilibrium in the economy. They freely admit that the Plan is subject to a considerable number of uncertainties, but argue that this strengthens rather than weakens the case for having a plan.[1] The Plan is presented, not as a 'rigid predetermination of the future growth of the economy', but as 'the outline of a medium-term economic policy'. It is more than a coherent, qualified projection; it is an amalgam of policy measures aimed at ensuring the attainment of certain objectives for production, investment and other variables. Many of these measures may be long-term ones, such as modifications in the structure of an industry, widening of the capital market, promotion of technical education and training, and increased mobility of labour. Others may fall within the scope of traditional short-term economic policy, such as monetary and fiscal policy and action on prices.

The planners distinguish in some detail between the broad, general objectives of the Plan and the sector or industry targets. They admit that the targets may be wrong but argue that they can

---

[1] For a very full conceptual justification of indicative planning see *Préparation du V*e *Plan*, p. 45 ff. This detailed defence of indicative planning, appearing in an official document, indicates the pressures on the planners to clarify the contribution of a national indicative programme to the management of the economy.

be adjusted without requiring the whole plan to be redrawn so long as the main objectives are not prejudiced. This may well be the case if the failure to attain one target is balanced or, to use the planners' word, 'compensated' by the overshooting of another. For example, a shortfall in productive investment would not be serious if it were the result of an over-estimate by the planners of the capital –output ratio likely to obtain during the Plan. Similarly, the failure of the steel industry to reach its production target would not jeopardize the success of the Plan if imports of steel could be increased without adversely affecting the balance of payments. Again, if production in any industry exceeds the planners' forecast, and the amount that the home market can absorb, this need not be a misallocation of resources if the extra goods can be exported.

The planners are clearly at pains to emphasize the flexibility of an indicative programme and to show that a certain degree of fluctuation in economic activity does not mean that a four-year plan is impossible or useless. Nevertheless, there are limits to the amount of flexibility which can be tolerated in the context of a given set of general objectives. If an industry fails to achieve its target this will mean that industries providing inputs for it will find their markets reduced below the level which the Plan suggested and this in turn will affect industries supplying them. Similarly, client industries will find themselves short of supplies. It might be argued that equilibrium will be restored as the less efficient firms in the supplier industries go out of business and the more efficient find alternative markets and client industries alternative suppliers. But the adjustment may be slow and wasteful, particularly if new capacity has been or has to be created, and the fact remains that one justification of a coherent indicative programme, namely the reduction of uncertainty, is considerably weakened if its forecasts or targets go too far wrong. The permissible amount of flexibility or error has therefore to be defined fairly carefully.

With this problem in mind the planners have for some time been considering the adoption of a system of sliding or rolling plans which would enable the Plan to be checked and revised each year and corrected targets set for a further five-year period, thus ensuring that corrections are always made in the context of a long-term plan. This, however, is now rejected as clumsy and too demanding of the skilled manpower necessary for the task. Moreover, machinery already exists for annual reassessments, in the form of the annual review of public investment by the Council of the Fonds de Développement Economique et Social, the annual *budget économique*, which sets the background for the budget, and the annual reports on the execution of the Plan. All of these documents review the Plan in the light of the developing economic situation. Rolling programmes are also open to the serious criticism that they mask the original targets of the Plan, casting doubt on their feasibility and the intention of the Government to adopt them as basic criteria.

Indicators of alert could avoid some of these difficulties. They can set out fairly precisely the degree to which certain constraints have to be observed and thus enable any short-term intervention to operate more selectively.[1] The original targets of the Plan should either remain as the long-term policy goals or should be altered in the light of previously defined situations. The planners stress the importance of retaining the longer-term perspective of the Plan. The advantage of the new approach is that necessary changes in strategy such as the Intermediate Plan of the spring of 1960 or the Stabilization Plan of the autumn of 1963 will not represent unplanned reactions to events or even the reversal of previous policy, but will be worked out in the context of a permanent plan. A further and even more important contribution is that the agents in the economy will be forewarned of these changes and as a result the approach to the limit of a constraint will influence their attitudes.

The emphasis on stability implied in these new departures may seem at variance with the traditional objectives of the Plans. It is indeed ironic that other countries are currently adopting planning systems to a greater or lesser extent based on the French model as a means of achieving more rapid and steady expansion, while the French planners appear now to be shifting the emphasis of planning

[1] The indicators in the Fifth Plan are:

(a) An annual rate of increase of 1 per cent in French retail prices over those of competitors for three consecutive months.

(b) A coverage of imports by exports (yearly moving average) of less than 90 per cent for three consecutive months.

(c) A rate of growth of GDP of less than 2 per cent per year and an annual rate of increase in industrial production seasonally adjusted (excluding building) of less than 2 per cent for three consecutive months.

(d) A rate of growth of productive investment of less than 2·5 per cent per year.

(e) Unemployment of more than 2·5 per cent of the working population for three consecutive months.

See *Vᵉ Plan*, Tome I, pp. 24–6.

from growth to the promotion of an organized policy of 'stop–go'. But the paradox is only partly real. The present reforms in the French system are a recognition of the fact that a medium-term indicative plan in an open economy where technical change is rapid and two thirds of the national production is consumed cannot hope to be totally successful in promoting growth with price stability. The earlier Plans testify to the validity of this view although some commentators have blurred this point with over-simplified versions of the Plans' contribution to French economic growth. The planners, faced with much narrower constraints and more effective economic policy measures than in the 1950s, are adapting the Plan accordingly.

CONTROLS AND INCENTIVES

The argument, so far, has accepted the term 'indicative' as a reasonably accurate description of French planning methods. This itself is a controversial issue. The planners have always been able to influence economic policy by means of a varying range of controls and incentives used to ensure the implementation of the Plan targets by the nationalized industries and in the private sector. M. Massé has referred to these as the 'active' elements of French planning; 'There exists in France a whole range of measures which enable industries which conform to the Plan to be rewarded. There is access to credit. There are tax concessions and, in the context of regional policy, subsidies for equipment. There are, now and then, reductions in interest rates. . . .'[1] The way in which these measures have been and are now being applied is discussed in later chapters.[2] The point that is raised here is whether their existence means that the real influence of the planners rests on their ability to influence and coerce rather than simply to suggest that certain objectives be accepted.

A basic distinction may be made between selective and non-selective measures. If controls and incentives are applied selectively with the aim of pushing some sectors and holding back others in conformity with the sectoral targets of the Plan, then French planning becomes more than an exercise in national programming and persuasion. If, however, they are applied generally throughout the whole economy or varied in response to criteria other than simply the

[1] 'Planning' papers read at a Business Economists' Conference at New College, Oxford, April 1962, p. 18.
[2] A full discussion of their implementation is continued in Chapters 6 and 7.

Plan's industrial or sectoral targets then they cannot be said to be measures specifically used to make the quantitative programme more binding. The granting of tax advantages to firms taking part in a desired programme of mergers and concentration or carrying out approved projects of research and development is significantly different from the provision of credit on favourable terms to firms agreeing to undertake investment or production plans in conformity with the planners' target for the industry. Since the Fourth Plan the use of selective controls and incentives has been much reduced and directed towards qualitative rather than quantitative objectives. The wide-ranging controls over new issues and credit which were the planners' most powerful weapons in the early plans have been progressively dismantled and direct State aid to private industries in the form of reduced interest rate loans and interest subsidies for debentures is now of negligible importance. The recent measures taken to widen and stimulate a freely working capital market and the reduction in the proportion of savings absorbed and distributed by the State marks a further important move away from control over the supply of funds.

The planners' power to influence the use of undistributed profits has also been reduced in accordance with the policy of fiscal neutrality outlined in the Fourth Plan. (But see Chapter 7.) Tax advantages are still used as a means of encouraging certain specifically defined kinds of development such as regional development, research and development, concentration and regrouping in certain industries. But these are broad general objectives and are not tied to an acceptance of output targets set by the planners. There is, therefore, a trend towards more indicative and less imperative planning, in the sense that controls and incentives are not conditional on the achievement of quantified investment or output targets.

The planners have, however, in collaboration with the Ministry of Finance reserved the right to enter into contracts with firms or groups of firms promising certain financial and fiscal benefits in return for the execution of specific projects and policies in line with the Plan. These agreements known as 'quasi-contrats' or 'contrats fiscaux' involve detailed negotiations between the planners and individual firms or groups of firms and a deliberate policy of discrimination. This detailed interference like the capital market controls mentioned earlier is at variance with the emphatic pronouncements of the planners that they do not interfere with individual firms. It means that the planners are in fact prepared to enforce their view and discriminate against firms that cannot agree to the *quid pro quo* of financial assistance or those with whom the planners do not consider an agreement necessary, although only a few such contracts have so far been made.

Planning by contract is, however, being used in a new and perhaps very significant way in the Fifth Plan. At the start of the Plan the Government introduced a system of *contrats de stabilité*. These were agreements between the Ministry of Finance, the planners and individual firms whereby a firm was permitted, despite the general freeze on prices in force since September 1963, to raise prices of certain of its products provided it lowered the prices of others. This was an attempt to maintain price control but to mitigate its effects on exporters and firms whose investment plans were being affected by the squeeze on profit margins. In July 1966, concern about the effects of price control on the objectives of the Plan led the Government to introduce a much wider ranging agreement known as a *contrat de programme*. Firms entering into this agreement are required to satisfy the Ministry of Finance and the planners that for the period of the Plan they will respect the earnings guidelines laid down in the Plan and that their production, investment and export plans are in conformity with the Plan's objectives. In return they will be given permission to raise prices if their financial situation makes this necessary. The trade associations of the car and electrical appliances industries have already signed contracts, and the general reaction of French industry is favourable. At the present time the *contrats de programme* can be considered as a sophisticated form of price control. But they form precisely the kind of procedure which the French planners and French industrialists could work and have worked very well, and after generalized price control has been removed they may be so numerous as to form the natural framework for ensuring that the economy develops along the lines set out in the Plan. Certainly in the course of the Fifth Plan it is unlikely that the planners will not see scope in the contracts for pushing and cajoling industry to increase exports, carry out the structural reforms required to make French industry competitive and increase its efforts in research and development. The French planners may develop an extensive system of specific agreements whereby firms and industries are given appropriate assistance to carry out approved schemes. The planners' influence will of course be reduced if the capital market continues to develop and allows increased scope for external financing, and if price control is removed, but the planners' anxiety to maintain long-term expansion and industry's shortage of finance may lead French planning back again by a different route to a more interventionist system.

CONCLUSIONS

The most obvious conclusion to be drawn from the discussion in this chapter is that in France, as in Britain, there has been a lively debate going on about the ways in which an indicative programme can make economic policy more effective. A closely related question is the place of the planners in the administration and the manner in which they should influence policy decisions. In Britain there are now few illusions left about the self-fulfilling power of an indicative programme and much of the earlier interest in French planning has evaporated. What this chapter has tried to show is that precisely the same doubts are being expressed in France and the planning system is undergoing important changes as a result of them. Because of these developments many of the studies of French planning published in English are now out of date and give the impression that French planning is a static and formalized system, which it certainly is not. The changes which are currently being made in France might be worth some attention before the very short-lived British experiment with an indicative programme is dismissed as a complete failure.

On the demand side the growth objectives of the programme serve as a criterion which must be set alongside stability in every decision of economic policy. In a sense the need for long-term planning is perhaps even greater now that the problem of price stability has assumed such importance. It is the job of the planners to ensure that if deflationary measures are necessary they should be implemented in such a way as to affect the longer-term prospects for growth as little as possible. By defining in advance indicators of instability in the context of a long-term growth programme the planners are aiming to influence expectations so as to avoid over-expansion and at the same time prevent the dampening effects on investment of irregular and apparently unplanned cutbacks. The introduction of contracts aimed at maintaining control over prices and at the same time encouraging investment is an example of the delicacy and difficulty of the planners' job. The French planners are now having to argue with other government departments more than ever before and they will have to use all their accumulated experience and influence to keep expansion in the forefront of policy.

On the supply side the Plan provides an established and highly developed framework within which a co-ordinated study of obstacles to growth can be made and action taken to remove them. The planners have given up some of the controls which they operated in earlier Plans; but the problems of ensuring stability by means other than a general deflationary policy and the importance of getting the co-operation of industrialists in their schemes to make French industry more modern and competitive may well lead the planners to attempt to extend the system of formal agreements and contracts with industry which they have used sparingly but appositely in recent years in relation to structural objectives.

This account of indicative planning in France has been kept brief and has tried to concentrate on an outline of the most important aspects and developments. The subject of national programmes is further discussed, in relation to the United Kingdom, in Chapter 4, and in a general assessment in Chapter 5 to which the reader is referred for a critical evaluation of French planning. More detailed aspects of French planning are examined in Chapters 6, 7 and 8 and, in connection with regional policy, in Chapter 10.

The following is a selection of general works on French planning:

In English:

P. Bauchet, *Economic Planning: The French Experience*, Heinemann, 1964.

J. and A–M. Hackett, *Economic Planning in France*, Allen and Unwin, 1963.

Vera Lutz, *French Planning*, American Enterprise Institute, May 1965.

P. Massé, French Methods of Planning, *Journal of Industrial Economics*, November 1962.

P. Massé, The French Plan and Economic Theory, *Econometrica*, April 1965.

PEP, *French Planning: Some Lessons for Britain*, Planning No. 475, September 1963.

PEP, *Economic Planning in France*, Planning No. 454, August 1961.

UN Economic Survey of Europe in 1962 (Part 2) *Economic Planning in Europe*, Geneva, 1965.

F. Perroux, *The IVth French Plan*, National Institute of Economic and Social Research, Translated Monographs No. 1, 1965.

J. Sheahan, *Promotion and Control of Industry in Post-war France*, Harvard University Press, 1963.

A. Shonfield, *Modern Capitalism. The Changing Balance of Public and Private Power*, Oxford University Press, 1966 (especially Chapters 7 and 8).

S. Wickham, French Planning: Retrospect and Prospect, *The Review of Economics and Statistics*, November 1963.

B. Belassa, Whither French Planning? *Quarterly Journal of Economics*, November 1965.

In French:

J. Bénard, *Problèmes et Instruments de Synthèse d'un Plan Indicatif*, Cahiers de l'Institut de Science Economique Appliquée, Série D, No. 10, 1958.

B. Cazes, *La Planification en France et le IVe Plan*, Paris, Les Editions de l'Epargne, 1963.

B. Cazes, *Capitalisme et Planification, sont-ils Compatibles?* Cahiers de l'Institut de Science Economique Appliquée, Série M, No. 4, 1959.

J. Fourastié et J-P. Courthéoux, *La Planification Economique en France*, Presses Universitaires de France, 1963.

J. Gruson et F. Bloch-Lainé, Information, Prévision et Planification, *Encyclopédie Française*, Editions Larousse, Vol. XX.

P. Massé, *Le Plan ou l'Anti-hasard*, Paris, Collection Idées, Gallimard, 1965.

P. Massé, Prévision et Prospective, *Prospective* No. 4, November 1959.

P. Massé, Une Approche de l'Idée de Plan, *Encyclopédie Française*. Editions Larousse, Vol. IX.

P. Massé, La Planification Française, *Problèmes Economiques*, October 3, 1961.

Very useful discussions of the current problems of French planning are to be found in the following official reports:

Préparation du Ve Plan, Rapport sur les Principales Options, *Journal Officiel*, December 23, 1964.

Ve Plan de Développement Economique et Social (1966–70), Paris, Imprimerie Nationale, November 1965.

Ve Plan. Rapport Général de la Commission de l'Economie Générale et du Financement, Tomes I and II (Appendices and working papers).

CHAPTER 4

THE UNITED KINGDOM[1]

In Britain over the past two decades popular usage has ascribed the term planning to two particular forms of intervention in the economic process, which have been thus distinguished from the general run of economic policy. The first was the general control and allocation of resources in the years of great shortages and stringent economic situation in the late 1940s. The second, and very different, use of the word has been to describe the initiatives taken in the early 1960s to secure a faster rate of growth of national output.

The planning of the use of resources in the late 1940s had the limited aim of distributing resources fairly and preventing overstrain of the economy and its probable collapse in view of the delicacy of the international payments situation. It was believed that monetary policy would be ineffective because of the extremely high level of liquidity; taxation was already very high; and there appeared little alternative to the tight control over imports and building, the allocation of some scarce materials, and the rationing that was needed for a fair allocation of consumer goods. As the situation became less critical, with the achievement of a reasonable balance on foreign payments, the apparatus of controls was gradually wound up during the last years of Labour Government and the first years of Conservative Government in the early 1950s. When rationing ended in 1954 all the more obvious features of this inevitably unpopular form of planning were removed.

This planning phase was not entirely limited to a holding operation. One way of keeping the claims on resources within the limits of the resources available was of course to increase the rate of growth

[1] Some parts of this chapter have appeared in PEP's Planning series: No. 488, *Planning for Growth*, and No. 493, *The National Plan, its Contribution to Growth*.

of output. Working parties were set up in a number of industries and the Anglo-American productivity teams visited the United States to study the reasons for the higher productivity there. There was also a largely abortive movement to establish Development Councils for individual industries.

But this early attempt to stimulate the growth of productivity suffered from association with the political disputes surrounding the nationalization of industry and with the frustrations caused by controls. The 1950s were a period of revulsion against planning, and an attempt to reassert the virtues of a *laissez faire* economy. The impetus behind any direct official intervention to improve the performance of industry was lost. The role of government was seen to be the maintenance of stability of prices and full employment with the help of monetary policy and Keynesian use of budget surpluses or deficits, but otherwise to leave the development of the economy to free enterprise. There was neither such a strong and persistent determination to intervene to make competition work and thus increase efficiency as in Germany, nor a policy for stimulating growth by target planning or structural reform, as in France; nor even a serious sustained effort to increase productivity by attacking obstacles to growth, as had been the aspiration in the early post-war period in Britain. Chancellors might take credit for the expansion of the economy in periods of boom, as Mr Butler did in 1954 in his reference to the possibility of doubling the national income in twenty-five years, but little was being done to encourage such desirable developments.

In the late 1950s, however, it began to be felt that the performance of the British economy was distinctly inferior to that of many other countries which had entered the period after the Second World War in an even less favourable condition than Britain. The comparative statistics of investment and productivity might be controversial; many explanations could be given as to why it was natural for the growth of output in Britain to be slower than in many other industrial countries; but the evidence piled up so high that notice eventually had to be taken of it. Furthermore, economic policy seemed unable to prevent the recurrence of severe payments deficits, prices continued to rise, and business expectations were repeatedly upset by the measures that had to be taken to tide over the crises. Academics, industrialists, and finally the Government, were gradually won over to the view that a more deliberate intervention in order to improve the performance of the economy was required.[1]

It would be a gross over-simplification to say that there had been no planning for the expansion of output in the preceding years. In the public sector, the nationalized industries and commercial departments of the administration had operated according to a series of long-term plans for investment and the growth of output, and many private firms, especially the large ones in expanding industries, also worked to long-term plans. It would not even be true to say that there was no co-ordination of plans; a great deal of consultation naturally went on within the public sector, between private firms and public enterprises, and among the private firms themselves. Yet it was felt that the lack of nation-wide organized co-ordination of investment programmes was a serious weakness in British economic management. There was no effective machinery, it was argued, for ensuring the consistency of the plans being made in different parts of the economy; in particular, the Treasury was not suited, by its traditional functions as a financial controller of the other departments and by its preoccupation with urgent short-term economic problems, to play a very positive part in securing a faster rate of growth. Nor was it thought that any other government department had the kind of relationship with private industry that could have enabled it to stimulate, assist and co-ordinate investment projects.

THE NATIONAL ECONOMIC DEVELOPMENT COUNCIL

Such was the prevailing mood of dissatisfaction in which, in July 1961, measures were taken to tackle the latest in the series of economic crises. The Chancellor of the Exchequer, Mr Selwyn Lloyd, then announced that he proposed to set up a new organization to bring together the 'various processes of consultation and forecasting with a view to better co-ordination of ideas and plans'.[2]

This new initiative in planning, though it was to some extent en-

---

[1] In November 1960, PEP published a survey of these problems, *Growth in the British Economy*, Allen and Unwin, 1960. In January 1961, the Federation of British Industries held a seminal conference at Brighton. French economic achievements and French economic planning in particular captured attention in Britain and in April 1961 the National Institute of Economic and Social Research organized a three-day conference on French planning, attended by influential officials, industrialists and economists. The report of the conference was published by PEP: *Economic Planning in France*, Planning No. 454.

[2] House of Commons Debates, July 25, 1961, Col. 220.

cumbered with the incubus of unpopularity of the earlier form of planning, was quite different in both motives and methods. Its aim was to influence the policy, particularly of the Government, but also of firms and individuals, and other economic institutions, in ways which would bring about an acceleration in the rate of growth of the national output and of national output per head. Its method was to identify an attainable target for a rate of growth of output, higher than the average of earlier years, to specify the requirements for and obstacles in the way of achieving this aim, and to influence the relevant instrument of economic policy in directions that would help to raise the rate of growth.

In his statement announcing the intention to set up the National Economic Development Council, the Chancellor explained that he wanted something 'more purposeful' than the existing advice and comment from bodies such as the Economic Planning Board and the National Production Advisory Council on Industry. In an explanatory statement he outlined the task to be attempted by the NEDC:

'I envisage a joint examination of the economic prospects of the country stretching five or more years into the future. It would cover the growth of national production and distribution of our resources between the main uses, consumption, government expenditure, investment, and so on. Above all, it would try to establish what are the essential conditions for realizing potential growth.

'That covers, first, the supply of labour and capital, secondly, the balance of payments conditions and the development of imports and exports, and thirdly, the growth of incomes. In other words, I want both sides of industry to share with the Government the task of relating plans to the resources that are likely to be available.'[1]

Consultations with industry and the trade unions went on through the latter part of 1961, and in December of that year the Chancellor was able to announce the appointment of the Director General of the Office of the NEDC, Sir Robert Shone, who as Executive Member of the Iron and Steel Board had been responsible for some years for the co-ordination of investment plans in the steel industry, and had taken a leading part in the public debate that led to the founding of the NEDC. In February 1962 the names of the employers' representatives on the Council were announced. The attitude of the Trades Union Congress was for some time in doubt, since they were concerned

[1] House of Commons Debates, July 26, 1961, Col. 439.

about the role which the new Council would be expected to play with regard to incomes policy, but in February 1962 they also agreed to join, and six trade union representatives were nominated early in March.

The Council, with representatives of the TUC and of private and nationalized industry, together with the Ministers most closely concerned with general economic affairs—the Chancellor of the Exchequer, the President of the Board of Trade and the Minister of Labour—had a fairly traditional membership for an advisory body on a subject of national importance. But a most important innovation lay in the establishment of the National Economic Development Office.

The Council met occasionally and gave general guidance for the policy and work of the Office. Divided between an economics and an industrial section, the staff of the Office was recruited largely on temporary secondment from government departments, from industry and from the universities. The appointments were intended to be normally for short periods of two to three years. By this policy, as well as through the membership of the Council, close relations could be maintained both with the Civil Service and with industry and the trade unions.[1] Some work was also done on a part-time basis, mainly by university people, and the NEDO also commissioned a considerable amount of research in the universities.

The organization of the Council and particularly of the Office, together with the drawing up of the first national programme, was enough to occupy the greater part of 1962 and 1963. Initially no attempt was made to establish any formal machinery for individual industries, and such consultations as were needed for the first two years' work took place through traditional channels such as trade associations, or directly with firms. Separate planning bodies were, however, envisaged for each industry, and these Economic Development Committees began to be established in 1964, with terms of reference to:

1. examine the economic performance, prospects and plans of the industry and assess from time to time the industry's programme in relation to the national growth objectives, and provide information and forecasts to the Council on these matters;
2. consider ways of improving the industry's economic performance,

---

[1] Letter from the Chancellor of the Exchequer to employers' associations and the TUC, September 1961.

competitive power and efficiency and formulate reports and recommendations on these matters as appropriate.[1]

The membership of these Committees was a reflection of the membership of the NEDC itself, with representatives of management, trade unions, the appropriate government departments, other experts, and a member of the staff of the Office. By November 1967 twenty-one Economic Development Committees had been established for: chemicals; food manufacturing; distributive trades; electronics; machine tools; electrical engineering; mechanical engineering; paper and board; wool textiles; building; civil engineering; food processing; rubber; hotels and catering; newspapers, printing and publishing; clothing; hosiery and knitwear; agriculture; the Post Office; motor vehicle distribution and repair, and the movement of exports. In addition there were two other bodies: a Process Plant Working Party and a Construction Materials Group.

For the first two and a half years of its existence, the NEDC was the main body concerned with planning for growth. Following the change of government in October 1964, some of its functions were taken over by the Department of Economic Affairs, but it has continued to play an important part. It is therefore necessary first to assess its role as the sole organization and then to examine its position after the establishment of the DEA.

Apart from the vital matter of disposing of the services of the NEDO, the NEDC was distinguished from the typical advisory committee by one other important difference. Most other advisory bodies at this level have had highly generalized terms of reference. They may be used by the Minister for advice and to sound out opinion on all kinds of problems relating to their general field. But the NEDC had, and has, the valuable distinction of possessing a definite aim for all its deliberations. It was established deliberately to act as a new pressure group, to influence government and industry in a pre-arranged direction. This made it potentially a much more important body than others with an apparently similar membership and function.

The NEDC decided at its first meeting in March 1962 to carry out a study of the implications of a 4 per cent per annum rate of growth of the Gross Domestic Product for the period from 1961 to 1966. The result of this study was published in February 1963. A further

---

[1] Terms of reference approved at a meeting of the NEDC on December 4, 1963.

report discussed general problems arising out of the industrial inquiries and the study of the economy as a whole, and policies that might be adopted to overcome these obstacles to growth.[1]

The 4 per cent target was put to the first meeting of the NEDC by the Office, and was accepted as the basis for the first 'plan' without previous detailed examination or discussions. It was in fact a rough estimate arrived at by the NEDO staff. Anything less than 4 per cent was regarded as being an insufficient improvement on the previous growth rate. Anything above 4 per cent, say 4.5 or 5 per cent, would inevitably, it was thought, raise insuperable difficulties for the balance of payments. Hence 4 per cent soon emerged as the right target to aim for in this first exercise in planning for growth. (Four per cent also represented the rate that would probably have been achieved in previous years if there had not been periodic stagnation.)

This rough target was tested during 1962 and early 1963 in two ways. First, an inquiry was made among a cross-section of seventeen important industries to see whether their output could grow at a rate appropriate to a 4 per cent average for the economy as a whole. Secondly, in order to check whether 4 per cent growth could be achieved with the resources that would be available in the economy as a whole, the target was tested more generally for its overall feasibility in relation to the main economic aggregates: manpower, productivity and technical change; consumption, savings and investment; and exports, imports and the balance of payments.

The industrial inquiry among the seventeen industries covered some 50 per cent of industrial production and of fixed investment excluding dwellings, and some 40 per cent of the GDP and of employment and visible exports. No formal machinery was set up at this stage, though the carrying out of the inquiry stimulated the construction industry to set up advisory bodies for building and for civil engineering, with the prime objective of liaison with the NEDO. Mostly the discussions took place with existing trade associations, with individual private firms, with government departments, nationalized industries and trade unions. The industries were asked to provide information about their existing plans, about the output foreseen for 1966 on the basis of current expectations, about the output they could achieve in 1966 on the assumption that the Gross Domestic Product was in fact increased by 4 per cent per annum,

[1] *Growth of the United Kingdom Economy to 1966*, HMSO, February 1963, and *Conditions Favourable to Faster Growth*, HMSO, March 1963.

and about the particular problems that would arise, and how these could be overcome. It was assumed that Britain would enter the EEC about half-way through the period, but the breakdown of the negotiations just before the report was published, though it affected individual industries, did not appear to make any significant difference to the general outcome.[1] The seventeen industries were selected on the basis of their importance in the economy, the need to cover a good sample of private and of public industry, of consumer and capital goods, of services, of industries where rapid growth could be expected, and of industries where opportunities for expansion were not so good. The industries chosen were: coal, gas, electricity, the Post Office, agriculture, chemicals, chocolate and sugar confectionery, building, civil engineering and building materials, heavy electrical machinery, electronics, iron and steel, machine tools, motor vehicles, paper and board, petroleum and wool textiles. The NEDO also made its own study of the distribution industry.

The general programme for the whole economy was therefore made up of fairly detailed estimates of what might be possible in the industries that were investigated, together with broader guesses about the possibilities in other industries. The total outcome for all the seventeen industries in the inquiry was that, on the basis that the economy as a whole would grow at 4 per cent a year, they expected that their output would increase by 4·8 per cent a year in the period 1961 to 1966, as compared with an actual increase averaging only 3 per cent a year in 1956 to 1961. If the 4 per cent target for the GDP was to be achieved, the rest of industry would have to grow at 3·5 per cent a year, compared with an actual 2·5 per cent in 1956–61. This requirement for the other industries, which had not been studied in any detail, seemed feasible in relation to their previous performance and in relation to what the seventeen major industries had said they could do, and this confirmed the 'rightness', so far as this first test was concerned, of the 4 per cent target, subject to one or two qualifications.

While the outline of the developments of the economy published in *Growth of the United Kingdom Economy to 1966* did not in any way commit any institutions to their actual implementation, neither were

---

[1] The main reason given in October 1967 for the postponement of the DEA's proposed second National Plan was uncertainty about the British proposals for entering the EEC. The economic situation must also have had considerable weight in this decision.

they regarded as merely a statement of what would happen even in the absence of any new planning initiatives. Not only were the target rates for the seventeen industries higher than the rates achieved in 1956–61, they were also considerably above the rates of growth of output that the industries forecast on the basis of 'current expectations', that is, without assuming the 4 per cent growth of the economy as a whole. The preparation and the publication of the report was itself thought of as a policy weapon on the grounds that it would make industry think in terms of a rate of growth that would otherwise have been regarded as extravagantly optimistic. The report was expected in this way to have a substantial influence towards the fulfilment of its own indications. For example, in May 1963 the electricity supply industry decided, with government approval, to plan its investment on the assumption that the 4 per cent growth would be achieved. It is difficult to find other examples but a wider influence, though not easily proved, is probable.

Although the NEDC had not revealed in public a great deal of its thinking about the nature of its work, it was clearly relying to a certain extent on the psychological impact of indicative target planning. It was aware that the success of the programme would depend partly on whether industry could be brought to believe in the possibility that it might succeed. There are, of course, limits to the self-realization of targets. Faith in the possibility of the developments outlined in any programme depends on the credibility of the details, of output in each industry and of developments in manpower, productivity, savings and investment, exports and the balance of payments, and on the consistency of each particular indication with every other. The programme tried to achieve this credibility and consistency, while at the same time identifying the less credible indications, and the possible obstacles to growth at the planned rate. There were, however, grave doubts whether the NEDC programme was in fact sufficiently credible to be convincing.

The credibility of the NEDC's programme for 4 per cent growth pivoted upon the question of whether the balance of payments could be maintained in a satisfactory state at this rate of growth. The programme envisaged an improvement in the balance of payments to an average surplus of £300 million on current account by 1966. Imports, it was assumed, would grow at 4 per cent per annum[1] if 4 per cent growth of GDP was achieved. The improvement in the current

[1] This optimistic estimate had later to be revised to 4·7 per cent.

balance, and the growth of imports at 4 per cent, were estimated to require a 5 per cent per annum increase in the volume of exports over the period.[1] The difficulty of this task could be judged by the fact that the past trend rate of growth of exports had been only 3 per cent a year. This increase in exports could be effected only, as the NEDC duly recognized, if Britain succeeded in halting the previous steady decline in her share of world trade in manufactures. This in turn implied a substantial improvement in the competitiveness of British exports, which would require, among other things, that the British price level should be held down at least as successfully as Britain's competitors could hold down theirs. This reasoning led logically to a statement of the need for an incomes policy, with which, however, the NEDC signally failed to make progress, and it had to content itself with a statement of the need for a generalized sense of responsibility. The balance-of-payments assumptions of the programme were, therefore, nothing less than heroic. The NEDC programme, though it was probably realistic enough on the side of the industrial appraisal, thus appeared to consist largely of wishful thinking so far as the major constraint on growth was concerned.

What the NEDC programme showed but failed to recognize was the unlikelihood rather than the credibility of 4 per cent growth, until the competitive power of the British economy had been drastically increased. To base plans for the expansion of public consumption and, through incomes policy, of private consumption also, on the assumption that 4 per cent growth would in fact be attained was in these circumstances quite unjustifiable.

THE DEPARTMENT OF ECONOMIC AFFAIRS AND THE NATIONAL PLAN

The return of the Labour Government in October 1964 resulted in substantial organizational changes, and some reorientation of policy in the light of experience in the period 1962–4. The organizational changes related to problems encountered by the NEDC and the NEDO as a consequence of their position on the edge of the administrative machine, and problems of staff recruitment. The NEDC's unique position 'under the aegis of but not in' the Government, to quote Mr Selwyn Lloyd, gave it the opportunity to develop close rela-

[1] This method of obtaining the export figure as a 'residual' to balance the expected imports was similar to that used by the French planners. See p. 88.

tions with both sides of industry, but at the same time raised problems for its relations with government departments. Though the Chancellor of the Exchequer was Chairman of the Council, the Office was intended to be independent of the Treasury. Yet it had access to confidential official documents, and this implied that its freedom to publish had to be restricted. Moreover, in the last analysis the Government had to take decisions based on the advice of the Treasury, with its executive responsibility for financial control as well as for economic policy. With a staff made up largely of seconded university and business economists, together with some civil servants, this small body, without executive responsibility, had to compete for the ear of the Chancellor with all the weight of the Treasury's experience. Since the Council to which its reports were submitted represented sometimes diverse interests, there was a further inhibition on the publication of work done in the Office.[1] Thus the position of the NEDO as neither a part of government, nor an independent research institute, was not entirely comfortable.

Partly because of its somewhat ambiguous position, the staffing of the NEDO also raised difficulties. Secondments from industry and from the universities were an obvious first step, in order to build up an experienced and highly qualified staff quickly, and to maintain the independent position *vis-à-vis* Whitehall. Yet this policy created uncertainty about career prospects among the essential core of permanent staff. Moreover, the small size of the Office also meant that the staff had to be spread over a wide range of subjects. Appointments were for short periods, usually two years, and many of the staff kept their links with the institutions they came from. This policy led to high turnover of staff, which was aggravated by uncertainty about the role and future of the organization, and by competition from the rapidly expanding universities. Although the important work of setting up Economic Development Committees for individual industries made good progress in 1964, these 'little Neddies' could not be expected to have a practical effect in such a short time. The organization was therefore troubled in 1964 by four major factors: its ambiguous position in the existing structure of government; the uncertainties about staff; the speculation about the future organization under either a Labour or a Conservative Government; and the developing economic crisis.

[1] Andrew Shonfield stresses this point in his discussion of the NEDO in *Modern Capitalism*, Oxford University Press, 1965, Chapter 8.

It was in these circumstances that the new Government decided to bring the economic planning side of the organization inside the Government. They argued that this did not require, as did the industrial division, intimate relations with industry, and would be in a better position for making its views heard in Whitehall and in the Cabinet if it were in a recognized and clearly defined position. To put it within the Treasury would have been an improvement from this point of view but the Government went further in setting up the Department of Economic Affairs, which took over most of the division of the Treasury concerned with economic growth policy, as well as most of the economic division of the NEDO, including its head, Sir Donald MacDougall, who became Director-General in charge of economic planning in the new Department. Not only did economic planning for growth thus obtain a clearly defined position in Whitehall, but it also acquired a separate political head in the Secretary of State for Economic Affairs, Mr George Brown, who was not only in the Cabinet, but also, as First Secretary of State, higher in Labour's hierarchy than the Chancellor of the Exchequer, Mr Callaghan. There was thus a much more influential direct voice representing planning for growth in the new administration. There was also an attempt to separate responsibility for long-term economic policy from the Treasury's more routine and detailed functions such as the control over spending.

Advantages were seen in keeping the industrial division of the NEDO in its independent position, rather than sweeping the whole organization into the new Department; and the economic division, though shorn of its quantitative planning function, was also retained. While it was believed that the planning function could be more effectively carried out within Whitehall, it was considered desirable to retain the tripartite involvement in economic policy which the NEDC had achieved. The Government wished to keep the Council itself as an independent forum for discussions about national plans and other government policies affecting the unions and industry.

Following its decision to establish the Department of Economic Affairs, the Government announced in the autumn of 1964 that the Department was to start drawing up the new programme for economic growth, to supersede the plan of the NEDC for 1962 to 1966, on the basis of the same 4 per cent growth rate. Political considerations probably bulked large in the decision to retain this target. In opposition the Labour Party had pressed for a more ambitious target, and while the economic situation precluded any raising of the sights, and many of the short-term measures could be blamed on the previous administration, the political repercussions of announcing a medium-term target lower than the Conservatives had subscribed to would have been serious. Britain thus retained, for no very good economic reasons, a growth target that had been nowhere near achieved in 1962–4,[1] and appeared to have even less chance of being achieved over the following two years. The Government did in 1965 accept the probability that the rate of growth in 1965 and 1966 would be slow, by amending the target to a 25 per cent increase on the 1964 Gross Domestic Product by 1970.[2] Although this restatement of the target quietly scaled it down from 4 per cent to 3·8 per cent per annum, it still implied a higher rate of productivity increase than under the original NEDC target, because of the slower growth of manpower expected in 1964–70. The 25 per cent target did, however, help to remove any impression that this rate had to be achieved each year. It was in fact recognized that growth would average less than 3·8 per cent in the early years, but it was intended that the rate would accelerate to above 4 per cent by the end of the period, thus achieving the aim of 25 per cent for 1964–70.

Before examining the Plan itself, it is necessary to deal with one or two ancillary matters that have a bearing on the way it had to be judged. First, it is probably true to say that the Plan could never have hoped to live up to the expectations placed on it. After the installation of a new government, the great changes in the structure of the planning organization, and coming at the end of a year of economic crisis, it was inevitable that too much should have been expected from this 'blueprint' for the future development of the economy. While advance publicity may have contributed to these excessive expectations, the Government had also given warnings about the obstacles to the fulfilment of the Plan, and the document itself was liberally

---

[1] It has sometimes been suggested that the 4 per cent target was in fact achieved in these years, by looking only at the output figures and ignoring the balance-of-payments crisis in the autumn of 1964 and the consequent slowing down of the rate of growth as a result of the restrictive measures in 1965 and 1966. Naturally 4 per cent can be achieved by ignoring the balance of payments, but not for long unless this constraint is dealt with by means of import quotas and exchange controls or devaluation, as was the case during the first three French Plans.

[2] House of Commons Debates, February 1965, Col. 1017.

sprinkled with reminders that great efforts would be needed if its targets were to be hit. The National Economic Development Council, who considered the Plan before its publication, issued a statement in which they commended it in cautious terms:

'[The NEDC] considers [the National Plan] a valuable analysis of the problems to be overcome in achieving a growth in the national market of 25 per cent between 1964 and 1970. The Council considers that such an increase within that period is within the nation's capacity, but given the situation likely to exist over the early years of the period it is clear that the achievement of this objective will require a major national effort.'

'Clearly the solution of the balance of payments is crucial to the achievement of more rapid economic expansion. In particular, the export performance required to meet the objectives of the plan is considerable and will require an intensive effort by all concerned.'[1]

Secondly, due allowance must be made for the fact that the Department of Economic Affairs had existed for only nine months when the Plan was completed. This does, of course, raise the question of why the exercise was rushed through so quickly. There were strong political pressures to publish a Plan at the earliest possible moment, as well as to cling to a target as ambitious as the one outlined by the NEDC and accepted by the previous administration. The time schedule for the planning process in France has, however, been much longer than that so far allowed in this country, either under the NEDC or the DEA. For the moment we shall merely note that the Plan was a rushed job, and that the potential value of the work of the DEA and of the NEDC should not be judged on it alone.

Thirdly, not all the actual or imminent policy decisions relevant to the Plan figures could be published by the DEA. Some, already taken, were regarded as the property of the executive department concerned, which would not want all its plans revealed by the DEA. For example, the White Paper on Housing[2] later indicated the proposed policy changes underlying the target of 500,000 houses per annum by 1970. Other policy decisions, clearly required to make sense of the Plan figures, were still under discussion when the Plan went to press, and it was obviously difficult to say anything positive about them at this stage in the formation of policy. It was in fact

[1] NEDC Statement issued on August 5, 1965.
[2] HMSO, *The Housing Programme, 1965 to 1970*, Cmnd. 2838, November 1965.

necessary, with this as with many official publications, to read between the lines.

While the National Plan had therefore to be seen within the whole context of the development of administrative machinery and policy, and while overmuch importance could not be attached to some of the infelicities deriving from its genesis in a multiplicity of committees, and from the burden of interdepartmental rivalries, it had nevertheless to be assessed primarily on what was in the document; and this gave considerable scope to those who are hostile to national plans, and cause for doubt among those who are well disposed towards them. One of the Plan's defects was that it had several different purposes which were only imperfectly distinguished. The impression left with the reader was that the planners might have been so engrossed in the technical problems of assembling the mass of data that they either failed to take time to think out exactly why they were doing it or neglected to explain this.

The Plan described itself in several different ways, for example, 'a statement of Government policy', 'a commitment to action by the Government', and as 'a guide to action' (by management and trade unions and individuals). No doubt the Plan had, and needed, elements of all these. But the early section on 'the nature and purpose of planning' illustrated the danger of failing to distinguish between them. After a fairly traditional statement of the need for intervention by the Government in maintaining a satisfactory balance of payments, speeding up the working of the market mechanisms, maintaining competition, and providing social goods, this section concentrated on describing the Plan as a co-ordinated national market forecast or projection.[1] 'Projections', 'forecasts' and 'plans' were used throughout these paragraphs as though they were synonymous. But the Plan was not merely a projection, or even a forecast, for, while it rested partly on extrapolations of past trends, supplemented by forecasts of changes in these trends which there was reason to believe might come about before 1970, it also called for expansion beyond these indications. To take the most important macro-economic example, past performance in respect of the growth of exports by volume was estimated at 3 per cent per annum. A simple *projection* would therefore have given this figure for the growth of exports to 1970. By disaggregating the projections to indi-

[1] HMSO, *The National Plan*, Cmnd. 2764, September 1965, Chapter 1, paras. 13–15.

vidual commodities and markets and by taking credit for certain improvements in the prospects for exports, the Plan *forecast* a growth at 4 per cent per annum to 1970. But the expansion of exports required to achieve the surplus on the balance of payments planned for 1970 was 5·25 per cent. This then was the *planned* growth of exports, on which the rates of expansion of output and consumption, etc., were expected to depend. The juxtaposition of these projected, forecast and planned figures for the growth of exports was valuable because it revealed the magnitude of the policy changes and their effects which would be needed to fulfil this part of the Plan. But it also showed that to describe the Plan as merely a set of projections, or at the most as a set of forecasts co-ordinated on a national scale, was inaccurate. The NEDC, which had produced very similar figures for exports, had not claimed that their figures were a forecast, only that they were an assessment of the 'impact and feasibility' of a national growth rate of 4 per cent. The DEA appeared, without any real justification, to be making more ambitious claims.

An upward bias, dictated by political considerations, was in fact a prime feature of the DEA's exercise, since a single rate of growth considerably in excess of what had previously been achieved was decided on before any information had been assembled from industry, so that it is hard to see what changes could have been made if, for example, the firms and trade associations' export forecasts had been less optimistic or if the DEA had been sceptical about them. These bodies were asked to fill in the questionnaire on the assumption that the Gross Domestic Product would grow at the chosen rate of 25 per cent over the period 1964 to 1970. It is true that they were also asked about present plans and expectations in the years 1965 to 1967, and even later where appropriate. And in respect of investment they were asked to state their definite commitments in 1965 and 1966. But the figures embodied in the Plan were those submitted on the assumption of 25 per cent growth by 1970; and in order to allay doubts about the prospects for breaking the balance-of-payments constraint, the Plan stressed the need for an incomes policy to hold down the level of prices relative to those in world markets. The issue of the role of an incomes policy in relation to a national plan is discussed in detail in Chapter 9; but it is relevant to point out here that there was never much reason to believe that the voluntary incomes policy that was in question at the time when the National Plan was drawn up and published would be able to improve Britain's competitive position radically enough to make achievement of the Plan's targets possible.

This is not to conclude that the National Plan should not have been based on assumptions. Alternative assumptions should have been used in two or more hypotheses of the future development of the economy, thus allowing the actual target to be chosen realistically as and when actual developments were seen to be corresponding to one or other of the alternative assumptions. Certainly, to try out one particular set of assumptions, deliberately departing from what past experience and current trends indicated to be the most probable outcome, was neither the same thing as forecasting the future of the economy, nor a sound method of mobilizing the economy for faster growth.

The question how far it was correct to describe the Plan as a forecast may be further clarified by reference to a set of figures showing the possible development of the economy to 1975, given certain assumptions, which was published by the National Institute of Economic and Social Research shortly after the National Plan appeared.[1] This study was very careful to forestall any possible misconception that the figures represented even 'a forecast of what is most likely to happen'. On the contrary, they presented only a 'possible picture' of the economy in 1975, on the assumptions, which were made quite explicitly, that productivity would grow faster, and that industry would become more competitive internationally. And the NIESR refrained from claiming that their figures were forecasts despite the fact that there are reasons to believe that these longer-term indications stood a better chance than the Plan targets of being fulfilled. For the problem of the influence of the restrictive measures taken in 1964–5 on the growth rate for 1964–70 overshadowed the DEA's Plan long before its publication, but did not affect the NIESR's estimates to the same extent. Further, although the Plan and the Institute's estimates both required that fairly similar assumptions be made about the growth of productivity, the success of an incomes policy, and consequent improvement in the competitiveness of the British economy, these were much more reasonable assumptions in the case of the NIESR's figures than of the DEA's, for they depended for their realization on policies that were above all long-term. These policies may have some effects by 1970: they are

[1] W. Beckerman and associates, *The British Economy in 1975*, NIESR, Cambridge University Press, 1965.

likely to have much more in 1970-5. It is possible to maintain that the DEA were correct in emphasizing the description of their Plan as a forecast on the grounds that it had the support of an industrial inquiry, that is, it had been 'tested' (as the NIESR's figures had not). But this test did not constitute solid evidence with respect to the crucial constraint of the balance of payments, and to put foward the Plan's figures as a forecast was therefore not legitimate. This misuse of words must be interpreted as part of the effort to change expectations. In line with frequent expressions of the Government's determination to take the action required to see that the 'forecast' came true, the figures represented a statement of intention and an expression of determination rather than a scientific prediction.

The Plan showed a keen awareness of the existence of constraints, whose removal was a precondition of faster growth. The Plan was, therefore, not merely indicative, but also a study of the feasibility of the target. It assessed in considerable detail the physical requirements for growth of 25 per cent by 1970. Yet it is as a feasibility study that the Plan was most unsatisfactory, for, like the NEDC inquiry, it showed the improbability rather than the feasibility of growth at the planned rate. A good study of feasibility would not necessarily have had to show that the planned expansion would not run up against obstacles, but it would have had to indicate far more precisely than the National Plan how they were to be surmounted. A Plan whose feasibility depended on what were little more than general aspirations for the improvement of export performance, and on the success in practice of a prices and incomes policy which had only just begun to operate, was not convincing.

Like the NEDC's report on the *Growth of the United Kingdom Economy to 1966*, the Plan was not excessively ambitious so far as the internal economy was concerned. The proposed increases in the annual rate of expansion of output and of output per head were quite high but, given appropriate policies, and some change of attitudes to which the Plan may have contributed, these targets might well have been achieved but for the external payments constraint. The increase proposed in the rate of growth of output per head was, for example, from the actual 2·7 per cent in 1960-4 (leaving aside the question of whether this period was a good basis for comparison) to 3·2 per cent in 1964-70, for the whole economy; though for industry, the increase required was from 3·1 per cent to 4·1 per cent, which is certainly a big jump. If performance fell short of the target rate of growth by no more than 0·1–0·2 per cent, however, nobody would be seriously hurt; and an increase from the previous 2·7 per cent to, say, 3 per cent did not seem impossible. So far as the capital investment requirement for this rise in productivity was concerned, this is a factor amenable to some degree to operation on expectations, and if the remainder of the Plan had been sound there would have been no reason for undue concern on this score. The DEA were clearly following the demand expectations theory at this point: 'The most important single factor affecting industry's investment plans is its assessment of future demand. Even though it has been necessary for the Government to take steps to ease the pressure of demand in the short term, the publication of the Plan, and further discussions in the Economic Development Committees and elsewhere of its implications, should encourage firms to plan for the longer term on a expansionist basis.'[1] They recognized, however, that special incentives to investment might be needed in addition.

The so-called 'manpower gap' also attracted the attention of sceptics. This was, however, as much a matter of presentation as of economics. The gap was one of some 400,000 workers, obtained by subtracting from the forecast of 800,000 more workers needed in 1970, derived from the industrial inquiry, the increase of 400,000 expected in the total working population. With credit allowed for the potential supply of 200,000 additional workers from the less prosperous regions, the gap was reduced to 200,000, though in the absence of any firm indications for this successful outcome of regional policy, this was only hypothetical. The gap was actually derived from estimates of the desire of employers to recruit and to release labour (net) between 1964 and 1970. It represented the difference between the expectation of eight industrial sectors that they would need to recruit another 1,200,000 workers if the GDP was to grow by 25 per cent and the expectation of three sectors—agriculture, forestry and fishing; mining and quarrying; and transport and communications—that they would lose, net, some 400,000 workers. Assuming the full success of regional policy in increasing employment in the less prosperous areas, the gap was thus some 16 per cent of the additional labour requirements of the expanding sectors, and with the removal of this assumption, it was about 33 per cent. But this was only another way of saying that industry did not expect its productivity to grow as fast as the

[1] *The National Plan*, Chapter 5, para. 25; also see pp. 133–9.

DEA's target of 25 per cent national growth assumed. Adding 0·1 or 0·2 per cent to the annual rate of growth of output per head would have eliminated the manpower gap; so would setting the growth target at 23·4 per cent, instead of 25 per cent. But even if to speak of the manpower gap was merely an indirect way of saying that industry expected its productivity to grow a little more slowly than the Government would have liked, it may well have served a useful purpose, as a reminder to firms of the importance of economy in the use of labour, that is, of reliance on increasing productivity rather than on hopes of increasing the labour force as output expanded in the light of the overall growth target.

One of the changes promised by the Labour Party, to remedy some of the deficiencies of the NEDC's approach, was the firm use of the Plan as a directive. It was for this reason, among others, that the planning function was removed from the National Economic Development Office and put into the DEA, inside the machinery of government instead of on its fringes. In opposition Labour spokesmen talked of giving planning teeth: of firmly taking all those decisions within the public sector that were necessary to hit the targets, and being prepared to enforce the necessary changes on private industry. The Foreword by Mr George Brown stated that 'the plan for the first time represents a statement of Government policy and a commitment to action by the Government'. The National Plan has since been abandoned, but there is good reason to believe that the DEA can have more influence on the policies of executive departments than the NEDC could have had: exactly how much will depend on the development of the continuing relationship within Whitehall between the DEA and other departments concerned with economic affairs.

However, there are also reasons for believing that future plans will prove to be less than full directives. First, although the executive departments are closely involved in the planning, many estimates in plans must represent compromises between conflicting views and interests, and it is highly unlikely that the insertion of a particular figure in a plan will be regarded as having settled finally all contentious issues up to the terminal year. So far as the private sector is concerned, there was little indication in the Plan of effective new measures to encourage change in private industry, let alone enforce it. The Plan was called a 'guide to action', and it admitted that 'it must show who is responsible for what'. But the action programme, though it included some specific measures already taken, and others intended, was rather a progress report on the setting up of committees and a statement of what these committees would try to do, than a statement of what precisely would be done. The Plan was not (nor is it likely that it was ever intended to be) really a directive for the private sector in that it did not explain what actions had to be taken by private firms, and what would be the required quantitative effects, to plug the gaps in the programme for 25 per cent growth by 1970. As far as any idea of administrative direction of private firms by the Government may have been extant, there was no trace of it in the Plan. The figures were estimates prepared largely by trade associations for their industry; and the actions referred to were largely actions on the part of committees which contain only a few representatives of their industries, or of industry in general. These committees have the task of disseminating information, provoking discussion, and influencing those who take the real decisions. These will finally be taken by firms, by individual trade unions or 'unofficial' groups of workers, and by the Government. But the Government is also in a position, through its decisions on fiscal and monetary policy, and various other instruments, directly to influence the action of private firms. It is by the use of its policy instruments that the Government can direct the economy to faster growth. The National Plan may properly be regarded as an additional instrument which may affect decisions in more subtle ways, and the same is true of a voluntary incomes and prices policy except in so far as public sector incomes or prices are directly controlled by the Government. Apart from any direct controls of this sort, those instruments certainly do not operate as a directive to anyone.

Although this discussion of the work of the NEDC and the DEA has concentrated on the role of the quantitative programmes for growth, it must not be forgotten that the NEDC initiated and continues the study of 'obstacles to growth', and that much of the work of the DEA lies in this area. Indeed, an important function of the quantitative programmes, and some would say the only proper function, was to help to indicate these obstacles so that policies could be devised to surmount them. In the industrial inquiry preceding the NEDC's Plan, the firms and organizations consulted were asked to indicate not only their expected output and investment but also what would be, in their opinion, the main obstacles in the way of, or requirements for, the rate of growth they envisaged. The

NEDO itself also studied more general questions and problems raised by the overall survey of the adequacy of resources, and published its findings in *Conditions Favourable to Faster Growth*. Considerable action has since followed, and since 1964 the Labour Government, building in some areas on foundations laid by the previous administration, has developed a many-sided effort to stimulate productivity and exports. Many aspects of these policies are discussed in detail in later chapters, and it is therefore unnecessary to provide a full account of this side of planning here. It is, however, desirable to give a brief summary of the main policies, in order to avoid any tendency to conclude from a reading of this chapter alone that British planning has concentrated on quantitative programmes at the expense of other policies.

The excessive inflation of Britain's prices in relation to those of its main competitors in world markets was recognized as one of the main reasons why the balance of payments was such a crucial obstacle to growth. The establishment of the Prices and Incomes Board and the statutory incomes policy were major elements in the Government's response to this problem, and may perhaps be seen in the future to have been the most significant consequence of the planning movement.

The following have been among the other main features of the 'obstacles to growth' approach. The Economic Development Committees and the industrial division of the DEA have examined problems in individual industries, and contributed to a change in attitudes conducive to the finding of solutions to long-standing problems. The Prices and Incomes Board, in addition to its work in trying to hold down increases in prices and incomes, has done complementary work to that of the EDCs by stressing in its reports the need for firms to absorb rising costs by greater efficiency, using the pressure of publicity to induce firms to act on these possibilities, and helping by pointing out practical ways in which this might be done. The Ministry of Technology has played a special role in relation to its 'sponsored' science-based industries, especially by accelerating government contracts for the supply of equipment. Research and development over a wider range of industry has also been further encouraged by the substantial increase in the funds available to the National Research Development Corporation for the financing of inventions and innovations. New business schools have been established to improve the standards of training and education in

E

management. The Industrial Training Boards have begun to step up the financing of industrial training and thus the effort devoted to it. The Redundancy Payments Act has gone some way towards making redundancy, and therefore mobility of labour, more acceptable. Regional Planning Boards and Councils have been set up as an aid to the formulation of regional policies and the development of their regional economies. Overseas investment and overseas government expenditure have been curtailed, some small incentives have been given to exporters, and other policies have been introduced to encourage exports. Fiscal reform has been initiated with the intention of putting more of the burden of taxation on to costs rather than profits, thus providing greater incentives to economy in the use of factors of production. The inevitable short-term fiscal and monetary restrictions have been applied with some discrimination in favour of productive investment and exports.

This broad movement to identify the obstacles to growth and to adapt a wide range of policies will probably be seen in retrospect to have been a more important part of the work of the NEDC and the DEA than the writing of the quantitative programmes, and may prove to have contributed more to the growth of productivity, when enough time has elapsed to make a judgment of these developments feasible. But the two sides of the work of the new planning institutions of the 1960s cannot be entirely separated. If the attempt to draw up quantitative programmes has contributed to the enthusiasm for and the range of policy adaptations to remove obstacles to growth, it will have been of long-term value, whatever the short-term damage that may have been done by the misuse of the NEDC and DEA programmes to encourage an unduly fast expansion of both public and private consumption, and to justify a rate of growth of production that went far beyond what the external payments constraint would allow and thus led to the use of orthodox measures in July 1966 to bring that growth once more to an abrupt stop.

After these 'July measures' the National Plan, already seriously discredited at the time of its publication, was assumed to have been finally abandoned. Subsequently the Government announced that it was engaged in a reappraisal of the approach to national plans.[1] This reappraisal was overshadowed by the short-term situation, which remained so discouraging throughout 1967 that further restrictions on the domestic economy had to be imposed in July. In

[1] See, for example, DEA, *Progress Report*, December 1966.

October the second National Plan, announced for the end of the year, had also to be postponed. In November the pound was devalued by 14·3 per cent, thus removing one of the uncertainties that had made quantitative forecasting extremely difficult.

The Conservative Party has also, in opposition, been reconsidering its attitude to planning institutions and methods that it originated in the early 1960s. There seemed a danger that, in the mood of disillusionment prevalent in 1967 following the failure of these early experiments, much that is valuable might be rejected in favour of extremist approaches on either side: towards renewed emphasis, in the Labour Party, on State ownership and direction of private firms,[1] and towards a blind reliance on *laissez faire* policies, regardless of their effectiveness, on the part of the Conservatives. To veer to either extreme would, as will be made clear in later chapters and especially in Chapters 12 and 13, be to run counter to the experience and evidence from the two other countries whose policies are examined in this book. There is therefore no attempt at this stage to draw conclusions from this brief outline of the development of planning for growth in Britain, which is to be regarded only as an introduction to the fuller treatment of particular policies which is found in Chapters 6 to 11. A more thorough critique of national quantitative programming itself is found in the next chapter, which draws on both British and French experience.

Some of the more important publications on British planning are:

NEDC, *The Growth of the Economy to 1966*, HMSO, 1963.
NEDC, *Conditions Favourable to Faster Growth*, HMSO, 1963.
NEDC, *The Growth of the Economy*, HMSO, 1964.
HMSO, *The National Plan*, Cmnd. 2764, 1965.
W. Beckerman and Associates, *The British Economy in 1975*, NIESR, Cambridge University Press, 1965.
W. Beckerman and K. J. Wigley, The National Plan, *Journal of the Royal Statistical Society*, Series A, Vol. 129, Part I, 1966.
J. Brunner, *The National Plan, a Preliminary Assessment*, Eaton Paper No. 4, Institute of Economic Affairs (2nd ed.), July 1965.
H. F. R. Catherwood, *Britain with the Brakes off*, Hodder & Stoughton, 1966.

---

[1] An Industrial Expansion Bill, to enable the Government to acquire shareholdings in private firms, extending the work in this direction of the Industrial Reorganization Corporation, was introduced in November 1967. See pp. 180–6.

A. Day, The Myth of 4 per cent, *Westminster Bank Review*, November 1965.

P. D. Henderson (ed.), *Economic Growth in Britain*, Weidenfeld and Nicolson, 1966.

J. Mitchell, *Groundwork to Economic Planning*, Secker & Warburg, 1966.

PEP, *Planning for Growth*, Planning No. 487, March 1965.

PEP, *The National Plan: its Contribution to Growth*, Planning No. 493, November 1965.

PEP, *Inquest on Planning in Britain*, Planning No. 499, 1966.

CHAPTER 5

THE CONTRIBUTION OF INDICATIVE PROGRAMMES

The contribution of a national programme to an economic policy aimed at maintaining a sustained high rate of growth has been widely discussed in France during recent years. The special conditions of the period before 1958, the growth in the influence of external factors on the French economy with the development of the Common Market, and the increasingly difficult problem of containing inflation without sacrificing long-term expansion, have served to provoke a conceptual justification of the plans, most notably by the former Commissaire Général du Plan, M. Massé.[1] In Britain there has been a continuous discussion since 1961 as to what kinds of national planning are valid and what they can hope to achieve, and in Brussels the working out of a Medium-Term Economic Policy Programme for the EEC has given rise to an international debate about planning for growth. This chapter examines four issues which are vital to our assessment of indicative programmes: how they operate on demand expectations, the reduction of uncertainty, the role of industry-level targets, and the relationship between planning and competition.

THE RAISING OF DEMAND EXPECTATIONS

The origin of the theory of demand expectations was M. Monnet's concept of the 'economic Malthusianism' into which the prewar French economy had declined owing to the pessimism of entrepreneurs, and his determination to inject some optimism into them by means of plan targets. A more up-to-date statement was provided

[1] See P. Massé, *Le Plan ou l'Anti-hasard*, Collection Idées, Gallimard, Paris, 1965. See also Préparation du Vᵉ Plan, *Journal Officiel*, December 22, 1964.

by Mr Beckerman in the introductory chapters of the NIESR study.[1] The central thesis is that the chief cause of growth is the expectation of growth: that the alteration of demand expectations is more important than any other single factor in accelerating the rate of growth: ' . . . the productive system, at least in most of industry, is believed to be very flexible, and the rate of growth that can be achieved is, within limits, partly a matter of the growth rate that the relevant bodies in society (particularly entrepreneurs) expect to be achieved.'[2] and, 'In an economy that has been growing slowly, it is difficult to expect acceleration if future growth expectations are simply extrapolations of the past. Persuading the community that a 4 per cent growth rate will be achieved may not, alone, ensure that it is achieved, but persuading them that only 2·8 per cent will be achieved is a fairly safe way of ensuring that 2·8 per cent will not be exceeded. Capacity will not grow fast enough to sustain a prolonged acceleration of the growth rate, unless the acceleration is accompanied by changing expectations concerning the longer run prospects.'[3]

This conclusion is so well qualified as to be unexceptionable, but Mr Beckerman is led, by a rather uneven chain of reasoning, to exaggerate the importance of expectations in relation to other factors. First, by econometric analysis it is shown that the combined contribution of capital and labour inputs to growth explains only about half the observed growth in selected advanced industrial economies, and that in the faster growing economies labour and capital inputs explain a smaller proportion of the total growth than in the slower growing countries. Secondly, it is assumed that since the 'residual' element in growth (that is, the proportion of growth that cannot be explained in terms of the size of capital and labour inputs) is so large, it cannot be ascribed in any large part to education. It is accepted that this analysis does not by any means eliminate supply factors as an explanation of growth, but rather shows that other factors should be influenced as well if growth is to be promoted as effectively as possible. (The actual figures suggest that for all nine selected countries, labour and capital are responsible for rather

[1] W. Beckerman and Associates, *The British Economy in 1975*, NIESR, Cambridge University Press, 1965, Chapters 1–3. Part of the following discussion of this theory has already appeared in PEP, *The National Plan*, Planning No. 493, November 1965.

[2] W. Beckerman, op. cit., p. 46.

[3] Ibid., p. 49.

more than half the growth.) With some honestly expressed mis-givings Mr Beckerman, however, comes down on the side of expectations: 'However, to cast doubt on the strength of the evidence in favour of autonomous supply factors by no means disposes of all or any supply-determined growth hypothesis. The question of how far growth is determined by supply rather than by demand is, of course, not merely of academic interest: it must greatly influence policies for growth and, for this study, the overall growth prospects which we need to assume in proceeding to the subsequent projections. It will be apparent from the above that we have given considerable weight to the demand expectations and, in particular, export demand.'[1]

The early chapters of Mr Beckerman's study, although it is not their intention to make out a case for target planning, do constitute a statement of the importance of demand expectations and therefore of the desirability of changing them in order to get faster growth. There are, however, considerable weaknesses, which are recognized, in this case. First, it comes very near to ascribing to expectations the whole force of the 'residual' element in growth. The fact that education may not be a large part of the residual does not mean that demand expectations are an even larger part. Is it not still more probable that the residual consists, as its name suggests, of mana-gerial efficiency, technological progress, education, labour relations and many other factors? The evidence for the importance of ex-pectations in the residual is slight, since it rests heavily on the coincidence of a high residual with rapid growth in two countries: Germany and France. This evidence is also consistent with the residual consisting of other elements besides demand expectations. Certainly, while we have some statistical measures, however un-certain, of the quantitative importance of capital and labour in promoting growth, we have no reasonable measure of the quanti-tative contribution of expectations as compared with that of other elements contained in the 'residual'. While the evidence suggests, therefore, that we would be foolish to concentrate all our efforts on increasing the quantity of capital and labour inputs, it does not appear to lead to any very certain conclusions about the relative importance of expectations as compared with other factors, and therefore about the extent to which reliance should be placed on the effort to change them.

[1] W. Beckerman, op. cit., p. 67.

It may nevertheless be accepted that demand expectations have some importance, but it is necessary to consider them in relation to the constraints that may check the expansion of production that would be induced by higher expectations. Another way of putting this is to say, quite simply, that operating on demand expectations at home will increase the rate of growth only if growth is constrained by home demand and not by other things: a rather obvious remark, but one that may perhaps bear repeating. Thus the validity of efforts to change demand expectations cannot be considered in isolation from the supply of labour and capital. Changing the expectations of those responsible for investment decisions would, of course, increase only the demand for capital, and not its supply. Misgivings have been expressed on this matter, lest an increase in both consumption and investment demand should lead to demand inflation (see p. 145). In a fully employed economy with a working population that is growing only slowly, expansion is likely to run quickly up against a supply constraint on the side of labour. This can of course be avoided if consumption is kept in check until production grows enough to provide for a faster growth of consumption as well as of investment, or if the growth of labour productivity is accelerated sufficiently. But there is nothing inherent in the operation on expectations of increased demand and therefore of faster growth of production which will lead businessmen to concentrate on raising productivity. The fact that any businessman is persuaded that faster growth of the GDP is probable is no reason why he, individually, should save labour in order to meet the overall labour requirements for faster growth. The Plan can try to work on expectations of labour shortage so as to encourage labour-saving investment, as the National Plan did by stressing the probability of a 'manpower gap'. It is, however, doubtful whether this will usually be sufficiently effective, and direct incentives or sanctions are probably required in addition to publishing the likelihood of labour shortages. A general sanction of this kind has been provided in Britain by the Selective Employment Tax introduced in the 1966 Budget. Given, moreover, that measures are taken both to keep consumption in check so as to allow for higher investment, and to accelerate the growth in labour productivity, it is still necessary to assess soberly the limits of what can be achieved by such methods, and not to try to raise expectations beyond these limits that are imposed by the supply constraints.

Likewise, the indicated growth rate can succeed in accelerating growth by changing expectations only to the extent that there is no external constraint to growth at that rate. But both the NEDC's inquiry and the DEA's Plan have indicated that for Britain the balance of payments is a very narrow constraint on growth above about 3 per cent. With some variations the NIESR estimates produce a similar conclusion, while the events of 1964–7 provided empirical confirmation of the existence of this constraint. The expectations theory is not directly relevant here, for no amount of altering expectations at home would be likely to make foreigners buy more of a nation's exports. Ironically enough, demand thus appears to be a leading element in growth in a sector where the target element in national plans is least capable of directly affecting it. In highly competitive world markets exports depend on relative price and quality and delivery dates, that is, on supply factors, not only at home, but in competitor countries. In any one country, unless these are relatively favourable, the balance-of-payments position becomes a constraint on growth, whose importance is related (though not directly) to the proportion of output that is traded. Action on supply factors to improve the competitiveness of exports appears more important than targetry (though, as is suggested below, the embodiment of policy changes in a comprehensive plan may aid in their acceptance and implementation).

Mr Beckerman did in fact stress the importance of overseas demand and, in assessing the feasibility of his hypothetical growth rate, considered various changes in economic conditions in Continental countries that could make British exports more competitive. Mr C. T. Saunders, in his introduction to the NIESR study, warned that the foreign trade figures were 'neither forecasts nor statements of policy', but 'statistical illustrations of what is meant by increasing competitiveness, which we regard as the fundamental condition for faster economic progress'.[1] But the DEA, to judge by the content of the National Plan (see pp. 119–128), supported indicative planning in terms that appear to have exaggerated the relative importance of the demand expectations theory of growth so far as it relates to home demand, and failed to take full account of the fact that, in so far as it relates to overseas demand, this factor is amenable to policy only through operation on the supply side.

The rate of growth cannot, in fact, be altered merely by incanta-

[1] W. Beckerman, op. cit., p. 46.

tion of the magical desired number; clearly the constraints have to be removed, which requires the necessary improvements in the quantity and quality of factor inputs and the financing of imported machines and materials. Unless this happens, it is worse than useless for businessmen to believe in the targets, because they will become disillusioned about planning if the constraints cause the investment boom to end in a crisis. Indeed, unless policies are seen to be having the required quantitative effects, the targets are not likely to be considered credible in the first place.

None of this should be taken to imply that the demand expectations theory was not applicable in the French economy in the 1950s. On the contrary, it was extremely relevant since, as explained in Chapter 3, output was not constrained by supply factors, and the French Government was willing to use import and exchange controls to prevent a payments deficit from checking growth. But it might be argued that, where exports rather than home demand are, as they have been in Britain, the leading constraint, it is the removal of constraints itself that will alter expectations, and that a national target cannot contribute anything additional. It seems probable that it can, however, by easing the process of removing some of the constraints through its effect on attitudes. A set of policy changes, required of government, trade unions and employers, is probably more easily put across if it is wrapped up as a co-ordinated programme for the achievement of some specific and quantified objectives. It is easier to mobilize opinion in favour of 25 per cent growth by 1970 than in favour of a vague 'faster growth'. However, while indicative target planning may have some significance in this way, it is clearly not so important as has been suggested by those who have over-emphasized the importance of demand expectations and under-emphasized that of the supply and external constraints. Instead of playing a major independent role, target planning is reduced to an adjunct (though possibly a valuable one) of policies that act more directly on supply factors, at least until the balance-of-payments constraint has been removed. The plan as a set of targets is thus best regarded as a catalyst of change, rather than a direct agent in itself. This implies that policy changes must be carefully interwoven into the fabric of the Plan, and the temptation must be resisted to regard the Plan itself as more important than the instrumental changes it is intended to facilitate.

The theory of demand expectations also appears to have some

validity from the point of view of stabilizing investment, even where, as in Britain, the balance of payments rather than demand expectations has almost certainly been the main constraint. If a national target can help to stabilize investment by persuading investors and the Government to 'stick to trend' and ignore short-term fluctuations in demand, it will make a valuable contribution to growth, because it will become possible to expand home demand without rapidly running up against limits of capacity that are all the more stringent because in the previous recession investment was curtailed. It may also help to expand as well as stabilize the rate of investment. Both greater stability and higher investment will help to improve the balance of payments and thus, in the case of Britain, to shift the main constraint.[1] So if targets were to help stabilize and/or increase investment while respecting the constraints, they would make a valuable contribution to growth; but if the constraints are neither shifted nor respected then it would be better not to raise expectations in the first place, only to have them dashed by restrictive measures later on.

THE REDUCTION OF UNCERTAINTY

The case for indicative target planning does not, of course, rest solely on the psychological effect of the targets in inducing more optimistic general expectations about the growth of demand. An indicative plan is also conceived to be a detailed means of reducing the element of uncertainty inherent in a market economy. This uncertainty becomes greater as the rate of technical progress increases and the gestation period of investment projects grows longer. In such circumstances, present market prices may, as the French planners have argued, be inadequate and even misleading guides for investment decisions, especially in sectors where investment is carried out in large blocks. The planners believe that businessmen will not, unaided, be able to make the best estimates of future price movements and they therefore attempt to establish what future relative prices are likely to be by estimating the probable changes in demand and available resources in the economy. The limitations of the 'signals' of the market are stressed by M. Massé: 'Prices have a two-fold function: a medium- or long-term function which is to direct and guide the decisions of economic agents, and a short-term function which is

[1] See T. Wilson, Instability and the Rate of Growth, *Lloyds Bank Review*, July 1966.

to direct and guide the formation of income. Governments are often compelled to act on the basis of effects on income rather than long-term effects.'[1]

To be effective the plan has to be a reliable guide to future demand and production patterns. The French planners seek to make it so through the Modernization Commissions and the British Economic Development Committees could eventually play a similar role. The main contribution of these bodies is to relate the development of one sector to that of the others and ensure that each industry's plans are reasonably consistent or, to use the planners' word, coherent. In this way, the inter-relationships of the economic system are made known for each branch of industry. If each industry adheres to the plan, then supplies and markets for inter-industry transactions will automatically be assured. The uncertainties of final consumer demand still remain, but there is at least a reduction of uncertainty for industries selling raw materials or equipment and the planners claim that this gives businessmen confidence in the feasibility of the target rate of growth and facilitates investment planning.

The French planners do not, of course, ignore the fact that many firms, particularly larger firms, carry out their own market research. But they seem to believe that such research is likely to be very limited in scope. M. Massé, for example, has cited the effect of an increase in agricultural incomes on steel production as farmers take advantage of their increased prosperity to introduce more mechanized techniques. To extend market studies to this extent, he argues, would not be normal practice for an individual firm. This raises the question whether French target planning did not reflect, at least in part, the under-development of business economics and market research in French industry, particularly in the early years of French planning. This has been, at least in part, a consequence of the structure of the French economy, where the continued predominance of small and medium-sized firms has inevitably limited their capacity to undertake or commission wide-ranging national market surveys and analyses of the effects of broad economic policy decisions. It certainly would be normal practice in the steel industries of, for example, the United States or Britain to make a serious forecast of the demand for steel from any significant customer industry, such as the manufacturers of agricultural machinery. This does not necessarily dispose of the argument of indicative planning as a means of

[1] P. Massé, The French Plan and Economic Theory, *Econometrica*, April 1965.

concerting the results of industrial market forecasts at national level, which helps to avoid inconsistencies due to ignorance in one industry of the plans of another, or in order to shift economic growth to a higher level by increasing the propensity to invest throughout industry. But it does mean that certain arguments of the French planners, based on the belief that industry does not make sensible forecasts of price or market trends where these are necessary for its investment plans, cannot be transferred as they stand to economies which are more oligopolistic in structure and where market research and business economics are more highly developed. Indeed, such arguments have decreasing validity in France itself where these activities have been evolving rapidly in recent years.

Some critics of national planning take the view that any attempt at the co-ordinated national forecast is doomed to failure. Thus Mr J. Brunner has poked fun at the DEA's questionnaire, referred to the lamentable failure rate of economic forecasts in general, and concluded that: 'No amount of statistical expertise and technical virtuosity is any substitute for ... "feel" for the course of events.'[1] The word 'feel,' and the 'judgment' he frequently invokes, are not defined, so that it is difficult to know what exactly Mr Brunner would wish to replace forecasting with in the process of arriving at decisions on, for example, investment proposals. If such decisions are not informed by the best possible estimates of future outcome based on carefully considered assumptions, then the 'judgment' seems likely to be definable as a guess whose inadequate basis is concealed by an implicit reference to some clairvoyant power on the part of the person exercising it. To condemn forecasting in this sweeping manner appears to be simply obscurantist. Forecasts must be useful because it is found necessary, at every level of the economy from the individual to the Government, to make them. And there is a very real sense in which not to make a forecast *is* to make one, an inadequate one, in which the best possible information about the present has not been carefully collected, assumptions have not been clarified, and in all probability it has been unconsciously assumed that things will continue much as before.

However, to condemn extreme attacks on forecasting is not to suggest that there are not many difficulties and dangers in the way, especially, of national forecasts, or that one can use them without

[1] J. Brunner, *The National Plan, a Preliminary Assessment*, Eaton Paper No. 4, Institute of Economic Affairs (2nd ed.), July 1965, p. 35.

proper care. The DEA has certainly been well aware of these difficulties . They admit that 'some of the forecasts or projections for particular industries will inevitably turn out to be wrong'. It is not then really necessary to warn them that many forecasts made in individual industries in the past have been proved wrong in the event. There is, of course, considerable room for improving the scope, the speed, and the reliability of information about the present and the recent past[1] (though these are conflicting requirements and choices will continue to have to be made between speed of publication and the necessity of subsequent revision). There is no *a priori* reason why the collection of information about intentions, and the preparation of a national forecast, should detract from existing statistical services, and it could improve them by emphasizing their relevance in decisions. There are dangers in the interpretation of answers to questions about the future, for many respondents may try, through their answers, to influence others' actions to their own individual advantage, but it is not impossible to guard against well-known dangers of this kind in the devising of questionnaires and the interpretation of the answers. It is also doubtful whether trade associations, which are essentially pressure groups for their own industry's interests, are the best sources of information in preparing plans, but the development of the Economic Development Committees may alleviate this problem. We should also note that, regardless of the value attached to the final figures, the process of carrying out an inquiry of this kind, and publishing its results, has some significant advantages. Any firms that have not been in the habit of making long-term forecasts may be induced to think ahead more, while those progressive firms that already have well-developed forecasting procedures may benefit from more information about other industries and the economy as a whole. The influence of a single growth target also varies considerably among different sectors. For the steel industry and the electricity industry, for example, good indications of future national growth rates may be of great specific value for investment planning. In other less concentrated industries it may afford a helpful but very vague guide for firms, especially if the technical conditions of the industry are changing rapidly. It is, of course, possible to argue, as Mr C. R. Pratten does, that the more detailed the plan targets become the less accurate they are likely to be.[2] But this is to a large

[1] Jeremy Bray, M.P, *The New Economy*, Fabian Tract 362, July 1965.
[2] C. R. Pratten, The Best Laid Plans, *Lloyds Bank Review*, July 1964.

extent an argument for improving forecasting techniques, while taking care not to place undue reliance on detailed figures.

In France, Mr F. Bloch-Lainé has stressed the need for co-operation between government and industry to create an *économie concertée*, 'in which the representatives of the State and enterprises meet in an organized manner to exchange information, to compare their blueprints for the future and to act together both in taking decisions and in establishing points of view on the intentions of the Government'.[1] This process of consultation between industry and government, thoroughly established as a basic feature of French planning, is in Britain being developed in the EDCs. In particular, the EDCs are carrying out studies on the main problems facing the various industries, especially those which impair competitiveness and hinder export performance. This kind of study is likely to be most effective if it is done on an industry-by-industry basis; the obstacles to expansion in the chemical industry are very different from those in the shipbuilding or machine tool sectors. A programme is likely to be much more effective if businessmen are actively involved in it and if the programme is expressed in terms that are meaningful and useful to them. It can be argued that these problems could be handled by separate industry studies and the introduction of tax concessions and financial aids where necessary. But the study of an industry's problems specifically within the framework of a national programme for growth and in conjunction with studies of other industries may well highlight obstacles to growth and assess the effectiveness of measures to overcome them more precisely than a series of uncoordinated studies unrelated to any estimates of the potential increase of production in the economy as a whole or in other sectors.

The French planners argue that, without industry-level planning to provide information and facilitate communication between firms and between industry and government, there would be much greater risk of under or over capacity occurring throughout the economy, because of faulty investments made by inadequately informed businessmen. Supply and demand would eventually be brought into balance but at the expense of waste and distortion which in the case of large-scale projects could be considerable. This point has also been developed by Mr G. B. Richardson, who distinguishes between 'general profit potential' and particular profit opportunities. The

[1] F. Bloch-Lainé, *A la Recherche d'une Economie Concertée*, Editions de l'Epargne, Paris, 1959.

decision to invest will depend on a businessman being assured that he will benefit from an increase in demand for a certain product. If he is to believe this, argues Mr Richardson, 'he will have to be assured that the volume of investment undertaken by his competitors will not be so great as to cause a substantial excess of supply over demand'.[1] Unless he possesses information about the plans and strategies of his competitors he may be reluctant to invest in case they do so also and thus create a situation of excess capacity. The higher the fixed costs and the longer the gestation periods in an industry, the greater will be the wastage, either through loss of output or excessive investment. The natural consequence of this situation is that firms will seek to improve their information about each other's plans, and collusion may well result. The self-regulating forces of the market may therefore result in a loss of potential output, the creation of excess capacity, or collusion. Collusion need not necessarily hinder the expansion of output, but equally, it cannot be proved in general terms that it will not. This is not an unfamiliar argument in favour of programming or planning. But it is important to note that it does imply that the type of planning adopted will be sufficiently powerful to lessen the particular type of uncertainty discussed above, providing some co-ordination at the industry or branch level of individual firms' plans and at the national level of different industries' plans in the form of a quantitative programme. If the planning system is required to reduce this type of uncertainty, it cannot do so on the basis of a purely global target, such as may be used, without the apparatus of 'industrial planning', as a guide for national economic policy.

GLOBAL TARGETS AND INDUSTRY-LEVEL TARGETS

The distinction between a system of industrial target planning and reliance on a few global and public sector targets is very clearly brought out in the Medium-term Economic Programme for the EEC, discussed in Chapter 12. The Medium-term Programme abjured, on German insistence, any attempts to influence industrialists by means of industry-level targets. Their forecasting exercise is rather designed as a framework for public policy and as a broad indication to industrialists as to future expansion at macro-economic level. Mr Dow

[1] G. B. Richardson, *Information and Investment*, Oxford University Press, 1960, p. 50.

had a similar conception of the function of targets in relation to the private sector when he wrote that 'the institution of the National Economic Development Council is likely to affect the conduct of fiscal and monetary policy in future. It would be neither possible nor necessary for the Chancellor to give pledges about future rates of taxation. But it would seem necessary for the Government to give a general idea of the rates of expansion in both consumer and investment demand which—subject to capacity growing as planned—budgetary and monetary policy aimed to produce'.[1] The growth target might have to be altered in the light of short-term fluctuations and other unforeseeable or uncontrollable developments; but there is a significant difference between a series of *ad hoc* policies which are formulated in terms of solutions to crises and a basic government commitment to continued expansion at a given rate which may have to be modified from time to time.

It has been suggested that if the existence of a target growth rate leads to government policies aimed at stimulating and maintaining demand at a high level, the result may be to push output to the limits of available capacity and create inflationary pressures. Thus Sir Roy Harrod has expressed the fear that if demand for consumer goods and investment goods is deliberately raised to the level required by the growth target, total demand may rise to a level above the supply potential of the economy. It will be difficult to increase the supply potential because the higher demand 'will not have left behind sufficient savings to finance the investment required for the growth process'.[2] Professor Day shares this critical view. In an economy operating near to full employment no amount of psychology can get around the physical necessity that if investment is to be increased and prices held stable, savings must increase by the same amount. Indeed, if demand is stimulated in line with a target rate of growth the resultant increase in consumer demand may actually hold back investment. He is, therefore, sceptical of the efficiency of a single overall growth target and sees it as a 'facile way of complacently escaping from hard thought. If the NEDC target of 4 per cent were treated as a target which could be achieved only at a price of sacrifice of current consumption and of severe disturbance to vested interests

[1] J. C. R. Dow, *The Management of the British Economy*, NIESR, Cambridge University Press, 1964, p. 411.

[2] Sir Roy Harrod, Neddy and Growth: a Theoretical Question, *Bankers Magazine*, June 1964.

and economic and social rigidities it would serve a useful purpose.'[1]

These are, of course, criticisms of ways in which a growth target can be misused, not of the proper use of a target as a guide for public policy or private investors. As far as the private sector is concerned, it may indeed be argued that judiciously selected industry-level targets can help to prevent inflation. The function of the targets is to stimulate the right amount of investment by indicating that demand will grow at a certain rate. Inflation will not be caused if all sectors of the economy adhere to output targets which when aggregated produce the desired rate of growth of capacity as well as of demand; investment may be encouraged without stimulating the general level of demand before the capacity is created. If each sector adheres to the programme, output and demand will expand together. The targets will thus help to ensure that the necessary conditions for a certain rate of growth are respected.[2]

There are, however, two crucial gaps in this tidy circular argument. The planners can reasonably hope to influence demand in the public sector, and via Modernization Commissions or EDCs the demand for raw materials and semi-manufactured goods in the private sector. But final consumer demand for the products of a given industry is much less controllable; it is the residual element in the planners' calculations. This must be accepted as a fact of life in a free society. But at the same time the consequences of an excessive general growth of consumption should be made clear. This is what an indicative plan can do. It can indicate fairly precisely the growth of consumption that is consistent with the targets of the programme and thus establish a framework within which indirect regulation of consumption may be carried out. Two obvious means of regulation are an incomes policy, and the manipulation of direct and indirect taxation. Here a programme should, if it is realistic and properly used, allow a more informed and consistent approach. The second gap concerns foreign demand. Even if balanced growth of demand and capacity were achieved as far as domestic demand is concerned, this still leaves export demand. Here even industry-level target

---

[1] A. C. L. Day, The Myth of Four Per Cent, *Westminster Bank Review*, November 1964.

[2] This is of course not by any means the only way in which Harrod's and Day's point is met. Building into the Plan expectations of manpower shortage can also help towards the same end. See above, pp. 126–7.

planning becomes much less powerful. The planners cannot with any firmness forecast the future level of foreign demand, and demand for exports is influenced by many factors which are beyond the influence of any national policies. The French planners, the Department of Economic Affairs and the NEDC have all recognized this fact and have devoted special attention to ways of increasing productivity and lowering costs, thus striking at both the balance-of-payments and inflationary problems at the same time. In view of the importance of the prices and exports constraints, this 'supply side' aspect of indicative planning, undertaken at the level of the industry or firm (e.g. much of the work of the Ministry of Technology) or at global level (e.g. the export rebate or the Selective Employment Tax), has become increasingly important in the thinking of planners.

THE PROGRAMME AND COMPETITION

The possibility that indicative planning will lead to a reduction of competition and even actively encourage restrictive agreements between firms raises the extremely important question of the co-existence of programmes with competition. This possibility exists even if there is no policy of incentives used to ensure adherence to the plan, although obviously the more prevalent such discriminatory arrangements the stronger the likelihood of serious infringement of conditions of competition. The reduction of competition is one of the strongest criticisms which German neo-liberals direct against indicative planning. The problem has been posed by Professor T. Wilson: 'Planning after the French model with its twenty industrial committees may encourage restrictive practices. To talk about discussions between the State and "industry" can be misleading. For what is "industry"? In practice what is likely to happen is that the officials will discuss industrial developments with representatives of the larger firms, and it is perhaps significant that planning is more popular with the large firms in France than with the small. If the small firms are to be brought into the discussions, they must choose representatives and this is likely to involve, in turn, fairly strong trade associations. When firms are linked together in this way in order to meet the needs of the planners, they may find it all the easier to maintain prices, to keep out newcomers, to blunt the edge of competition.'[1] A more optimistic point of view but one reflecting a

[1] T. Wilson, *Planning and Growth*, Macmillan, 1964, p. 40.

similar concern is expressed by Mr J. Sheahan. 'The great blessing in practice is that group goals have not been made binding on individual firms, that disorderly and consequently vigorous movement has been favoured instead of the deadening goal of rational coherence.'[1]

These are undoubtedly serious criticisms. Industry-level planning must necessarily involve an exchange of information between firms on matters such as investment, output, research and manpower needs. This immediately raises the question of how the plans of individual firms are related to the forecasts or targets for the industry. Some allocation of markets between firms must take place either as a result of competition or of discussions between firms in which the planners may or may not participate. Professor Granyk claims that, in at least one of the Modernization Commissions, sharing out of markets was done by the large firms; the planners stayed out of the discussion.[2] Precise information on this aspect of French planning is, however, extremely difficult to find. No study has been made of the extent to which even the larger firms take account of the plan targets in formulating their own plans. In general, the French Employers' Federation have been favourably disposed towards planning although the National Federation of Small and Medium-Sized Firms has continued to suspect that the planning system legalizes agreements amongst the larger firms. There would seem indeed to be some reason for this suspicion. It is shared by Professor Perroux who argues that the Plans *depend* for their success on the co-operation of the large firms.[3]

The encouragement of agreements or cartels by a system of indicative planning need not be considered *per se* to be an obstacle to economic growth. Within the framework of a growth plan cartels would be formed in the context of an expanding economy. Their object would not be to share out a static or declining market, but to arrange the orderly distribution of a growing market. In these circumstances the pressures on the efficient firms to compete in terms of quality and product innovation might still be considerable. At the very least it can be said that the cartel will not halt the expansion of

[1] J. Sheahan, *Promotion and Control of Industry in Postwar France*, Harvard University Press, 1963, p. 170.

[2] D. Granyk, *The European Executive*, Weidenfeld and Nicolson, 1962, p. 154.

[3] F. Perroux, *The IVth French Plan*, National Institute of Economic and Social Research, Translated Monographs No. 1, 1965.

output[1] and agreements will not necessarily be biased in favour of inefficient firms.

It is also important to remember that the structure of industry in France still poses the problem of excessive fragmentation rather than excessive concentration.[2] This concern is reflected in the emphasis laid in the Fifth Plan on the need for structural reform in certain sectors. In 1958, a study by INSEE showed that 85 per cent of industrial establishments employed fewer than six wage earners, 12 per cent between six and fifty and only 0·2 per cent more than 500. In the engineering sector 89 per cent of establishments employed fewer than six persons. A similar situation existed in the building and textile industries. The efforts of the planners in these sectors have since the Second Plan been directed towards concentrating and rationalizing the industries, although with only limited success. The danger of cartels formed by big firms must not, therefore, be exaggerated in the context of the French economy, and this has probably accounted at least in part for the lack of weight given to this problem in the planning reports and the French literature on the planning system.

The ill-effects of cartelization are not, however, removed simply by ensuring that any collusion is accompanied by the expansion of output. There is the obvious risk that expansion may be less than it would have been had competition or oligopolistic strategies been the rule. The well-known defence of restrictive practices on the grounds that they encourage the investment required to take advantage of technical progress by providing some degree of balance between security and the pressures of competition may become less convincing if account is taken of the influence of indicative planning. The argument rests on the assumption that price competition will be replaced by product competition particularly through innovation. It can be argued that in several ways planning may militate against this non-price competition.

First, if firms accept the Plan targets as reasonable the onus is on the planners to prepare accurate and ambitious targets. If the

[1] For a discussion of this point see T. Wilson, Restrictive Practices, published in a symposium *Competition, Cartels and their Regulation* (ed. J. P. Miller), Harvard University Press, 1963.

[2] French legislation on restrictive practices is equally sympathetic to the argument that in certain circumstances agreements and mergers may improve and not damage efficiency. The planning system is not, therefore, in any sense in opposition to the law.

stimulus of competition is to be removed it must be replaced by targets that indicate within certain constraints the maximum potential of the industry. It is not difficult to quote cases where this has not been done. All forecasting or planning exercises must rest to some extent on extrapolation from past trends of productivity. The estimation of forces which will cause the trend to alter is always difficult, particularly if technical progress is rapid. The Second French Plan offers a clear example of a general under-estimation by the planners of the economy's potential.

Secondly, the output targets of the Plan are set after consultation with businessmen. Inevitably this means consultation with the largest firms in each industry either directly or through the medium of trade associations. Professor Wilson makes the point that the largest firms need not be the most dynamic and there is a danger that smaller but efficient and fast-growing firms will be left out of the planning process.[1] The result of this could be a conservative estimate of the industry's potential. This may put the case too strongly, but it is useful as a reminder that innovation and rapid expansion is not the monopoly of large firms. It is interesting to note that M. Massé, commenting on Professor Perroux's argument that the plan depends on and reinforces monopolistic structures, agrees that it is important to distinguish between 'monopoly profits which tend to raise prices and the profits of innovation which tend to lower them', although he insists that arguments about the effects of monopolistic competition must be conducted in dynamic terms.[2]

While it is clearly a risk, the danger of conservative industry forecasts should not be too much exaggerated. It is in fact a common feature of both the French and British experience of indicative planning that the first round of industry estimates can in some cases over-estimate productive potential and under-estimate the constraints on expansion in relation to the planners' benchmarks. In the Fourth French Plan the Modernization Commissions successfully pressed for an increase in the target rate of productivity and also produced export estimates which the planners consider much too optimistic. Perhaps even more dramatic was the very high forecast of exports which the Industrial Inquiry produced in the British National Plan. There is, therefore, some evidence that industrial forecasting is not uninfluenced by 'animal spirits' and that

[1] T. Wilson, *Planning and Growth*, Macmillan, 1964, p. 43.
[2] F. Perroux, op. cit., preface.

industrialists are prepared seriously to discuss and compute on the basis of benchmark figures which, as in the National Plan, were considerably higher than past performance. Similarly, it is not always the case that the planners' own figures are unambitious and neglectful of possibilities of increased productivity. To the extent that they are not, the independent review of the industry forecasts by the DEA or the Commissariat du Plan can lead to upward as well as downward revisions. The opportunities for upward revisions are likely to be increased the greater the number of variants considered in the forecasting operations. The existence of a 'high' variant will at the very least lead the planners to examine in a more formal and informed way industry estimates which they think to be on the low side. They are, therefore, forces which can operate to offset over-cautious forecasts by industry.

Thirdly, if the plan does lead to an agreement to share the projected increases in markets the entry of new firms to an industry may be made very difficult. It will also be more difficult for individual firms within the industry to move ahead more rapidly than the target rate for the industry and thus ignore any 'rules' of market sharing. The French planners stress that they do not hold back firms who choose to disagree with the plan, but powerful, if not necessarily direct, methods of dissuasion have been and are still being employed. A danger here is that the planners, despite their penetration of the industrial community, may not be fully abreast of the changes in the methods and attitudes that have occurred. Mr Sheahan suggests that this could well be so: 'Intelligent government officials can probably score high in picking the most efficient of the largest firms of the moment. They are unlikely even to know about the smaller ones which could come up fast given an equal chance, and decidedly unlikely to know the key sources of possible radical change in the future.'[1]

This criticism of 'active' indicative planning is a particularly serious one in view of the tendency both in France and in Britain for the State to intervene to an increasing degree to promote faster growth of productivity by encouraging changes in the structure of industry. Such intervention is bound to conflict with the rules of the market and involves the planners in making decisions about the desirable size and structure of industries. It would seem, therefore, that planning and competition have tended to become more and

[1] J. Sheahan, op. cit., p. 248.

more incompatible and that the dangers of detailed planning are being heightened. In one sense this is true. Less reliance is being placed on the competitive process; but whether this is necessarily all loss is less clear-cut, for there are several arguments which suggest that more planning of the kind that relates to the structure of industry can be beneficial.

It has first to be made clear that what we are discussing is not the imposition of planning for any doctrinal reason but the introduction of an alternative method of allocating resources which may be better able to deal with the changes which rapid technological advance is forcing on all Western economies. We are in fact back to one of the basic principles of the French planners. In industries where fixed costs are high and the gestation period of investment long, research and development costly and essential, and international competition strong, the market mechanism left to itself can lead to the creation of extremely wasteful excess capacity or to equally serious delays in investment decisions due to uncertainty about future developments or unwillingness to take the enormous risks involved. The competitive process in such circumstances may still eventually ensure the survival of the most efficient and adaptable, but the costs to the nation in time and resources of the working out of the struggle are likely to be considerable. They may be as in the past reduced or obviated by firms coming together in collusive agreements or forging more permanent links by means of take-overs or mergers.

Recent government policy on these matters in both France and Britain has certainly accepted that increased concentration in certain industries may be necessary and advantageous, even though there is some detriment to internal competition.

Given these developments the objection to French-style indicative planning on the grounds that it is a government-supported cartel system loses some of its force. The planners may by promoting or underwriting industrial reorganization exclude potentially efficient entrants to the industry in question and block the expansion of some smaller firms within it. But the barriers to entry were by no means non-existent before their intervention and the costs of leaving changes in industrial structure to take place competitively have some chance of being reduced. Furthermore, the planners can bring to bear on the question of industrial grouping and regrouping a wider set of criteria than the participants in such operations would be required or inclined to consider if left to themselves. The consequences of a particular agreement or merger in a particular industry, for other industries and ultimately for the performance of the economy as a whole, will at least be taken into account by people with some experience of the industry and knowledge of its role in the economy. It is not easy to argue that such a system would be more disadvantageous to economic expansion than one in which the Government was careful to avoid any and every detailed, *ad hoc*, intervention.

It is important to note at this point that the kind of activities that have been mentioned as a legitimate field for the planners are not the same as, or even dependent upon, the division of an industry output target among different firms. Neither the French planners nor their British counterparts now see their prime task as ensuring the achievement of certain predetermined output totals. Rather they are concerned to promote, by a variety of methods, a reduction in costs and the improvement of efficiency. Industry output estimates are thus considered not as firm objectives but as benchmarks which may be altered either upwards or downwards. As was pointed out in Chapter 3, there are limits to the flexibility that a plan can tolerate without losing its usefulness as a guide to the future. But the French planners' distinction between compensated and uncompensated forecasting errors does indicate the direction in which flexibility is greatest. Increases in certain industries' outputs above the 'planned' figure, which are due to increased productivity, may alter the pattern of inter-industry relationships which will require certain adjustments by both the planners and industry. The adjustments required are, however, of a totally different order from those necessitated by the expansion of capacity in an industry as a result either of an over-optimistic view of demand or of competitive pressures to secure a larger share of the market. In the former case, for example, the macro-economic consequences are almost bound to be favourable (i.e. 'compensated' in the French planners' language) in an open economy facing reasonable conditions in world markets; whereas in the latter case there is likely to be distortion both at the macro- and micro-economic level. The planners' concern with industrial structure, and therefore capacity, while leaving output open-ended, is a strategy which allows coherent industrial expansion to be combined with an acceptance and indeed a search for '*un*-planned' increases in efficiency.

It may still be argued that the planners are able to limit entry to the industry and prevent firms from undertaking new investment projects which could yield significant gains in productivity. But this is simply restating the basic problem of setting the gains of competition, frequently conducted with insufficient information, against the waste of resources it involves. Moreover, the emphasis on productivity and structure rather than output will tend to encourage the ambitious firm to demonstrate its superior efficiency in order that it may establish for itself the right to a larger share of the industry's capacity in the future.

Finally, it must always be remembered that the picture of active indicative planning as a tight cartel arrangement takes no account of the impact of foreign competition either in the form of trade or capital movements. No planning system in an open economy without specially protective tariffs can overlook the need to maintain competitiveness and, if in addition the movement of capital is free, the possibility that foreign firms may severely limit its control. In the absence of any supranational planning authority there is therefore a constant and considerable competitive pressure to be set against any protectionist effects which a tightly organized domestic planning system may encourage. There are several very clear instances of these pressures in France and the French planners have frankly admitted that the fact of the European Economic Community has significantly loosened their control over certain industries.

CONCLUSIONS

It will now be apparent from this chapter that it is difficult to make firm general statements on the role of indicative programmes. Much depends on the circumstances of the particular economy or industry to which they are applied. This lack of clear recommendations is unsatisfactory, but in a sense it is also salutary. It should serve to dispel the notion which gained ground as a result of some rather uncritical examination of the experience of French planning, that the very formulation of a coherent national forecast could by its effect on expectations lead to a faster growth of output and capacity. Enough has been said already in this book to make it clear that such a model can be applied only to an economy where supply-side constraints are either negligible, can be widened by the expectations effect itself, or can be circumvented by special measures. The French economy from 1946–58 came near to satisfying these very severe conditions, but since 1958 it has ceased to do so and no other Western European economy has at any time in the postwar period been able to meet them.

This is not to say that the national indicative programme ought to be removed from the arsenal of economic policy measures in Western economies: considered as something less than a panacea for the problems of economic management it can be usefully employed in a variety of ways. It can, following the French planners, help to reduce uncertainty and the errors and waste to which it gives rise in a period of rapid technical change. It can also enable economic policy to be applied in a more informed and selective way. However, this requires at least tentative industry-level forecasts which are compatible with each other. A purely global target is not only of much less specific use and relevance to any particular sector or industry and to policies which are intended to be selective in their effects; it may also lead to an over-expansion of aggregate demand as different sectors of the economy react differently to the overall target.

Even when the programme is disaggregated to industry level there remains the objection that if the really important constraints on growth are the balance on external payments and the competitiveness of industry, there is little that an indicative programme can contribute. In terms of direct influence this is true. But if the promotion of competitiveness and the removal of factors which impede it are to involve any direct intervention in industry by the State, it is desirable that this be done in a co-ordinated way. For productivity in any one industry in a sophisticated industrial economy is closely bound up with productivity in related industries. Measures to increase productivity are, therefore, more likely to be effective if they take account of this fact than if they are considered either in terms of across-the-board effects, or of individual industries. An industry-level indicative programme could be a uniquely useful framework for such *inter-industry* productivity studies by providing access to the potential and problems of the whole range of industries. This point is especially significant in relation to that area of industrial economic policy concerned with altering the structure of industries in the light of technical and other developments. Given that it has been decided that responses to such changes cannot always be made efficiently through the market mechanism, the State is under obligation to ensure that its substitute for the market regulator is more efficient. It is unlikely that such efficiency will be achieved if the problem is tackled in piecemeal fashion by a variety of different institutions examining and reacting to changes in industrial organization according to very different criteria. A planning commission should be involved in any review or judgment of take-overs, mergers or allegedly restrictive agreements, applying the widest criteria of possible improvement in the overall performance of the economy.

Much of this conclusion will sound very ominous to the ears of those who see an active form of indicative planning involving 'supply-side' interventions as a serious threat to the competitive order and efficiency. There is a very real dilemma. It centres on the ability of the market mechanism to operate effectively in a situation where increased productivity requires considerable and rapid changes in the size of firms and industries, and the nature of their products. Intervention by the State in the context of an indicative programme has been justified in this chapter if it promotes these changes at a lesser economic cost than the market mechanism, either left to itself, or even if it is realistically adapted to suit particular situations. This chapter has suggested that there is a case for using such planning but acknowledges that the choice poses many problems.

These problems have been discussed basically in terms of the erosion of incentives to produce more or better output which could result. Such a risk clearly exists. Planners can be and have been dampening influences under the guise of superior organizers. But it has been noted that French planners, the oldest exponents of the art, have now accepted that output forecasts over a wide range of industries must be treated as highly flexible. The notion of an indicative plan as a cartel is in these circumstances much less plausible. The planners do still have the power to select and promote certain industrial structures and they may be as slow as the market to spot the sources of beneficial improvements, or worse, be the cause of their non-emergence. But by leaving industrial output targets open-ended in so far as they may be exceeded owing to productivity increases, there is still an incentive for a firm to increase its efficiency and stake its claim to a larger share of its industry's capacity and markets. The 'dead hand' of the planners is thus no longer an accurate representation.

Finally, while this chapter has concentrated on the impact of quantitative programmes directly on industry, it is not intended to suggest that this is their only significance. Even if there were no question of using programmes either directly to influence firms' decisions, or as a guide to State intervention in industry, governments would nevertheless find medium-term programmes indispensable as a guide to their decisions on economic policy. A medium-term forecast is necessary both as a framework for longer-term policies, such as a re-modelling of the tax system, or a permanent prices and incomes policy; and as a context within which short-term policies must be developed.

CHAPTER 6

MONETARY AND CREDIT POLICY

Discussion of monetary policy in West European countries since the war has tended to concentrate on two central and related questions. First, should monetary policy be aimed solely at the objectives of maintaining price stability and balance-of-payments equilibrium, or should it also be adapted to the furtherance of other objectives, such as regional balance, full employment and, most notably, faster growth? Secondly, what is the correct role of monetary policy in relation to other methods of pursuing these objectives? Concentration on the former, more traditional, objectives to the exclusion of the latter leads to the operation of global monetary measures controlling the price and availability of money which are intended to have minimal effects on the working of the price mechanism. The adoption of the newer objectives has influenced governments to operate more selective monetary measures designed to affect the allocation of investment and consumption expenditures as well as their aggregate levels. Depreciation of monetary policy in relation to other instruments has also tended to follow from the adoption of the growth objective.

There has been much controversy about the success with which the two main types of monetary policy can be operated. The critics of the global approach have questioned whether global monetary policy alone can cure inflation or balance-of-payments deficits and certainly whether it can do so without in practice having serious discriminatory effects on different parts of the economy. Thus the Radcliffe Report analysed the impact of monetary policy and found that it was frequently very uneven, and there were doubts as to its effectiveness.[1] Mr J. C. R. Dow has written that: 'It was often employed as if it and it alone would cure inflation, or, alternatively,

[1] HMSO, Committee on the Working of the Monetary System (Radcliffe Report), Cmnd. 827, 1959.

right the balance of payments; and as if it would do so without impinging openly or painfully on any specific class of demand.'[1] It has also been suggested that the attempt to operate global monetary restrictions in the face of the difficulties described by the Radcliffe Committee led to the sacrifice of growth on the altar of monetary stability, since monetary restrictions impinge most severely on investment. These criticisms of global monetary policy resulted in two reactions: the first, to re-order priorities to permit the sacrifice of some stability in the interests of growth, and the second, to operate monetary policy, when restrictions must be imposed, in a selective way, encouraging activities that would contribute to growth or regional balance or exports, and discouraging less socially useful activities. Proponents of the global approach have counter-attacked by arguing that the avoidance of monetary discipline in the effort to secure faster growth must in practice imply the surrender to inflationary pressure and probably balance-of-payments difficulties, and is therefore very likely to be self-defeating.

Recently, there have been signs of compromise from both sides of this debate. In Germany, where the Government has favoured global monetary policy with the emphasis on stability, and where it has been regarded as sufficient to keep prices stable, growing inflationary pressures and increasing international constraints have led to a greater acceptability of supplementary methods of controlling the economy, especially fiscal measures. In France and Britain the tendency is, while accepting the need for monetary discipline, to regard monetary policy as an instrument that can and should be used selectively, with due regard to its effects on different sectors of the economy, and with a view to securing objectives such as full employment and economic growth as well as the soundness of the currency.

FRANCE

The French, up to 1958, gave greater priority to expansion and less to price or balance-of-payments stability than most of their European neighbours and in particular the Germans and the British. The use of monetary policy to regulate overall demand was not a major feature of economic policy for a number of reasons of which the chief

---

[1] J. C. R. Dow, *The Management of the British Economy*, NIESR, Cambridge University Press, 1964, p. 258.

was a willingness to accept inflation and its consequences. Balance-of-payments crises were tided over by the inflow of dollars under the Marshall Aid programme and later by offshore purchases by the NATO forces, by tariff surcharges, quantitative import restrictions and export subsidies, and by devaluation. Thus France was one of the last countries to lower tariffs and remove quotas under the OEEC agreements. In addition to special import restrictions, favourable exchange rates for exporters in 1957 amounted to a devaluation of 20 per cent; and in December 1958 the franc was formally devalued by 17 per cent.

Even after 1958, when monetary policy found greater favour with the French Government, belief in its efficiency was modified by recognition of the inability of global restrictions on demand by themselves to deal with the inflation caused largely by the upward push of costs. The high costs and archaic structure of much of French industry, which had been sheltered by the high protection of the 1950s, the disorganized distribution system exemplified in the anachronism of Les Halles, the pressure from farmers and agricultural workers for higher farm prices and incomes, and the runaway growth of incomes in both the private and the public sector were all potent sources of inflation. France is not unique in this respect but analyses of the acute inflation of 1958 and 1963 and the measures taken to deal with it do indicate the crucial relevance of structural and institutional reforms to increasing efficiency and reducing pressure on costs. Thus, by virtue of their interest in such reforms, the planners feel they can contribute towards the achievement of price stability. At the same time they have been able to exercise influence over the operations of financial institutions and use them to some extent to secure the implementation of the Plans.

During the period of the First Plan, credit policy was designed specifically to encourage the programmes of reconstruction and development.[1] Qualitative controls were imposed to ensure that bank loans were not used to finance stock-building or to expand production of consumer goods. Absolute priority was given to those sectors outlined as the basis of the First Plan (see p. 82). This policy, when combined with the backlog of consumer demand that typically follows a period of war and the inflationary effects of war-time finance, rapidly produced serious inflation. Savings, eroded by

[1] For a more detailed discussion of this early period see J. G. S. Wilson, *French Banking Structure and Credit Policy*, G. Bell and Sons, 1957.

the uncertainty and depression of the 1930s and reduced even further by the prospect of continuing inflation, were inadequate to finance the large-scale investment projects outlined in the Plan. Accordingly, the investment programme had to be financed largely by the State. The rise in prices, however, had to be slowed down and a strict system of credit rationing was instituted in September 1948. For the first time quantitative controls were imposed. First the banks were required to hold certain minimum amounts (*planchers*) of Treasury bills. This measure was aimed at reducing the volume of private credit and tightening government control over bank lending. Secondly, *plafonds* or ceilings were imposed on the amount of finance that could be obtained by rediscounting bills at the Bank of France. Funds could still be obtained above the ceilings, but only at penal rates of interest. Monetary policy in the 1950s, such as it was, centred round the manipulation of these two controls. Although the bank rate was varied from time to time it was not regarded as a major weapon. Price controls were also imposed over a wide range of products, and these severely reduced the possibilities for self-financing.[1]

Within the context of these quantitative credit controls, the prospect of obtaining credit from State-controlled sources was a major inducement to firms to carry out projects that helped to fulfil the Plan. Access to bank credit and the capital market was effectively restricted to firms carrying out projects essential to the Plan's success. In 1948, a special fund, the Fonds de Modernisation et d'Equipement, was made responsible for financing the investment programme of the Plan. The fund issued long-term loans on favourable terms. This system of controls made it difficult for firms not contributing to the programme of the Plan to expand. Housing suffered most in the public sector and the whole range of consumer goods industries found expansion very difficult.

The exigencies of the period of the First Plan and the absence of an adequately developed statistical or conceptual apparatus made it impossible for the planners to measure the costs and benefits of the allocation of resources they so vigorously promoted. But they argued that it was clearly necessary to concentrate on long-term

[1] Good short accounts of French monetary policy are given in M. Lagache, *La Politique du Crédit*, Les Editions de L'Epargne, Paris 1963; and H. Fournier, The Problem of Controlling Liquidity in France, *Banca Nazionale del Lavoro*, Vol. XIII, 1960.

investment projects in the basic sectors, in order to lay the foundation for future growth, even if the neglect of housing needs and the strict limitation of the output of consumer goods worsened the inflationary situation, delayed an increase in real consumption per head and severely strained the balance of payments. Though such a choice was perhaps justified in the circumstances, it is not relevant to more normal times when the choice of alternative strategies is a more subtle one, because the requirements of the economy are more complex and the information available to the planners is more detailed and precise.[1]

The allocation of scarce resources then, mainly through the control of credit, was used most successfully in order to secure the fulfilment of the objectives of the First Plan. In the public sector the easy access to finance led to considerable expansion of the railway system and the coal and electricity supply industries. The nationalized Renault car firm also benefited and used the finance to carry out a very ambitious expansion programme. The situation of the steel industry provides yet another example. In the immediate postwar period the French steel industry was insufficiently concentrated, and duplication between firms and regions denied obvious economies of scale. In pressing for reform on these points, the planners ran into opposition, particularly from the smaller producers, who were called upon to give up their independence or to undertake large-scale conversion operations. But the planners had a remarkable degree of success, in which the allocation of finance and scarce commodities played a large part. 'The reasons for which the producers co-operated are not mysterious. Co-operation assured essential financing help on favourable terms in a very capital-tight period. It provided assistance in obtaining materials and equipment. And perhaps not least the Plan was drawn up in order to strengthen the industry, by changes that the producers had not achieved themselves but agreed to be desirable.'[2]

Their influence with the sources of finance continued to be an important weapon of the planners, particularly in relation to large-scale projects in both the public and private sectors. In 1955 the Fonds de Modernisation et d'Equipement was replaced by the

[1] This point is discussed in W. Baum, *The French Economy and the State*, Princeton, 1958.

[2] J. Sheahan, *Promotion and Control of Industry in Post-war France*, Harvard University Press, 1963, p. 70.

Fonds de Développement Economique et Social (FDES). The Directing Council of this body and its specialized committees, on which were represented the Commissaire Général du Plan, the Minister of Finance and the Governor of the Bank of France, are responsible for the control of all publicly financed investment. Its terms of reference are 'to advise on the order of priority and rhythm of the execution of the project as well as the method of financing applicable . . . taking into account the directives of the Plan'. It is empowered to grant long-term loans at a reduced rate of interest, and to subsidize part of the interest charges on the bond issues of public enterprises and large private firms or groups of firms. Loans are repayable over thirty-three years, and the rate of interest is 4·5 per cent. The majority go to public enterprises, and in view of the high cost of raising capital in France and the inflationary conditions prevailing in the 1950s, the preferential terms constituted a real advantage.

Private industry has benefited hardly at all from these loans, but the planners have influenced private investment through the official apparatus for the distribution of credit. While, as in Britain or Germany, the central bank, the Bank of France, is the central organ of monetary policy as the lender of last resort to the banking system and to the State, a distinctive feature of the French monetary system is the importance of official specialized credit institutions such as the Crédit Agricole, the Crédit Populaire, the Caisse des Dépôts et des Consignations and the Crédit National. Of these the Caisse des Dépôts and the Crédit National are particularly important.

The Caisse des Dépôts holds all the funds accumulated in local savings banks, the pension funds of the nationalized industries and any unspent tax revenue. Its main function is to 'transform' this large mass of short-term, highly liquid savings into medium-term credits to industry. It also acts as an official underwriter for bond issues by firms on the capital market. It is in effect a large public bank thoroughly in the centralist tradition of French economic institutions. As a depository for government funds it collaborates closely with the Commissariat du Plan. Its president, until 1967, was M. Bloch-Lainé, a distinguished civil servant and a prominent participant in the discussion and practice of indicative planning.

The Crédit National is a semi-public bank which supervises medium-term credit. Since 1943 it has filled the gap created by the increasing demand for medium-term credit which could not be met by the banks, which are unwilling to hold a large volume of illiquid assets and are required to maintain a certain liquidity ratio. The Crédit National is prepared to guarantee a medium-term loan of up to five years in approved cases to the client of a commercial bank. The commercial bank then proceeds to grant an automatically renewable short-term credit which it can discount at the Crédit National if its liquidity position requires it. The Crédit National in turn can rediscount this credit at the Bank of France as lender of last resort.

All requests for medium-term credit (two to five years) for industry and commerce, involving more than 0·5 million francs, are vetted by the Crédit National and the Bank of France in conjunction with the Commissariat du Plan. The same procedure is applied to demands for long-term credit (five to twenty years) for sums over 2·5 million francs. Since there has to be unanimous agreement on the worth of loan requests the planners appear to have the power to postpone or veto a request which seems incompatible with the Plan's objectives. Two recent commentators definitely take this view. Mr Shonfield concludes that 'French firms have learnt that it is not worth putting up a scheme for a loan of any size to their bank without clearing it first with the Commissariat'.[1] M. Fradault considers that the procedure for granting medium-term credits provides the planners with a most effective instrument for controlling investment.[2] Thus while it is not clear how much weight the planners carry in relation to the Bank of France, they are certainly in a position to see that the compatibility of an investment project with the Plan is at least brought into the discussion as well as a banker's view of its prospects. There is on the other hand less agreement about the methods for co-ordinating the operations of the various credit agencies. M. Bauchet, who is sceptical of the ability or willingness of the Bank of France to see the planners' viewpoint, has this to say: 'The present system is anything but unified. There is indeed a certain amount of contact between the specialized institutions but their credit policy is unco-ordinated and in some cases conflicting.'[3] The same point is made by M. Bloch-Lainé,

---

[1] A. Shonfield, *Modern Capitalism*, Oxford University Press, 1965, p. 169.

[2] P. Fradault, France's Plan and the Part of the Banking System in its Drafting and Execution, *Banca Nazionale del Lavoro*, December 1965.

[3] P. Bauchet, *Economic Planning: the French Experience*, Heinemann, 1964, p. 105.

who has been advocating for some years that the various credit agencies should be brought under the supervision of a Credit Directory.[1]

Chapter 3 has shown how the role of monetary policy was strengthened after 1958. The Stabilization Plan of 1963 was a serious threat to the Fourth Plan. To halt the rise in prices some restrictions on demand were required but their effect on investment was weighed very carefully. Foreign competition and a general upward pressure of costs were already seriously reducing profit margins and investment plans. It was argued that a traditional dose of deflation would aggravate this situation and at the same time be of doubtful efficiency in restraining costs. In order to limit these undesirable effects as much as possible M. Massé wrote a letter on September 12, 1963, to the Conseil National du Crédit, the body charged with general surveillance of financial policy, in which he advocated a very selective squeeze on credit. 'If the basic conditions for expansion are to be respected, our credit policy must be selective. In particular, as far as medium-term credit is concerned, there is a case for giving privileged treatment to the most dynamic firms serving foreign markets and to sectors especially hard-hit by foreign competition and for giving privileged treatment to the financing of projects for the reorganization of production.' M. Massé was particularly concerned that industries open to foreign competition should not be deterred from carrying out necessary modernization. He singled out chemicals, steel, aluminium, paper, mechanical engineering and electrical equipment for particular attention. Also the element of 'cost push' in the 1963 inflation made it imperative not to discourage schemes for concentration and specialization in French industry. His plea that the Plan should be respected was based not on the thesis that the economy could produce its way out of inflation but on the need for modernization and increased productivity as a way of lowering costs. The Conseil National du Crédit issued this letter to the banks with instructions that its recommendations be carried out. This is a striking example of the adoption of the Plan's objectives as a specific criterion for credit policy. How far it is effective does, however, depend again on the ability of the planners to press their case in the consideration of individual applications for credits.

The whole question of the planners' role in credit policy has

[1] F. Bloch-Lainé, Pour une Réforme de l'Administration Economique, *Revue Economique*, No. 6, November 1962.

assumed even greater significance with the introduction of 'value-planning' in the Fifth Plan[1] and the Government's decision to reduce the role played by the Treasury as the 'transformer' of short-term savings, in the form of purchases of three- to five-year Treasury bonds, into long-term credits for industry and commerce. The need to expand and stimulate the market for longer-term securities and to reduce the traditionally high liquidity preference of the French investor has long been recognized. The increased investment required in the Fifth Plan, at a time when profit margins are being reduced, gives the problem added urgency. 'Of the savings available for investment in 1970 about two-thirds will be short-term and one-third long-term. The forecast demand for capital by households, firms and administrations will, on the other hand, be two-thirds long-term and one-third short-term.'[2] The problem of 'transformation', therefore, remains. The authorities have decided no longer to rely entirely on the Treasury to perform this task but to attempt to encourage more savings to move directly into longer-term assets and to stimulate longer-term savings in such forms as life insurance. The role of the banking system is also to be expanded. The volume of medium-term credits to industry is planned to increase considerably as the Treasury reduces its issues of short-term bonds and lowers the minimum amount of this paper which the banks are required to hold. The present five-year limit on medium-term credits is to be extended by two years. These changes will inevitably loosen the control which the authorities and therefore the planners have over the sources of finance. The building up of a more effective capital market, less dominated by the Treasury and the Caisse des Dépôts, will loosen the planners' most effective weapon: control over firms' external financing. The proposed expansion of the banking system to an extent unknown in postwar France will mean that the weight of the planners' influence in the banking system will become for them a matter of still greater importance. For if their essay in value planning is to be successful they must be in a position to influence the flow of finance in the economy.

In view of the low level of savings aggravated by inflationary developments, the underdeveloped capital market and the resultant high cost of borrowing, the authorities have hitherto, throughout

[1] See pp. 93-9.
[2] Le Rapport de la Commission de l'Economie Générale et du Financement for the Fifth Plan quoted in Le Monde, January 22-3, 1966, p. 9.

the postwar period, kept a tight control over capital issues. The bond market in France has constantly been too small to sustain the demands made upon it at prevailing rates of interest. Since 1945 the timing and amount of new issues has therefore been regulated by the Ministry of Finance in consultation with the Commissariat du Plan. This has been a powerful lever of control, for the main borrowers are large firms or groups of firms such as the Groupement des Industries Sidérurgiques and the Groupement des Industries Electroniques. A firm not given formal approval may have to wait a considerable time before it can obtain access to the market.

Until 1959 the market for shares was subjected to similar control. Since then the Ministry of Finance has required only prior notification of new issues. The financing of investment by increasing capital has always been costly in France, and although there are now no direct controls certain fiscal advantages are granted to firms wishing to increase their capital. Until 1957 interest payments to bondholders only were considered as expenses and not subject to tax, while dividends to shareholders were treated as distributed profits and taxed at a rate of 50 per cent. This kept dividends low and further weakened the market. In 1957 the planners successfully recommended that a firm should be permitted to set off against profit tax dividends of up to 5 per cent on new issues for seven years. This advantage, however, is granted only if the planners approve the firm's expansion plans.

The power to control the capital market has undoubtedly been the most useful weapon the planners possessed. It has given them a large measure of control over sectors like the steel industry which are chronically short of capital. It has, however, not been effective in cases where firms can finance expansion out of retained profits. The French motor car industry and the oil companies are the classic examples of the freedom which self-financing confers. This has led certain proponents of active planning to argue against the extension of self-financing because of the loss of influence which it entails.[1] The Fifth Plan, however, is emphatic about the need to increase the degree of self-financing in order that private investment will not be held back through lack of finance.[2] To encourage

[1] P. Bauchet, op. cit., p. 106.

[2] The proportion of investment financed out of retained earnings in industry and commerce is required to increase from 66·5 per cent in 1965 to 70 per cent in 1970. Vᵉ Plan de Développement Economique et Social (1966–70), Tome I, Paris, Imprimerie Nationale, November 1965, p. 187.

this development, certain fiscal incentives and reforms of the tax system which will increase firms' liquidity are proposed.[1]

The Fifth Plan marks a decisive change in French planning. The growing influence of the Common Market, the re-establishment of monetary discipline and the normalization of the French capital market are all factors tending to lessen the planners' influence over the allocation of finance for investment. They have in fact themselves proposed measures likely to further this tendency but which they felt the economic situation demanded. The question that remains is the extent to which the planners can retain and develop by indirect methods an effective influence on decisions of monetary policy.

GERMANY

As Chapter 2 showed, the German neo-liberals have regarded monetary stability as the first priority for a competitive order, and Eucken advocated that as far as possible an 'automatic stabilizer' should be built into the monetary system to ensure this. Since the 1948 Currency Reform monetary stability has been given high priority in Germany. As the German Economics Minister said at the opening of the Frankfurt International Fair in 1965: 'If you were to ask me what the top priority is both now and at all times, the answer could only be: the preservation of stability. The Government finds itself in accord with public opinion on this matter, in that all the opinion polls for some time past have shown that monetary stability is seen by our population as the most important political problem.'[2] That the public, as indicated, have generally endorsed the priority of monetary stability can of course be partly ascribed to Germany's experience of catastrophic inflation in the 1920s, and of suppressed inflation in the years 1945–8.

In accordance with Eucken's doctrine monetary policy has also, until recently, been seen as the main instrument for achieving stability. This is not to say that Eucken's 'automatic stabilizer' has come into operation. Neither the postwar international monetary system nor the German Central Bank's internal policies are based on the principle of complete automaticity. An 'autonomous stabilizer' has, however, been established in Germany in the form of

---

[1] For details see pp. 202–3.
[2] Kurt Schmücker, statement at Frankfurt, February 1965.

a Central Bank formally entrusted with 'safeguarding the currency', and endowed with very considerable independence.

The peculiar status of the German Central Bank is brought out by the 1957 law establishing the Bundesbank. (Until 1957 the German Central Bank was the Bank Deutscher Länder, and the Länder Central Banks were legally independent. The 1957 Law centralized the organization of the Central Bank and transformed the Länder Banks into its agencies. The autonomy of the Bank Deutscher Länder was however as sharply stamped—if anything more sharply —as that of the Bundesbank which succeeded it.) The Board of Managers of the Bundesbank is indeed nominated by the Government, but their term of office is, as a general rule, fixed at eight years, thus giving them considerable independence. Furthermore on the highest organ of the Bundesbank, the Central Bank Council, sit not only the Board but the eleven Presidents of the Länder Central Banks nominated by either the Bundesbank or the Länder authorities. Members of the Government can attend meetings of the Council and propose nominations, but they have no vote, and are empowered only to defer the taking of a decision for a maximum of two weeks.

The Bundesbank has to advise the Government on monetary matters, and the Government for its part invites the President of the Bundesbank to discussions of matters which have implications for monetary policy. Although the Bundesbank has to support the overall economic policy of the Government (not particular measures) it is obliged to do this only in so far as it is consonant with its express task of safeguarding the currency. Nor is it bound to follow instructions from the Government.

Other clauses emphasize the Bundesbank's independence. The loans which the Bank may grant to the public sector are subject to fixed ceilings. Apart from the usual instruments of discount policy (including the use of rediscount quotas), minimum reserve policy and open market policy, the Bank is also empowered to exercise what is known as 'deposit' policy. According to Article 17 of the 1957 Act, the Government, the special federal funds, and the Länder 'shall deposit their liquid funds, even when cash balances are earmarked under the Budget for some special purpose, at the Bundesbank on current account. Funds shall not be deposited or invested elsewhere without the consent of the Bundesbank; in this connection the Deutsche Bundesbank must take into account the interest of the

Länder in maintaining their State and Land banks.' This interesting and original instrument is intended as an additional means of influencing liquidity; it is also intended to oblige the 'State itself, and those public authorities which it enables by law to have a significant revenue, to observe the requirements of monetary policy in the management of this money'.

The Bundesbank then has some claim to represent an 'autonomous stabilizer', able to pursue the objective of monetary stability without being subject to political pressures. It has not, however, had an easy task in doing so.

The system is seen working in its full rigour during the first phase of reconstruction when, at a time of massive unemployment, the Bank Deutscher Länder continued to preserve price stability. The Bank's action during the Korean crisis, when it held to a restrictive policy until prices were seen to be falling, that is from October 1950 to May 1952, is also particularly worthy of mention. During the first post-Korean boom of 1955-6, the Bank again intervened vigorously, if slightly late, using bank rate, minimum reserve and open market operations to prevent prices rising. This was the classic period of the 'stabilizer'. Since 1957, however, the German Central Bank's task has become considerably more complicated. The overall strategy of price stability has remained the same but the tactics have had to be drastically altered. The turnabout has paradoxically been caused largely by the very effectiveness of the earlier policy. From 1952 onwards, helped by its comparatively low price level, Germany began to build up enormous export surpluses. To these surpluses was added, as the liberalization of capital movements went ahead, a large inflow of speculative money, attracted by the soundness of the German position and hopes of a revaluation of the mark, as well as by fears of a devaluation in the deficit countries. As a result, in 1957 Germany's monetary reserves grew to gigantic proportions. In that year, Boarman has observed, the increase in the gold stock alone exceeded that of all the other West European countries put together and was greater than the total proportion of gold newly mined in all Western countries that year.[1]

From that year the problem of 'imported inflation' became a major issue in Germany. This problem was caused by two factors. First, there was the danger that the increased liquidity in the

[1] Patrick Boarman, *Germany's Economic Dilemma*, New Haven, Yale University Press, 1964, p. 80.

economy, caused by surpluses of foreign exchange, would be transformed into inflationary demand. Secondly, there was the contagious
process, caused by market forces alone, by which extensive trade
with inflationary foreign countries led to rising prices at home.

It is extremely difficult for orthodox monetary policy to deal with
this problem. In the first place, the increased liquidity from abroad
gives private credit institutions greater independence from the
Central Bank, and thus makes it more difficult for the latter to use
restrictive measures effectively. Secondly, if the Central Bank
attempts to use bank rate to combat this kind of inflation it only
aggravates the problem by attracting more capital from abroad.
Thirdly, orthodox monetary measures cannot counter inflation imported through market forces without intensifying the balance of
payments disequilibrium, which market forces have also caused.
The fact is that the classical model, on which orthodox monetary
policy is based, is designed to ensure stability of the balance of
payments, not of the internal price level. Indeed, the orthodox response to an increase of reserves is to let internal prices rise until the
net inflow of foreign exchange is checked. The addition of internal
price stability as an equal or superior objective therefore makes it
impossible to maintain balance-of-payments stability by orthodox
measures. The only really effective monetary remedy is the unorthodox one of revaluing the currency. It is surprising that people
familiar with classical economics should have failed to realize from
the outset that orthodox monetary policy could not be expected to
fulfil both objectives at the same time.

The danger of imported inflation explains, then, the ambivalent
policy pursued by the Bundesbank from 1957 to 1959: a policy of
lowering the bank rate to discourage the inflow of hot money, but
of using minimum reserve and open market policy to restrict liquidity at home, while at the same time encouraging the export of
capital. In 1959 when Germany experienced its first balance-of-
payments deficit since 1950 it seemed as though this policy had
succeeded. But in 1960 another boom at home was accompanied by a
further massive inflow of capital from abroad. To begin with, the
Bundesbank gave first priority to restraining the boom at home and
returned to a policy of tight money, but it soon became apparent
that this served only to aggravate the balance-of-payments problem,
by attracting more liquidity from abroad.

In November 1960 German monetary policy experienced what

has been called a 'Copernican Revolution' but was in fact a return to the classical tradition: by reducing bank rate and relaxing its minimum reserve requirements the Bundesbank formally acknowledged that balance-of-payments objectives had to take priority over internal requirements. Finally, in March 1961, the Government and the Bundesbank agreed to revalue the mark by 4·7 per cent. This policy had been recommended by the Advisory Council to the Economics Ministry as early as 1957, and was agreed only after a long controversy.

The revaluation, however, did not solve Germany's problems for long. In 1961 there was indeed a large movement of capital out of the country, and an overall deficit of 1,900 million marks appeared in the balance of payments, as opposed to the surplus of 8,000 million marks the year before. In 1962 external payments were more or less in balance. In spring 1963, however, the trouble started again when inflationary trends in Germany's EEC partners, France and Italy, and later in the Netherlands, caused massive trade and payments surpluses to accumulate in Germany. At the beginning of 1964 it seemed as though the situation was getting even worse.

In the face of this problem the Bundesbank found itself in difficulties. It could not use bank rate, which had been reduced between November 1960 and May 1961 to 3 per cent and was to remain there for almost four years. Instead, in March 1964 it introduced a variety of measures to discourage the inflow of foreign capital and stimulate the outflow of German capital, and later that year it used minimum reserves and rediscount quotas to restrict internal liquidity. These measures seem, however, to have been of only marginal importance in bringing about the remarkable change in the balance of payments in 1964. More important, as the Bank itself recognized, were the deflationary measures taken by Germany's neighbours, together with the 25 per cent tax imposed in March 1964 on capital earnings on non-resident holdings of German fixed interest securities.

During the following year, however, the surpluses vanished and the Bundesbank was again free to act. In the face of price rises at home it intervened vigorously, raising bank rate in January and August, and again in May 1966 (to 5 per cent). In the second half of 1966 the pressure of internal demand began to slacken appreciably and—almost predictably—large export surpluses reappeared. Concerned lest the weakening of internal demand should turn into a recession, the Bundesbank rapidly relaxed its restrictive measures from the end of 1966 onwards. By May 1967, bank rate was back to 3 per cent.

In sum then, German monetary policy has been directed since the 1948 Currency Reform at maintaining price stability. But orthodox monetary policy has clearly been unable to achieve this. It is for this reason above all that since 1960 increasing attention has been paid to the possibility of using the budget more actively as an anti-cyclical weapon, something to which Eucken and the early neo-liberals had given little attention. It explains, too, why Germany has pressed in recent years for increased monetary co-operation at the EEC level and beyond. It is for this reason too that not a few voices have recently been raised in Germany in favour of the adoption of flexible exchange rates. In the same way that the freeing of trade and payments causes difficulties for the French planners, it also presents problems for those who wish to use monetary policy to achieve both price and balance-of-payments stability.

This section has so far concentrated mainly on the actions of the German Central Bank. What of the other credit institutions within the economy? How far have these been controlled by the State and how far has this control been exercised in accordance with neo-liberal objectives? In the following discussion the money market and the capital market will be examined with a view to answering these questions. The money market is defined for this purpose as the market for short- to medium-term credit, that is credit for a period of up to four years, while the capital market embraces credit which extends beyond this period.

Before looking at the money market, it is worth recalling that Eucken considered that tight control over private credit institutions was essential for the effective working of the monetary system in a competitive order. The important point then is not whether German credit institutions have been controlled or not, but to what extent this control has allowed competition. Until the end of 1961, the German market for short- and medium-term credit was regulated by provisions inherited from the Third Reich. Largely as a result of Allied pressure, these regulations were administered on a decentral-ized basis, through supervisory boards established by the Länder, though there was a co-ordinating committee on which the federal authorities were represented. The regulations laid down *inter alia* the ratio between liquid resources and liabilities which credit institutions had to observe, similarly the ratio between advances and an institution's capital, the requirements to be met by new establishments, and the special procedures for credits over a certain size. The provisions did not permit the Länder authorities directly to fix interest rates. This was done through an agreement, the so-called *Mantelvertrag*, dating from before the war, between the main credit institutions, the result of which was officially sanctioned by the Länder authorities. By the *Mantelvertrag* maximum rates of interest were fixed for deposits, scaled according to the different kinds of deposit. There can be little doubt that this part of the cartel effectively excluded interest-rate competition for deposits. On the borrowing side the restriction was not so complete. The agreement set 'normal' rates for borrowers which could be exceeded only with the authorization of the Länder authorities. As credit institutions could lower their rates freely below the 'normal', however, competition could, and did, flourish. Those who profited chiefly from this side of the agreement were in fact the small or weak borrowers who were protected against exorbitant rates.

With effect from the beginning of 1962, the old provisions were replaced by the Law regulating the Credit System. This Law made two significant changes. First, it replaced the decentralized system of administering the rules regarding credit institutions, which had led to differences of interpretation, by a centralized one, thus bringing the system back into line with the prewar one. An independent federal supervisory office for the credit system was set up in Berlin, under the aegis of the Minister of Economics. As will be seen it has certain links with the Bundesbank. Secondly, the task of fixing interest rates was removed from the credit institutions themselves and granted to the State. Thus Article 23 of the new Act laid down that in future ordinances would decide the limits for the interest rates and conditions of deposits and borrowing, the main reservation being that such ordinances must be designed to support the credit policy of the Bundesbank. The Minister of Economics is given the power to issue these ordinances, but he can delegate it to the Berlin office, which must, however, work in accord with the Bundesbank.

Apart from these two major changes the law does not deviate greatly from the earlier regulations. The supervisory office ensures that new credit institutions satisfy certain requirements regarding capital and organization; it watches over the liquidity and capital ratios of credit institutions and can, in conjunction with the Bundes-bank, lay down certain guidelines for them (this is more flexible than the old provisions which specified certain percentages); it can intervene to prevent credit institutions abusing their position and either endangering the security of the funds entrusted to them or disrupting the orderly conduct of business. Large credits, that is, credits to a single borrower which exceed 15 per cent of the credit institution's own capital, credits of over a million marks to a single borrower, as well as 'organ' credits, which are made to persons working in the credit institution or having a share in it, all have to be notified to the supervisory office via the Bundesbank (in the case of 'organ' credits directly). Naturally the supervisory office is also entitled to receive a considerable amount of information from the credit institutions regarding their positions.

Has the new Act brought greater competition into the German money market? In the first three years of its operation the answer could only be negative. The State used its new powers simply to endorse the agreements already reached by the main credit insti-tutions. In February 1965 a significant change was made. By an ordinance issued in this month only interest rates for deposits up to two and a half years, and not, as previously, up to four years, were made subject to maximum rates. Fines were established for disregarding this new regulation, which marked a new development in the organization of the German money market. Finally in 1967 it was decided that bank interest rates should be completely freed. This decision, which took effect on April 1 of that year, marked the end of over thirty-five years of official regulation, and brought a new element of competition into the German banking system.

So much for the official supervision of the German money market. It has been shown that until recently interest-rate competition for deposits was effectively restricted, but that these restrictions have now been swept away. How far has the structure of the market, that is, the size of the participants, served to restrict competition? It is well known that there have been some significant moves towards greater concentration among German banks. In particular, the attempt of the occupying powers in 1947 to break up the 'big three' German banks, the Deutsche Bank, the Dresdner Bank, and the Commerzbank, was completely without success, in that ten years later they had each re-formed into their original shape. This does not, however, mean that concentration in the money market has increased. The report of an enquiry into concentration, published in 1964,[1] showed that there was still a considerable degree of concentration in the banking sector. But it was less than in 1954, and this reduction was due above all to the diminishing share of the five largest banks (from 30 per cent to 22 per cent). The reduction in the share of the 'big three' was even more marked. It should also be noted that the various groups of institutions have abandoned their traditional areas of specialization. Since 1948 they have been moving more and more into each other's market, and competition has shown itself in the very large number of new branches and subsidiaries, the development of new services by the various institutions, and the low interest rate margins. The process was greatly assisted by the decision of the Federal Administrative Court, in 1958, that the old regulation by which new establishments in the credit market had to prove a need before they were permitted was incompatible with the freedom to choose one's profession guaranteed by the German Basic Law. Between 1958 and 1967 no less than 10,000 new bank branches have been opened. The removal of restrictions on bank advertising and the freeing of bank interest rates in April 1967 have also led to increased competition.[2]

As far as the capital market is concerned, the position in 1948 must first of all be recalled. At that time this market was in a state of chronic disequilibrium, a gigantic demand for capital pressing on a very limited supply of funds. In such circumstances it was inevitable that there had to be extensive State intervention both to ration existing funds and to stimulate an increased supply.

By the 1949 Law regulating Capital Transactions a capital issues committee was established and specifically empowered to direct the market for securities in accordance with the 'European Recovery Programme, the needs of the economy as a whole, the requirements of regional reorganization and the basic principles of an ordered monetary policy'. The most important means by which this committee directed the flow of capital was through a ruling which limited the rate of interest on mortgage bonds to 5 per cent and that

[1] *Bericht über das Ergebnis einer Untersuchung der Konzentration in der Wirtschaft*, op. cit., 1964, p. 36.

[2] For evidence of increased competition in these areas see the articles Der Bankkunde wird mündig, in the *Frankfurter Allgemeine Zeitung*, May 27, 1967, and Eine neue Wettbewerbs-Phase im Kreditgewerbe beginnt, in the same paper, October 14, 1967.

on industrial bonds to 6½ per cent. This restriction both effectively blocked the development of the capital market, and favoured the government-sponsored housing programme.

To offset the inadequacy of the capital market many fiscal privileges were introduced to spur capital formation by individuals and firms: self-financing was favoured; accelerated depreciation allowances introduced; individual savings with savings or credit banks, insurance companies and building societies were encouraged; and loans to housing and shipbuilding given special advantages. Savings by the Government were a further substitute for an effective capital market, the savings thus generated being used primarily to further the housing programme. The Kreditanstalt für Wiederaufbau was set up in 1949 to provide medium- and long-term credit for those areas of the economy which were in particular need and could not raise funds elsewhere. It was financed through Marshall Aid and also through budgetary surpluses. Finally, the Investment Aid Law of 1952, by means of a levy on industry and additional fiscal privileges, generated an investment of 4,750 million marks in the basic sectors of the economy, primarily coal, steel and energy.

By the First Law for the Furthering of the Capital Market of December 1952 the direct fixing of interest rates on mortgage and industrial bonds was replaced by a whole scale of tax advantages for different kinds of securities. These tax advantages particularly favoured government fixed-interest securities and considerably distorted and fragmented the capital market. Although they were successful in generating an increased number of new issues they were strongly opposed by industry, and the law ran out at the end of 1954. The Capital Transactions Law itself, which was reformulated in 1952, ran out at the end of 1953.

With the expiry of these two laws the German capital market was free. The supervision which the Economics Ministry has exercised since then has been concerned solely with ensuring the reliability of new issues and not with directing the market. The 'Capital Market Committee' which was established in 1957 by the German credit institutions is similarly an instrument for regulating the timing of issues and ensuring consistency in their terms rather than directing it for any other purpose.

The removal of controls from the capital market was an important step. The market was, however, still distorted by many tax privileges for specific kinds of savings and loans, and during the

1950s steps were taken to remove or rationalize a number of them. Tax discrimination in favour of retained profits was gradually transformed into discrimination against them, thus encouraging firms to have recourse to the capital market. A number of special tax privileges for savings were replaced in 1959 by the Savings Premium Act which, by introducing a uniform premium for most types of long-term saving, prevented competitive distortions. Tax relief for loans to housing was considerably reduced in 1954.

This brief sketch of the development of the German capital market shows the general trend of government intervention. At a time of severe disequilibrium there was considerable State direction of the flow of capital. The Government put its emphasis, however, not on direct investment planning in accordance with targets, but on the more *marktkonform* method of fiscal encouragement. The nearest that it did reach to the former method was with the Investment Aid Law of 1952. When the market returned to normality controls were removed and measures taken to encourage fair competitive conditions. Some neo-liberals have argued that the transition could have been made more swiftly, and that in particular the 1952 Law for the Furthering of the Capital Market was a mistake; but the movement towards decontrol was in any case not slow.

BRITAIN

This section will be kept brief since the subject is one that is familiar to British readers, and on which there is a very adequate literature.[1]

Like the French and the Germans, the British have experienced several phases of monetary policy since the war. The first was the 'Dalton' period of cheap money despite the acute postwar shortage of capital, with the pattern of investment controlled by the restriction of access to the capital market and the allocation of supplies of materials. During the 1950s, however, a more active monetary policy was adopted.

This policy varied from a reliance on the global instruments of bank rate and budget balance, based, at least when Mr Thorneycroft was Chancellor, on a crude 'quantity of money' theory, to the use of selective measures such as restrictions on hire purchase terms for particular commodities. Mr Dow and the Radcliffe

[1] An authoritative account of British monetary policy is to be found in J. C. R. Dow, op. cit.

Report have already been quoted (pp. 158–9) to indicate the growing awareness of the discriminatory effects of monetary policy, but despite the greater sophistication of analysis and to some extent of action that resulted, dissatisfaction with the failure of policy either to halt inflation and prevent recurrent balance-of-payments crises, or to stimulate a rate of growth comparable to that of Britain's neighbours on the Continent, led to the demand for a new departure in the form of a system of planning for growth.

It might have been argued that monetary policy had failed partly because it had not been pushed to its logical conclusion, or had been unaccompanied by a coherent strategy to overcome obstacles to growth. As Chapter 4 relates, however, it was decided to adopt a 'French' system of indicative target planning combined with an in-comes policy that was intended to resist cost-push inflation at its source.

It was at the same time widely agreed that monetary equilibrium should have a lower priority than in the past and the growth of out-put a higher priority; and that, when restriction might be required, it should not take the form of general deflation but should, rather, be as selective as possible. It followed that, during the gathering pay-ments crisis in 1964, and to a greater extent than would otherwise have resulted from the temptations of an election year for the party in power, the Chancellor attempted to avoid, or at least to delay, the imposition of monetary restrictions, in order not to interrupt the growth of output. The emphasis, when action had to be taken, was on selective measures to adjust the trade balance, not on general deflation by either monetary or fiscal means. Within the monetary control that had to be imposed in the exchange crisis in November 1964, the banks were, as on previous similar occasions, asked to be helpful in granting facilities to firms that would contribute to productive investment and exports, while restricting more sharply credit for less worthy purposes. With the intensification of credit restrictions in 1965, moreover, the banks were further requested to discriminate against imports in considering requests for credit.

However, the Government was not willing to press to its logical conclusion the high priority for growth and the rejection of de-flation: namely to accept, as the French did during the 1950s, the consequence of import controls and/or devaluation should external payments get too far out of balance. When it became clear, therefore, that the selective measures of restriction were not enough, resort was had once more in July 1965 and still more strongly in 1966 to a policy of general deflation.

Although the highly developed British capital market makes it harder for British planners to influence the flow of finance into individual investment projects than it is for the French, it has been shown in recent years that credit restrictions can, largely by means of directives to the banks, discriminate more generally in favour of activities such as exports and investment or against imports. Moreover, selective credit is, as it has been for many years, available on favourable terms to firms in order to persuade them to move to areas of high unemployment. While this has usually taken the form of generally available credit or grants on standard terms, some of the most important successes of this policy have taken the form of 'bargains' with large firms, as for example the major diversion of investment in the motor industry to Merseyside and Scotland in 1960 and the location of sheet-steel mills in Wales and Scotland, which can be compared with the French quasi-contracts (see p. 201).

Too often such credit has been provided to bolster up uncompetitive sectors such as cotton, shipbuilding or agriculture. But another area in which the provision of government finance has been important, and is particularly relevant to planning for growth, is research and development. The valid criticism is not so much that too little has been spent on this in the past, as that expenditure has not been planned with a view to its effect on the growth of the economy and has therefore been concentrated too much on a few 'prestige' sectors such as aircraft and nuclear power. Greater attention is now being paid, through the Ministry of Technology, to computers, electronics and machine-tools, which can not only contribute to the generation of exports and the replacement of imports, but are also important suppliers of equipment for the modernization of other industries.

A notable innovation in the provision of credit for ventures which the Government feels are strongly in the national interest was the founding of the Industrial Reorganization Corporation (IRC) in 1966. The immediate intention, as it emerged from a White Paper[1] and subsequent parliamentary debates, was to encourage desirable mergers by filling a gap in credit facilities which arose when substantial sums were needed over long periods. Such funds were not always

[1] HMSO, Industrial Reorganization Corporation, Cmnd. 2889, January 1966.

available within the firms concerned in a merger, nor were the merchant banks, the traditional midwives of mergers, willing to tie up very large sums for long periods, often amounting to taking a semi-permanent and sizeable minority holding in major companies. Both a neo-collectivist and a neo-liberal case could therefore be made for an official body, disposing of public funds, but in close contact with the private capital market, to help in such cases. Unfortunately, however, subsequent events showed that the motives for setting up the IRC were mixed if not confused, and the actual operations in which the IRC indulged during 1967 contributed little to the clarification of its role. Some light was thrown on the Government's intention in the field of industrial finance by the introduction in the autumn of 1967 of an Industrial Expansion Bill, which, by enabling the Government to take a permanent holding in companies, went far beyond the basic IRC concept of a revolving pool of finance for mergers (though the IRC had in fact already been used for this kind of operation). Since these new moves represented the first British steps in the direction of a permanent system of discriminatory finance for industry on the French model, and many commentators have also drawn parallels with the operation of the Italian State Holding Company, IRI, some discussion of the (admittedly rather thin) experience down to the end of 1967 is called for.

First, it is essential to put the discussion in perspective by remarking that the IRC was only the latest in a considerable number of specialist public and semi-public financial institutions which complemented a very diversified and (by European standards) highly developed capital market. Since the Second World War the Industrial and Commercial Finance Corporation (ICFC) provided finance for small firms for projects costing less than £200,000, and the Finance Corporation for Industry (FCI) for medium-sized investments over £200,000. These corporations were set up to fill the famous 'gap' in the capital market revealed by the Macmillan Committee in the 1930s. The Estate Duties Investment Trust (Edith) dealt with the special problem of the small business faced with the prospect of death duties. More recently, the Technical Development Corporation (TDC) was hived off from the ICFC to finance particularly important technological developments. The National Research and Development Corporation (NRDC) concentrated on the finance of inventions and innovations, such as the Hovercraft, and its funds were markedly increased following its absorption into the Ministry of Technology. The IRC must, therefore, be seen as only one of a number of financial intermediaries. However, it had the potential for a new positive intervention in the finance and structure of industry. Whereas the earlier bodies may have been regarded as filling gaps in the market, the IRC, and the new investment agency proposed in the Industrial Expansion Bill in November 1967, appeared to represent the beginning of a decisive move towards a form of joint State/private enterprise. It is, however, difficult to interpret exactly what the Government considered the role of these new institutions should eventually be.

We should note, first, that the role of the IRC was not restricted to the supply of finance; it was also intended to act as a pressure group for mergers and to encourage firms in other ways to bring them about. Markets or profitability criteria are not the only consideration in motivating businessmen to seek or reject mergers; pride of ownership or control, security of employment, desire for a quiet life: all these inhibitions are involved and need to be overcome where mergers can be profitable. In the case of the take-over of Associated Electrical Industries (AEI) by General Electric (GEC) in November 1967, for example, there was no question of the need for IRC finance. The IRC was engaged at the early stage in trying to persuade AEI to accept a merger, and when these discussions broke down it threw its influence behind GEC in the take-over struggle.

But it was certainly felt that the chief justification for the IRC was that its financial help could be decisive in bringing about certain desirable mergers. What was not so certain was on what terms such help should be given. It could be argued that the IRC ought to accept less than a market rate of return on its investments, since the national interest could be secured even by mergers that were not justified in the interests of the parties. But this case was more controversial than the superficially similar case for subsidizing investments in development areas, since there was no clear-cut social benefit in the case of the mergers, nor any obvious economic advantage such as the utilization of previously unemployed resources. Something was made of the point that mergers could be valuable for the overall development of the inter-industry structure of the economy, even though not for the firms participating in them. But since inter-industry trading is carried on through the market, one would assume, in the absence of evidence to the contrary, that a merged enterprise making a valuable contribution to other industries would also find this financially rewarding to itself. Only if some macro-economic case in terms of import-saving was introduced did this line of reasoning begin to be plausible, but this also raises many problems.[1]

The institutional gap is not for short-term funds, but for finance that will be needed for a number of years until the merger begins to pay off. The Government may well be able to take a longer view than the market, but institutional gaps cannot be entirely divorced from economics, and the same considerations that lead to the existence of a gap in the market should lead to some hesitation in accepting too readily that the Government can afford to wait longer. Waiting has a cost for public as for private bodies, and this cost should be reflected in the rate of return expected on IRC investments. The IRC is in a sense a 'lender of last resort', a body whose role is to provide the last section of finance without which a merger cannot go ahead. As such, it is economically and financially sound to charge a higher rate except in so far as a clear case may be made out for a subsidy in order to overcome the resistance to change and any failure of the market to make the private and social benefits of mergers coincide. The Government was certainly prepared on the contrary to let the IRC be a soft lender. For example, under the terms of the English Electric and Elliott Automation merger, the IRC was to receive only 8 per cent per annum for the last six years of the eight-year term of the debenture. With the first two years interest free, this worked out at a yield below the estimated 7·8 per cent market rate. In order to break even, that is, to obtain the market rate, the IRC would have to sell at the end of the eight years for £18·6 million the £15 million debenture it put up in 1967, and it is by no means certain that it will be able to do this.[2]

If the fund of £150 million of which the IRC disposes is to revolve quickly and enable it to play a significant part in the finance of mergers, the early investments will have to yield a quick return. Yet the market gap is precisely one of medium- and long-term funds. There is some confusion, therefore, about the way the IRC will in fact operate. Locking funds into long-term holdings need not imply the end of the IRC's usefulness, for at the end of 1967 it was in a very experimental stage, and if the Government saw fit to extend its operations it would not be impossible to increase the £150 million limit on its Treasury funds, or to remove the prohibition against its

[1] See pp. 350–2.
[2] *The Economist*, July 1, 1967.

raising money from the market, or both. Whether the transition, which this would imply, into a large State holding company similar to the IRI in Italy would be desirable is another matter, discussed below. But neither of these answers to the problem of keeping the IRC effective corresponds to the case for it in its original form. If the funds were made to revolve rapidly, the IRC could hardly fill the most serious gap in the market. If the funds were tied up for long (or even indefinite?) periods, the IRC would become a different animal. Its use to achieve a State participation in the Rootes Group/Chrysler merger, where the motives for an IRC investment were very different from those explained in Parliament in the debates on setting up the IRC, suggested that the Government did intend to acquire permanent holdings in major firms.

Although the main emphasis of the IRC's work in 1967 was on assisting the mergers of firms that were already very large, it was also intended to promote mergers among small firms, in order to rationalize the structure of industries typified by the existence of too many small and inefficient firms. Here, the typical form of merger had been a series of take-overs by a much larger firm, and the market had moved quite quickly to reconstruct several industries. For example, textiles had been considerably remodelled by Courtaulds and Viyella (the latter financed initially by ICI). Where the market had not succeeded so well was in cases where units were much larger, but where further amalgamations were needed to face up to international competition. Outstanding cases of this kind were the shipbuilding and aircraft industries. In both cases direct governmental intervention specifically designed to meet the problems of the individual industries was necessary. The IRC, therefore, would appear to fit into the area between industries of the textile type, and those of the shipbuilding or aircraft type. The scope of the IRC has, moreover, been constrained by the fact that it does not dispose of the staff and resources to enable it to investigate many industries in depth and initiate merger proposals where none existed previously. Its role has seemed likely to be confined to helping in discussing and financing mergers arising spontaneously among private firms. In the English Electric/Elliott Automation merger, both firms had liquidity problems, and IRC finance was probably decisive. In the case of GEC and AEI, finance was not a problem. The IRC's approval was clearly of some value to GEC, but it is hard to judge whether or not it tipped the scales in a close-fought battle. IRC approval has also appeared helpful as a guard against the possible disapproval of the Monopolies Commission.

The future of the interest which the IRC acquires in a concern by helping to finance a merger was another matter still clouded in obscurity at the end of 1967. If the operation of the market is to be assisted but not replaced by a mammoth State holding company, then IRC investments must eventually be handed back to private ownership. However, this runs into the objection that private capitalists would thus obtain the profits on a venture that would not have existed at all in the absence of State assistance. On the other hand, not all firms make profits all the time, and the State could find itself, through the IRC, holding shares of a lower market value than the original loan. Moreover, the prospects depend not only on the success of those parts of a business which the IRC has helped to finance, but also on all the other aspects of a business which may have little or nothing to do with a particular merger. For example, the profitability to the IRC of the English Electric/Elliott Automation merger depends also on the success of English Electric's heavy electrical equipment and domestic appliance interests. If this pattern is repeated, the State could find itself making a loss by financing a merger that in itself was successful, or a profit on one that was a failure. If it were accepted that the IRC should not hand back to private owners its interest in a 'profitable' merger, and could not very well force them to take back an 'unprofitable' one, the IRC would indeed seem destined to become a vast holding company. But such a development would saddle it with a mass of investments, profitable and unprofitable, for which there would be no current rationale. Greater clarity about the objectives of the IRC would enable this unsatisfactory outcome to be avoided. If, as argued earlier, the IRC's investments were made on terms which ensured a market rate of return on the State capital, the firms concerned could be left to bear the risks. (Unless, of course, it were held that firms would not be prepared to do this, a proposition that would raise many other issues not present in the discussions on the IRC in 1967.)

In sum, British monetary and credit policy has evolved quite rapidly in the 1960s in order to achieve a more sophisticated form in which, while not neglecting its primary purpose of managing the level of demand in the short term, it can make a contribution to the objectives of growth and regional balance. This has so far been done largely in a qualitative sense: of devising selective controls, or the selective credits of the IRC, for objectives such as the promotion of exports or the encouragement of concentration in certain industries. Further extensions of this approach are possible, as, for example, the frequently suggested advance payment for imports, a form of negative credit which has been applied in Italy and elsewhere. It is also possible that credit policy will in future be more closely related to the targets for individual industries in a national programme. But, since Britain has a highly developed capital market, it is unlikely that credit control could ever be such a powerful instrument for this purpose as it was in France in the 1950s. British planners are in any case more likely to harness credit policy, as the French have tended to do in the 1960s, to qualitative rather than quantitative ends; and, again like the French, to use their influence to ensure that short-term monetary policy is applied in such a way as to minimize any damage to long-term growth.

CHAPTER 7

FISCAL POLICY

———————

Taxation and social insurance contributions take about a third of the national income in most West European countries. The incidence of taxation consequently has a major influence with respect to the main issues with which economic planning and policy are concerned, such as the rate of growth, the business cycle, and the extent to which competitive conditions are neutral or distorted.

The French have, for some years, used selective fiscal incentives to stimulate growth. In Britain there has been much discussion on this subject and certain measures of this sort have been taken, but the British contribution has been more in the use of taxation as an instrument of cyclical policy. The Germans, for their part, have recently shown much interest in the latter aspect; but the main effort of the neo-liberals in the postwar period has gone into the attempt to make taxation as neutral as possible in its impact on the market system.

GERMANY

How far has the German tax structure been deliberately moulded in accordance with neo-liberal concepts? To answer this question it seems useful again to make the distinction between the first period of German reconstruction, that is from 1948 to 1952 or 1953, and the years following. The moulding of the tax system during the early period was based on rather different premises from that of the second.

To understand the first phase one must go back briefly to the years before the Currency Reform. In these years the Allies had increased taxes considerably in an effort to get rid of the huge excess of money in the economy which had been the legacy of the Nazi regime. In 1946, as Dr Roskamp has pointed out, income tax rates were the highest that Germany had ever seen.[1]

In order to resuscitate the economy, Dr Erhard and his colleagues in the Frankfurt Economic Council had argued that the Currency Reform should be accompanied by a major tax reform in which there would be drastic cuts in the income tax and certain indirect taxes and a transformation of the corporation tax from a graduated range of 35 to 65 per cent to a flat rate of 50 per cent. The Allies, however, disagreed with this programme on the grounds that it would probably lead to budget deficits and from there to inflation. Although the corporation tax was changed in the direction the Germans wished, the other tax cuts that took place in 1948 were only of a minor nature and consisted chiefly of certain concessions for lower income brackets.

Faced with this impasse, the West German authorities resorted to a host of special privileges and concessions, most of which were directed at stimulating capital formation as rapidly as possible.

There were firstly privileges designed to encourage individual savings. By the provisional reorganization of taxes of June 1948, savings contracted not only with insurance companies and building societies but also with savings or commercial banks could be deducted from taxable incomes. In 1952 special premia were introduced for savings contracted for house-building purposes and the purchase of specified kinds of fixed-interest securities was also favoured by tax concessions.

For industry there were special concessions. These included special accelerated depreciation, and in shipbuilding and residential construction the right to deduct loans from taxable profits. Tax exemptions for retained earnings were also introduced in 1949, and in 1951 a law was passed granting certain tax aids for exporting firms. Finally, by the Investment Aid Law of 1952 special accelerated depreciation was permitted for investment in the basic industries, chiefly coal, steel and electricity.

These special tax reliefs were costly but the 'increase in capital formation and the resulting increase in total income and taxes . . . were expected to offset, or more than offset, revenue decreases'.[2] In 1950 it was even decided to proceed with a reduction in the rate of

---

[1] K. W. Roskamp, *Capital Formation in West Germany*, Detroit, Wayne State University Press, 1965, p. 122.

[2] Roskamp, op. cit., p. 124.

income tax. But the Korean boom, and the concomitant balance-of-payments crisis, which followed almost immediately after this tax reduction, dampened the German authorities' optimism about tax reductions. In an effort to keep prices down, and to ward off a threatening budgetary deficit, several of the tax concessions had to be rescinded in 1951, and a number of taxes raised. The corporation tax was increased from 50 to 60 per cent, and the turnover tax from 3 to 4 per cent. At the same time the concessions for retained earnings were removed, the income tax allowances were restricted to those who had been persecuted by the Nazis (including refugees), and certain limitations were put on loans.

To what extent can the tax privileges introduced during this early period be said to be in keeping with neo-liberal principles? Given that West Germany in 1948 found itself, because of the shortage of capital, in an abnormal situation, and that overall tax reductions were not possible, the system of tax privileges that was adopted was a method of intervening which was certainly less *dirigiste* than fiscal or financial intervention that discriminates deliberately between firms. The question remains, however, how far the tax concessions and privileges were restricted to the period of disequilibrium.

Some of them were. As has been indicated a number were rescinded or curtailed in 1951. The special incentives for exports ran out at the end of 1955, and the law allowing tax privileges for the purchase of certain fixed interest securities expired at the end of 1954. The special accelerated depreciation was generalized for all equipment with a lifetime of more than ten years. In 1958 it was extended to include equipment with a lifetime of less than ten years.

But even if several concessions were restricted or generalized, others remained. It is doubtful whether, after the Equalization of Burdens Law[1] had been passed in 1952, there was any need to keep special income tax allowances at all, and yet they have continued to exist, in the form in which they were revised in 1951, right up to the present. The special concessions for individual savings were increased in 1956, and they were only transformed (except for savings contracted with building societies) into non-discriminatory aid for savings by those with low incomes by the Savings Premium Law in 1959. Until that time the concessions benefited mainly those with high incomes and thus encouraged the concentration of wealth

---

[1] This Law finally settled the problem of compensation to refugees, expellees and war victims.

well after the time when this was accepted because of the urgent need to encourage investment. Similarly, the concessions for shipbuilding mentioned earlier continued to exist up to 1958, after German yards had been fully employed for some time.

It is more difficult to assess the continuance of the concession for loans to housing. The restrictions imposed in 1951 were removed in 1953, but in 1954 further and more stringent limitations were imposed. Even in its attenuated form, however, this concession has been strongly attacked as favouring unnecessarily the concentration of wealth. The continuance of special accelerated depreciation for residential construction, revised in 1960 and 1964, can probably be justified as an integral part of the Government's housing programme, described earlier. By the latest reform it has been transformed in such a way as to give particular aid for owner-occupied and one- or two-family houses.

Taken as a whole, then, the fiscal regime of the early years conformed only in part to neo-liberal principles. It was compatible to the extent that the early period was one of disequilibrium, and this method of intervention avoided investment planning by the State at the level of the firm. It was incompatible in so far as many of the concessions were continued after the original need for them had disappeared and positively contributed to the concentration of wealth that neo-liberalism seeks to avoid.

The Report on Organic Tax Reform

In 1953 the Scientific Advisory Council of the Finance Ministry produced a Report entitled Organic Tax Reform[1] which examined the German tax structure as a whole and suggested the ways in which it could be reformed. In judging the tax system, it took as its criteria: the meeting of financial requirements in the most economic way; the compatibility of taxes one with another; the compatibility of the tax system with the basic economic order (that is with a market economy); and the compatibility of the tax structure with the German political order. This report of 1953 serves as a useful yardstick for assessing the concrete measures taken after that date.

The report began its analysis with a far-ranging critique of the structure and orientation of the German income tax. The essence of the argument was that, through the attempt to make income tax

[1] *Organische Steuerreform*, edited by the Bundesministerium der Finanzen, Bonn, 1953.

perform economic, social and purely financial objectives simultaneously, the tax had now become both divorced from its original purpose and riddled with internal contradictions. Instead of a tax of
moderate rates and a high threshold, it had become one of very high
rates which reached down to embrace broader and broader sections
of the population. Instead of a tax aimed essentially at the individual's income it had spread through the corporation tax to cover
industrial organizations as well.

The very high rates applying to individuals and corporations
had, in the Council's view, extremely undesirable effects on economic
activity, reducing the initiative to take risks or improve performance,
weakening the will to save, and channelling enterprise unnecessarily
towards tax avoidance, luxury spending by firms being simply one
manifestation of this. Attempts to reduce these economic disadvantages by creating tax concessions of one sort or another were only
partially successful. In the first place, they were socially undesirable
in that they tended to discriminate in favour of those in the higher
income brackets. Thus numerous concessions for economic purposes tended only to make income tax weigh proportionately more
heavily on lower income groups: a paradoxical result, if the social
objectives of the tax were borne in mind. Secondly, numerous concessions had psychologically undesirable results in that they tended
to make the tax so complex and opaque that no one really knew
where they stood.

The objective of an 'organic' reform, the report concluded, must
be to restore the income tax to its proper role in the tax system, and
this could not be done without heavy reliance on the regressive taxes
on consumption and expenditure. The first condition for such reform was to re-establish a rate of income tax which was not an excessive disincentive and which applied to incomes of equal height
and structure in a completely equal manner.

In concrete terms, the report called for a drastic reduction in the
rates of income tax, a raising of the lower threshold of the tax, a
smoothing out of the rate of progression in such a way that those at
the lower end of the tax scale could benefit fully from the gradual-
ness of progression and no groups suffered or benefited from dis-
proportionate jumps in the rates, and a removal of several of the tax
concessions introduced during the early period of reconstruction. To
keep the tax simple and 'transparent' it was recommended that the
global method of assessment should be kept in preference to one of

separate schedules, and that a unified rate of tax should be kept in preference to one based on 'normal tax' and 'surtax'.

Parallel with this reduction of income tax, the report recommended that the corporation tax should be reduced by a quarter. It also recommended that the so-called 'dependency' privilege (*Schachtelprivileg*), an important concession by which dividends or other income transfers received by a company from another company in which it has a holding of over 25 per cent were not subject to corporation tax, should be replaced by an overall provision that, no matter what the size or form of participation, any income received from another company, which had already been subject to corporation tax, could be deducted by the recipient from its taxable income.

The financial requirements remaining after this reshaping of the income and corporation tax would have to be met, the report stated, by the indirect taxes. But the report did not propose any major increase in these taxes. Rather it accepted the new position of the turnover tax, which, largely as a result of the drastic increase of 1951, now provided as much revenue for the Federal Government as the income and corporation taxes combined. The main aim, in the report's view, was not to raise this tax but to reshape it in such a way that it did not distort competition or encourage concentration. The report therefore suggested that the cumulative turnover tax, which was levied like a 'cascade', at each stage when a product is bought by one firm from another, should be replaced by an added-value or net turnover tax. All special concessions for different legal forms of company, or different spheres of production, should be struck out of the new tax, though the report recommended that concessions for certain essential goods should be allowed on social grounds.

The report estimated that all the changes it suggested would lead to a reduction in tax revenue, but argued that the social and economic benefits which would accrue would far outweigh this loss. 'Each basic change in the existing tax structure is . . . a financial risk', but 'no responsible doctor would argue against the move from sickness to health, because the process of transition involved certain difficulties'. The main task was to put through all the changes together, and to avoid piecemeal and disconnected tinkering.

This report has been described at some length because it seems to be a fair statement of the neo-liberal viewpoint on the way the German tax structure ought to be altered. Many of the various proposals included in it have been worked out and expounded at far greater length elsewhere, but this report provides a useful, comprehensive view of the whole. How far have its recommendations been implemented?

It is perhaps most convenient to consider first the clear failures of German fiscal policy before looking at the positive achievements. The failure to remove several of the tax concessions introduced during the early period of reconstruction has already been discussed. Apart from this there has been the failure to make a single 'organic' change in the system, as the report suggested. The reforms that have taken place have been spread out over a number of years, and the only one which can qualify as 'major' has been that of 1958. As one commentator has stated, 'permanent tax reform' is probably the best description of the changes since 1953, and the prolonged nature of the reforms has undoubtedly lessened their impact.

Of the more specific failures, the most important has been the delay over the introduction of an added-value turnover tax. No one in Germany doubts that the cumulative turnover tax encourages vertical concentration, as well as causing price distortions, and thus contradicts the basic principles of the competitive order. It was not, however, until 1963, after exhaustive discussion and debate, that the Government finally introduced its draft bill for an added-value tax on the lines suggested by the 1953 report. This Bill finally became law in May 1967. According to the Law's provisions an added-value tax at the rate of 10 per cent was introduced on January 1, 1968. A special rate of 5 per cent is envisaged for certain basic necessities, some professional activities and the entertainments world. By a decision taken soon after the Law was passed, the normal rate of the tax would be raised to 11 per cent in 1968. This was to help balance the budget.

Two lesser failures from the neo-liberal viewpoint have been the survival of the 'dependency' privilege and of the 'organship' privilege, both of which tend to encourage concentration. The 'dependency' privilege has been reduced, it is true, by the reduction in the rate of corporation tax on distributed profits, but it still acts as an incentive to firms, and in particular it seems to banks, to acquire a holding of 25 per cent or over in other corporate bodies. The 'organship' privilege is rather similar in effect. It was introduced as a general concession in 1958, after having been permitted for certain limited cases before then. In fact, the privilege goes back to prewar days, but it had been deliberately curtailed by the Allies

G

as part of their decentralization programme. The concession, as defined by the 1958 law, meant that a holding of 51 per cent or over in a company made that company an 'organ' or agent of the owning company, and that therefore business transactions between the two were exempt from turnover tax. In 1961 the privilege was made more difficult to obtain by raising the required holding to 75 per cent.

If the clear failures of German fiscal policy lie in the retention of certain privileges beyond the period of reconstruction, in the lack of a major, comprehensive reform, in the delay in the reform of the turnover tax, and in the retention or insertion of the dependency and organship privileges, the successes lie in the reform of the income and corporation taxes.

Reform of the income tax: tax privileges
The reform of the German income tax since 1953 has been a two-fold one, the first change being in the rates of the tax, the second in the technique of levying it. Both changes fulfil the basic principles enunciated in the Report on Organic Tax Reform.

The major tax reform of 1958 introduced the formula rate, under which the maximal rates within each range of income did not go up in a series of jumps but were calculated so as to rise continuously with even the smallest rise in income. It also created a new proportional 'entry stage', whereby for incomes up to 8,000 marks for single persons and 16,000 marks for married couples a single rate of 20 per cent applied. This change, according to Reuss, eliminated 95 per cent of all taxpayers at one stroke from progression—though with rising incomes a lot of these were soon to enter it again. Finally, the 1958 reform reduced the maximum rate of tax, which had already been reduced in 1953 and 1955, to 53 per cent. In other words, from 1958 onwards the German income tax rose in a curve between a proportional entry stage of 20 per cent and a proportional exit stage of 53 per cent. There was still a 'jump' from the proportional entry stage to the lowest level of progression, and the curve rose in three separate sweeps—each representing a range of income within which the tax rose with any rise in income.

In 1964 a further change took place. By the reform of that year the rate of tax for the proportional entry stage was lowered from 20 per cent to 19 per cent, the curve of progression was smoothed out and a tax-free allowance of 240 marks for manual workers was introduced.

The changes which have been made over the same period in the corporation tax may be more briefly summarized. Instead of an overall reduction such as the 1953 report had recommended, the Government reduced the level first and foremost on distributed profits. The object of this was twofold: first, to stimulate the capital market, and second, to counteract the concentration of wealth caused by self-financing. Forcing firms to the capital market does not of course by itself discriminate against 'bigness' in that big firms as a rule tend to be able to raise money more easily in the capital market. The Government has, however, reinforced this policy by further discrimination in the tax, in addition to its other measures of 'middle-estate' policy.

In discussing the German tax structure so far the accent has been on those areas where something has clearly been done to implement neo-liberal ideas and those areas where nothing has been done. There is also a large 'grey' area where a large number of special concessions for different sectors of, or groups within, the economy have been either retained or granted since 1953, and where it is more difficult to be categorical in making any assessment. In Chapters 2 and 6 the measures retained to encourage savings and capital formation were mentioned; and there are many other concessions.

The list of concessions existing in 1965, published by the Ministry of Finance,[1] indicates the most important of them in terms of value. First, there are exemptions from the turnover tax: for agriculture and forestry, for milk products from dairies, for the wholesale trade in solid fuels, for the supply by producers and wholesalers of certain petroleum products and non-solid fuels, for the wholesale trades in certain foodstuffs and in iron and steel, for the supply of water and, with some limitations, electricity and gas, for the renting and leasing of land, for certain medical and educational goods, and for firms in West Berlin. There are also low rates of turnover tax for certain other agricultural products, concessions for products used in and made by smelting, and allowances for the professions.

Of the concessions from income tax, a large number of the major ones relate to West Berlin and were introduced by the Aid to West Berlin Law of 1964. Of the others by far the most important are those which have already been mentioned, namely the relief for individual savings contracted with building societies, the special

---

[1] *Finanzbericht*, 1966, Bonn, Bundesministerium der Finanzen, p. 179 ff.

depreciation privilege for residential housing, and the free allowance for manual workers introduced in 1964. There are also less important income tax concessions in the form of Christmas allowances for manual workers, and exemptions (unspecified) for certain interest rates. As regards the other taxes, there is an important housing concession from the land tax, the dependency privilege from the corporation tax, a concession for local transport from the transportation tax, and an exemption for tractors from the motor vehicle tax.

These then are the main German tax privileges. Taken as a whole they undoubtedly contradict the basic neo-liberal principle that the tax system should be simple, transparent and neutral. This does not mean, however, that neo-liberals will condemn each of them as incompatible with the competitive order. No such sweeping condemnation is possible, for each tax privilege must be judged in relation to the particular purpose it is designed to fulfil. Thus some of the agricultural aids are legitimate in that they help agriculture to adapt; others merely preserve the *status quo*. Neo-liberals accept the desirability of discriminatory measures provided that they work to eliminate structural defects from the economy, or satisfy social aims, such as help for the needy or a wider distribution of property, with the minimum of interference in the working of the market. The problem of how far German State aids are legitimate, according to this criterion, will be considered again in Chapter 8.

FRANCE

Selective fiscal incentives

In France, as in Germany, there has been a debate about fiscal neutrality, particularly in the Fourth Plan. In France, however, it has centred on the justification of measures, supported by the planners, for the provision of selective incentives in order to encourage certain types of activity, such as exports or investment, and to induce individual firms to conform to the requirements of the plan.

The first problem, however, was not so much the desirability of favouring approved types of activity as the need to eliminate fiscal discrimination against them. Thus the most important general measure of the postwar period was the replacement in 1954 of the indirect taxes on production and sales by an added-value tax. This was intended to remove the bias against investment inherent in the old system, since the old tax, operating on the 'cascade' principle, had fallen on a firm's total value of production, thus including costs attributable to bought-in materials and equipment, which had already been taxed as part of the production of the firm selling it. It was calculated that the tax amounted to 25 per cent of the value of 'intermediate products'.[1] Following strong recommendations in the Fourth Plan, the added-value tax is to be extended in the Fifth Plan to non-manufacturing sectors (excluding agriculture) where so far it has not been applied. This is particularly aimed at stimulating investment required to modernize the retailing system. The tax is also varied as between different commodities as a matter of deliberate policy. This manipulation of the tax has been one of the major differences between the French and German views about its function as an economic regulator. Agreement has, however, been reached on the added-value tax at a single rate on all products as the basis of indirect taxation in the EEC.

In 1959 another disincentive to investment was removed in France, in that the revaluation of firms' assets was made obligatory so that depreciation could be calculated at the new accounting value. This enabled the effects of inflation on the cost of investment to be allowed for. A second exercise of this kind is now under consideration. A further measure introduced in 1959 positively discriminated in favour of investment. This was the provision for accelerated depreciation. The degree of acceleration increased according to the length of life of the new capital. Previous legislation granting only certain firms the advantage of this arrangement was abolished and the incentive was applied generally throughout manufacturing industry.

In February 1966 the Government introduced a new and more direct form of investment incentive aimed at stimulating private investment which was lagging owing to the effects of the stabilization measures on demand and profits. For the period to December 1966 firms were given special relief on profits tax amounting to 10 per cent of the value of new capital goods purchased. In order to reduce the possibility of wasteful investment this privilege was granted only in respect of capital goods with an accounting life of at least eight years, an exception being made of machine tools. This criterion was

[1] G. de la Perrière, *Le Plan et les Grandes Entreprises*, roneotyped note by Commissariat du Plan, p. 6. See also *La Politique d'Incitation*, a study by Bureau de Recherches et d'Action Economique, Paris, 1960, p. 28.

preferred to a distinction in terms of types of equipment, which, it was argued, would have been more arbitrary and capable of being interpreted too widely.

Apart from investment, the two most important activities which have been favoured by fiscal discriminations are exports and regional development. The preferential treatment of exporters was instituted in 1957 when the French economy was losing its high level of protection and ceasing to benefit from foreign aid. Exporters selling at least 20 per cent of their total turnover abroad above a minimum level of 500,000 francs (£36,000) were awarded a *carte d'exportateur*. This document entitled them to specially favourable depreciation provisions before these were generally available. They were, in addition, given priority access to the capital market and exempted from increases in the added-value tax. Such access was also extended to firms producing major import substitutes such as steel and chemicals. This latter incentive is still in operation and the planners are prepared to make limited and judicious use of it in the Fifth Plan. They did, however, state that it would be aimed at removing obstacles and delays for exporters and would not be employed as a form of subsidy.

A wide range of incentives are offered to firms moving to regional development areas, including numerous fiscal devices (as well as loans and subsidies) to aid their initial investment outlays. All such advantages are awarded on a selective basis after a careful examination by the planners, who by now have a major voice in decisions relating to regional development, of the contribution the firm is likely to make towards stimulating economic activity in the regions. A firm must, for example, fulfil certain strictly defined conditions as to the number of jobs it is likely to provide. A complete reform of the system of incentives was introduced in May 1964, in which France was divided into five zones according to the nature of the regional problem, and the form and extent of the incentives were varied to suit each case (see pp. 327–8).

The effectiveness of these fiscal incentives is not easy to gauge. The stimulation of exports coincided with the devaluations of 1957 and 1958, which removed the heavy disadvantage of an over-valued currency. It is probable, however, that the incentives did contribute to the remarkable resurgence of French exports after 1958. This is certainly the view of M. Niveau, who argued in 1961 that 'the increase in exports over the last three years has come essentially from firms benefiting from the privileges of the *carte d'exportateur*.[1] The relative growth of exports of manufactured and semi-manufactured goods over the same period is another indication of the increased competitiveness of French exports. The export incentives probably helped to encourage this move into new markets. Fiscal incentives are thought to have had a more limited effect in stimulating regional development, where the increasingly tight restrictions on factory building and extensions in the Paris region and the provision of adequate infrastructure facilities for decentralizing firms are believed to have been more important. The reforms of 1964 constituted an attempt to remove some of the weaknesses of the incentive system and make the incentives a more valuable aid to industrialists. They are discussed in detail in Chapter 10.

Incentives are also available to encourage structural reforms in industry, a constant preoccupation of the planners. The Ministry of Finance is prepared, under an agreement outlined in the Fourth Plan, to grant a number of privileges to firms introducing approved measures to rationalize and concentrate production. The 13 per cent 'transfer tax' on the acquisition of land and buildings is to be reduced in cases where firms are undertaking industrial regrouping. The taxable profits of the 'mother' company are reduced by an amount equal to the taxes paid by subsidiaries, if it holds a 20 per cent, and in special cases a 10 per cent, holding in the subsidiary. (This is known as the *mères et filiales* procedure.) Tax relief is given to small and medium-sized firms forming groups or associations to 'adapt to the necessities' of the Common Market or to carry out operations of conversion and rationalization. Other benefits are given to firms engaged in research and development operations of an approved kind.[2] These incentives are frankly discriminatory even if their cost in budgetary terms (and the planners emphasize this point) is not great. They are, however, considered necessary in view of the highly fragmented nature of French industry and the increasing incompatibility of this situation in the context of the developing Common Market.

The efficiency of these measures is, however, generally viewed with scepticism. The capital goods industry, in which the planners have, since the Second Plan, tried to encourage concentration and

[1] M. Niveau, La Planification Indicative en France, *Economie Appliquée*, Tome XV, Nos. 1–2, January–June 1962, p. 132.
[2] IVᵉ Plan, *Journal Officiel*, August 7, 1962, p. 71.

rationalization of production methods, lagged badly even in the period of inflationary expansion in the mid-1950s. A review of the operation of incentives concluded that 'bona fide concentration and specialization agreements involving two or more firms are extremely rare and the operations induced by the incentives are negligible when set against the continuous growth of ententes and mergers which has taken place spontaneously over the last ten years'.[1] The fragmented nature of the capital goods industry makes such forms of intervention harder to apply successfully than in the more concentrated industries such as steel, in which financial inducements to concentrate have proved quite effective. The traditional hostility of the family firm to State intervention, reflected in the generally suspicious attitude that the National Confederation of Small and Medium-sized Enterprises has maintained towards the planning system, is also a factor that must be taken into account.

In his survey of the capital goods industry[2] Mr Sheahan argues that the really effective pressure that has been exerted has come from the increased foreign competition produced by the Common Market, which provided a stimulus much greater than any incentive granted by planners to an industry that throughout the 1950s had enjoyed the twin advantages of an increasing domestic market and a high level of protection. The relative improvement of the industry since 1958 gives weight to this argument. The establishment of the Common Market combined with the more conservative tendencies of the Fifth Republic have, as in the case of credit policy, caused the Commissariat du Plan to moderate somewhat its enthusiasm for selective interventions. But the following quotation from the Report of the General Economy and Finance Commission of the Fourth Plan indicates something of a rearguard action by the planners to preserve some selectiveness in the face of the demands of fiscal neutrality. 'Is taxation to play a discriminatory role and to grant advantages to certain operations or methods of production judged by the Plan to be of particular significance? The Commission's answer must be a qualified one. In view of the attention paid by firms to tax problems this type of action can certainly be effective.[3] But it is not

[1] Bureau de Recherches et d'Action Economique, op. cit., p. 51.

[2] J. Sheahan, *Promotion and Control of Industry in Postwar France*, Harvard University Press, 1963, Chapters 13 and 14.

[3] This runs counter to the conclusion of the Richardson Committee in Britain that investment decisions were not greatly influenced by tax considerations. See below, p. 204.

always possible to determine with the degree of generality necessary
... the operation and production methods that are significant for the
Plan. It is also imperative to avoid a long-term reduction in the tax
base, and as far as possible the principle of simplicity must be maintained. In general, advantages will be the subject of individual
agreements or granted for only a short period.'[1] The selective incentives available to stimulate structural reform are a further practical instance of the planners' reluctance to relinquish this weapon.

The conflict between fiscal neutrality and French concepts of
planning is expressed more sharply by some commentators: 'The
principle of fiscal neutrality runs the risk of endangering the success
of planning if it is pushed too far. Fiscal and financial incentives
would then be granted in a rigid and systematic way without a prior
examination of particular cases to see whether they are justified and
likely to be effective.'[2] They go on to cite several instances in which
such incentives, awarded too rigidly and too generally, might not
achieve the results expected of them. To take an obvious example,
incentives intended to encourage exports might be used instead to
expand production for the domestic market.

Although finding it necessary to modify their planning methods, the
planners continue to emphasize the value of fiscal incentives that are
the subject of specific and detailed agreements, 'quasi-contracts' or
contrats fiscaux with individual firms or industries. The procedure of
the quasi-contract was first introduced in 1957. It takes the form of
an exchange of letters between the firm or the industry requesting
aid, the relevant Ministry (Industry, Agriculture, etc.) and the
Ministry of Finance. The final decision is referred to a sub-committee of the Fonds de Développement Economique et Social on
which the planners are represented. The advantage of this sometimes lengthy process is that firms given preferential treatment in the
financing of investment or research projects are assured of the continuity of this aid for a given period. There have in fact been relatively
few examples of this kind of contract. In 1957 the most ambitious
agreement was signed, between the automobile industry and the
State, in which the industry agreed to export two-thirds of its
additional production. In the Fourth Plan six quasi-contracts

[1] Rapport Général de la Commission Générale et du Financement du IVe Plan,
p. 59.
[2] J. Fourastié and J. P. Courthéoux, La Planification Economique en France,
Paris, Presses Universitaires de France, 1963, p. 122.

operated, two in the steel industry and four in the mechanical engineering sector. Four of these concerned aid for research and development. One gave a loan for a specific investment project and one provided temporary bridging finance to allow the closure of a steel firm in the south-west of France to be carried through without the immediate laying off of its employees.

The emphasis is now on 'fiscal contracts' rather than 'quasi-contracts'. The difference is that, with a small number of exceptions, aid under such contracts will be given entirely by fiscal means and not by loans or subsidies. They will, moreover, be reviewed annually and thus comply with traditional notions of budgetary policy in a way that the longer-term quasi-contracts did not. The commitment of the State in advance to financing long-term projects in the private sector is not popular and is likely to be used with considerable discretion, though major exceptions will undoubtedly be made in the field of regional policy.

There are some indications that the move away from selective incentives will not be pursued too vigorously in the Fifth Plan. There are two main reasons for this. First, the need to press ahead with structural reform in order to keep French industry competitive has led the Government to revert temporarily to a more interventionist policy. The following comment in the Fifth Plan makes this point very clearly. 'The reorganization of industrial structure requires exceptionally large resources, for such operations are not immediately profitable. The reformation of French industry is now such a high national priority that loans on special terms (interest rates, duration, deferred payment) will be granted to encourage important operations. Funds will be made available for this purpose under the management of the FDES.'[1] A second and closely related reason is the need to ensure and facilitate the financing of private investment.

The introduction of the Fifth Plan was accompanied by a series of measures specifically designed to improve firms' liquidity. A distinction was made between long-term and short-term capital gains. Gains resulting from the sale of shares or industrial land which a firm had held for more than two years are now taxed at 10 per cent, while shorter-term gains are taxed at 50 per cent, but the tax made payable over a period of five years. The rate of tax on distributed profits was lowered from 50 per cent to 25 per cent by means of a

[1] Ve Plan de Développement Economique et Social (1966–70), Paris, Imprimerie Nationale, November 1965, Tome I, p. 70.

system of tax credits which allowed French shareholders to set half the value of dividends against their income or profits tax liabilities. By thus increasing the effective yield on shares it is hoped to stimulate the capital market and increase the supply of external finance available to firms. The planners approved of both these general incentives to investment but argued that further encouragement was required. The generalized right to depreciate assets at an accelerated rate had not been taken advantage of as widely as it might have been and the squeeze on profits was anyway lessening its value to many firms, particularly exporters facing international competition. The planners advocated instead a system of investment allowances. They insisted, however, that they should be highly selective and used to aid such categories as exporters, and firms establishing in development areas. The scheme introduced in February 1966 was very much along these lines and indicates the reluctance of the authorities and the planners to deny themselves too drastically the right of selective intervention.

BRITAIN

The search for fiscal incentives

The chief aims of fiscal policy in Britain have traditionally been efficiency of collection, equity as between one taxpayer and another, and a fair distribution of incomes after tax. Since the war, the Treasury has pioneered the Keynesian use of a surplus or deficit in the annual budget in order to keep a balance between supply and demand in the whole economy; to this was added, in 1961, the power to vary at short notice the rates of indirect taxes and of a small payroll tax, so as to make finer cyclical adjustments as soon as an inflationary or deflationary tendency was detected. Investment and hence growth have also been stimulated by investment and initial allowances. Apart from this, however, there was little attempt to use taxation as an instrument of economic growth policy in the 1950s. The liveliest debates concerned proposals for an expenditure tax, a capital gains tax, or a wealth tax, to solve the problems of the unfair definition of income in the existing tax structure. The NEDC did stimulate the examination of ways in which tax changes might encourage growth,[1] but despite the stress laid on growth and efficiency as objectives of economic policy in recent years, the massive reforms

[1] NEDC, *Conditions Favourable to Faster Growth*, HMSO, 1963, pp. 10–13.

of the 1965 Finance Act, introducing the corporation tax and the capital gains tax, were largely, though not entirely, irrelevant to the objectives of competition and growth. Only with the introduction of the Selective Employment Tax in the 1966 Budget did Britain make a substantial, though still tentative, step towards reforming the tax structure in a way that will make it possible to take some of the weight off direct taxation and hence to reduce its disincentive effects.

Investment has been encouraged in Britain since 1952 by the granting of the initial and the investment allowances against company taxation. A virtue of this method is that, while it applies generally over the whole of industry, the tax relief is given only on evidence provided by firms' accounts that investment has actually taken place. The allowances have, however, been used very much for the short-term regulation of the economy, and the NEDC made a number of proposals for making them a more permanent encouragement to growth.[1] One of NEDC's suggestions has been put into effect. In the 1963 Budget the Chancellor for the first time introduced discrimination between regions in the granting of investment allowances. Free depreciation was allowed for firms in development districts, thus adding to the already wide measures for aiding areas of high unemployment. A further discrimination in the allowances, but one not clearly related to growth, has been the special rates used to encourage shipbuilding.

One drawback of the way in which the investment allowances have been administered is the delay between the actual outlay by the firm and the relief to its financial position brought about by the reduction of tax. Another is that uncertainty has been created by frequent changes in the rates allowed. A further problem, examined in the Richardson Report on Turnover Taxation[2] and again in the NEDC Report on Investment Appraisal,[3] is that in practice firms may not react to the incentives because their inadequate accounting procedures obscure the true value of the allowance. The NEDC recommended that the administration be speeded up and also that longer notice should be given of any intention to alter the allowances.

However, following the introduction of the corporation tax in the

---

[1] NEDC, *Conditions Favourable to Faster Growth*, HMSO, 1963, p. 42.

[2] *Report of the Committee on Turnover Taxation*, HMSO, Cmnd. 2300, March 1964.

[3] NEDC, *Investment Appraisal*, HMSO, 1965.

1965 Budget, the Government was obliged to revise the whole structure of investment allowances. The new allowances, which were announced in 1966, are given in cash and not in tax relief, thus solving the problem that had exercised the NEDC. In total, however, the new cash allowances appeared less generous than the value of the tax reliefs they replaced.

The NEDC also investigated the Swedish system of stabilizing private investment by the use of a tax reserve fund, which could help to meet some of the problems encountered in the operation of the British system, as a result of trying to use the same allowances both as an incentive to investment and as a stabilizer. The Swedish investment fund or reserve seems to have been quite successful in regulating private investment for anti-cyclical purposes in the last six or seven years, when it has been used actively as an integral part of economic policy. Under the present regulations, companies can set aside 40 per cent of their annual profits before tax as a special investment reserve. To prevent these allocations from expanding liquidity excessively it has been stipulated that 46 per cent of them (40 per cent before 1960), a proportion roughly equal to the amount that would have been paid in taxes, must be deposited in a blocked account with the Central Bank. The remainder must be kept sufficiently liquid to enable it to be used when required. Responsibility for deciding when and where the fund should be used for anti-cyclical purposes now rests with the Cabinet (until recently it lay with the Labour Market Board). The Government is free to fix a specific time limit for the investments, to attach whatever conditions it thinks desirable, and also to use the funds to stimulate particular areas of the country; for example, it has recently aimed at increasing investment in the north. If the companies concerned invest in accordance with the Government's wishes, they can write off the whole amount at once, plus 10 per cent. If, on the other hand, the funds are used without permission having been granted, 11 per cent of the amount used is immediately subject to tax, though if five years have elapsed 30 per cent of the money a company has set aside may be used without permission and written off. To give some idea of the size of the fund, the allocations which remained unused at the end of 1961 (during a period of restriction when the funds were not being released) amounted to about 2·4 billion Kr. or £168 million.[1] This is equivalent almost to one quarter of total gross investment (excluding

[1] Curt Canarp, *Skandinaviska Banken*, Vol. 44, No. 2, 1963.

houses) during a one-year period. The fund is larger than the combined reserve of government projects (described on pp. 238-9) which amounted in 1963 to a total of £140 million.

As the Swedish authorities stated in an OECD report: 'It is natural that the companies who set aside money in the investment funds are mainly those with ample liquid reserves, strong powers of expansion and long-term investment plans. This means that the anti-cyclical policy serves to stimulate efficient production rather than to keep declining firms and industries alive during recessions. At the end of 1960, 70 per cent of the funds had been deposited by firms with over 1,000 employees.'[1]

The investment fund has been used, for example in 1958-60 and 1962-3, primarily as an instrument to stimulate investment during a recession. As such it has undoubtedly been effective. As a method of restraining a boom it does not seem to have had the same automatic effectiveness. During the boom period of 1960-1, for example, further measures had to be taken. But the measures, consisting chiefly of additional tax concessions conditional on depositing, not 46 per cent, but 100 per cent of the fund with the Central Bank, were taken within the framework of the investment fund.

The OECD has commented on the Swedish investment fund system that it 'does not differ very much from that of allowing the undertakings to make extra provisions for depreciation in periods of economic depression'.[2] This seems altogether too crude a judgment. The investment fund system has two clear advantages over the system of varying depreciation allowances, one from the viewpoint of private companies and one from the viewpoint of the Government. From the point of view of the firms, there can be little doubt that a permanent investment fund subject to more or less fixed rules regarding tax concessions and penalties has a less disruptive effect on the calculations of firms, and on the continuity of their investment plans, than the arbitrary raising and lowering of depreciation allowances, even if the Government tries to give a preliminary warning about such changes. There are uncertainties in the investment fund system (for example, as to the time when projects will be started) but these are the unavoidable uncertainties of cyclical movements themselves. Instead of the whole of their investment programmes being suddenly exposed to a different effective rate of taxation, the firms

[1] OECD, *Labour Market Policy in Sweden*, 1963, p. 42.
[2] Ibid., p. 60.

can single out the more postponable of their projects to be the subject of the anti-cyclical policy. The Government in its turn is given greater certainty about the possibility of countering a slump in investments because it can determine precisely the value, timing, location and type of the investments that will be made, and can tailor them to the depth, timing, location and nature of the recession. A further, and most important, advantage is that the instrument of growth planning, the investment allowance, is separated from the instrument of cyclical planning, the investment tax reserve fund, so that either can be operated as circumstances and policy require. The two objectives and the two instruments will interact, but they will not contradict each other in the same way as the two objectives will if they have only one instrument to serve them both.

Added-value tax and purchase tax

Consideration has been given in Britain to the introduction of an added-value tax to replace the existing profits tax, and possibly also purchase tax. The NEDC estimated that a rate of $2\frac{1}{2}$ per cent on added value would have the same yield as the 15 per cent profits tax.[1] If the tax were also to replace purchase tax (which would clear up the untidiness inherent in having both taxes and alleviate the burden of purchase tax on growth industries) it would have to be levied at $5\frac{1}{2}$ per cent. A particular merit of the added-value tax, during a time of recurrent balance-of-payments difficulties, was thought to be the possibility that it could be charged on imports but not on exports, although it was feared that much of this benefit to the balance of payments would be lost since home prices might be increased by the amount of the tax, thus leaving the British exporter little better off even though he was relieved of profits tax and did not have to pay the new tax. Moreover, the discrimination of purchase taxes against some industries, including growth industries, could be avoided in a more simple manner by widening the scope, while lowering the rates, of purchase tax. And this extended purchase tax could still exempt necessities. The British purchase tax has in fact been adapted in this direction, and the case of the added-value tax been allowed to drop.

There is, however, reason to believe that the negative conclusion about the added-value tax was founded on too narrow an approach.

---

[1] NEDC, *Conditions Favourable to Faster Growth*, HMSO, 1963, p. 41.

The tax was examined, both by NEDC and by the Richardson Committee,[1] as an alternative to the existing purchase tax, and/or profits tax, and in the context of the maintenance of revenue; the possible rates were in consequence assumed to be the low ones of $2\frac{1}{2}$ per cent to $5\frac{1}{2}$ per cent. The question of fiscal neutrality and the possibility of using added-value tax to take some of the burden off income tax have not been given nearly enough attention; nor does the advantage to the exporter appear to have been given enough weight, at a time when the balance of payments has been the key constraint on economic growth.

The Richardson Report compared the purchase tax with the French added-value tax to make the important point that there is 'basic similarity of purpose' behind the two. First, the report stated that the French adopted the added-value tax as 'a conscious effort to make the French system more like the purchase tax'. The French tax 'was evolved as a result of conscious efforts to transform a generalized production tax, which had previously fallen on investment and certain other business costs as well as on consumer goods, into a tax falling on consumer goods only. Purchase tax from its inception was designed as a tax on consumers' expenditure . . .'.[2] Secondly, the rate of the French tax varies in relation to different categories of goods: there are in fact five different rates. This again makes it very similar to purchase tax.[3] Thus the basic difference between the two taxes was considered to be simply that the purchase tax is collected at one stage rather than at several, and that it does not at present have so broad a coverage as the French tax. The remedy for this, if a remedy is required, was also simple: to extend the coverage of the British purchase tax.

The Richardson Report is open to criticism in taking the French version of the tax, adopted as long ago as 1954, as its standard of comparison, and ignoring the exhaustive debate in Germany and the view of the Neumark Report, which was drawn up for the EEC Commission and was implicitly critical of certain aspects of the French

---

[1] *Report of the Committee on Turnover Taxation*, op. cit. This Committee of three members, including Sir Donald MacDougall, was appointed to follow up the findings of the NEDC by inquiring 'into the practical effects of the introduction of a form of turnover taxation either in addition to existing taxation, or in substitution for either the purchase tax or the profits tax or both'.

[2] Richardson Report, op. cit., para. 93.

[3] Ibid., para. 296.

tax.[1] The German thinking, outlined earlier on pp. 192 and 193, is that the added-value tax is a means of taking some of the burden off income tax, and thus of reducing its progressivity, and that it has the advantage of competitive neutrality. For these reasons the added-value tax is seen in Germany as intrinsically better than the purchase tax, though the French are criticized for levying their added-value tax at different rates on different goods.

The idea of shifting the burden of taxation away from income tax towards an added-value tax is not exclusively a German one. Largely with a view to reducing the shapelessness of the tax system the Swedish Minister of Finance appointed in 1960 a committee to make a comprehensive survey of the whole tax system, and to make proposals for reform. Its first Report, in June 1964, was 'The New Tax System'[2] which reviewed the taxation of individual income, indirect taxes and social contributions, but not the taxation of corporate profits. A substantial reduction in direct taxes was proposed, which would be compensated by a rise in indirect taxes, achieved primarily by the introduction of an added-value tax at a rate of 13 per cent. The Committee suggested that the rate of the tax could, if necessary, be increased to 20 per cent.

It is interesting that the alternative idea of extending the existing single-stage tax was explicitly rejected for a number of reasons, chiefly because a tax rate of 10 to 11 per cent was considered the maximum feasible for this kind of tax. Above this rate the technical problems of control became increasingly difficult. Not only the single-stage tax, but the energy tax and several excise duties would be absorbed by the added-value tax, which would thus lead to considerable simplification of the tax system.

The problem of collection, which has bulked large in British discussions on the added-value tax, did not deter the Swedish Committee. The method proposed for levying the tax was as follows: Every other month each enterprise would declare its sales and purchases. The tax included in purchases would be deducted from the tax assessed on sales, the difference being paid to the tax authorities. Deductions for tax included in purchases would be verified from copies of the suppliers' invoices, which could also be used by

[1] *Rapport du Comité fiscal et Financier*, EEC, Publication No. 8070, 1967, pp. 42-3.
[2] See *Index*, Stockholm, No. 4, 1964.

the tax authorities as a check on the declared sales of the suppliers. The Swedish 'tax from tax' system is not the only one that can be used for assessing an added-value tax; the system of assessing deductions on the 'purchase from turnover' principle can also be used. Nevertheless, the Swedish example shows that the method of collection need not be unduly complicated.

The Committee pointed out that the added-value tax had the interesting advantage of being a useful instrument of cyclical planning to influence the liquidity of the economy by postponing the right of deducting the tax included in the amounts paid for goods and services purchased. The large gross turnover of a 13 per cent added-value tax means that a relatively short postponement of the right to make deductions can have very significant liquidity effects throughout the economy. The measure ought perhaps to be regarded as monetary rather than fiscal, since the ultimate tax burden on consumption is not affected. A considerable effect on the liquidity of the banking system and of business firms can on the other hand quickly be achieved.

It is not necessary to accept wholesale the German or Swedish ideas in order to appreciate the force of their line of argument. There is little doubt that income tax in Britain is so high as to be a disincentive with ill effects on growth, and that no way of reducing it should be ignored. It is, moreover, of undoubted advantage to have a tax system that is basically neutral, even if substantial derogations from neutrality are desired; for the extent of the exceptions can then be known, and policy therefore decided on a more rational basis. The added-value tax, moreover, offers the possibility of increasing or reducing taxation without altering the desired balance between neutrality and discrimination, and in particular of increasing taxation, when necessary, without damaging effects on incentives and growth.

The Richardson Report's suggestion that similar results could be obtained by increasing the coverage of the purchase tax is open to serious objections. The Report quoted the figure of £9,600 million of untaxed consumer expenditure against £7,225 already covered by the purchase tax or other customs and excise taxation. But well over half the consumer expenditure which the Richardson Report suggested could be covered (i.e. food, coal, coke, electricity and gas, together with all the services which the report includes, a total expenditure of about £8,000 million) presents very real difficulties, which the report itself indeed often recognizes. Some are of a social nature. There are objections for purely social reasons to the idea of the purchase tax being levied at a substantial rate on essential foodstuffs. Food also raises an additional problem: if unprocessed food is to be taxed, the purchase tax must be extended either back to the farmer or forward to the retailer.[1] However, the same problems arise with the added-value tax.

But a number of the main difficulties spring from the nature of the purchase tax itself, and in particular its objective, which the Richardson Report endorsed, of taxing first and foremost 'consumer consumption' and excluding business consumption. In extending the tax in the way the Richardson Report suggested, the problem of demarcating the two types of consumption becomes acute, in particular in relation to coal, coke, electricity and gas, as well as to most of the services. The Report considered these difficulties and concluded that coal and coke 'would involve control at the retail stage', that for electricity and gas a 'special tax' might be necessary, and that for services, 'problems would exist whatever form of taxation of services were adopted'.[2]

Thus the extension of the purchase tax would appear to involve abandonment of its main advantage, which is the ease of collecting a tax at the wholesale stage only. And, even if the distortion of the pattern of production involved in the present one-stage system is tolerable, an attempt to increase revenue from the tax by raising the rates rather than extending the coverage would be liable to accentuate distortions to an unacceptable degree. By contrast the fuller coverage of the added-value tax enables it to raise sufficient revenue to take the burden off income tax while itself being levied at a moderate rate.

It is not intended in a book such as this to make definitive recommendations on a question as complicated and controversial as that of the added-value tax. But it is clear that the British discussion of this tax reform has been vitiated because its terms of reference have been too narrow; and that, furthermore, the technical aspects of tax collection appear to have been allowed to weigh too heavily and the economic implications too lightly. The problems of collection do not seem to frighten the Germans or the Swedes.

[1] Richardson Report, op. cit., para. 86.
[2] Ibid.

Payroll and selective employment taxes

Proposals for a payroll tax, payable by employers in respect of each worker employed, have been the subject of much discussion in Britain in recent years. Just as the investment allowances have been used for stabilization policy and to stimulate investment, the payroll tax has been put forward as an instrument to serve either purpose. It was, however, mainly for contra-cyclical purposes that the Chancellor, Mr Selwyn Lloyd, introduced a proposal for a payroll tax in the Finance Act of 1961, in the form of a flat rate tax on each employee at a level which was to vary, according to contra-cyclical requirements, up to a maximum of four shillings per employee per week.

The use of a payroll tax for this purpose has been suggested by, among others, J. C. R. Dow[1] and T. Balogh.[2] It had been argued that such a tax could be rapidly adjusted from time to time between budgets, would mop up cash very quickly from the economic system, and lead to economy in the use of labour at the most critical times, thus striking at a frequent cause of the curtailment of expansion. Mr Lloyd's tax was, however, widely criticized as ineffective for this purpose. First, the maximum rate proposed of 4s a week was considered to be inadequate. The addition of 4s a week to the gross wage paid to each employee would not have any decisive effect in inducing firms to economize in their use of labour, particularly since it would be imposed only temporarily, and at the time when their demand for labour was strongest. The maximum tax of little over 1 per cent on average earnings was thought to be far too small. Secondly, in so far as it might be effective in preventing the hoarding of workers, the flat rate tax that was chosen ran up against the criticism that its effect would be both inequitable and economically inefficient. A poll tax has the virtue of simplicity, but its impact is regressive. A 4s per week tax would have a bigger impact on the employment of lower paid, unskilled labour than on the higher paid skilled labour which was in particularly short supply. Similarly, it would affect poorer regions such as Northern Ireland, Scotland and north-eastern England more heavily than the prosperous regions where it was particularly important to release labour in times of

[1] J. C. R. Dow, Fiscal Policy and Monetary Policy as Instruments of Economic Control, *Westminster Bank Review*, August 1960.

[2] T. Balogh, The Morning-After Budget, *New Statesman and Nation*, April 2, 1960.

high activity. For these and other reasons, this section of the Finance Act met with considerable opposition, and in the event the Government refrained from using the power granted by Parliament.

The second use of a payroll tax was proposed by Sir Robert Shone, Director of NEDO from 1962 to 1966, and H. R. Fisher,[1] and mentioned in *Conditions Favourable to Faster Growth*. This was for a payroll tax to finance part at least of the social services, and to allow a reduction in other taxes on industry, in such a way that investment would be stimulated, and especially investment in labour-saving machinery. The proposal was in fact intended to make labour permanently more expensive relative to capital. In 1961 Mr Lloyd paid a certain amount of attention to this argument for the tax, talking instead of increasing the rate of economic growth by encouraging the use of capital instead of labour. But this can hardly be considered to have been a serious case in support of his specific proposal for a tax which, being a tiny percentage that would be imposed and lifted and reimposed and relifted in response to fluctuations in economic activity, could not really have been expected to give significant incentive to investment. Although Mr Lloyd's tax was never imposed, the Government, through graduated pension contributions and the increases in contributions to the National Health Service from the National Insurance Fund, did increase the burden of taxes on labour. And in the Budget of 1966 Mr Callaghan finally introduced a Selective Employment Tax[2] which was probably the main fruit of the discussion about fiscal incentives to growth initiated by the NEDC and the DEA.

This tax was much more substantial than the payroll tax that was proposed in 1961: it has been levied at a rate of 25s per week for men, and 12s 6d for women and boys. At such levels it can make a major contribution to broadening the tax base and could thus take part of the burden off income tax and corporation tax. The tax was discriminatory against the construction and service industries, in that it was refunded to other industries, and discriminatory in favour of manufacturing in that it was refunded at a rate, 32s, higher than that at which manufacturers will pay. As a result of the different proportions of service and manufacturing in different parts of the country, the tax was also discriminatory between regions,

[1] Sir Robert Shone and H. R. Fisher, Industrial Production and Steel Consumption, *Journal of the Royal Statistical Society*, 1958, Part VI.

[2] HM Treasury, *Selective Employment Tax*, Cmnd. 2986, May 1966.

against the south-east but in favour of the Midlands, and also against Northern Ireland. The tax was to act as a general relief to manufacturers, and thus, in a very broad sense, to exporters. It spread the burden of indirect taxation, which so far, in the form of purchase tax, has hit manufacturers particularly hard, to the service and construction industries which have so far been taxed more lightly. SET had, at least in the manner of its initial impact, anti-cyclical uses. It was announced that the tax would commence in September 1966, but the first refunds were to be paid only from February 1967. This was a method, therefore, of reducing liquidity temporarily. At the same time as the devaluation of November 1967, the removal of the premia for manufacturing industries was announced, except in the case of factories in the development areas.

Viewed in its aspect as a payroll tax, that is, as a means of altering the relative costs of labour and capital, the case for the tax rests partly on the evidence in the National Plan of probable manpower shortage (see p. 126). It is not clear whether the aim is to make wages plus fringe benefits and taxation reflect the actual cost of labour, that is, to use the tax as a corrective of an existing bias in the system; or whether it is deliberately to bias the system in favour of capital-intensive methods by increasing the cost of labour to the employer beyond this point. The NEDC had in mind the former aim, of fiscal neutrality, when they commended the changing of national insurance contributions on to a wage-related basis because this would help to finance higher rates of benefit, especially unemployment benefit, and 'would also bring more directly into industrial calculations the costs, in relation to the advantages, of a trained and skilled working force'.[1] If fiscal neutrality is the objective it is, of course, necessary that taxation should bear in equal proportion on the different factors of production, so that the cost to the employer of each factor after tax has been paid should reflect that factor's marginal productivity. It may be that labour has so far been under-taxed in this sense, and the NEDC claimed that 'to tax profits specially is to tax the reward of efficiency (though profits are not always a criterion of efficiency) and, generally speaking, of the use of capital intensive methods of production'.[2] In so far as this is true, the introduction of the new tax, and its use to avoid the increases in income tax and/or corporation tax that would otherwise have been

[1] NEDC, *Conditions Favourable to Faster Growth*, 1963, p. 43.
[2] Ibid., p. 41.

necessary in 1966, were certainly justified, although in this case it is right to tax manufacturing employment too.

If faster growth is an objective of planning, however, one way of securing it is to increase the annual increment of production derived from new investment, whether by raising the rate of investment or by investing more efficiently. There is little doubt that in the British economy there is room for improvement in both of these respects. This being so, it is necessary to decide whether taxation, in addition to other instruments of policy, should be used to this end. There is again little doubt that it should. But this does not lead necessarily to a payroll tax, or to a Selective Employment Tax on the service sector in particular, because other forms of taxation, and especially the investment allowance, can be used for this purpose. In deciding whether to select the payroll tax for this function, moreover, account should be taken of the extent to which the tax might be passed on to the worker, which could well happen in trades where the labour market is not dominated by a strong union, in which case the net cost of labour to the employers would not increase. There is also room for considerable doubt whether the SET was a really effective way to promote exports. For one thing, in favouring manufacturers, it applied equally to exports and home sales. A general incentive that would really apply to exports would of course be the remission of a value-added tax on exports. A lot of revenue would be lost in favour of firms that already, because of their product structure and conditions in world markets, have a high proportion of exports, and the incentive to the firm struggling to break into export markets may appear far too small just when encouragement is most needed. An even more effective method of obtaining increments of exports, rather than rewarding those who are already exporting, would be the *carte d'exportateur*. But this is less acceptable to international opinion.

Certain conclusions can be drawn from this review of the debate on fiscal changes in Britain and of the changes that have been made. Individual tax changes should be considered in the context of the whole structure of the tax system, and not, as they all too often have been in Britain, partially, tax by tax, or group by group of taxes. And whenever taxes are under review, for whatever purposes, the objectives of economic policy and in particular the aims of increasing productivity and competitiveness have to be given their full weight in relation to other requirements, such as equity, administrative economy and convenience, and the maintenance of revenue. These may appear to be very obvious precepts but, unfortunately, the inquiries that have been held in Britain since 1945 into a tax system that is crying out for reform have had largely negative results, partly because of the tendency to take too narrow a view. In the early 1950s the Royal Commission on Taxation allowed their terms of reference, or the way in which they interpreted them, to rule out the full consideration of schemes for replacing the National Insurance system. The discussion of the added-value tax and the payroll tax have suffered from a similar defect. In Germany, by contrast, tax reform has been aided by the existence of a consistent theory of the relationship between the tax system and the economic system.

It is disappointing to find how little the British tax system has been adapted in the interests of growth in the years following the foundation of the NEDC. The practical results to the end of 1967 of the debates on how to increase the fiscal incentives to growth were a number of measures whose influence on growth is likely to be slight, or indirect and uncertain: the introduction, in the 1963 budget, of free depreciation for firms in districts of high unemployment, the alteration of the system of investment allowances without increasing their value, the slender tax exemptions for exporters in November 1964 (withdrawn when the pound was devalued in November 1967), and the Selective Employment Tax in 1966 (with premia for manufacturing industries withdrawn on devaluation). The Finance Act of 1965 could not be regarded as a contribution to growth policy, except indirectly in that the discouragement of overseas investment, which is one of the implications of the introduction of a corporation tax, may help to overcome the international payments crisis and therefore enable growth to be resumed somewhat earlier. The capital gains tax could have been also an incentive to growth only in so far as it obtained trade union co-operation in the incomes policy; but this effect was very uncertain, and the more direct effects on the incentive to invest are probably adverse. The raising of the standard rate of income tax in 1965 merely strengthened the force of the arguments against excessive reliance on this tax. The 1965 budget was not merely largely irrelevant to the prospects for growth, it was probably actually harmful to them. For a major constraint on tax reforms is the capacity of the Board of Inland Revenue to absorb them, and the great administrative effort required to implement the

1965 Finance Act has imposed tremendous strain on the tax collection machinery, and pre-empted too much of its capacity for change for too long a period. From this point of view the Selective Employment Tax may be regarded as an ingenious way round the self-imposed administrative obstacle to fiscal reform in the interests of growth.

CHAPTER 8

PUBLIC EXPENDITURE

There has been a great increase in recent decades in public expenditure in all capitalist countries, both in total and as a proportion of the national product. This growth in the direct power of the State as a purchaser and employer is one of the most vital of the inter-related developments referred to in Chapter 1 as posing the problems under discussion in this book. The State has come to exercise a decisive role directly in the economy, not only through the sheer weight of its spending power, but also on account of the vital quality of much of its expenditure, especially on investment in infrastructure, research, education and training. The questions of the management of this investment and its possible manipulation in an attempt to influence the growth of the economy have therefore come to be given great prominence in discussion of economic policy. In one sense the divide between neo-liberal and neo-collectivist thinking is much narrower in this area than in some others; for in respect of public expenditure the State may be regarded much as a single vast enterprise, and the necessity of planning within the enterprise is accepted even by those who are most opposed to the superimposition of planning on a sector or industry made up of separate enterprises. There are still major differences about the desirable level and direction of expenditure, but in most West European countries in recent years it has become increasingly accepted that there should be more medium- and long-term planning both of public investment and of public expenditure as a whole. At the same time there has also been increasing support for greater flexibility in budgetary policy, including public spending, so that more of the responsibility for regulating cyclical fluctuations can be removed from monetary policy. This chapter will examine each of these developments and the problem of their mutual compatibility.

PLANNING THE LEVEL OF PUBLIC EXPENDITURE

Britain

There have been a number of reasons behind the move towards more medium- and long-term planning of public expenditure in Britain. First, there is the feeling that too much chopping and changing of public investment and of public expenditure as a whole not only leads to waste and inefficiency but has a damaging effect on business confidence as well. If government departments were to prepare more elaborate expenditure programmes for four, five or six years ahead, and if more was done to enable them to keep as closely as possible to these programmes, then some of these drawbacks might be avoided. Secondly, there is the motive of co-ordination, the feeling that it is not enough for each government department to draw up its own programme, but that each of these programmes, so far as this immense task is humanly possible, should be properly linked and co-ordinated with the others, and be made part of an overall plan or programme. Thirdly, there is the desire that the Government's expenditure plans should be properly related to the country's resources, so that these plans are kept within the limits of what the country can afford. Finally, it is felt that long-term planning of government expenditure will facilitate parliamentary control.

These four arguments can be seen running through much of recent discussion of British public expenditure policy, from the Report of the Select Committee on Estimates in 1958[1] to the Plowden Report of 1961[2] and beyond. Much has now been done to implement these ideas. In many government departments, for example defence, transport and education, the idea of a four- or five-year, or even longer, programme of both capital and current expenditure has now become firmly established, even if government changes still act as a disruptive force. More moves have been made to co-ordinate individual programmes, for example the Labour Government's decision to plan not only rail, but the transport sector as a whole. The 1960 White Paper[3] on public investment in Great Britain provided for the first time estimates of public capital investment in all sectors for two financial years. Full-scale surveys of prospective public expenditure in relation to resources began in 1961 and now take

[1] Select Committee on Estimates, 6th Report, *Treasury Control of Expenditure*, H. of C. Papers, Session 1957–8, No. 254.
[2] HMSO, *Control of Public Expenditure*, Cmnd. 1432, 1961.
[3] HMSO, *Public Investment in Great Britain*, Cmnd. 1203, 1960.

place annually. The December 1963 White Paper[1] gave estimates of total public expenditure in 1963-4 combined with an estimate of prospective expenditure in 1967-8.

The five-year estimates do not have the character of rigid targets, but are regarded as moving or 'rolling' programmes, which preserve a certain amount of flexibility. As Lord Bridges has written of the system, 'the plans for capital expenditure by public authorities are submitted on the basis of the plans for the ensuing two years being reasonably firm and those for the succeeding three years being more tentative. In this part of the field the five-year period is conceived not as a fixed quinquennium—say from 1965 to 1970—for which funds are allotted before the quinquennium starts, but rather as a continuing or moving period of five years which is rolled forward another twelve months each year.'[2]

Of the economic motives behind the development of the planning of public expenditure undoubtedly the most important at the outset was the third one mentioned above, namely the need to keep its growth in a 'proper' relationship with the growth of GNP. This was, for example, the view of the Chancellor of the Exchequer in 1961 when he announced the initiation of the full-scale surveys of public expenditure: 'If we look back for a decade, it will be found that, for a time after 1951, total public expenditure—and in this I include the whole of the public sector, central and local government, above and below-the-line, the national insurance funds, and the capital expenditure of nationalized industries—rose more slowly than the gross national product. This was largely due to a reduction in the proportion taken by defence. But the process was reversed three years ago, and the share of our total product taken for public purposes is rising again, and rising appreciably. The object of carrying out the study which I have just mentioned is to see how we can best keep public expenditure in future years in proper relationship to the growth of our national product.'[3]

Excessive ambition in the size of planned expenditure is one problem, but as serious is the failure to keep actual expenditure down to what had been planned. This issue has been often raised, but most authoritatively by Sir Richard Clarke: 'This confrontation of prospective public expenditure against the prospective national

[1] HMSO, *Public Expenditure in 1963-4 and 1967-8*, Cmnd. 2235, 1963.

[2] Lord Bridges, *The Treasury*, Allen & Unwin, 1964, p. 200.

[3] Mr Selwyn Lloyd, H. of C. Debates, 17 April 1961, Vol. 638, Cols. 793-4.

measures is the heart of the matter. The whole concept of long-term programmes for the development of the public services depends upon the effectiveness and realism of this confrontation. The most difficult technical problem which has been encountered is the tendency to underestimate the future cost of Government policies; and if at the same time an unduly optimistic estimate is made of the prospective growth of GNP, expenditure decisions are likely to be reached which, when they come to fruition, will lead to the over-loading of the economy.'[1]

In the same lecture Sir Richard Clarke pointed out that public sector expenditure, excluding debt interest, had increased from 36·5 per cent of GNP in 1959–60 to 39·7 per cent in 1963–4. Including debt interest, the corresponding figures were 41·6 per cent and 44·6 per cent respectively. The 1963 White Paper,[2] using the same definitions, estimated that, excluding debt interest, the prospective increase in public expenditure at 1963 prices on the basis of the Government's policies and programmes at that time would be equivalent to an annual increase of 4·1 per cent between 1963–4 and 1967–8. These programmes had been accepted on the assumption that the GNP would grow by 4 per cent a year; and, acting on a similar assumption, the new Government in 1964 proposed further increases in public expenditure. Now it may in itself be desirable to increase public expenditure at a rate faster than the rate of growth of GNP; the question of criteria for deciding the size and direction of public spending is discussed later in this chapter. But what cannot be justified is to decide the rate of growth of public expenditure as a whole on the basis of a target rate of growth of GNP when there is no solid evidence that this target is likely to be achieved. If a country seriously intends to achieve faster growth, indeed, it must surely plan public consumption at a level consistent with a conservative forecast of economic growth, so as to leave room for a faster growth of investment, both public and private, and of exports, even if the more optimistic prognostications are not fulfilled. Both Conservative and Labour Governments, however, ignored these requirements of prudence, with the result that public expenditure plans had to be suddenly and disruptively cut back in July 1965 and again in July 1966, when foreign exchange reserves were under pressure and it

[1] Sir Richard Clarke, *The Management of the Public Sector of the National Economy*, Athlone Press, 1964.
[2] Op. cit.

was obvious that a 4 per cent rate of growth of GNP could not be sustained. Finally, a major revision of commitments, especially for defence, followed the devaluation of November 1967.

Germany

The overall size of State participation in the economy in West Germany has been very considerable, and this raises the question of how far this participation is compatible with the neo-liberal principles on which German economic policy has been based. It is worth noticing at the outset that the control of the Federal Government over the size of public expenditure has been weakened by the fact that there are three distinct levels of public budgeting. At the top there is the budget of the Federal Government, together with the two 'special funds', the Equalization of Burdens Fund and the ERP or European Recovery Programme funds. Below this there are the ten Länder budgets. Finally, there are the budgets of the communes or local government units, of which there are some 25,000.

Each of these levels has its own sources of revenue. The Federal Government receives all revenue from the turnover tax and from the customs and excise duties (except that on beer), while it shares the revenue of the income and corporation taxes with the Länder. Originally the Federal Government's share of these taxes was fixed at 33·3 per cent; in 1958 it was raised to 35 per cent; in 1963 it rose to 38 per cent; and in 1966 it stood at 39 per cent. This steady increase has been necessary to offset the continuous shift in favour of the Länder due to the rising revenue of the income and corporation taxes. The Equalization of Burdens Fund, established in 1952 to compensate war victims, received its original resources through a capital levy on all those with an income over a certain level at the time of the Currency Reform. It finances its current spending on compensation through the income from the loans it makes, and also receives certain grants from the Bund and Länder. The ERP Fund was originally financed from the German counterpart funds for Marshall Aid. It has steadily increased in size over the years, because the burden of repaying Marshall Aid was assumed by the Federal Government, and secondly because of the income it receives through the repayment of the loans.

Besides their share of the income and corporation taxes the Länder receive the revenue from the property, traffic and beer taxes. The communes' main sources of income are the taxes on trading profits and on real property. In fact, the revenue from the latter taxes, which has not risen very fast over the years, has been insufficient for many communes to carry out their tasks, and they have had to receive considerable subsidies from the Länder. One of the objectives of current proposals for budgetary reform in West Germany is to strengthen their financial resources. Their share in the total tax revenue in 1965 was roughly 13 per cent, that of the Länder 32 per cent, and of the Federal Government 55 per cent.

What is the overall size of State activity in Germany? It may be summarized by stating that some 40 per cent of GNP passes through the State's hands; that the State has played a highly important role in the process of capital formation, though this role is now diminishing;[1] that the public sector extends beyond the traditional public utilities; and that the amount of visible and invisible subsidies granted by the State has represented in the past over 6 per cent of GNP, and it increased sharply during Dr Erhard's Chancellorship.[2] The Ministry of Economics has estimated, moreover, that the total proportion of capital investment which the State influenced—that is to say, not only investment directly financed by the State, but also private expenditure for investment purposes which was first made possible by financial assistance from the State—amounted to 'more than 50 per cent.'[3] This is interesting because it is also the usual figure given for the amount of investment which the State can influence in France.

Does the extent of State activity in Germany mean that the economy is not really a market economy? There are a number of economists in both Germany and Britain who maintain that there is a definite stage at which the quantity of State activity transforms a market economy into something different. Some would say that this

[1] German public authorities accounted for 36·6 per cent of net capital formation during the decade 1950–60, and 31·8 per cent of net capital formation for the years 1961–4. The first figure is provided by *Finanzbericht*, 1962, Bonn, p. 96; the second has been calculated from the data provided in the Monthly Report of the Deutsche Bundesbank, April 1965, p. 3 ff.

[2] The figures provided in *Finanzbericht*, 1966, p. 78 ff, show that the visible aids provided by the Federal Government, and the invisible aids provided by all levels of government, amounted to 6·8 per cent of GNP in 1963, and, provisionally, 9 per cent of GNP in 1965. Visible aids represent actual expenditure, invisible aids renunciation of income.

[3] *Nachtrag zum Wirtschaftsbericht*, 1964, Bonn, Deutscher Bundestag, supplement to Drucksache, IV/1752, June 1964, p. 16.

is happening when 30 per cent of GNP is represented by the State's income and expenditure, others would say 40 per cent, and yet others 50 per cent. The wide divergence between these figures shows the difficulty of basing any useful definition of a market economy on a percentage of this sort. Many neo-liberals lay emphasis instead on the way in which State activity is carried out. Is it—as the neo-liberal school demand—moulded so as to stimulate market forces, or is it designed to replace them? If one examines the German nationalized sector according to this criterion, neo-liberal principles appear to be largely fulfilled. Not only are many of the non-independent public corporations run on the same principles as private enterprise, but the independent companies in which the State participates almost invariably are. As the OECD report *Growth and Economic Policy* expressed it: 'The commercial companies which are wholly or partly owned by the public authorities are as a rule remarkably free from government control and intervention. They conduct their activities on the same principles as private enterprises. The central or local government is represented on the company board but by far the greater part of the supervisory posts are held by persons taken from private industry and business. The function of the competent minister is in most cases restricted to defining rules for auditing and appointing auditors.'[1] The Government's active policy of denationalization (see pp. 65–6) should also be remembered in this context.

It is more difficult to assess the effect of the considerable subsidies granted by the German State. Clearly there has been a major effort to adapt those granted to housing so as to conform as far as possible with market forces (see pp. 55–58). The various ERP subsidies may also be said to be in keeping with neo-liberal principles in that they are generally limited in time, and aimed at curing disequilibria as they arise. The substantial aids granted to small and medium-sized firms, both through the ERP Fund and by the Federal Government, are intended to prevent market forces from being weakened by excessive concentration, as are the measures taken to promote wider property ownership. It is true that much regional aid is aimed simply at preserving the *status quo*, but in view of the peculiar condition which the country, and Berlin in particular, found itself at the end of the war, this is understandable. Where German State subsidies seem to run most clearly counter to market forces is in relation

[1] OECD, *Growth and Economic Policy*, 1964, p. 30.

to agricultural and energy policy. Over 5,000 million marks was provided for German agriculture by the State in 1965, and although some of this was aimed at promoting rationalization, the great bulk of it was not. Similarly a large proportion of the assistance granted by the State to the German coal industry since 1958 has had the purely negative goal of protecting it against competition from other sources of energy. Transport subsidies are more difficult to judge. Since the legislation passed in the early 1960s to introduce more competition into the German transport system they are undoubtedly more in conformity with neo-liberal principles than they were earlier. Finally, the considerable grants made by the German State to the social insurance system have been strongly attacked by neo-liberal writers, on the grounds that they weaken the element of true insurance in the system and thus in turn weaken individual self-reliance and responsibility.

This brief survey of German subsidies shows that their effect on the market system can be assessed only with reference to their particular purposes and characteristics. Some of them have been strongly influenced by neo-liberal thinking, but German governments have often been unable or unwilling to resist the pressure of interest groups and electioneering requirements when they came to shape subsidy policy.

One point at which German expenditure policy can be said to have moved in a direction which brings it close to elements of French policy is in the adoption of medium-term financial or budgetary planning. The trend towards budgetary planning in Germany did not, however, spring from any desire to use the public sector as a motor for pushing the economy as a whole towards a target. It was rather part of a general move to use the budget more effectively as an anti-cyclical weapon, to prevent essentially long-term projects—road-building and education for example—from being distorted by what Dr Erhard has called 'annual contingencies', to prevent public expenditure from galloping ahead of the growth of GNP or causing inflation, and to knit together more closely the different levels of public spending in Germany.

The background of this movement may be briefly sketched. The active use of either fiscal or expenditure policy as an anti-cyclical weapon was very rudimentary in Germany during the 1950s. In the early years of reconstruction, that is up to 1952, the main objective of the Finance Minister was to keep the budget balanced, an

H

objective given additional weight by a stipulation in the Basic Law to this effect (Article 110). The vigour with which this principle was interpreted is shown by Finance Minister Schäffer's action at the time of the Korean crisis, when he raised the turnover tax by a third to prevent a budgetary deficit.

During the middle years of the 1950s, the anti-cyclical aspects of German budgetary policy are best described as 'unconscious'. Thus the period between 1952 and 1956 was that of the so-called 'Julius Tower', a period during which ever increasing budgetary surpluses were 'frozen' at the Central Bank by the Finance Minister. These surpluses were caused partly by an underestimate of revenue but mainly by an overestimate of Germany's future defence commitments. Schäffer regarded the freezing of these revenue surpluses as the height of 'good housekeeping'. In fact his policy had two unforeseen effects. First, the skimming-off of internal demand which the surpluses represented probably served as an additional incentive for German industrialists to look for overseas markets in the years following the Korean crisis. Secondly, they probably helped to damp down the boom of 1955–6, the period at which the Julius Tower reached its maximum. To this extent German budgetary policy can be said to have been unintentionally anti-cyclical during this period.

The dissolution of the Julius Tower in the years after 1956 can also be described in this way. It took the form chiefly of increased agricultural subsidies through the 'Green Plans', increased pensions through the reform of 1957, and increased expenditure abroad. Although many feared that it would have inflationary results, the economy had at this time quietened after the boom, and the increase in public spending did not in practice have harmful effects.

The year 1960 opened a new phase in German budgetary policy, conditioned largely by the inability of the Bundesbank to counter the problem of imported inflation. The limitation of degressive depreciation in the 1960 tax law; the power given to the Government by the 1961 tax law to introduce special depreciation allowances; the power given to the Finance Minister in the budgets of 1961, 1962 and 1963 to block budgetary expenditure if necessary in the interests of stability; and finally the use of this power in 1962 and 1963 to block building expenditure by 20 per cent: these are all indications of a new determination to use fiscal and expenditure policy for anti-cyclical purposes alongside monetary policy. During this period Dr Erhard also enunciated the principle that public spending should not increase faster than the national product.

Ironically the period which witnessed this new orientation also witnessed the steady increase both in the Federal Government's expenditure and, even more strikingly, in the expenditure of the other two levels of government, to a point where it began to endanger price stability. Thus from 1963 onwards three tendencies began to show themselves: first a tendency for public expenditure as a whole to increase far more rapidly than the national product; secondly, a tendency for federal expenditure to exceed in practice the amount laid down in the various budgets; and lastly a tendency for federal expenditure to increase more rapidly than income, leading to increasing budgetary deficits. In 1965 a critical point was reached. This was an election year and, as might be expected, federal expenditure rose much faster than the Government had originally intended. It was also a year of slower growth in Germany, and the tax income of the Government fell. The result was an even larger deficit than hitherto, and inflationary trends. In the autumn of that year special measures had to be taken and a law for safeguarding the budget (*Haushaltssicherungsgesetz*) was passed, which cut back expenditure quite considerably.

Even this was not enough, however, and it was largely because of Dr Erhard's seeming inability to prevent public expenditure and public income from moving apart that this Government fell in 1966 and was replaced by the 'Grand Coalition'. The new Government in January 1967 took vigorous steps to prune public spending and to raise public revenue, and its proposals for the 1968 budget followed the same pattern. It was again ironic that while this effort to balance the budget was being made the German economy was showing signs of moving into a recession. To counter this trend the Government, during 1967, implemented two special public investment programmes, as well as introducing special depreciation allowances for a limited period. In other words, during this year the new Government was in the unhappy position of having to pursue two goals simultaneously, one of cutting back overall public expenditure, and the other of stimulating the economy by increased expenditure. Fortunately by the end of the year the recessional trends seemed to have disappeared.

It is against this background that the reform of the German budgetary system in 1967 must be seen. A start had been made towards such a reform during Dr Erhard's Chancellorship. In 1964 a Finance Committee had been set up to study the problem, and its recommendations, published early in 1966, provided the basis for the 'Stabilization Law' introduced in that year. This Law was still pending when the 'Grand Coalition' took office, and it was finally passed in June 1967, under the changed name of 'The Law for Promoting Stability and Growth in the Economy'. (The change of name itself is symbolic of the change of emphasis in economic policy which the new Government has brought.) The new Law, which required a change in Article 109 of the German Basic Law, made the following stipulations. First, the federal budget is to be drawn up in future within the framework of a five year financial plan which will 'roll' forward each year. This plan will set forth the projected development of expenditure and revenue over this period, relating it to the likely development of the economy's productive resources, and if necessary making use of alternative projections. The plan will be drawn up by the Ministry of Finance on the basis of the medium-term investment programmes presented by the various departments. Second, the Government can, by means of ordinances and with the agreement of the Bundesrat, vary income and corporate taxes by 10 per cent up or down. It can also introduce special depreciation allowances for a limited period, and similarly restrict allowances if need be. In time of recession the possible incentives that may be granted are huge, namely an investment premium of up to 7·5 per cent over and above 100 per cent depreciation. Third, an anti-cyclical reserve fund is to be established at the Bundesbank. The Government can (again by means of ordinances, and with the agreement of the Bundesrat) instruct the Federal and Länder authorities to place up to 3 per cent of their tax revenue of the previous year into the fund. Apart from this, increased revenue caused by an anti-cyclical raising of the income and corporation taxes will be automatically paid into the fund. Money in the fund can be used only for anti-cyclical expenditure, which again may be implemented by Government ordinance with the agreement of the Bundesrat. Fourth, the Government can by the same procedure restrict, for a period of up to a year, credit granted by the Federal authorities, the Länder, and the Communes. Fifth, a Council for Anti-Cyclical Policy is created, bringing together representatives of the Federal Government, the Länder, the Communes and the Bundesbank. It has the right to be consulted over the restriction of credit, and over payments into or out of the anti-cyclical reserve fund. Sixth and finally, the Government must now draw up an annual report setting out its quantitative economic and financial goals, and, every two years, a full account of all the subsidies it grants.

This Law provides the Government with a wide range of instruments with which to counter undesirable cyclical movements; it links the three levels of government budgeting more closely together, and it should bring greater coherence into the formulation of the Federal budget. The Council for Anti-Cyclical Policy rapidly became active, and the budget for 1968 has been placed within the framework of a financial Plan reaching forward to 1971. This Plan estimates that between 1968 and 1971 the German GDP will increase in real terms by 4 per cent per annum, and in nominal terms by 5 per cent or 5·5 per cent per annum on average. These figures are based on the assumption that total public expenditure will increase by 6 per cent on average. No great shift is envisaged from Federal expenditure on consumption to Federal expenditure on investment. The latter will be only 1·5 per cent higher (19·2 per cent) as a proportion of total expenditure in 1971 than it was in 1968. The major shift evident in the Plan is to greater Federal expenditure on research. This will increase annually by 16 per cent, though in 1971 it will still amount to only 3·1 per cent of total expenditure. Finally, the Plan envisages that the salaries of those employed by the Federal Government will rise by 4 per cent in 1968, 5 per cent in 1969, 5 per cent in 1970, and 5 per cent in 1971. As was noted in an earlier chapter, the projections upon which the budgetary plan is based have been stated by the Economics Minister, Professor Schiller, to be a 'political programme', and have been used as the basis for this policy of 'concerted action'.[1]

France

In a discussion of the relationship between public expenditure policy and a policy for promoting economic growth the postwar French experience is a particularly interesting case. In France the authorities accepted from the outset that the planned development of public expenditure must be the basis of any national plan for growth and accordingly allowed the Commissariat du Plan a considerable voice in determining its distribution and growth. It is, therefore, not unreasonable to assume that after twenty years the

[1] For details of the Plan, see *Finanzbericht*, 1968, Bonn, p. 99 ff.

French planners would be able to offer their British and German counterparts some methods of solving the problems of deciding between the competing claims of the various public agencies on the national resources, ensuring a reasonably efficient and democratic control over public funds and manipulating public expenditure so as to reduce fluctuations in economic activity and promote and facilitate the growth of national output. This section attempts to outline to what extent and with what success public expenditure programmes have been integrated into the five postwar plans.

The First Plan was essentially a loosely co-ordinated series of public investment programmes with particular emphasis on reconstructing and expanding the basic industries of the economy: coal, steel, cement, energy, transport and agriculture. The proportion of investment financed by public funds was very large, particularly in the early years of the Plan.

PUBLIC INVESTMENT AS A PERCENTAGE OF TOTAL INVESTMENT
(1952 PRICES)

1947	1948	1949	1950	1951	1952
52	55	64	47	39	39

Source: R. Martinot, La Place de l'Investissement Publique dans l'Economie Française, Revue de Science Financière, 1958, No. 4.

A large part of this investment was financed by various special funds and not by budget appropriations. The amount of investment which appeared in the budget accounts during the First Plan was very much smaller than that financed by the Reconstruction Fund and the Fonds de Modernisation et de Développement Economique (FME) established in 1948 as the financing agency for the Plan's investment programmes. The large investment programmes were by far the most important influence on the growth of public expenditure. Public spending on current account was severely restricted and in 1948 and 1949 the orthodox budget actually showed a surplus. Not until 1951 when military expenditure in Europe and Indo-China was increasing did public current expenditure begin to grow faster than was allowed for in the Plan.

In 1954 and 1955, the first two years of the Second Plan, the rate of growth of public expenditure slackened. In 1955 the war in Indo-China ended, allowing a reduction in military expenditure. The termination of American aid and the impossibility of continuing the high rate of investment reached in the First Plan led the Government to remove the financing of the nationalized industries altogether from the budget and to act only to a limited extent as underwriter of those industries' capital issues.

There were, however, other pressures which caused public expenditure to rise well above the Plan's forecasts and to exceed the level compatible with stable prices. There was, first, the Algerian situation, which by 1956 had become a full-scale war and replaced Indo-China as a heavy drain on resources. A second factor was the large increase in expenditure on social welfare. After the concentration on 'productive' investment in the First Plan the Government in 1954 adopted ambitious building programmes for schools, hospitals, and State-financed, low-rent housing. These were, on paper, a part of the Second Plan but the planners' ability to control or co-ordinate government departments was very limited and expenditure on 'social' investment in the Second Plan exceeded the forecast by 28 per cent. Productive investment on the other hand barely attained its target although it included the research expenditures of the oil industry and a supplementary atomic energy programme. The subsidies granted to the nationalized industries and farmers in order to hold down the prices of their products provided a further claim on public funds.

The relatively uncontrolled expansion of public expenditure during the Second Plan was a major cause of the rapid rise in prices after 1956, which became a critical issue with the advent of the Common Market. Although they were well aware of this the planners were not prepared to advocate wholesale cutbacks in public expenditure and the Third Plan, which came into operation in January 1958, set high targets for certain categories of public investment. To reduce France's dependence on imported fuel and to provide the energy required for a fast rate of expansion, electricity generating capacity had to be considerably expanded and the natural gas deposits at Lacq in south-western France exploited. There were, too, schemes for the electrification of the railway system. Also, in spite of the efforts in the Second Plan, housing, educational and health services were still inadequate and the increase in the birth rate immediately after the war was now raising both problems and opportunities which required, in particular, a rapid increase in secondary school places.

The inflation and the worsening balance of payments could

not be allowed to continue and in September 1958 M. Pinay, re-called to the Ministry of Finance by General de Gaulle, formed a Committee of Experts under the chairmanship of M. Jacques Rueff, whose task was to prepare a programme of financial recon-struction. The committee began by diagnosing the basic problem of the French economy as inflation brought about mainly by the ex-cessive growth of public expenditure.[1] The committee was presented with an estimate of the total budget deficit for 1959 of 1,200 billion francs, more than double the amount the Treasury had been able to borrow in previous years. The committee reckoned that to remove the inflationary pressure this must be reduced to 600 billion francs by increasing taxation and cutting public expenditure.

The committee strongly recommended that the cuts in public expenditure be made selectively. The Algerian situation made reductions in military expenditure impossible while current ex-penditure on civil administration could not be substantially reduced in a short period. The committee were firm in their refusal to hold back capital spending although this was estimated to increase by 26 per cent in 1959. They accepted the planners' argument that the public investment programmes of the Third Plan must be carried through in the interests of long-term expansion, particularly since the increases necessary in taxation would have a dampening effect on private investment as consumption was reduced. The major cuts were in fact made in expenditure on subsidies. This selective use of public investment as a contra-cyclical weapon allowed the Third Plan's public investment targets to be attained.

The growth of public expenditure was an issue of central im-portance in the Fourth Plan. The planners were clearly and explicitly averse to the prospect of France becoming a mass-consumption economy on the model of the United States. The Plan, therefore, gave priority to social investment at the expense of productive investment and private consumption.

The inflationary developments of 1963 and the Stabilization Plan introduced to remove them inevitably affected the Plan's progress. The traditional supplementary credits to the 1963 budget were considerably reduced and the estimates for 1964 fixed the overall budget deficit at 4·74 billion francs, the lowest figure since 1952,

[1] *Rapport sur la Situation Financière*, Imprimerie Nationale, Paris, 1958. The Report also recommended that the franc be devalued by 17·5 per cent. This was done in December 1958.

part of a policy of moving eventually towards a balanced budget. Public expenditure programmes were frozen at their 1963 level but the planners' influence enabled exceptions to be made for educational and public health programmes which the Fourth Plan had emphasized. 'Productive' public investment and current expenditure were more severely restricted and again, in line with the planners' wishes, private consumption suffered most of all.

The planners must be given at least some of the credit for the actual outcome of the Fourth Plan which show that the public investment targets were on the whole achieved despite the retrenchment required by the stabilization measures. There were, however, serious shortfalls in the education programmes and the schemes of urban redevelopment, which the planners considered could not all be attributed to the exigencies of 1963–4. They held that the programmes were not completed on time at least partly because, despite some improvements, the methods employed by the departments to

RESOURCES AND USES IN THE FIFTH PLAN (1966–70)
(ANNUAL PERCENTAGE RATES OF GROWTH)[1]

	1954–62	1960–5	1965–70
Total Resources	5·4	5·3	5·3
Consumption	4·7	5·2	4·7
of which:			
Private	4·8	5·2	4·6
Public	2·8	5·9	6·5
of which:			
Civil	4·4	6·0	4·9
Military	1·6	5·8	7·8
Gross Fixed Capital Formation	7·6	8·3	4·9
of which:			
Productive	7·7	6·0	5·0
Housing	7·1	12·3	3·3
Administration[2]	7·3	10·6	7·9

Source: Vᵉ Plan de Développement Economique et Social, Tome I, Imprimerie Nationale, Paris, November 1965, p. 182.

[1] In 1962 prices. The 1970 estimates take account of estimated differences in the movement of relative prices of goods and services under the various headings.

[2] This is mainly social investment. The low figure for housing is due to the exceptional increase in housing investment in 1965.

carry out projects 'are not always suited to the number and importance of the operations'.[1]

The Fifth Plan continued to emphasize the importance of 'social' investment, and was prepared to sacrifice some increase in private consumption in order to promote the expansion of publicly provided services.

There are, however, several factors which during the Fifth Plan may well make it difficult for the planners to achieve their aims.

The first problem is the resources available. The planners have already had to reduce the amount of resources to be allocated to social investment in order to allow a faster rate of growth of productive investment, and even then this investment is to grow at a slower rate than in any previous five-year period. The lag in productive investment in the Fourth Plan can be attributed in part to the temporary effects of the stabilization measures on private investment but it is also arguable that the French are over-estimating the capacity of the economy to sustain increased social expenditure together with the rate of growth currently aimed at.

A second constraint over which the planners have no control is the increasing amount of resources devoted to defence. This type of public expenditure can of course be used to stimulate growth by encouraging expansion in certain industries but a large part of it is consumption expenditure which must be considered as directly competitive with private consumption and social expenditure.

Then there is the stress in the Fifth Plan on the need to keep prices stable. The planners and many of their critics are clearly concerned about the feasibility of financing the plan's investment programmes by non-inflationary methods. They are, therefore, anxious to increase private savings in order to reduce the burden on the Treasury and avoid the need to increase taxation. The high liquidity preference of the French investor has long been a preoccupation of the planners and has induced the Government to act as a substitute for the capital market by borrowing on attractive short-term paper and lending on a long-term basis to private industry and the nationalized industries (see pp. 159–68). The recent decision to discontinue this practice in order to allow the capital market to develop is a sound long-term measure. It may, however, result in a shortage of savings as investors take time to weigh up the new situation, and thus make the financing of investment difficult. The decision to make the

---

[1] *Rapport sur l'Execution du Plan en 1963 et 1964*, p. 29.

nationalized industries to a much greater extent self-financing, again entirely justifiable, is open to the same objection in the short term.

A comparison of the three countries

The three countries under study differ considerably in their attitudes to the total level of public expenditure. There has in Britain been the good intention to keep the total growth in a 'proper' relationship with the growth of GNP, combined with vagueness as to what constitutes a proper relationship and a damaging lack of realism in expectations about the growth of GNP on which expenditure plans have been based. Public spending has been adjusted a number of times since the war in the interests of contra-cyclical policy, but there has been some resistance to this procedure. In France there was, at least until 1963, an expansive attitude towards public expenditure that contributed to the inflation of the 1950s. The planners still recommend an increase in the share of GNP devoted to 'social' expenditure and a decline in the share of personal consumption, and there is strong resistance to any cuts in public investment, which accounts for as much as a half of total investment; but the Government appears determined to pursue a less inflationary budgetary policy. In Germany in the 1950s there was little effort to plan the overall level of public expenditure, but through good fortune rather than good judgment the budget worked in an anti-cyclical manner. In the 1960s this good fortune ended and despite efforts to check public spending it increased at an inflationary pace. This has now led to a radical reform of the budgetary system and the inauguration not only of medium-term 'rolling programmes' for public expenditure which are to link the latter to the economy's total resources, but, in addition, of a number of special devices which will enable budgetary action of a short-term anti-cyclical nature to be taken.

It cannot be said that a study of the three countries, although it elicits many interesting details about public expenditure, uncovers much in the way of principles to guide this aspect of budgetary policy and its relationship with economic policy and planning. The realization in Britain, France and Germany that public expenditure plus private expenditure must be kept within the limits of total resources is salutary, even if performance has fallen short of precept; but it is no more than the most elementary of first principles of public sector planning, and does not carry one far towards better planning of expenditure in the public sector, particularly in relation to economic objectives such as growth or competition. The lack of thinking on this subject is strange in view of the fact that many people believe (see for example the Medium-term Programme of the EEC discussed in Chapter 12) that the planning of spending in the public sector is one of the main tasks, if not the main task, of economic planning. There is, however, one more positive conclusion. In France and to some extent in Britain the advent of a national programme has produced a more selective approach to the short-term manipulation of public expenditure. The problem of how the selection should be made is still much in need of analysis but at least policy has advanced beyond the crude variation of total expenditure.

It may be useful to bear in mind, when planning the total level of expenditure, the simple lesson from postwar experience, in both Britain and France, that public expenditure and private consumption have both tended to increase faster than planned, so that consumption has frequently pressed in an inflationary manner against available resources. It would seem prudent, therefore, at least in the early stages of an effort to increase the rate of growth of GNP, and while the policy is to raise productive investment to a level that will provide enough capacity to cater for demand if the maximum feasible growth rate is achieved, to aim at a rate of growth of consumption plus non-productive investment that will not be excessive even if faster growth fails to materialize.

This means that the NEDC programme and the National Plan would have been realistic only if they had aimed in the first instance for investment, both public and private, that would support a growth rate of 4 per cent, and for consumption, public and private combined, which would allow for some diversion of resources into exports even in circumstances where growth remained at its postwar average of 2·5 per cent. In France, the Fourth and Fifth Plans have made it very clear that the growth of private consumption has to be held back if investment and military expenditure are to increase. The proposed increases in social investment in the Fifth Plan are in the circumstances very ambitious, but the planners have formally recognized the price that must be paid in terms of lower private consumption given the rapid rate of growth of military expenditure.

Provided that a reasonable prudence is observed, and provided that the tax system allows a greater proportion of GNP to go into collective expenditure without negative effects on growth, there does not seem to be any reason, as far as the growth and efficiency of the economy are concerned, for preferring private rather than public consumption. The choice between the two would in these circumstances, as has already been suggested, be one to be made on its own merits, and one in which the techniques of survey and sociological research and of cost/benefit study can play a valuable part. It is, moreover, desirable that decisions on social expenditure, which account for a substantial percentage of the national income and which consequently deeply affect the evolution of other types of consumption and investment, should be properly related to economic policy and planning as they are to a growing extent in France. There is accordingly much to be said for the argument that those responsible for the social services should be represented on economic forecasting and planning bodies such as the NEDC.

THE USE OF VARIATIONS IN PUBLIC EXPENDITURE FOR STABILIZATION POLICY

In contrast with the tendency towards longer-term planning of public expenditure is the concept of varying it at short notice as an instrument of contra-cyclical policy. The British Government has used public expenditure in this way a number of times since the war, but recently the trend has been towards less reliance on this device rather than more. The Plowden Report of 1961, for example, discussing both public investment and public expenditure as a whole, expressed the following view:

'It must be accepted that some changes in plans for government expenditure policy are inevitable. The Government are required by public opinion to seek to manage the national economy with only small variations in the level of employment. It is natural, therefore, to explore the possibilities of using variations in public expenditure to help in this task. Experience shows, however, that government current expenditure cannot be varied effectively for this purpose. Attempts, at moments of inflationary pressure, to impose short-term "economies" (or to make increases at moments when "reflation" is called for) are rarely successful and sometimes damaging, and we think that these attempts should be avoided.

'There has been a tendency in the past to overestimate the possibilities of useful short-term action in public investment, and to underestimate the indirect losses caused by sudden changes. Experience shows that at least six to nine months (and often more) must elapse before short-term changes in either direction take full effect. In the two-year period from high to low, which seems to characterize postwar fluctuations in the economy, the effect of the action taken may well appear at the very moment when the economy is already on the turn. The remedy may, therefore, be worse than the disease, and we would endorse the cautious view expressed in the White Paper on Public Investment of last November.'

However, it is interesting that the report concluded:

'Nevertheless there must be some possibility of achieving small, but significant and timely, variations in public investment to help to keep the economy stable, and we hope that they will be examined in discussion with the various public authorities. It is only by specifying in advance the fields to which short-term action can and will be directed, and explaining it fully to those in charge of the specified programmes, that the variations can be made without damaging the wider objectives of control and economy of public expenditure.'[1]

The new anti-cyclical reserve fund in Germany has already been described. Sweden too has developed a system of varying public expenditure for anti-cyclical purposes that seems to justify the more optimistic tone of the Plowden Report's conclusion. The Swedish system is based, first, on special appropriations in the ordinary national budget which are to be used only if measures to increase employment are required, and secondly on a special or 'General Emergency Budget', which finances public works projects for the same purpose. The first of these funds amounted to about £32 million (2 per cent of total fixed investment) in 1963, and the second to £108 million (6 per cent of total fixed investment and 8 per cent of ordinary budget expenditure) in the same year. A large part of these funds, once voted, can be used without further reference to Parliament.

The Labour Market Board both plans and proposes the projects which are to be started. Projects are selected for inclusion in the Public Projects Reserve if they are of such importance that they can be expected to get under way in any event during the next few years. Planning thus aims at making it possible, in a certain situation, to

[1] Plowden Report, op. cit., paras. 22–3.

carry out important central and local government projects somewhat earlier than would normally have been intended. The projects included in the Public Projects Reserve comprise industrial building, construction of dwellings, forestry works, and the manufacture of industrial products. The choice of projects is made in consultation with the appropriate central government authorities, in addition to which annual planning conferences are held with the municipalities, the employers' and employees' associations, the associations of country and municipal councils, etc.

It cannot be pretended that this kind of emergency budget system serves in any way as an automatic guarantee of cyclical stability. It depends for its effectiveness very largely on extensive and accurate employment forecasting, and mistakes in timing can be and have been made. It nevertheless represents an interesting addition to the instruments at the disposal of governments for dealing with cyclical movements. Although the Swedish system is directed towards the release of funds when required to prevent unemployment, moreover, one can envisage a similar stock of projects to which the reverse process could be applied: a flow of spending that could be cut when it was desired to disinflate the economy, either generally or in specific trades or places. Such a concept is, indeed, similar to the proposals in the second quotation from the Plowden Report, above.

In France the planners have until recently successfully resisted the indiscriminate cutting of public expenditure as a means of correcting short-term fluctuations. Public investment was cut back in 1953 and 1958 but there had been an extremely heavy concentration of investment in the public sector in the years preceding 1953, while in 1958 the Rueff Report made it clear that restrictions on public investment must be devised so as to keep to a minimum the interference with long-term expansion. The influence of the planners is acknowledged in a United Nations study of the public sector. The authors state that the Commissariat du Plan has helped to introduce short-term changes in investment with the minimum hindrance to the achievement of long-term objectives.[1] They have a fair measure of influence over the management of public funds. In the first place, they have the right to be consulted. The Commissariat du Plan is represented on the Council of the FDES which, as has been explained earlier, determines each year the selection and methods of financing

[1] See, for example, the United Nations, *Economic Survey of Europe in 1959*, Chapter V, p. 37.

of all investment projects directly or indirectly financed out of public funds. The planners are also consulted by the Budget Directorate of the Ministry of Finance during the preparation of the annual budget and the Commissaire Général is a member of the National Accounts and Economic Budget Commission which each year reviews the economic situation and forecasts the development of the economy one year ahead. In the Fourth Plan the Minister of Finance, M. Giscard d'Estaing, gave explicit instructions to Ministries to prepare their estimates in the light of the Plan targets and was himself sympathetic to the arguments of the planners. The French planners have therefore established for themselves a position which allows them the opportunity to present their views both formally and informally on public expenditure policy.

The impossibility of planning effectively in the public sector if credits were voted for only twelve months led M. Mendès-France to introduce programme laws (*lois programmes*) which applied mainly to the nationalized industries and guaranteed to the industries a fixed amount of funds for specific, approved projects for the duration of the plan, thus sheltering them from interference by the budgetary authorities. For various reasons discussed later, this procedure was not entirely successful. It did, however, indicate the acceptance by the Government of the need for continuity in public expenditure programmes and at the time this contrasted sharply with the disruptive, *ad hoc* policies pursued in Britain. In the interests of more effective management of the public sector the powerful and time-honoured tradition of an annual parliamentary vote on public spending was put aside.

It is, however, misleading to conclude that short-term policy in France is perfectly integrated with the long-term programmes of the plans. There are several difficulties. First, the rapid growth of public investment in the earlier plans was not all planned. The over-fulfilment of social investment targets and the unforeseen rise in military expenditure in the Second Plan is a major example. Account must also be taken of the special conditions in which the French economy operated up to 1958 when assessing the priority given to a steady expansion of public investment (see pp. 343-4). The absence of restrictions which during this period so severely affected public sector programmes in Britain was to a considerable degree a reflection of the much easier circumstances of the French economy. The restrictive measures of 1963 and subsequent years give some indication of the advantages which the planners enjoyed in the earlier period and the difficulties involved in pursuing an expansionist policy in the presence of the kind of constraints which have limited British economic growth since the war.

Although the planners have been admitted to all the agencies concerned with the control of public expenditure, doubts are still expressed about their position. One of the most persuasive critics is M. Bloch-Lainé, who argues that no amount of consultation can overcome the fact that the Budget Directory and the Treasury Directory of the Ministry of Finance have the final decision concerning public expenditure.[1] Since these agencies are primarily concerned with the equilibrium of the economy they are likely to oppose the more expansionist views of the Commissariat du Plan. What Bloch-Lainé advocates is a Ministry of Planning which would incorporate the sections of the Ministry of Finance that exercise financial control, thus ensuring that the annual budget would be properly integrated with the four-year plan. Attached to the Ministry would be a Directory of Investment which would operate as a national investment fund and an inter-ministerial committee with the task of co-ordinating the plans of different departments in the context of the plan. An essential feature of this scheme is the creation of a single agency responsible for both long- and short-term policy rather than a separation of the two as in the present British system.

There are of course objections to such a proposal. It involves a radical change in the role of the Ministry of Finance and it would complicate the very important work of the Commissariat in its relations with the private sector. At the same time despite present experiments with inter-ministerial committees the planners do have difficulties in getting other departments to co-operate. M. Massé has spoken very plainly on this point. 'Day-to-day action can be said to be a compromise between the short-term and the long-term views. To overlook the latter is to sacrifice the future to the present. Unfortunately such an attitude is only too readily adopted, and the Commissaire Général in implementing the plan must combat it sympathetically yet firmly.'[2] The shortfalls in some of the public

---

[1] F. Bloch-Lainé, Pour une Réforme de l'Administration Economique, *Revue Economique*, No. 6, November 1962.

[2] P. Massé, *Histoire, Méthode et Doctrine de la Planification Française*, La Documentation Française, Paris, 1962, p. 9, quoted in the United Nations, *Survey of Europe in 1962*, Part 2, Economic Planning in Europe, Chapter V, p. 6.

sector programmes during the Fourth Plan which the planners claim are due to administrative delays indicate the importance of this aspect of planning procedure.

The narrow constraints under which the Fifth Plan is operating demand considerable ingenuity from the planners. The stabilization measures and the reduction in the proportion of investment financed by the Treasury are going to make it more difficult for them to implement long-term programmes. The Fourth Plan recommended that a list of public investment projects be prepared, very much on the Swedish model, which could be brought into operation in the event of a recession. The Fifth Plan may well require the planners to adopt the process in reverse and thus ensure that any further cuts in public expenditure are made as selectively as possible and that lists of projects which are most suitable to postponement or reduction are prepared in advance.

Whether flexibility is compatible with the longer-term planning of public expenditure is, then, one of the important questions of economic planning. If long-term planning were to consist of the imposition of rigid, imperative targets it would, of course, be totally incompatible. Economic processes are not, however, predictable enough for such rigid planning to be possible, so that public expenditure programmes are in fact, as explained earlier, largely rolling programmes. The requirements of contra-cyclical policy, in particular, cannot be foreseen a long time ahead; contra-cyclical measures are therefore necessary from time to time; and there is no reason why they should fall solely on private consumption, still less on private investment. The most suitable incidence of measures of restriction on expansion in the various sectors of the economy (private consumption, private investment, public consumption, public investment) at any time will depend on the relative benefits or disadvantages deemed likely to ensue from the changes in each sector. In a time when growth of GNP and strengthening of the balance of payments have high priority, for example, measures for expansion would tend to be directed at productive investment, whether public or private, and at the encouragement of exports, while restriction would be aimed rather at consumption, whether public or private, and at the sectors with a large import content in particular, bearing in mind, of course, that too severe or lengthy restrictions will react on investment. Thus long-term planning of public expenditure should, as the Plowden Committee finally accepted, provide for a margin of expansion or contraction in the interests of contra-cyclical policy.

The way of doing this that is most compatible with longer-term planning is, clearly, to select for expansion or contraction those items of expenditure that are the most amenable to such changes; and the Swedish method of setting aside a stock of projects that are to be subject to cyclical manipulation seems to be the most convenient administrative technique. This amounts, in fact, to the separation of a country's 'cyclical budget' from its long-term budget. The cyclical budget would, of course, be of relatively small size, but within those limits cuts or boosts could be decided upon at short notice and with the minimum disruption to long-term plans.

The problem of political control naturally emerges. On reflection, however, this appears to be a false problem, at least in Britain. Apart from the fact that, as many recent studies have demonstrated, Parliament now exercises very little budgetary control in practice, it would be highly impracticable for it to try and reassert its 'power over the purse' where cyclical policy is concerned. The optimum timing, direction and extent of normal contra-cyclical measures are technical questions, and it would be better if this were clearly acknowledged and for Parliament to concentrate its attention on the pattern of long-term expenditure. A similar development has been accepted on the side of revenue with the introduction of the fiscal regulator (see p. 203). The best way to make the operation of cyclical policy effective while at the same time securing its ultimate responsibility to Parliament would be to institutionalize it and make it subject to more or less clear-cut rules. Those responsible for cyclical policy should be made to follow as far as possible objective criteria in deciding when and how to intervene. Such objective criteria might consist of unemployment figures, broken down by trade and locality, in times of recession, and of capacity or delivery-date figures in time of a boom. The instruments to be used could include not only variations in public expenditure but also limited tax variations and monetary measures designed to affect private consumption or investment.

PUBLIC AND PRIVATE INDUSTRY

In deciding how big public expenditure should be, the first question to ask is what activities are to be in the public sector. The answer depends partly, of course, on a political choice as to the preferable point on the spectrum between individualism and collectivism. It is not the purpose of this book to take a view on this subject, but merely to point out the relationship of the choice with some aspects of economic planning. In so far as publicly owned productive enterprise is concerned, much depends on the legal form of the enterprise and its relationship in practice with the central government and hence with economic planning. Where the enterprises are monopolistic or oligopolistic, or where they are directly controlled by the central government, there are obvious implications for competition policy, which is *pro tanto* weakened; there are, on the other hand, greater possibilities for the imperative planning of investment and even production, with a view to reaching numerical targets or removing obstacles to growth. It may be noted, at the same time, that there is no necessary correlation between public ownership and monopoly or oligopoly, and that there are many gradations in the degree of control and indeed of ownership by the central government. In so far as publicly-owned enterprises are not in practice controlled by the central government, their decisions to expand are likely to be taken in a way comparable to those of private firms, and the size of their contribution to public expenditure is not, therefore, a matter for 'public sector planning'. Such would seem to be the case with, for example, British Petroleum.

Where expenditure on goods and services other than those produced and sold by nationalized industries is concerned, the decision regarding what should be in the public sector and what should not is more predominantly one of political choice. It may be worth pointing out, however, that at least a part of the basis for a decision may be the way in which the citizen prefers to obtain the commodity in question—a matter which can be investigated by modern techniques of survey and psychological research, which have, however, been applied with very much greater energy in the form of market research in the private sector. Such investigation is of an objective nature, and is thus the legitimate province of the economic planner confronted with problems of planning in the public sector. The planners may not, however, be allowed a final decision on this question. This is certainly so in France where in the Fourth Plan the Government opted to reduce the growth of consumption in favour of increased 'social' investment and in the Fifth Plan to increase by a considerable amount the expenditure on defence. The existence of a national programme does, however, mean that the implications of a given policy on social expenditure for the rest of the economy can be worked out in some detail.

Before considering how, once it has been settled what should be in the public sector and what should not, the amounts to be spent on each activity should be fixed, it is worth noting one basic constraint that operates with some force in Britain today. This is the taxable capacity of the economy, given its existing tax system. Here, the questions of fiscal policy discussed in Chapter 6 become very significant. It is most undesirable, when faster growth is a major objective, to expand public expenditure at the expense of private investment. But with the existing British tax structure it is extremely difficult to devise ways of increasing the diversion of resources from private to public consumption without incurring severe effects on incentives and pressure on the price level, both of which are inimical to growth. Colin Clark[1] and others have generalized this predicament in suggesting that the proportion of GNP which it is permissible to raise in taxation has a rigid upper limit; but this is to ignore the possibilities of tax reform, which may enable a larger share to be diverted to public spending while avoiding loss of incentive due to high marginal tax rates, inflation, or misallocation of resources. It is reasonable to suppose, rather, that the permissible proportion of the GNP diverted to public spending is in part a function of the tax structure. This proportion could be increased if further broad-based taxes in addition to the experiment with the Selective Employment Tax were introduced that would allow bigger transfers without such harmful marginal effects; but it would be inadvisable to do so in advance of a radical tax reform.

It is, then, necessary to decide how much is to be spent in the public sector, within the limits set by the ability to raise taxes without damaging economic growth through the diminution of incentives. A further constraint is set by the total resources available to the economy (the GNP) less the amount that goes to the private sector, both consumption and investment, and less the balance of foreign payments. But the public sector is not just a residual after the other sectors have taken their share of the available resources; each item of public expenditure should be of such a size that the marginal pound brings the same benefit as does the marginal pound spent on the products of the private sector. The essential question is, of

[1] C. Clark, *The Cost of Living*, Hollis and Carter, 1957.

course, of how much benefit is the publicly spent marginal pound and on whom is the benefit conferred? The theoretical formulation about marginal benefit does not begin to answer that; but it does indicate that the size of public expenditure cannot legitimately be fixed according to some *a priori* relationship with GNP, but should be based on a detailed evaluation, item by item, whose results would certainly differ from time to time and from country to country, depending on the values and the economic condition of the people at the time and in the country concerned.

The first stage of analysis, if faster growth is a major objective of policy, is to define those branches of public expenditure whose expansion is a necessary basis for the expansion of the economy. In Britain and France the most important of these are the nationalized industries providing the economic infrastructure of power and transport (although this infrastructure includes also the roads whose building and maintenance are under the direct control of central and local government). There is also a correlation with expenditure on industrial training and on some aspects of education; and expenditure on labour market policy (see pp. 285–8) may likewise be directly linked with plans for faster growth, particularly in a country such as Britain where resistance to industrial change represents a critical brake on economic progress.

These branches of public expenditure all have the character of investment, and a serious intention to increase the rate of economic growth must be accompanied by investment at the level required to support the consequent demands. Earlier in this chapter British governments have been criticized for committing themselves to the expansion of public expenditure at a rate that would be justifiable only on the assumption of a rate of growth of GNP of 4 per cent a year. This criticism must not, however, be applied to expenditure on 'productive' investments of the type defined above, i.e. such as necessarily accompany the expansion of production. It is advisable to expand such expenditure at a rate that would provide the facilities required if a reasonably optimistic forecast rate of economic growth were to be fulfilled. Policy towards productive investment in the private sector should be guided by similar principles, and the remainder of resources will then be available for other types of expenditure, which are mainly those classed in the statistics as public or private consumption but which also include some 'non-productive' investment, both public and private, such as housing. It is not suggested that productive investment should have this priority because it is intrinsically 'better' than other ways of spending money; but that if faster growth is wanted, investment at the appropriate level is a necessary means to that end. Planning of public consumption and non-productive investment within the limits of the resources thus available will be discussed below, but it is first necessary to consider further the planning of public investment of a productive nature.

First, the question arises as to how the decision should be made to increase capacity by a given amount. Is the GDP growth target set by the planners to be a mandatory framework for this decision and, given the assumption for the rate of growth of GDP, who is to decide in practice what expansion is required for the goods or services produced by a given public enterprise? Boldness in the basic industries of the public sector laid the foundations for the postwar growth of the French economy, and it would seem that, when it is intended to create a substantial change in the economic environment, such as an increase in the rate of growth, it is desirable to allow the planner to coerce the publicly owned industries by means of imperative targets, if they do not spontaneously adjust their thinking to the new line of policy, as the French basic industries in fact did, and as the British electricity industry did in relation to the 4 per cent target. In times when it is not a part of government policy to increase the rate of growth substantially or otherwise radically to alter the economic environment, however, there seems to be no good reason why the boards of nationalized industries should not form their investment policies in much the same way, and in a similar relationship with the economic planners, as do the boards of private companies of equivalent size. Normally, then, decisions about the growth of these branches of the public sector should not be the subject of special rules or principles relating to public sector planning.

Secondly, however, there is the question of the efficiency of investment in projects to increase capacity in the public sector, as well as that of the size of the capacity to be installed. Here the situation of public enterprises is different from that of private ones, in both France and Britain, because of their dependence on public finance rather than the capital market. It is not always remembered that the Treasury has replaced the capital market as the source of finance for a substantial sector of the British economy, and that in this sector the efficiency of the employment of capital is, therefore, ultimately the

Treasury's responsibility. Criticisms have been made that, apart from errors of judgment in the broad allocation of funds (too much on expanding the coal industry, too little on docks and roads), individual projects are proposed by the nationalized industries and passed by the appropriate ministry and the Treasury that are generous in their costing to an extent that is not necessary to the efficient execution of the project and would not be tolerated by boards or by sources of finance in the private sector.[1] While it is beyond the scope of this book to investigate such criticisms, it does not seem inherently unlikely that there should be room for improvement in this function of a government machine which has since the war been charged with vast responsibilities that were formerly the province of private industry and the capital market. It is certainly a vital element in the planning of expenditure in the public sector that there should be an efficient instrument not only for deciding what increases in capacity should be financed but also for ensuring the efficient use of capital in the relevant projects.

In France the nationalized enterprises are financed to varying extents by the Finance Ministry in the form of direct subsidies to cover deficits, and by long-term loans and interest subsidies from FDES to aid development. This ensures that the planners have influence over the expenditure of the nationalized industries. Some of the nationalized industries in France, particularly electricity and gas, have established a reputation for technical dynamism and even when the planners' influence has not been too powerful there has been vigorous expansion. The industries have also pioneered sophisticated methods of price and investment appraisal. The successive management teams of Electricité de France have made particularly important contributions in the form of the famous *Tarif Vert* which applies the rules of marginal cost pricing more faithfully than any other public enterprise, and in the use of discounting methods to assess the merits of alternative investment projects. The latter technique has been generalized and in the Fourth Plan a discount rate of 7 per cent was adopted as a measure of the return that could reasonably be expected on capital investment over the economy as a whole. These measures are, of course, open to many criticisms and not all sectors are so capably run as Electricité de France, but the point that is relevant here is that some of the major French nationalized industries have made considerable efforts to use resources efficiently.

[1] For a discussion of this question see PEP, *A Fuel Policy for Britain*, 1966.

There are, however, problems. Although the FDES does an important job of co-ordination the development of the nationalized industries in the plans is considered by separate Modernization Commissions and there is not sufficient cross-reference in the earlier stages of the Commissions' work. A second point is that the planners' control over the nationalized sector is purely financial. The FDES controls the supply of funds provided by the State and requires the nationalized industries to give detailed plans of their operations. It then communicates the decision to the Ministry of Finance and to the ministry responsible for the industry which has the task of supervising the detailed implementation of the project. At this point the financial control of FDES ceases to be effective. The project becomes the subject of discussions between the industry and the ministry and can differ in both timing and content from the original proposals approved by the planners. The autonomy of the industries is increased if they have a surplus on operating account, since these funds are not controlled by FDES and only in theory by the relevant government department. The use of credits for purposes other than the original approved scheme was one of the factors which caused the planners to modify the system of programme laws in the Fourth Plan. They are now used only in cases where the placing of orders over a long period will lower the cost to the industries supplying the materials and thus lower the cost of the projects. As a means of ensuring continuity in the development of public sector programmes they are no longer considered to be effective.

The budget restrictions which are likely to operate during the Fifth Plan have persuaded the Government to reduce the amount of financial aid it gives to the nationalized industries. This will mean that the prices of the goods and services produced will very probably increase. The planners have faced up to this possibility and indeed have made a virtue out of necessity by urging the industries (Electricité de France is of course an honourable exception) to adopt pricing policies which more nearly reflect costs. This reversion to the market as the regulator in the public sector marks a definite break with previous policies which to a notorious extent preferred to meet the needs of the industries by taxation and subsidies rather than increased charges. It will reduce the degree of direct control exercised by the planners but, in a time when there is no need for a massive reconstruction of the basic industries in the economy and in the light of the difficulties of managing the public sector without reference to the market, it may lead to a more efficient allocation of a large section of the economy's resources.

Apart from the provision of the public services required by an expanding economy, there are a number of ways in which public expenditure can be used in the interests of faster growth. The financing of industries concerned with advanced technology has already been mentioned in Chapter 6. There is no clear-cut line dividing the provision of finance at advantageous rates from the provision of government subsidies. In addition to projects that are either too big (aircraft, atomic reactors) or too speculative (the hovercraft) to get finance from the private sector, the British Government does, through the Science Research Council and the National Research and Development Corporation, provide funds for a very wide range of research and development projects in order to stimulate industrial progress. Since January 1966 when the new investment grants replaced investment allowances in manufacturing and extractive industry, public expenditure has also taken over most of the stimulation of private investment previously done through tax allowances.

It has frequently been pointed out that the Government can encourage the growing points in the economy by purchasing, for normal official requirements, products that incorporate advanced technology, even if the balance of advantage in terms of cost and probable efficiency would tend to favour the purchase of a more traditional or an imported product. This might apply, for example, to items such as computers and advanced machine tools. In considering such proposals it is as well to stress, first of all, that it is dangerous to go far in the direction of requiring those who buy goods for the public sector to take into account considerations other than economy, which represents the optimum combination of quality and price in a product and is therefore the best working criterion of high productivity on the part of the producer. Indeed, the greatest contribution that those who buy goods and services for the public sector could make to the efficiency and hence the growth of the economy would probably be to become more effective purchasing officers on severely orthodox lines: changing suppliers whenever an advantage is to be had by doing so, exacting penalties for late delivery, breaking price rings whether by taking them to the court or by finding a supplier who will not be bound by their restrictions, and so on. The use of the US Federal Government's power as a major consumer of steel to prevent the American steel industry from raising its prices has provided a striking illustration of the possibilities. But the public sector in Britain now spends some 40 per cent of the national income, and the proportion in other Western countries is not far different, so that the continued and undramatic pressure of an active purchasing policy throughout the public sector could do a great deal to invigorate the competitive atmosphere and hence the growth of productivity.

Within limits, however, and for important and clearly defined objectives, it seems legitimate to use purchasing policy in a less orthodox way. The purchase of advanced items of equipment has already been referred to, and it should certainly be possible for some industrial sectors, selected on the grounds that the encouragement of their technological progress will be particularly conducive to growth, to be encouraged in this way. It should likewise be possible to strengthen the balance-of-payments position, when this is required, by, for example, instructing purchasing officers in the public sector, including the nationalized industries, to give some preference to products that are likely to develop export markets, when these are at least equally suitable for the purpose in hand and not substantially more expensive. The possibilities of export creation and import savings are further discussed in Chapter 11.

CHAPTER 9

PRICES, INCOMES AND THE LABOUR MARKET

Nowhere does the increasing scale of economic decision-taking units referred to in Chapter 1 raise more far-reaching problems than in the labour market. The driving force for centralization of decisions has not been the rate of technological progress, as in many commodity markets, so much as the search for more and more powerful institutions to match the bargaining strength on the other side of the labour market. The outcome of the growth of national trade unions, of monopolistic enterprises, and of national associations of employers, forming systems of collective bargaining, coupled with the maintenance of full employment as an objective of governmental policy since the Second World War, has been a persistent inflation of money incomes and therefore of prices in almost all Western countries, and not least in Britain. These circumstances have given rise to the adoption of national incomes policies in most Western countries.

An incomes policy may be defined as an attempt to influence the growth in the general level, and the distribution, of money incomes by central intervention in the processes of income determination. A similar intervention may also be made, either independently or simultaneously, in the formation of prices. The objectives of such interventions are threefold. First, in countries that have little foreign trade, or which have a favourable balance of payments, an incomes policy may be desired solely in the interests of internal price stability, in order to avoid the economic and social problems posed by long periods of continuously rising prices. Secondly, countries seeking to maintain a fixed exchange value for their currency, and to avoid deflating the domestic economy, may have recourse to an incomes policy as an alternative means of tackling balance-of-payments difficulties. This second objective is often the most urgent, and it is in this connection that incomes policy is most clearly related to planning for growth. Thirdly, in addition to the desire for internal price stability and external balance, the objective of the just distribution of the national product, or the fair determination of the relative levels of incomes in different occupations, while it may not be in recent experience a primary motive for establishing incomes policies, is inevitably involved in the exercise, since it is impossible to restrain the general increase of incomes and prices without affecting relative incomes.

Just as there are various motives for an incomes policy, so the institutional pattern for effecting this central intervention takes many forms. This is not the place to give a full description[1] of the many different kinds of incomes policy institutions in various countries. Probably the main distinctions lie between special arbitration courts, as in Australia and New Zealand, permanent bipartite or tripartite conferences, as in Holland and Sweden, and special committees, councils or commissions, which have been favoured in Britain. In addition to the complexity of institutions, the actual method of operation of an incomes policy varies very considerably, both between countries and within the same country at different periods. Some of the most useful distinctions can be made between permanent and temporary incomes policies; between voluntary and compulsory policies; and between intervention in the process of negotiating agreements and intervention in their implementation.

Voluntary incomes policies are those which are agreed by national bodies representing, and securing the approval of, the majority of employers and employees. Compulsory incomes policies are those enforced by governments without the active co-operation of such representative bodies.

Permanent incomes policies, whether voluntary or compulsory, are intended to operate continuously for an indefinite period. Temporary policies are designed to meet a particular situation, and frequently have a fixed term of months set on them, at the end of which, though they may be renewed, at least they must be debated afresh.

Direct intervention of incomes policy in the process of wage determination occurs, for example, where arbitration courts decide on a particular wage claim, or where a central body determines the size of wage increases for particular industries. Intervention in the

[1] For such an account see the Appendix to OECD, *The Problem of Rising Prices*, Paris, 1962. Also, B. C. Roberts, *National Wages Policy in War and Peace*, Allen and Unwin, 1958.

implementation occurs when no attempt is made to intervene in the processes by which wages are determined in particular industries, but where investigations may be made and pressure or even legal compulsion brought to bear on the parties to dissuade them from implementing an agreement they have made or are about to make. But it should be stressed that these distinctions, though useful, are difficult to make in practice. Permanent incomes policies break down; temporary policies have a habit of lasting for long periods; it is not easy always to distinguish between the 'persuasion' required for a voluntary policy and the powers taken to enforce a compulsory one; while seemingly indirect policies may in practice involve a very close intervention in particular wage decisions.

INCOMES POLICY IN BRITAIN

There has hardly been a year since the Second World War in which it could be said that there was no incomes policy at all in the United Kingdom. In the early postwar years reliance was placed largely on compulsory arbitration of wage claims and other industrial disputes, which had been instituted during the war under the National Arbitration Tribunal, and extended until 1951. But since this institution was increasingly ineffective, it was transformed into the weaker Industrial Disputes Tribunal in 1951 and completely abolished in 1958. Only one vestige of compulsory arbitration remains in British industrial relations: in the 'issues' procedure by which collective agreements can be enforced on a minority of recalcitrant employers. Compulsory arbitration in peacetime was very unpopular with trade unions, and a request to the arbitrators to 'take into account the national interest' came to be regarded as an invitation to throw out all wage claims. However, the possibility of a further resort to this method, even in the face of union opposition, could not be ruled out, if other methods of controlling the rise of money incomes had failed, and the situation was serious enough.

Apart from this postwar hangover of compulsory arbitration, British incomes policy between 1945 and 1966 has taken the form of a series of temporary policies to meet particular crises. On three occasions the situation has been deemed to require a temporary, but complete, cessation of all except the most exceptional wage increases: the 'wage freeze' of 1948–50, the 'pay pause' of 1961–2, and the incomes and prices freeze of 1966–7. The first was supported by the TUC, and initially secured widespread co-operation from the trade unions. It eventually broke down when the pressures became too great and union co-operation evaporated. The second was imposed by the Government, and was most effective in the public sector where the Government is the employer. The third obtained reluctant acceptance by both the TUC and the CBI, though with strong minority opposition on both sides of industry, and indeed in Parliament. There have also been three periods in which the Government has tried to impose some restraint on the rate of increase of incomes, without freezing them entirely. In 1957–9 the Council on Prices, Productivity and Incomes, an entirely government-appointed body, tried to influence particular wage decisions by investigating and publishing reports. In 1962–4 the 'pay pause' was followed by a period of restraint in which the National Incomes Commission, a body which contained employers' but not trade unionists' representatives, performed a similar function. Finally, in 1964–6, this time before the wage freeze, the Government attempted to restrain the rise of incomes and of prices through the National Board for Productivity, Prices and Incomes. This time the Government had secured the co-operation of the TUC, as well as of the CBI.

Before the formation of the NEDC in 1962, the various incomes policies were not specifically linked to a growth objective, though the connection had begun to be realized. Even without a plan for growth, intervention in the determination of incomes had been seen to be necessary for price stability and for balance-of-payments equilibrium. But the need for an incomes policy becomes more explicit in the context of a national programme, and the establishment of the new planning machinery in Britain intensified the search for a permanent incomes policy. In the British context, the balance of payments was seen as undoubtedly the prime constraint on growth; price differentials between Britain and her chief foreign competitors were seen as a major influence on exports and the balance of payments; and, following the rather unsatisfactory experience of monetary policy in the 1950s, governments tended to turn more and more towards incomes policy as a means of holding down British prices.

The NEDC expressed the need for stability of prices in the interest of achieving faster economic growth first and foremost in terms of shares in world trade. Their plan for the growth of the economy to 1966 required that, if exports were to reach the necessary level by 1966, the British share in world exports of manufactures had to be maintained, if not increased. This share had in fact fallen since the early 1950s, from 21 per cent in 1953 to 15·2 per cent in 1962. Although due attention was paid to competitiveness on non-price factors such as quality, design, sales effort, delivery dates and credit, a key factor was thought to be the relative prices of British exports.[1] Even in the previous years of fairly rapid price increases in some of the main competitors in Western Europe, British exports had shown no appreciable improvement in competitiveness. It appeared, there-fore, all the more important, since inflation was being brought under control in several European countries, for the British price level to be kept down. This was all the more urgent in that there was evi-dence of a tendency for British export prices to be depressed below the level of prices in the home market, a tendency which made ex-porting unattractive to businessmen compared to selling in the home market. Relating the problem of export prices to the growth of out-put and earnings, the NEDC noted that between 1953 and 1961 British export prices rose faster than those of our competitors largely because wage costs per unit of output rose about 3 per cent per annum faster. They did so for two reasons: first, because productivity rose between 1·5 to 2 per cent more slowly, that is because the British economy grew more slowly; and secondly, because money wage earnings rose from 1 to 1·5 per cent faster. The NEDC's plan for 4 per cent growth, if achieved, would itself have helped to create the relative price conditions in which its export requirements could have been met. But the increase in the rate of growth of productivity would not have been enough to fill the whole gap between Britain and her competitors in respect of the growth of productivity. A gap of 0·5 to 1 per cent would still have been likely. Moreover, the operation of the economy at a higher level of demand (also recom-mended by the NEDC) might tend to increase the pressure for wage increases. To fill the remaining gap in the increase of productivity, and the continuing and possibly worsening gap in the rate of increase in earnings, it was natural to turn to some form of incomes policy. According to the NEDC plan for 1962–6 productivity would rise at 3·25 per cent per annum between 1962 and 1966, which would

[1] There is sometimes a remarkable confusion between the 'real' factors of quality, delivery, etc., and the 'economic' factor of price. It is implied that evidence could show that one or the other is the cause of sluggish exports. But both are involved at all times: they are not rival but complementary explana-tions of the volume of exports.

permit an increase of earnings at about the same rate while keeping prices stable. If prices continued to increase in other countries, there might even be some improvement in the competitive position. But earnings had in the past risen by 5 to 6 per cent per annum, leaving a gap of around 2 to 2·5 per cent above even the planned rate of increase of productivity. Unless the growth rate could be put up to as high as 6 to 7 per cent, which was impossible on account of other constraints, an incomes policy appeared essential to the logic of the plan for growth.

The NEDC, therefore, always regarded prices and incomes policy as one of its major concerns, though it was forced to tread warily on this delicate ground. Attempts merely to make pronouncements on the need for restraint in the determination of incomes were rejected by the TUC representatives at a meeting of the NEDC early in 1964. A report, published shortly after, did no more than restate the necessity of an incomes policy.[1] Though understandable, this was not a very satisfactory result. There was not much point in repeating that everyone shared the responsibility of avoiding inflationary price and wages increases, when there was no machinery even for influencing specific determination. That the NEDC was not able to make progress in 1963–4 on working out any such detailed arrangements was not surprising. What was dangerously unrealistic was the apparent dependence of the whole programme on the assumption not merely that there would be an effective incomes policy, but that it would actually succeed in making British exports more competitive within the period of the plan for growth.

The role of incomes policy in the DEA's National Plan was very similar to the part it had played in the NEDC's pioneering venture. The planned growth of the gross domestic product to 1970 of 3·8 per cent per annum, plus the objectives of maintaining some overseas aid and investment while transforming a balance-of-payments deficit into a substantial surplus, required that the volume of exports should grow at 5·25 per cent per annum, in contrast to the growth of only 3 per cent per annum in the previous decade. Part of this gap could, it was thought, be filled as a result of favourable trends in the pattern of exports by commodites and by markets, but over half would have to be made up by an improvement in competitiveness. The DEA, though presented with a problem similar to that of the NEDC, came on it at a much less favourable phase in the business cycle. Whereas

[1] NEDC, *The Growth of the Economy*, HMSO, March 1964, paras 40 and 41.

I

the National Incomes Commission had become more and more disregarded in 1963-4, it was urgently necessary to have an effective incomes policy to see the country through the economic crisis which became apparent on the formation of the new Labour Government. At the same time, the Government took the decision to attempt to create the conditions for a permanent and voluntary incomes policy, with a view to the needs of the whole period of the National Plan and beyond, rather than to impose a freeze that could only be temporary and might jeopardize the chances of establishing a more permanent policy. The necessary compromise between the immediate and the long-term requirements took the form of establishing the long-term policy at great speed so that it could make as early a contribution as possible to the solution of the immediate difficulties. By December 1964 the Government had obtained what no previous government had: an agreement in principle by both the CBI and the TUC on the setting up of a new incomes and prices policy.[1] This was rapidly followed early in 1965 by agreement on the machinery for the policy, and by an agreed statement of the principles which should govern it.[2] In April 1965 the National Board for Productivity, Prices and Incomes (PIB) was established under the chairmanship of Mr Aubrey Jones. It was given the powers of a Royal Commission to demand evidence, and was to operate in two Panels, one for prices and the other for incomes. The 'norm' for wage increases was 3·5 per cent, which was the same rate of increase as that indicated for productivity in the National Plan. The board produced its reports with commendable speed[3] and, though it had no formal powers to enforce its conclusions, undoubtedly helped the DEA and other departments to exercise effective pressure, especially on prices. On the wages side a collision with the National Union of Railwaymen was averted at the last moment, but in May 1966, after the Government had been confirmed in office by a second election, an attempt to apply the policy to a wages and hours claim by the National Union of Seamen resulted in a prolonged strike. The Government held firm, however, refusing to allow the employers to offer more than was thought

[1] Joint Statement of Intent on Productivity, Prices and Incomes.

[2] HMSO, *Machinery of Prices and Incomes Policy*, Cmnd. 2577; and HMSO, *Prices and Incomes Policy*, Cmnd. 2639.

[3] To February 1968 no fewer than fifty-five reports had been published, roughly equally divided between wage and price references. They covered a wide range of issues: productivity, wages and salaries, professional emoluments, costs and prices, in public and private firms.

consistent with the policy. But the overall experience on the wages side had been unsuccessful. In 1965 hourly wage rates rose by 7 per cent,[1] that is, at twice the norm, and prices had risen by 2·5 to 3 per cent. As a result a process of escalation occurred, as the policy was tightened up in a series of steps. First, the Government introduced, with the consent of the CBI and the TUC, a voluntary 'early warning system', whereas all price increases, and all wage claims, would be notified in advance, to give an opportunity for them to be referred to the Prices and Incomes Board if this should be thought desirable.[2] For this purpose the TUC acted as a vetting agency on behalf of the Government in respect of wage claims. When it appeared that voluntary notification would not be adequate, the Government introduced a Bill to give itself powers to require notification and to delay any increases pending a report from the PIB, and providing penalties for non-compliance. Then, while this Bill, delayed by the General Election of March 31, 1966, was still before Parliament, the exacerbation of the economic crisis in July 1966 led to the superimposition of a complete freeze on all incomes and prices for a period of six months, to be followed by a further six months of severe restraint through the operation of a 'nil norm'; all of this was effected by amending the Prices and Incomes Bill already before Parliament. Thus the attempt to establish a voluntary and permanent indirect prices and incomes policy had to be interrupted. While the introduction of compulsion was not on the face of it helpful to the longer-term exercise, the Government's intention was to take up the permanent policy again at the end of the emergency period, and it would be a mistake to be so influenced by the events of 1966–8 as to write off the whole effort of 1964–6 as a failure. This phase was a logical development in the postwar history of economic policy, and, though always controversial, reflected widely held feelings in all political parties, and on both sides of industry.

INCOMES POLICY IN FRANCE

The state of industrial relations in France after 1945 was extremely backward and chaotic. The trade union movement was bitterly divided at every level on religious and political grounds, in marked contrast to the well organized National Employers' Council. Wages

[1] DEA, *Progress Report* No. 12, December 1965.
[2] HMSO, *Prices and Incomes Policy: an Early Warning System*, Cmnd. 2808.

were fixed by the Government during the war and not until 1950 was the principle of collective bargaining introduced as the basis for wage determination. Even after 1950 the State retained very considerable powers both as the employer in a large public sector and by means of a series of laws defining the conditions for wage agreement including the appointment of the workers' representatives at factory level. In practice, however, actual earnings were the outcome of detailed bargaining between employers and trade unions (by-passing the appointed representatives) at the level of the individual plant or firm, and in many cases were much higher than the wage rate determined by collective agreements at district or national level. In the public sector the Government was in sole control and on several occasions deliberately held back wage and salary increases in an attempt to halt the general rise in prices.

The official approach to an incomes policy was one of the many aspects of French economic life which was profoundly altered by the Common Market. In the 1950s, although incomes grew faster than productivity, the problem in France was demand rather than cost inflation, and the import and exchange controls and devaluation made the economic effects of the rapid rise in prices a less serious matter than in other countries. The increased foreign competition introduced by the Common Market compelled the authorities to pay much closer attention to the relative level of French costs and prices. The Fourth Plan noted that 'some Western countries such as Holland, whose dependence on international trade makes it particularly sensitive to instability of prices, apply an incomes policy. In view of our increasing participation in international trade the same cause will tend to produce a similar effect in France.'[1] A second source of pressure was the desire of the planners in the Fourth Plan to encourage social investment at the expense of private consumption. This could be achieved only by keeping the growth of incomes under some kind of discipline.

The planners, under pressure from the Ministry of Finance, were extremely discreet about proposing any action. Emphasis on the need for an incomes policy in the Fourth Plan was coupled with a strong denial of any intention to interfere in the process of free wage bargaining.[2] The plan proposed both the establishment of a special

[1] IVᵉ Plan, Tome 1, p. 48.
[2] See P. Bauchard, La Mystique du Plan, Paris 1963, Chapter 9. In this stimulating and entertaining discussion of French planning M. Bauchard points out

commission to examine the statistical and conceptual problems involved in working out an incomes policy (French trade unions are deeply suspicious of government calculations in this field), and a *rendezvous* in September 1962 under the aegis of the Conseil Supérieur du Plan between the Government, the employers and the trade unions, which would be repeated annually. The meeting was held in a reasonably favourable atmosphere despite strong reservations on the part of both employers and trade unions, but no concrete recommendations were made. In March 1963, the widespread strikes in the public sector led to the appointment of a three-man *comité des sages*, chaired by M. Massé, to act as arbiter in the dispute.

In his settlement of the dispute M. Massé emphasized the urgent need to introduce some reasonable negotiating machinery in the public sector. The absence of any such procedures and slower rate of growth of incomes in the public sector (excluding the civil service) had created an atmosphere of intense distrust among the trade unions and made industrial action the almost inevitable outcome of any dispute. In October 1963, the Government appointed M. Jean Toutée, a Conseiller d'Etat, to head another three-man inquiry into the problems of wage negotiations in the public sector. The report of the inquiry suggested regular meetings involving the official statistical agency the Institut National des Statistiques Économiques et Financières (INSEE) in order to work out an agreed statistical basis on which discussions and negotiations about incomes (and costs and prices) could proceed. This was far from being simply a technical point for, as has been pointed out, French trade unions have long been sceptical of the official price and income indices and much time was spent on detailed, inconclusive statistical argument. Secondly, the Toutée report proposed that the Government should fix annually the total amount that each public corporation should grant in wages and salaries within which more detailed negotiations could take place.[1]

---

that the planners were anxious to have a firmer commitment by both the Government and the trade unions to an agreed rate of growth by incomes, but the Ministry of Finance were concerned that the unions would not honour any agreements.

[1] For more detailed accounts see the Toutée Report: *Mission sur l'Amélioration des Procédures de Discussions des Salaires dans le Secteur Publique*, La Documentation Française, Notes et Etudes Documentaires, No. 3069; and J. E. S. Hayward, Interest Groups and Incomes Policy in France, *British Journal of Industrial Relations*, Vol. IV, No. 2, July 1966.

Both M. Massé and M. Toutée prefaced their recommendations by an insistence that in both the public and private sectors a permanent incomes policy had to be worked out and they went on to argue that it should be done in the context of the National Plan. The Government had accepted this argument after the Massé enquiry and took steps to implement it while the Toutée Commission was carrying out its work by convening a second incomes conference.

The second incomes conference was held from October 1963 to January 1964 at the conclusion of which M. Massé, the chairman, presented a personal report outlining his views on the future shape of an incomes policy.[1] He put forward three main proposals. First, the Fifth Plan (1966–70) would contain forecasts formulated in value as well as volume terms if the necessary statistics could be produced sufficiently quickly. Parallel to the investment and production targets, calculations would be made for the different categories of income and expenditure, including profits and public sector transactions, indicating the rates of growth compatible with the objectives of the plan. The key job of working out the criteria on which these growth rates should be based was to be given to the Conseil Economique et Social. Secondly, the annual economic budget, which reviews the annual progress of the plan, would include a review of these calculations in the context of the performance of the economy and the circumstances of particular sectors. Thirdly, Massé recommended the establishment of a Collége d'Etude et d'Appréciation des Revenus (CEAR) composed entirely of independent representatives selected by virtue of their competence. This body, which represented a conscious attempt to construct a French counterpart to the National Incomes Commission in Britain, was to examine the functioning of the policy for incomes outlined above. It would conduct inquiries into particularly significant cases and publish the results, although it would have no executive power.

The attitude of the trade unions to these proposals varied. The three main federations emphasized again their difficulty in participating in a plan which was in fact designed to increase investment and production. The most co-operative, the Catholic Confédération des Travailleurs Chrétiens (CFTC), agreed that an incomes policy was a necessary element in economic policy, but it had to include some regulation of profits, and the State must limit its activities to setting income guide lines. They accepted that the financing of the

[1] This is the Massé Report referred to on pp. 94 and 268.

plan's investment programmes had to be assured, but they wanted to see more control over the amount and utilization of retained profits and the level of prices.[1] The Communist Confederation Générale du Travail (CGT) and the Socialist Force Ouvrière (FO) opposed any integration of incomes policy into the Plan on the grounds that this would mean that incomes were controlled at the same time as profits were increased in order to finance the Plan's investment programmes.[2]

ANNUAL AVERAGE RATE OF GROWTH OF INCOMES (PERCENTAGES)
AND OF PRODUCTION

	1954–62	1965–70
Wages, salaries and social benefits	6·3	5·0
Gross incomes of individual firms	4·1	3·1
Retained profits (gross of tax)	4·4	6·4
Other incomes (interest, dividends, etc.)	4·1	8·6
Gross domestic product	5·3	5·0

Source: Vᵉ Plan, Tome I, p. 189.

The long-term incomes policy ran into further trouble with the introduction of the Stabilization Plan in 1963. The Government was still sympathetic to an incomes policy integrated with the National Plan but in order to hold down costs it felt compelled to take direct, shorter-term action. In accordance with the Toutée proposals very similar norms for wage increases were set in 1965 for the publicly owned industries, gas, electricity, coal and railways, and pressure was brought to bear on employers in the private sector not to exceed this figure. Despite increases in the minimum industrial wage and promises to strengthen the role of the trade unions in the bargaining procedures, the trade unions saw in this action exactly the authoritarian approach they feared.

---

[1] This was a restatement of the position outlined in the report produced by the CFTC in 1959 in which it stated in detail the difficulties in the way of effective trade union participation in the Plan. See *Rapport sur le Programme Economique de la CFTC*, Paris, 1959.

[2] For a good short summary of the three viewpoints, see *Le Monde*, August 5–6, 1962, p. 5.

The Fifth Plan, not surprisingly, continued to be discreet. The major technical innovation of 'value planning' indicated that the growth of various categories of incomes which the planners had calculated were compatible with the proposed growth in the volume of national output and an annual increase in the general price level restricted to 1·5 per cent (see table on preceding page).

No attempt was made at more detailed indicators although work on this was continuing. The above figures were not 'targets' to be imposed on any section of society; indeed, the Plan specifically stated that even a contractual incomes policy based on them was not at the time feasible. There was to be an annual examination of the growth of incomes as part of the economic budget, and the Government, in consultation with employers and trade unions, would try to agree on the desirable growth rates for the following year. M. Massé's proposal for an independent commission on the lines of the British National Incomes Commission is still in abeyance, having been rejected by the Conseil Economique et Social, but the Fifth Plan proposed a variant of it in the form of a Centre d'Etudes des Revenus. This body would examine test cases either on its own initiative or on the basis of suggestions from the Conseil Economique et Social. The Government would, however, reserve the right not to implement its proposals and to withhold publication of any of its reports. An active incomes policy has, therefore, still to come despite the increasing technical sophistication of the planners. The option of the Fifth Plan for a large increase in productive investment, which requires both distributed and undistributed profits to grow faster than wages, and the very low 'target' for price increases look impossible to achieve without one. But the idea of holding down the rate of growth of wage and salary incomes and consumption in order to allow public and private investment to expand is hardly one to which the trade unions are likely to prove amenable.

PROBLEMS OF PERMANENT INCOMES POLICIES

All that has been attempted up to this point has been to give a description of the connection between incomes policies and planning for growth in Britain and France. Central intervention in the determination of prices will be discussed later. Meanwhile, some examination of the problems involved in securing a permanent incomes policy is desirable. The policies described so far have been indirect: designed to bring pressure to bear on wage determinations from outside the collective bargaining system. There is reason to believe that a truly permanent policy would have to be a direct one: that is, that employers and trade unions would have to come together in some form of conference to allocate wage increases between different industries. The organizational structure of the trade unions, and to a lesser extent of the employers, poses great problems for the detailed working out of such a permanent incomes policy both in Britain and in France. In Britain the unions' structure is amorphous, with overlapping forms of craft and general unions, and a minority of industrial unions. Neither the TUC nor the CBI have significant powers over their affiliated organizations. Where incomes policies of the kind under discussion have been attempted in other countries, they have been based on a structure of industrial relations and institutions much more favourable to central decisions than exists in Britain. These countries, for example Sweden and Holland, are also much smaller than Britain. In Sweden the State has remained aloof from the collective bargaining process as far as possible. But the existence of a powerful central Labour Federation (LO) and a similarly powerful Swedish Employers' Confederation (SFA) has allowed the development of national wage negotiations for the whole economy. A central meeting of these two bodies sets a 'frame agreement' for an average percentage increase in wages, and it is then up to the individual industries to negotiate how to distribute this increase among different classes of workers. The LO and the SFA both have considerable sanctions against any unions or employers who move out of line with the frame agreement. The SFA pays out of its funds compensation for firms which are hit by strikes, if it approves their policy, but equally may levy fines for non-compliance with the central policy. The LO similarly holds a large central strike fund, and unions wishing to call out more than 3 per cent of their members have to get permission from the LO. Under Swedish labour law unofficial strikers face the prospect of legal action by employers for losses suffered. The internal organization of unions in Sweden also puts much more power into the hands of the leaders. The national executives have powers of decision on strike action, without a ballot of their members, and union officers are elected by delegates to annual conferences on a representative basis, and not by votes of the whole membership as in many British unions. Tremendous changes in internal union organization, in the powers given by the individual unions and employers' associations to their central organizations, and in the legal basis of industrial relations, would still be needed before Britain could apply a Swedish type of incomes policy.[1]

These problems can be highlighted by considering the implications of any attempt to set up a 'frame' agreement for incomes in Britain. A bipartite conference of unions' and employers' representatives, or a tripartite conference including government representatives, would have to come to an agreement on the average percentage increase in wages that could be paid without causing inflation. Such an agreed average percentage would have to be related to the average expected increase in productivity over the whole economy. But this would be only the first, and easiest, step. It would also be necessary to make at least some broad decisions about how the average increase was to be shared out among different classes of workers or among different industries, and possibly in different regions. These decisions could not be too broad, or they would leave too much uncertainty in the crucial stage at which decisions of the conference were translated into actual wage bargains by individual unions and employers' negotiating organizations. The central conference would also probably decide such issues as whether, in general, that part of the increase of productivity to be allocated to labour should be taken out in the form of shorter hours instead of in fringe benefits or a straight wage increase. The delegates to such a conference would have to commit their members to specific proposals, with figures quoted. Some room for manoeuvre might be left, in the division of increases among different classes of workers, for example, and by allowing a certain amount of wage drift, but the biggest decisions on wages would be taken in this new body and not by the traditional collective bargaining machinery. At present neither employers' national associations nor the national executives of trade unions in Britain have the power to commit their members in this way. There is usually some provision in these very democratic bodies for reference back to the members of any decision arrived at in negotiations by the delegates. Even particular wage increases are often subject to ballots. Radical changes would be needed within employers' associations and within trade unions before the members would allow their leaders to commit them as far as would be necessary in carrying out a wages policy of this kind.

[1] The Report of the Royal Commission on trade unions was expected early in 1968.

Further changes would also be needed in the powers of delegates sitting on national bodies.

Economic planning under the NEDC and the DEA, and the effort to establish an indirect incomes policy, have drawn attention to these organizational problems, created a climate in which progress on them is more likely, and have already resulted in some advances. For example, in 1965 the Confederation of British Industries was created by an amalgamation of the previous three national organizations of employers: the Federation of British Industries, the National Association of British Manufacturers, and the British Employers' Confederation. This body is now able to speak for employers with at least the degree of authority that the TUC has in relation to the trade union movement. Although a merger of this kind had been discussed for some years, the fact that it finally took place owed something to the way in which the NEDC's and the DEA's work on the role of an incomes policy in relation to a plan for growth revealed, more clearly and urgently than before, the harm done by dealing with wage questions through the BEC and non-wage matters through the FBI and the NABM. There have also been a number of steps towards union amalgamations which will help to rationalize the structure of industrial relations in several industries where this is most urgent, above all in shipbuilding. The PIB has played its part in stimulating this progress, for example in its recommendation that the various unions in the printing industry should merge to form a single union for the whole industry.[1]

The second major problem in a permanent incomes policy concerns the principles on which the national incomes conference would allocate the permissible increase among different industries. If growth is taking place unevenly it would obviously be impossible to operate the same global criterion for all industries. Even if growth should, by some miracle, take place evenly across the economy, there might still be a case for faster increases in incomes in some industries than in others. There are two major principles on which increases may be allocated to different industries and groups of workers: on the basis of productivity and on the basis of comparability. Those concerned in planning for faster growth have tended to support the principle of productivity, since it enables them to use wage and salary settlements as levers in pressing for improvements in efficiency and faster growth of productivity. In

[1] PIB, *Report on Wages in the Printing Industry*, August 17, 1965.

Britain it has been stressed that the incomes policy is a policy also for productivity, and the PIB has concentrated attention in several of its reports on ways in which wage and other cost increases can be absorbed by greater productivity without leading to higher prices. The 'productivity agreement', the wage settlement in which increases in earnings and reduction in hours worked are related to and dependent on changes in working practices to improve the efficiency of utilization of labour, has become popular. Similarly in France, M. Massé recommended a system whereby the growth of incomes in each sector would reflect to some limited extent different rates of growth of productivity, and saw the existence of a long-term plan operating at the sector level as an opportunity to introduce greater rationality into wages policy.[1] But he insisted on a recognition of the many problems that are involved in using productivity as a criterion for wage increases. One danger, widely recognized in Britain, is that the productivity agreement often exchanges actual wage increases for promises of co-operation in increasing productivity, and it is necessary to see that these promises are fulfilled; otherwise the agreement is merely a device for avoiding the operation of the incomes policy. Moreover, productivity is not always easily measurable, and it does not always increase. There is a danger that wage increases in some industries, matching no more than the full increase of productivity in those industries and therefore apparently not inflationary, would spark off, on the basis of parity, claims in other industries which could not pay the increase without raising prices. This method might solve the problem of determining wages in a few favoured industries, where the rapid increase of productivity removes the difficulties anyway, without solving the overall problem, which is as much a problem of relationships between industries as it is of fixing wages within each industry. The productivity criterion is, therefore, of no value and indeed positively dangerous, unless it is clearly understood that workers in dynamic industries have to accept increases considerably smaller than the increase in productivity, and thus leave room, even if full parity is not granted for workers in less dynamic industries, for wage rises in sectors where there is inherently less scope for the growth of productivity (for example, nursing, teaching, police). As M. Massé puts it: 'An industry in which productivity is growing faster than the national average rate can increase the

[1] P. Massé, *Rapport sur la Politique des Revenus*, La Documentation Française, Receuils et Monographies, No. 47, p. 9.

remunerations of its factors of production so long as it plays its part simultaneously in lowering prices.'[1] Prices could then be reduced, given competition, in industries where the rise in productivity was large, thus counterbalancing the increased costs of those sectors where the growth of productivity is necessarily restricted, through no fault of those who are employed in them. On balance over the whole economy, prices could then remain stable.

The alternative criterion for dividing the permissible increase in incomes is that of parity or comparability of incomes between different industries for workers doing similar jobs. In principle this criterion includes all that is valid from the point of view of the individual worker in the productivity argument, for it takes account of the net advantages of one job as against another. Any extra effort, responsibility or mental strain, any improvement or deterioration in working conditions, that may be necessary to achieve high productivity, is taken into account in calculating the wage that is set on the basis of parity with other trades. In Holland the wages policy since the Second World War has been based largely on a national 'job evaluation' of this kind, though with some reference also to variations in productivity. In Britain this method has been widely employed in the public service, where productivity measurement is difficult or impossible, and a stream of official reports on incomes in government departments and public corporations in the late 1950s and early 1960s gave the impression that the Government were moving steadily towards the acceptance of the parity principle in determining incomes. However, with the emphasis on productivity since incomes policy has been linked closely with a programme for economic growth, the comparability principle has come into disfavour. It would certainly be impossible to recommend unconditionally that incomes policy should be based on comparability alone.

This is also very much the official view in France. M. Massé referred in his report to the problem of 'combining parity and differentiation', of finding the appropriate combination between a basic remuneration which could grow at the same rate throughout the economy, and varying surpluses taking into account the particular conditions and evolution of each activity. Too rigid an application of the parity criterion would have a negative effect on economic growth by removing the incentives to greater efficiency and flexibility,

[1] P. Massé, op. cit., p. 9.

which are required in a growing economy, with a changing industrial structure and changing manpower needs. The same point is made with some emphasis in the Fifth Plan. The indicated rates of increase for different categories of income set out in the 'value planning' exercise are not based on the parity principle. 'The norm for each category must be considered by itself, and not with reference to other categories. More precisely, no category can justify an increase above the norm set for it on the grounds that other incomes have changed in a certain way.'[1] The parity argument contains quite enough contradictions within itself to keep cost inflation going. It is always possible to find good arguments why, on the grounds of parity, group A should be paid more than group B, and equally, why group B should be paid more than group A. While productivity is a potentially quantifiable criterion, parity is essentially qualitative. The market mechanism, though it works very imperfectly, is superior to any committee in deciding how much extra should be paid for danger, dirt, inconvenient times, or any of the other advantages and disadvantages of different occupations. It is therefore not surprising that the PIB in its report on railway wages[2] rejected the comparability approach enshrined in the Guillebaud Report of 1960,[3] and strongly opposed the extension of this method of determining incomes outside the public sector. While there may be much truth in the contention that the reports of various committees and commissions recommending increases in the public sector on the basis of comparability were merely publishing convincing reasons for doing what everyone knew was necessary in order to overcome the shortage of labour in those occupations, it is perhaps salutary that the resulting tendency towards an uncritical acceptance of the comparability principle for less justifiable reasons has been reversed in recent years.

A basic requirement of whatever criterion is chosen for deciding wage increases is that it should encourage the movement of labour out of low-productivity and declining industries into high-productivity industries. If wages are based on revenue productivity, that is, not on physical productivity but on the value of the output as sold on the market, then labour is attracted to the industries where demand is growing fastest and the technical conditions impose

[1] Ve Plan, Tome I, p. 19.

[2] PIB, *Pay and Conditions of Service of British Railways Staff*, Cmnd. 2873, January 1966.

[3] Railway Pay Committee of Inquiry, Report, March 1960.

fewest obstacles to its being supplied. The physical productivity criterion is not so good from the point of view of the allocation of labour since it ignores the state of demand and also other elements, such as varying costs of other inputs, which affect the profitability of an enterprise and therefore its need to attract, and ability to pay, more labour. If the strict parity argument is used, there is no means of distributing labour through the economy into the most efficient places except negatively, as a result of the need to curtail output and lay off labour where the parity wage is greater than can be paid without increasing prices to a level at which revenue will no longer be buoyant enough to allow profitable operation. But redundancy can be a slow and painful business, and this leads to the demand for compensation arrangements to ease the process.

To operate on both criteria at once seems to complicate the business of arriving at decisions, and to open up possibilities of 'leapfrogging' as between increases based on productivity and others based on comparability. In practice, however, it is unlikely that any incomes policy would be able to avoid using both, since each represents a strong real pressure for wage increases. Since other elements that trigger off wage claims, such as the cost of living, and the sheer habit of an annual increase, are unlikely to be eliminated altogether, the final result is likely to be an unsatisfactory compromise, based on too many contradictory principles, and resulting in an increase greater than is appropriate to the growth of national productivity. In other words, the pressures for wage increases cannot be abolished over-night by setting up an organization. The same pressures which now operate through a multiplicity of organizations, and through the market, will still be at work in a single central national body.

PRICES AND PROFITS

A very significant feature of the development of thinking about incomes policy in relation to growth in recent years has been the attention paid to non-wage incomes and to prices. In Britain one of the main barriers to the implementation of earlier proposals for incomes policies was that they had been concerned only with wage and salary incomes, and not to any serious extent with the impact on prices of profits and other non-wage incomes. They tended to neglect the third objective of an incomes policy: that of a 'just' distribution of incomes. As the Trade Union Advisory Committee of the OECD argued: ' . . . there is nothing at all to be said for planning or guiding half the incomes and leaving the other half unguided and unplanned and subject to market forces of varying degrees of monopoly control.'[1] To be established, certainly to be effective over a period exceeding a few months, an incomes policy must extend from wages and salaries to cover other incomes, especially profits, and may well also need to be complemented by a policy for the regulation of prices.

Since there are such enormous obstacles in the way of direct control over non-wage incomes, proposers of a balanced incomes policy have often contented themselves with suggestions for indirect, usually fiscal, measures against non-wage incomes, as the *quid pro quo* for wage restraint. Thus the British Labour Party argued for years the need for tightening up the loop-holes in the income tax, imposing an effective capital gains tax, and possibly a wealth tax, in order to introduce the climate of 'fiscal fairness' in which it might be possible to hold fruitful discussions with the trade unions about wages. In so far as these fiscal measures would reduce net profits they would be open to many of the objections facing the direct measures of profits or price control, as well as introducing their own distortions. From the point of view of growth, the wealth tax seems to have most to recommend it, and it was indeed specially commended by the NEDC.[2] It would not only avoid the disincentive effects of a really effective income tax, and of the capital gains tax, but could be devised so as to give an incentive to the productive use of wealth, including all forms of assets. To those who feel that fiscal fairness already requires that tax reforms on these lines should be carried out, their use as a bargaining counter in discussing incomes policy with the unions is perhaps not very attractive, but such difficulties could be surmounted by levying the new taxes at appropriate rates.

At the end of the 'pay pause' of 1961–2, and the beginning of the period of restraint which followed it, Mr Macmillan promised to use fiscal and other indirect methods to restrain any excessive growth of profits which might arise out of the limitations set on the increase of wages and salaries. The Conservative Government had already

[1] OECD, *Policies for Prices, Profits and other Non-Wage Incomes*, Paris, August 1964, p. 17.
[2] NEDC, *Conditions Favourable to Faster Growth*, HMSO, 1963, para 170.

introduced a short-term capital gains tax in the 1962 budget. This was converted in the 1965 budget into a full capital gains tax applying to long-term gains also. The introduction in the same Finance Act of the corporation tax, separating company taxation from personal income tax, provided the Government with a further fiscal weapon that could be used in the indirect control of profits. As compared with the 1950s there has, therefore, been a considerable increase in the ability of the Government to impose sacrifices on profits. (The 1965 Rent Act may also be deemed to have a similar potential so far as incomes from rents are concerned.) But such general controls over profits have serious weaknesses. An increase in the rate of corporation tax, for example, levied at the end of a year in which profits as a whole are deemed to have risen too fast, would admittedly avoid the difficulties of individual profit controls, while keeping profits down to a 'fair' share in the national income. But its effect on incentives to invest is uncertain. While the prospect of a high average rate of tax on all profits might give an incentive to individual companies to raise their own profits to the highest possible level, a general feeling that tax would take an excessive bite out of profits might lead to a curtailment of investment and a reduction of efforts to increase efficiency. Moreover, this general manipulation of tax rates could do nothing to prevent individual price increases intended to increase individual profits: in so far as the prospect of a high rate of tax was an incentive to greater efforts to raise individual profits, it might indeed serve to accelerate such price rises.

In the development of British incomes policy since 1964 the Government has not, therefore, relied only on these indirect means of controlling profits. The 'freeze' of July 1966 applied not to profits, but to dividends. To the extent that the economic situation still allowed some companies to increase their profits, and therefore still gave them the desire to raise dividends, this control was a useful concomitant to the wages and salaries freeze. But control over dividends does nothing to restrain the growth of profits, which, if retained, add to the appreciation of capital, and may be received in the form of a capital gain on realization. Control over individual profits would be exceedingly difficult to administer, and so far as prices are concerned, would mean only that any autonomous rise intended to increase profits could be prevented. The policy would thus be limited to preventing any speeding up of the inflationary process arising on the side of profits: it could prevent firms from raising prices to a level beyond that necessary to offset a previous rise in wages or other costs; but assuming that a cost push inflation was already in being, this policy of controlling profits could, on its own, do nothing to stop it.

The difficulties of operating any of these proposals for controlling profits have led to a direct attack on prices. Again, there are grave problems. Direct controls over prices have been accepted in wartime and postwar emergencies and continuously up to the present time in France, but are highly unpopular in peacetime since they are administratively complex, tend to operate arbitrarily so as to cause great injustices, and are difficult to enforce. If people want something badly enough they are likely to find some means of paying more for it even though the Government says they should not. Price controls may also have a serious effect on innovation and improvements in design and the quality of goods, because it is not possible to adjust the controlled prices often enough to take into account such changes. Another problem is that most prices have to be adjusted from time to time, and long and costly investigations would be needed into the circumstances that justified increases. Such investigations could take so long that industry would be harmed by not being able to cover its costs in the interim, as happened for many years in the case of nationalized industries subject to delays in approval for price increases.

One way out of these difficulties of price control is to attempt to control only certain 'key' prices, such as those of basic industrial materials and fuel and transport, although this kind of partial price control operates inequitably as between one industry and another and could distort the profitability of industries and therefore the allocation of investments. Certainly, it appears as open to the criticism of unfairly sacrificing one sector as does the crude wages policy which does not apply to other incomes.

Another solution is the one that has been adopted in Britain under the PIB. It takes the form of controlling prices only indirectly, through the method of investigating particular price increases or proposed increases, and mobilizing public opinion in general, and consumers in particular, against increases that are found to be 'unjustified', by publication of reports and other forms of pressure and publicity. To a considerable extent this policy has secured the voluntary co-operation of business. Voluntary control of prices had been discussed in the NEDC, and it was accepted in the Statement of Intent in December 1964. A voluntary early warning system for price increases was also accepted at the same time as the similar system for wage claims. The CBI also reluctantly acquiesced in the prices 'freeze' that accompanied the wage freeze in July 1966. In judging price increases in the cases submitted to it, the PIB has pursued its objective of stimulating productivity by stressing the need to absorb cost increases, wherever possible, by increased efficiency. The fact that wages, or import prices, or any other cost, had increased, has not been accepted as automatically justifying an increased price. So far the PIB has, by Herculean labours, produced its reports with admirable celerity, thus helping to minimize the damage done by any delay in implementing justified increases.

Since the war official control over prices has been a much used weapon in France and is administered by the Office of Price Control in the Ministry of Finance. The Government also has the power to freeze prices, even if they have been decontrolled, to meet a particular situation. No restriction is put on the methods used and a number of methods are employed, involving both direct action on prices and varying degrees of limitation on profit margins. The regulations are enforceable at law and violation can result in closure of the offender's premises, imprisonment or fines.

After a period of widespread control after the war prices were gradually freed, though periodic use was made of temporary 'freezes'. By the end of the 1950s the area of control had narrowed to basic commodities such as wheat, coal, aluminium and steel. The reappearance of inflation in 1963, however, resulted in the reimposition of price controls on food products and some industrial products. Finally, in September 1963, producer prices for all industrial products were frozen. The machinery required to carry out this wide-ranging operation already existed.

The Massé Report emphasized the illogicality of having a plan for production, investment and foreign trade, which left incomes to be determined by market forces or monopoly power. M. Massé was at the same time cautious about advocating any generalized form of price or profit control. Certain proposals have been made that the profit margins required to finance the investment programmes of the plan should be calculated and inserted as target figures in the plan, but M. Massé did not go so far as this. The plan was aimed at achieving the fastest possible increase in production per head; this meant that the investment required to produce the increase must not fail to appear through lack of finance; it was therefore important that profits should not be too severely curtailed. A possible solution was one that the French trade unions demanded: the Government should exercise more control to ensure that retained profits were in fact used to finance necessary investment. The increasing importance of retained profits as a source of finance added weight to this argument. But M. Massé was not inclined to accept either global measures of control or widespread detailed controls on individual products, but to treat each sector as a specific case. He was sympathetic to the argument of the French Employers' Federation, that firms subjected to the intensified foreign competition introduced by the Common Market were already experiencing a very rigorous form of price and profit control. As a means of dealing with the problem in a selective way he recommended the creation of a Price Tribunal, which (like the PIB) would consider particular prices in the light of general economic conditions.

The Stabilization Plan brought the issue of price control to the forefront as the Government felt compelled to introduce a wide ranging price freeze on industrial products and later services mainly affecting industrial firms. This generalized imposition of controls was in marked contrast to the very nuanced proposals of the Massé Report and came under very critical scrutiny by the OECD. The report on Prices and Non-Wage Incomes gave a very hedged approval of the measures, seeing them as 'expedients aimed at correcting or reducing the effects of temporary disturbances of the market; they do not imply general and concerted action on the volume and distribution of non-wage incomes. Corrections by price controls such as these are usually temporary in nature and are not intended to cause radical changes in structure'.[1]

In view of the French history of controlled prices this conclusion smacks more of hopeful prophecy than objective judgment. It is in marked contrast to the opinion of Mr Shonfield who points to the price controls as an example of the ability of French officials to behave in an 'extraordinarily imperious' manner and to seize every opportunity to widen their control over the economy.[2]

Even if the point is not made as forcibly as it is by Mr Shonfield, recent developments make it difficult to disagree with his judgment of the planners' philosophy and strategy. At the start of the Fifth

[1] OECD, op. cit., p. 60.
[2] A. Shonfield, op. cit., p. 148 et seq.

Plan in January 1966, the Government modified the price controls by introducing *contrats de stabilité*: agreements between the Ministry of Finance, the planners and individual firms which allowed certain firms to raise the prices of some of their products provided they lowered the prices of others.[1] This procedure was extended in July 1966 with the introduction of *contrats de programme*. Under these much wider contracts firms or industries recover the freedom to determine the prices of their products on the condition that they discuss periodically with the Government and the planners their production, investment and export programmes and that they accept the earnings guidelines laid down in the Fifth Plan. Almost immediately the car, aluminium and electrical appliances industries accepted these conditions and further agreements have been concluded. In its survey of the French economy in 1966 the OECD observed that: 'It would be desirable to speed up the relaxation of price controls, and to attain, eventually, through the new approach to price policy expressed in the *contrats de programme* the complete removal of price controls. Conceivable as an emergency in periods of strain, such controls can in the long run only create distortions and irrationalities which defeat their original purpose.'[2]

There are several good reasons for doubting whether the French planners will in fact regard these agreements as a purely temporary measure. First, they were introduced in order not to jeopardize the investment targets of the Fifth Plan through an insufficiency of finance. Much of the investment programmes of the Fifth Plan are, however, very closely related to the objectives of structural reform, the promotion of exports and the provision of aid to increase expenditure on research and development. In order to achieve these objectives the planners have explicitly accepted the need to depart from the market mechanism. They may well, therefore, regard the *contrats de programme* as a very convenient method of pursuing these objectives while at the same time using the agreements as a means of avoiding some of the disrupting and distorting effects of permanent, *unselective* price controls. This is particularly likely given the other factors which are tending to weaken the planners' control over the private sector and given the importance of the industries which have accepted the new agreements.

It should be remembered, in the second place, that the French

[1] See p. 104.
[2] OECD, *Economic Surveys*, France, May 1967, p. 36.

planners have had long experience of dealing with private firms on the bases of contractual arrangements conferring benefits on both sides and, equally important, that French industrialists have also had a long time to learn the advantages and disadvantages of this kind of control. At a time when finance is in short supply they may prefer co-operation with the planners to the illusory freedom of an, as yet, inadequate capital market and the threat of general action on prices in the event of inflationary pressures reappearing.

Finally, the planners are likely to be reluctant to give up a measure of control which permits them to mitigate the effects on investment and growth of unselective anti-inflationary policies whether in the form of price controls or the reduction in the level of domestic demand. They are, as has been pointed out, extremely keen to expand their influence on the short-term management of the economy as the uncertainty surrounding medium-term developments increases. A system of agreements involving prices and incomes at the level of the industry (and by strong implication the individual firm) may allow the planners to develop the 'productivity bargaining' approach to incomes and prices policy recommended by M. Massé and at least partly successful in Britain.

INCOMES POLICY IN GERMANY

So far this chapter has centred the discussion on incomes policies in Britain and France. No attempt has been made to integrate German attitudes and experience, since their approach to the subject has been until recently very different from that of the French and British. During the period up to 1966 it cannot be said that either the authorities or the public in Germany were so convinced of the desirability of attempting an incomes policy as they were in Britain or France. There seem to be two main reasons for this. First, the problem of inflation in Germany had not, until 1965–6, approached the dimensions it had reached in France and Britain; and secondly, the attitude of the German Government, employers and workers has not seemed conducive to the introduction of any elements of central control into wage bargaining. It would be far from the truth to suggest that there had been no 'wage problem' in Germany before 1965. Wages have in fact outrun productivity in most years since 1950. Before 1955, however, the disparities were only minimal. Even after 1955, when the gaps became bigger, and gave more cause for concern, they did not cause any acute difficulties. This was largely because of the sensitivity with which wage movements reacted to economic expansion, rising as production expanded and slackening as the rate of expansion fell. Thus the biggest wage rises accompanied, and were largely absorbed by the booms of 1955–6, 1959–62, and 1964–5. During the first two booms it was significant that wage increases were matched (in 1955) and even out-stripped (in 1959) by rises in productivity in the initial stages of the upswing, and only caught up with and overtook productivity in the later stages. The 1964–5 episode was different, and more serious, in that wages outstripped productivity at both the start and the finish of the boom.

A number of factors help to explain the differences between the German and the British situations. In the early years of the social market economy there was of course a steady flow of workers into Germany and the demand for labour was easily supplied. This helps to explain the relatively modest wage increases during this period. After 1955, however, Germany reached and maintained a level of full employment frequently higher than that in Britain, and this factor clearly no longer applied. A more lasting and compre-hensive explanation is to be found in the attitude of the German unions. Although violent views have been expressed from time to time by the German unions (by Dr Viktor Agartz, for instance), they have on the whole remained moderate in their campaign for higher wages and have nearly always had regard for the state of the economy as a whole. This was true particularly in the very early years of the social market economy when they were under the able leadership of men such as Herr Böckler, who saw that in those early years unemployment was caused by structural deficiencies rather than by cyclical factors, and that the only cure for it was more widening investment. To secure this increased investment Böckler was prepared to restrain the unions' demands for higher pay. Also, at this time the unions had turned their main attention to the struggle for co-determination rather than to the struggle for higher wages. Even since the achievement of full employment the unions have generally shown a keener awareness of the interaction of wage increases, productivity and the price level than most of their Euro-pean counterparts, and moderated their demands accordingly. It is significant that at the height of the inflationary difficulties ex-perienced by Germany in 1964–6, the expert committee on economic development noted that 'now as before the demand for labour has had a greater effect on wages than the pressure of collective bargaining by the unions. Even in the most recent past the unions have not pursued an aggressive wage policy, although the scarcity in the labour market has benefited their efforts'.[1] The very low number of working days lost through strikes and lock-outs in Germany— much lower proportionately than in France, Britain or the United States—is further witness of the German unions' more moderate approach.

The moderation of the German unions has sometimes been attributed to the 'weakness' of their organization. This is by no means proven. Although it seems generally agreed that German unions are less strongly organized at the plant level than their British counterparts, it can also be argued that German unions, of which there are only sixteen, organized on an industry-wide basis, are far less fragmented than in Britain and are correspondingly stronger. As early as 1950-1, the battle over co-determination showed that the German unions could fight powerfully and determinedly when they wished to. A more convincing reason for the comparative moderation of the unions with regard to wage increases is the greater sensitivity which both they and the Government and indeed most Germans share towards the dangers of inflation. The effect of inflation has been brought home much more forcibly to Germans than to most other European peoples. As a chairman of the German Trade Union Federation, Herr Rosenberg, has stated: 'You must realize what people in Germany understand by inflation. By inflation they mean one billion marks for a tram ride.'[2] If the shock of 1923 (and the suppressed inflation of 1945-8) was terrible, it has had some long-term advantages in that it has led to the unanimous agreement of employers, employees and the Government, that prices must be kept reasonably stable. If such a sensitivity could be induced, by less drastic but none the less forceful means, into other countries, the problem of cost-push inflation might be eased there also.

One further factor contributing towards greater wage restraint in Germany is the gradual introduction of automatic arbitration schemes in wage disputes. After several years of failure, representatives of the unions and of employers' federations were able to agree

[1] *Sachverständigenrat: Jahresgutachten*, 1965, pp. 7-9.
[2] Quoted by H. Götz, *Weil alle besser leben wollen*, Düsseldorf, Econ-Verlag, 1963, p. 264.

at Margaretenhof in 1954 on a system of automatic arbitration. This system had two elements: first, the automaticity of arbitration if wage negotiations broke down, and secondly, the obligation that no aggressive measures should be taken until the arbitration procedures had been exhausted. The Deutsche Gewerkschaftsbund (TUC) in Frankfurt in October 1954 endorsed this agreement, despite the opposition of the large Metal Industry Union. Soon after, the Metal Union itself entered into an arbitration agreement with its employers, though this did not contain any provisions for automaticity. When the metal workers struck in Schleswig Holstein in 1956–7, in the most serious strike that Germany has experienced since the war, the employers warned that they had broken the arbitration clauses of the agreement, and it was significant that the Federal Labour Court in October 1958 awarded damages against the union for this very reason.

One further institutional factor which has probably helped to moderate industrial disputes in Germany is the existence, as a result of the successive co-determination laws passed in the 1950s, of excellent machinery for consultation between employers and employees in most German firms.[1]

Turning now to the policy of the German Government vis-à-vis excessive wage increases before 1966, it may be said to have comprised three elements: the use of monetary policy, wherever the external situation allowed it, to prevent 'overheating'; the use of appeals for moderation and responsibility (Seelenmassage); and the policy of spreading property ownership. Of the first two instruments little need be said, for they are similar to those which have often been used in Britain in the past. The main difference would appear to be that whereas British governmental appeals for moderation have usually been greeted with scepticism, in Germany exhortation has evoked a better response as a result of the greater national consensus regarding the evils of inflation.

The third instrument of German policy deserves further mention. It is based on the belief that one major way, first, of preventing wage increases from leading to inflation, secondly of ensuring that sufficient savings are generated for investment purposes without the

---

[1] It is an error, however, to suppose that co-determination, as opposed to the provision of consultative machinery, is a neo-liberal objective. The strongest attacks on the idea of co-determination have in fact come from neo-liberal writers.

danger either of credit inflation or of excessive concentrations of wealth, and thirdly, of ensuring that labour's share of national income does not decrease in absolute terms as the returns from capital tend to increase, for example through the advent of automation, is actively to encourage and stimulate the participation of as many people as possible in the creation and holding of capital.

This is the basic premiss of the German Government's energetic and largely successful campaign to encourage savings by people of all income levels by means of extensive tax reliefs; to encourage by special premia the building of private dwellings as opposed to publicly-owned houses; to denationalize publicly owned companies and spread the ownership as widely as possible by means of 'people's shares' (*Volksaktien*); to give fiscal privileges to workers' shares; and to give incentives to employers, through both the tax and national insurance system, to provide workers with bonuses in the form of shares, savings certificates, etc. As Herr Theodor Blank of the German Labour Ministry has said: 'The Government is determined to work towards formation of wealth in the hands of employees . . . a plan of which one will say in the future that it was a turning point of social development.'[1] This so-called 'property policy' (*Eigentumspolitik*) is echoed by the slogan familiar in Britain of a 'property-owning democracy', but the Germans have pursued the objective with great thoroughness.[2] Although it has not been the major factor in abating cost-push inflation in Germany, it has undoubtedly played a subsidiary role.

What is the likelihood of some form of incomes policy being adopted in Germany? The idea of a productivity-orientated wage policy has been actively discussed there since 1955. It was firmly rejected in memoranda by the Scientific Council of the Economics Ministry in 1955 and 1960. The Council recommended instead a more energetic policy of spreading property ownership. Nevertheless in 1959 the Government made a tentative move toward establishing a guideline for wage increases when it asked the President of the Bundesbank to prepare a forecast of the growth of the economy during the coming year, chiefly with a view to providing an objective background for wage negotiations. The result was unfortunate. The Bank's report completely underestimated the future growth rate:

[1] Quoted by F. G. Reuss, op. cit., p. 247.
[2] See also pp. 66–8, where some of the action taken is discussed more fully.

instead of the estimated increase of 4–5 per cent at constant prices during 1960, the German GNP rose in fact by some 8·8 per cent. It was possibly as a result of this that Dr Erhard's Government did nothing to implement the subsequent recommendations of the expert committee on economic development, set up in 1964. In each of its first three reports (1964, 1965 and 1966) this committee recommended that guidelines based on productivity should be established for wage negotiations.

With the formation of the 'Grand Coalition' in 1966, the recommendations of the expert committee received official endorsement. In its declaration of December 13, 1966, the Government declared its support for voluntary 'concerted action' by both sides of industry to preserve stability in time of a cyclical upswing. The Government stated that it would carry out all the necessary preliminaries for such an action, and would in particular, in co-operation with the expert committee, place data at the disposal of both sides of industry to guide them in making their decisions, and discuss these with all concerned.[1]

A start has now been made on this policy of 'concerted action'. A number of meetings took place during 1967 between the Government and both sides of industry to discuss ways and means of keeping wage increases in line with productivity during the period 1968–71—that is, the period of the first medium-term budgetary plan—and at the same time to ensure what is called in Germany 'social symmetry'. These discussions have been based on the Government's programme that nominal gross national product should increase annually by 5·0 per cent or 5·5 per cent, the net income of employees by 4·4 per cent or 4·8 per cent, net business profits by 4·1 per cent or 4·6 per cent, and the net income of independent persons by 3·9 per cent or 4·3 per cent. At the time of writing no concrete decisions had emerged from these meetings.

A NEO-LIBERAL SOLUTION?

So far it has been assumed that an incomes policy must take the form of accepting that collective bargaining is organized through monopolies, and that what is needed is to control the monopolies in the public interest by even greater centralization. However, there

[1] The declaration of the Grand Coalition, *Frankfurter Allgemeine Zeitung*, December 14, 1966.

have been suggestions for what may be regarded as a fully neo-liberal solution: to press for structural changes in the direction of breaking up the monopolies.[1] Briefly, what is suggested is that wage bargaining at the industry level should be restricted to the setting of a national minimum rate, and that each individual firm should be left to set its own actual rate above this minimum. Of course, this is precisely what happens already, but the proposals involve one significant change from the present practice. At the moment, an increase in the nationally negotiated minimum rate is a signal for all the special local rates to be increased as well. The 'drift' is thus consolidated at each wage round. Under the proposals, local wage rates would be quite free of the minimum so long as they were above it, and an increase in the national minimum would not necessarily mean an increase in all the local rates. Each would be subject to negotiation between the individual employer and the workers in his establishment, and no employer could assume that if he increased wages, his competitors would do the same. The suggestion is therefore one for moderating the present centralized structure of wage negotiations and leaving more freedom for really individual bargaining. Such a step could cause more, rather than less, inflation if aggregate demand were excessive and the demand pull, the bidding of employers against each other for labour, strong. At such times the existence of truly centralized bargaining might even restrain the growth of wages. But assuming that suitable policies are used to moderate the demand pull and that the national minimum is so low as to contribute little to cost push, local bargaining would help to stop the tendency for wages to increase each year faster than the rise in productivity.

But this effect would depend on moving to real localized wage negotiations. In the United States employers are frequently 'localized', but the unions remain national monopolies. Negotiations take place between a union and the individual employer, but the unions concentrate on the 'key bargain' and the other firms in the industry usually fall into line. The individual employer may fear to be isolated as the one employer who grants an increase, so that his costs get out of line with those of his competitors, but he equally fears the strike which is directed against him alone, when his competitors may steal his market. So through the following of the 'key bargain', the results of firm-by-firm negotiations in the United States are commonly not

[1] See for example, D. J. Robertson, *A Market for Labour*, Hobart Paper No. 12, IEA, 1961.

very different from those of industry-wide bargaining in Britain. The reason for the lower rate of increase of prices in the United States may be sought rather in their much higher percentage of unemployed than in differences in the industrial relations structure.

The case for localization of wage bargains is not so much their effect on the general wage round, as the possibility that industry and unions might be made more productivity-conscious by the linking of wage increases to actual or potential growth in output per man. The examples culled from the United States, and the few cases so far in Britain, of which the Fawley Blue Book is outstanding,[1] show that firm-by-firm bargaining may be most valuable in obtaining productivity agreements for the removal of restrictive practices. The broad theoretical connection between productivity and real wages may be easily seen at the national level, but it is at the level of the individual firm that the exact relationship between 'practices' and the wage level that can be attained is observed, and a mechanism for linking the removal of restrictive practices with immediate benefits in wage rates, hours of work or fringe benefits can be most readily devised. National organizations of employers and workers, and national determination of wage rates, sometimes prevent local agreements which could transform the prospects of several British industries. These possibilities may be obvious to those concerned at the local level, but the need to refer everything to London can prevent any real attempt to overcome the obstacles in the way of such agreements.

LABOUR MARKET POLICY

Labour market policy is a concept that could with advantage be adopted in Britain to comprise the wide variety of methods of improving the market for labour in order to be able to run the economy to finer tolerances, to increase the productivity of labour, and at the same time to fulfil some very important aims of social policy. One of the most significant items to emerge from the examination of obstacles to faster growth is the need for a comprehensive and systematic planning of the supply and use of labour. This has been especially true in Britain, where the growth of the total working population, even with the immigration of the early 1960s, has been slow. While regional planning is largely concerned with using

[1] See A. Flanders, *The Fawley Productivity Agreements*, Faber, 1964.

previously unemployed labour resources in certain parts of the country, it is also concerned with many matters other than the supply of labour: for example, the prevention and relief of congestion, the supply of suitable sites, and economies in expenditure on social capital (see p. 295). Similarly, labour market policy is concerned with many other aspects of the supply of labour than merely the mopping-up of unemployment and underemployment in development areas. It may be defined as that group of policies, so far too little co-ordinated, that are concerned with the efficient utilization of labour resources. Labour market policy thus embraces not merely the maximization of the crude numbers of the working population if this is found to increase growth of output per head, but also education and training, mobility, attitudes to change, and everything affecting the overall efficiency of the labour force over the whole country. Many of the individual policies may be designed for particular social purposes, but it has become clear that a policy of maximizing the growth of the gross national product requires an overall labour market policy. The link between labour market policy and a prices and incomes policy is that anything that increases the overall productivity of labour probably increases the chances of fulfilling wage aspirations without inflationary effects, while it is impossible to plan the improvement of the quality and flexibility of the labour force without considering the financial counterpart to the real factors.

The OECD, in their report on Labour Market Policy in Sweden, defined it as: 'a necessary element of an economic policy that aims at full employment, stable money and a higher standard of living. The labour market policy must try to even up the different parts of the market, both geographically and occupationally. Its functions can be described as a continuous striving to eliminate unemployment and satisfy the demand for labour by promoting adjustment between sections of over-supply and sections of over-demand.'[1]

The main objective of the Swedish policy is defined as to operate the economy much nearer to full employment than would be possible without this kind of direct intervention in the labour market, and to increase the productivity of labour. 'Attempts are being made to achieve these objectives through general economic policy measures and this would keep employment at a rate (say, 95 per cent) which would not give rise to any inflationary tendencies. The task of the

[1] OECD, *Labour Market Policy in Sweden*, Paris, 1963, p. 20.

labour market policy is then to provide employment for the remaining labour force through selective means directly affecting the individual worker and employer, so that a state of full employment is maintained.'[1]

The NEDC defined a similar requirement in their chapters on the level of demand, on education, and on mobility and redundancy, in *Conditions Favourable to Faster Growth*. They concluded that, though there were risks to the balance of payments, especially in the transition from a lower to a higher level of demand, on the whole it appeared that in the long run the balance of payments would not suffer from planning the economy at a higher level of demand, but might even improve because of the probable faster growth of productivity. They therefore aimed at raising the level of employment substantially over the period of the plan from the low level of 1962–6, especially by a vigorous location of industry policy designed both to lower the rates of unemployment and to raise the activity rates in the less developed regions. At the same time, they suggested that productivity could be increased by other measures which would reduce workers' resistance to change. In Britain then, as in Sweden, it is realized that general fiscal and monetary controls, however discriminatory between industries and between areas, need to be supplemented by more direct activity in the labour market, and considerable progress has been made in recent years in several areas: for example, compensation for redundancy and unemployment benefits, industrial training, and management education.

Sweden, however, appears to be somewhat more advanced both in recognition of the nature and role of a labour market policy and in its application in a systematic way. A National Labour Market Board (*arbetsmarknadsstyrelsen*) and twenty-five County Labour Boards consist of representatives of employers' and employees' organizations, and of the Government. Although, under these Boards, the detailed aspects of labour market policy are pursued by agencies similar to those in Britain, for example, labour exchanges, training centres, and vocational guidance offices, according to the evaluation by the OECD there is a great advantage to be found in co-ordinating policies through a central Board: 'The clear definition of their employment policy tasks has converted the labour market agencies from passive agents able to serve only limited sectors of the labour market; they now form an organization which seeks to anticipate the

[1] OECD, op. cit., p. 51.

changes in supply and demand for labour on a broad scale and to facilitate the adjustments of individuals and enterprises to oncoming changes. This policy has inspired confidence among workers in the probability of their placement in new jobs after loss of employment, and in financial maintenance during the adjustment period. The result has been a greater willingness on the part of trade unions and the people as a whole to support technological and economic changes which will benefit the national economy.'[1]

Many of the functions of the Swedish Labour Market Board are carried out in Britain by the Ministry of Labour, but a more positive and systematic labour market policy could be very important in helping to raise the rates of growth of productivity while at the same time keeping the price level more stable. It should recruit the support of neo-liberals as well as of neo-collectivists, since it implies breaking down the imperfections of the market and improving the supply of a factor of production. A particular example may be taken from the problem of general (not specific) training in industry. Here it would seem that the market tends to produce the worst rather than the best solution. In a free market, the most profitable course of action for the individual firm is to train no workers, and rely for recruitment on poaching from those who have been foolish enough to train them. Not having been put to the expense of training, the firm can afford to pay enough to attract them away from those who have. Hence no one firm has an incentive to train workers, and market processes minimize rather than maximize the supply of trained men. In this case collective action, enforced by legislation, to set up Industrial Training Boards and raise money for training by a levy on all firms in the industry, though it implies a restriction on the freedom of the firm, is necessary and desirable in the interests of the firms, the workers and the nation.

INCOMES POLICY: AN ASSESSMENT

The problem that incomes policy is designed to alleviate is, to put it very simply, that of a gap between the customary expectations of wage and salary increases based on monopoly power of trade unions, and the attainable rate of growth of productivity. It may be useful to spell out the logical possibilities for closing this gap. There appear to be three. First, an attempt can be made to alter the market structure

[1] OECD, op. cit., p. 69.

that has given rise to the excessive increases in the past. This neo-liberal solution is theoretically attractive, but, while something might be done by judicious reform of the law relating to the labour market, and by pressure for internal changes within trade unions and employers' associations, and in their negotiating procedures, it would seem unlikely that it would be possible to reverse the trend of the past century towards collective bargaining between nation-wide monopolies on both sides of industry. Certainly, there is no substantial body of opinion in favour of such an attempt, even in Germany where it would be consistent with other aspects of neo-liberal philosophy.

The second logical possibility is to restrain the rise of money incomes to bring them into line with the productivity increases. This requires the kind of institutional intervention defined as an incomes policy. The third possibility is to accelerate the growth of productivity up to the level of the growth of money incomes. A combination of the first two possibilities is to apply a norm for national wage bargains, through an incomes policy, so much below the rate of growth of productivity that plant bargaining necessarily becomes a much more important feature in the determination of wages. But it should be stressed that the norm required would be well below those that governments have ever attempted to apply (if the 'emergency' nil norms that have sometimes been applied are disregarded), in order to leave adequate room for this deliberate wage drift.

So far as the incomes policy approach is concerned, two main lines of objection have been put forward: that econometric analysis shows that it could in any event be helpful only in rather special circumstances in any country; and that the policy has not succeeded in the countries where conditions have been most favourable and where it has been most consistently pursued. We shall now consider these two objections to incomes policy, before going on to examine the prospects for the third solution.

Many economists have argued the first objection to any attempt to operate an incomes policy: that it is worth while only if the economy is to be operated at such a level of demand that unemployment lies within a very narrow band. For example, Professor Paish has suggested that above $2\frac{1}{4}$ per cent unemployment an incomes policy is unnecessary for the British economy since the pressure of demand is inadequate to create inflation, while below 2 per cent unemployment the pressure of demand is so great that it cannot possibly

K

succeed in preventing inflationary increases in incomes.[1] Within the band of 2–2¼ per cent the annual increase in wage rates is under 3 per cent and roughly equal to the rate of increase in annual output per head. While the econometric basis of this calculation is open to serious doubt, there is much to be said for Professor Paish's distinction between a minimum level of unemployment below which incomes policy is ineffective, and a maximum level above which it would be unnecessary. But this does no more than to set certain limits to the discussion of incomes policy, for there are good social and economic reasons for believing that it is precisely in the probably rather broad area between an ineffective and an unnecessary incomes policy that the economy should operate. There is evidence to suggest that these particular figures underestimate the pressure of wage demands even when unemployment is quite high. For example, the 1965 Report of the US President's Council of Economic Advisers concluded that 'Powerful unions can and sometimes do obtain wage increases that outrun productivity, even where the labour supply is relatively abundant.' To operate the economy with unemployment above the limit is to waste labour resources and reduce the volume of output, quite apart from the social objection; operation below the limit is impossible to maintain for any length of time. It is a matter of some doubt whether stabilization policies can keep the economy within this range but this would certainly seem to be their object. The British economy has frequently operated even within Professor Paish's narrow band in the 1950s and 1960s, and one may assume that greater success in combating cyclical fluctuations would lessen the fluctuations in unemployment. Moreover, the relevant range could not be a datum for all time, but must be shifted by alterations in the labour market. Indeed it should be expected that labour market policy will gradually increase the degree of utilization of labour by matching supply and demand in different sectors of the market, thus lowering the previous minimum of unemployment above which incomes policy is relevant. Labour market policy would not increase the pressure on incomes and prices, nor of course would it do anything to reduce it. But with labour market policy ensuring that the economy was operated to the finest tolerance so far as labour resources are concerned, incomes policy could then help to prevent this resulting in inflation. Incomes policy is

[1] F. W. Paish and J. Hennessy, *Policy for Incomes*, Institute of Economic Affairs, Hobart Paper No. 29, 2nd ed., January 1966.

therefore certainly relevant; the question is whether it can work.

Sweden and Holland are the two countries usually named as examples of the permanent operation of voluntary incomes policies over many years. Different methods have been used, appropriate to the institutional and social conditions in these countries, and many changes have been made within each country over the years. Whatever policies have been tried have failed, except on rare and brief occasions, to moderate the rise of money incomes sufficiently to stop the rise of prices. These small countries are, of course, highly dependent on international trade, they have probably 'imported' much of their inflation, and this makes it extremely difficult to assess the effectiveness *per se* of the operation of their incomes policies. But considerable internal problems certainly exist. Although the central machinery has usually succeeded in establishing agreed norms for wage increases in different sectors, these have been treated as minima to which the various local extras and bonuses have been added. The incomes policy has therefore failed to impose effective maximum earnings. Moreover, even centrally agreed minima have been raised faster in periods of high aggregate demand, which suggests that the pressure for wage increases has continued to operate through the central institutions as it does through the less centralized British organizations, though it may have been moderated. It has proved impossible for the LO-SFA in Sweden, or for the College of Arbitration in Holland, to stand out against these pressures without risking the breakdown of the whole machinery. So the only way to keep the policy in existence in these periods has been to keep it ineffective.

It would, however, be foolish to dismiss these attempts at incomes policies out of hand. There is some evidence that they may have succeeded in temporarily holding back the rise in wages at times when it was particularly urgent that they should do so: for example, in Holland in 1951–2, during the world-wide inflation that followed the outbreak of the Korean War. Such a temporary effect of an incomes policy could be especially relevant in helping the transition of an economy from a low to a significantly higher rate of growth: that is, during the period when investment is being expanded rapidly, and before it begins to yield higher productivity. A similar temporary restraint has been achieved in Britain without a permanent machinery for incomes policy by the 'wage freeze' of 1948–50, by the 'pay pause' in 1961–2, and by the incomes and prices freeze of 1966–7,

But such temporary restraints produced resentment and recrimination because of their inequitable effects, which could be avoided by a consistent and permanent policy. There is a significant difference between a permanent policy which includes a low or even zero 'norm' in a crisis, and a freeze imposed from outside the framework of a permanent policy.

The alternative possibility for closing the gap between wage expectations and productivity growth is to accelerate the latter. This is, of course, an objective of the quantitative national programmes with which incomes policies have become closely associated in Britain and in France. In addition to being an alternative solution, the planned increase of productivity can assist the effort to establish an incomes policy, since it makes it possible to describe the policy as one for the 'planned growth of incomes', rather than for wage restraint. The practical difference, if the economy fails to grow faster, is nil, but the case for an incomes policy is more readily accepted by the unions in the context of an economy at least theoretically geared to faster growth. A national programme, if realistic, also allows a more accurate assessment of the scope for increases in incomes, and provides some of the data about the economy which is needed in order to formulate the policy. The plea for an incomes policy is also much more effective if it can be argued to be a necessary condition for the attainment of a higher rate of growth.

From this point the argument has shifted towards the raising of productivity, not as an ancillary to an incomes policy, but as a separate policy in its own right, still with the same objective in mind: the avoidance of inflation. The higher the actual rate of growth, the more likely it is that expectations of wage increases that have become built into the economic system can be met without inflationary consequences. The target rate of growth of productivity in the plan published by the DEA in September 1965 of $3\frac{1}{2}$ per cent per annum was clearly inadequate to meet expectations of increases in money wages and salaries of about 5–6 per cent on average which have become habitual in Britain. Hence the need for an incomes policy. A more ambitious target, such as was suggested at one time by the Labour Party, would make the necessary limitation of incomes less drastic. For example, in the unlikely event that productivity could be accelerated to 6–7 per cent per annum, there might be no need for any direct limitation on the rate at which wages grew.[1] It was on

[1] Faster growth might cause some acceleration of wage increases, especially

this point that open disagreement occurred within the Labour movement concerning the crisis measures of July 1966. Mr Cousins, whose union, the Transport and General Workers, had been the outstanding opponent of the incomes policy from the beginning, and his supporters took the view that to deflate the economy, thus slowing down the growth of productivity, while freezing wage increases was harmful not only because of the immediate loss of output and damage to longer-term growth prospects, but also to the cause of price stability itself. The alternative they proposed was to do everything possible to accelerate the growth of productivity, thus bringing its rate of increase as near as possible to the expectations of wage increase. This dispute is another of the clashes of short-term and long-term considerations, and of internal and external requirements, which are brought out by the attempt to achieve faster growth.

Virtually every country in the world, whether or not it is adopting quantitative planning, is now operating, or attempting to establish, an incomes policy. It is just possible that all these countries are mistaken in pursuing price stability by this method, but the case for an incomes policy also appears very strong. There does, however, appear to be some danger to the general development of economic policy in the search for an incomes policy. There was an outstanding example of this in the advance announcement in Britain in 1964 of the new corporation and capital gains taxes before details had been sufficiently worked out. This was probably done in order to secure union co-operation and thus to help surmount the first hurdles in the race to an incomes policy. But the premature announcement led to serious embarrassment for the Government, as well as contributing to uncertainty in industrial and financial circles, and possibly also to speculation against sterling. The attempt to get an incomes policy clearly should not be allowed to lead the Government to accept too many sacrifices in other fields of policy. Attempting a permanent long-term incomes policy also has more general drawbacks, which are emphasized by the fact that the prospects of success are small. Provided that attention is not diverted from other, more certain, policies and provided that the prospects are properly discounted in any programme for the development of the economy, no

---

if it was brought about in part by productivity agreements. Hence it is not possible to assume that growth at the same rate as previous wage increases would be adequate.

harm may be done. Unfortunately, it is next to impossible for a government to talk about the possibility of a permanent incomes policy without giving the impression that it is hoping to remove the necessity of doing other more unpopular things, or of making greater efforts in other directions. When setting out to persuade employers and unions, the Government can hardly start by admitting that the chances of success are slight.

It is also important that a programme for growth should not take any credit for a not-yet-realized incomes policy, of whatever variety, into account in setting its targets. This mistake seriously affected the credibility of both the NEDC's and the DEA's programmes. There is always pressure on the Government to include the effects of an incomes policy in the programme, for the chances of getting an incomes policy agreed are improved if the incomes policy can be seen to be an integral part of a plan for growth. But the experience of the NEDC in 1962 to 1964 and of the DEA in 1964 to 1966 has shown that it is dangerous to juggle with too many hypothetical variables at the same time. If 4 per cent growth can be achieved if everyone believes it will be, and in order to believe this they must believe also in an incomes policy, which in turn is not possible unless you also believe in the plan for growth, the outcome is, to say the least, uncertain. In economics as in horse-racing, risks are multiplied by cumulative acts of faith. A surer procedure would seem to be to draw up a basic programme on the assumption of no incomes policy effect, together with supplementary plans showing the alternative growth paths on various assumptions about the effects of an incomes policy. The appropriate variant can then be taken out of its pigeon-hole as and when an incomes policy, together with other factors, is seen to be having sufficiently favourable effects on the balance of trade.

Incomes policies are just as relevant in countries which do not attempt to use quantitative programmes for influencing growth rates. A neo-liberal growth policy, emphasizing market forces as the best way of removing obstacles to growth, cannot ignore the monopolization of the labour market and its consequences. Measures to increase competition in commodity markets—for example, tariff liberalization, anti-monopoly policy, and control over mergers— have their corollary in policies to make the labour market also operate more efficiently, since an incomes policy is an intervention intended to help to avoid the inflationary consequences of monopolization of both sides of the labour market.

CHAPTER 10

REGIONAL POLICIES AND PLANNING

Regional policies have a longer history in Britain than that of national planning for economic growth, whereas in France both started soon after the Second World War. There is, however, a great gulf between such policies and full regional planning as part of a national plan for economic growth. Four stages may be distinguished in policy as it has actually developed. The first is the use of *ad hoc* policies to cope with particular locational problems, such as unemployment or congestion, in the particular areas or districts where these problems arise. The second stage is the assessment of locational problems as problems concerning whole regions, and requiring a policy for the region and in some sense a regional plan, as a framework for particular interventions and incentives. This, however, still does not constitute a fully integrated regional policy. The third stage is the integration of intra-regional plans for particular regions, whatever their problems, into a national plan bringing out the interrelationships between regions, and the impact in each region of what is happening in the others. The fourth stage may be described as the full implementation of regional policy, the breaking down of a national programme for growth into a series of regional programmes, so that the part of each region in contributing to the maximum growth of the economy as a whole can be organized. At the beginning of this spectrum of policies, the aim is primarily to solve a particular social problem, whether it be heavy unemployment or congestion, or the need for urban renewal, encountered in a particular area. At the end, the approach is different: it is to see that each region makes its full contribution to the national plan, though fulfilling its part in a national programme may also help to solve the particular problems of a region. In order to show the impact of national planning for growth on regional policy, and the contribution of regional plans to the overall national programmes, it is necessary to give some account of the development of regional policies in Britain and France, and to a lesser extent in Germany, both before and since the connection with national planning for growth became as prominent as it is today. This chapter will describe the policies in each country separately, starting with the relatively under-developed regional policy in Germany, continuing with an account of British policy, and concluding with France, where the regional policy is highly developed and closely integrated into national planning.

REGIONAL POLICIES IN GERMANY

In contrast to France and Britain, West Germany is a federal State, and according to the Basic Law responsibility for regional policy rests primarily with the Länder. This formal stipulation has not prevented the Federal Government from taking considerable action to promote regional development, and today it is probably true to say that Bonn represents the 'motor' of German regional policy, the Länder having shown little dynamism of their own. The Government's policy is not, however, in any sense as elaborate or ambitious as the French. Its main features would seem to be flexibility, decentralized administration and heavy reliance for incentives on special credit terms.

The main landmark in the Federal Government's policy was the regional development programme launched in 1951, with the objectives of helping the areas along the border of East Germany, lessening the gap between the economically advanced and backward areas in the country, and counteracting the wholesale exodus of population from predominantly agricultural areas. The programme's overall aim was to raise average incomes in backward areas by creating new employment possibilities, together with the infrastructure and services necessary for new employment.

Special areas were marked out to receive federal assistance through the programme. They were of three kinds. First there were the border territories (*Zonenrandgebiet*), which consisted of a strip of land about 40 kilometres wide running the whole length of the border with East Germany. There were several reasons, economic and political, why this area had to be assisted. Much of it had been cut off from its natural economic hinterland by the border; much of it was far from the main economic centres of West Germany and relatively backward; and prestige considerations demanded that

West Germany presented a good front to East Germany. For all these reasons aid to this area was, and has remained, an important part of the Government's programme. Second, there were 'development areas' proper, originally 'readjustment areas', which were considered to be economically backward. These were redefined in 1963 on the basis of three criteria: (1) the gross national product per head of working population; (2) the presence of industry (number of jobs per 1,000 inhabitants); and (3) the movement of population into and out of the area. It is estimated that these areas account at present for about one-third of the total area of West Germany, and that about one-tenth of the population live in them. Thirdly, there were 'development towns'—small and medium-sized towns situated in primarily agricultural or structurally weak areas, which were particularly suitable to be built up into economic centres for these areas, because of the functions they already performed. Since 1959 the express purpose of aid to these towns has been to help them to launch into self-sustained growth.

The most important of the Federal Government's regional policies has been the provision of long-term credit at favourable rates. Firms wishing to establish factories in development areas or towns receive credits at a rate of 3·5 per cent for fifteen years. Loans at a rate of 4 per cent are available for the modernization or extension of firms already situated in development or border areas. Loans at a rate of 2 per cent for a period of twenty years are available for local authorities and corporations to carry out regionally desirable infrastructure projects. Apart from these loans, made available from the Federal Government's budget, mention should be made of the credits for regional purposes which are provided by two federal authorities: the ERP fund, and the Federal Labour Office in Nüremburg.

The Länder Governments have the main responsibility for implementing federal policy. The authorities in Bonn—the Ministry for Internal Affairs is at present responsible for regional policy—lay down the priorities of federal policy each year and the Länder Governments receiving funds from the central Government must observe these priorities. The Länder have always been consulted during the formulation of federal policy. A regional planning law of 1965 attempted to achieve greater integration of Länder and federal policy by laying down certain general principles which both have to follow. It also formally provided for joint consultation between the two levels of government on regional problems, and established a consultative Council for Regional Planning which brings together about fifty representatives of interest groups and of the different levels of government, as well as experts, and is attached to the Ministry for Internal Affairs. The Government is also obliged by the law to present an annual report on regional planning to the Bundestag.

As has been mentioned, strong initiatives of their own have not been very noticeable amongst the Länder, and the Federal Government has frequently tried to jog them into doing more. It was not until 1964 that the first comprehensive Land Development Plan emerged, that for North Rhine-Westphalia, the most populous of all the Länder, and one of the most highly industrialized. The Plan was aimed first and foremost at reducing the extreme congestion of the Ruhr area.

The lack of initiative shown by the Länder can be at least partly excused by the gradual convergence of their levels of economic development in recent years. This was not so in the early years of Germany's postwar growth. Between 1950 and 1957 it was the traditional centres of Germany's industry and commerce which expanded the fastest: in particular North Rhine-Westphalia, Baden-Würtemberg, and Bremen. The rates of growth in the relatively backward agricultural Länder—Rhineland-Palatinate, Bavaria, Lower Saxony and Schleswig-Holstein—were all below the national average. Since 1957, however, this process has been reversed. Between that year and 1964 the rates of growth of North Rhine-Westphalia and Bremen have been well below the national average, while those of Bavaria, Lower Saxony and Schleswig-Holstein have all been above. In terms of production per head the position of these three Länder is now much closer to the national average than in 1957. Only the position of Rhineland-Palatinate has remained fairly static. Unfortunately an exact comparison of incomes in the various Länder is not possible, but the indications are that wage levels throughout Germany have also tended to come closer together and that this has been the result, not of concerted union action, but of competition for manpower in the less-developed areas, and of the diminishing significance of certain locational advantages possessed by the big industrial centres.

The tendencies for regional productivity and income differences to diminish has been accompanied by a lessening of structural differences. The recent advance of the traditional agricultural areas has not been made at the cost of an exodus of population and since the mid-1950s, when Germany reached full employment, the number of industrial establishments and those working in them has actually increased more rapidly in agricultural areas than elsewhere. Only those areas with a very high proportion of agricultural workers indeed have continued to show losses of population. Nor has this structural change represented simply an expansion of the traditional industries of these areas—much of the new industry has come from outside.

The incentives provided by the Federal and Länder Governments have undoubtedly helped this movement of industry into the less-developed areas. It would be rash, however, to relate it simply to these. The very period at which the movement started would seem to indicate that the search for reserves of manpower, combined again with the lessening attractions and advantages of the highly industrial areas, have provided the major impulse.

In conclusion, the regional policy of the Federal Government is a comparatively flexible one, which aims essentially at encouraging the industrialization of backward areas by means of credit at favourable terms. The policy is implemented by the Länder who also carry out their own, hitherto modest, regional programmes. There is only a small problem of regional backwardness in Germany at the moment in that for the last decade the more backward areas have been growing faster than the more advanced ones. The nature of the first Land Development Plan would suggest that the main problem at the moment is one of overcrowding and that it will be to cure this that future initiatives will be primarily directed.

REGIONAL POLICIES IN BRITAIN

In Britain, the legislation as far back as the 1930s had been based on aid to 'special areas', which were in fact quite large regions. The Distribution of Industry Act of 1945 extended these regions, and its aim was to secure in each of them a well-balanced and diversified industrial structure, in order to prevent unemployment.[1] The re-named 'development areas' were, if some smaller and later additions are excluded, large industrial regions, and, though there was at that time no formal concept of 'growth points', the new industrial sites

[1] *Report of the Royal Commission on the Distribution of the Industrial Population* (Barlow Report), Cmnd. 6153, 1940.

were in practice largely confined to the more favoured parts of these regions, as indeed had been the industrial Trading Estates of the 1930s. Thus, although there was no full regional policy for the whole country, the social problem of heavy localized unemployment was treated as a regional problem. The Distribution of Industry Act of 1958 and the Local Employment Act of 1960 abandoned the regional approach, and took a step backwards to the first stage defined on p. 296, namely, an *ad hoc* policy of bring aid to small 'DATAC' areas and unemployment districts, where unemployment was defined as being heavy. Although some of the previous development areas, especially in Scotland and the north-east, were liberally scattered with districts which were on the list maintained by the Board of Trade, the policy appeared, particularly in the recessions of 1958 and 1962, as a kind of 'fire-brigade', rushing help from one district to another, as districts rose above or sank below the official criterion of heavy unemployment.

The influence of the more recent emphasis on growth is seen in the reversal of the previous trend in policy for the location of industry. This change, which may be dated about 1963, implies, in part, a return to the regional policy employed in 1945 to 1955, but abandoned in the legislation of 1958 and 1960.

Official thinking has now returned to a regionalism not unlike that of the 1940s. Recent reports have considered the economic future of the whole of these regions, and envisaged the attraction of industry to 'growth areas' within them, rather than merely trying to alleviate unemployment when and where it is heavy. Thus we seem to be returning to stage two of the development of regional policy.

At the same time, the Report on the South-east especially, showing as it does the likely development of a rapid expanding region, has been seen to have serious implications for the remainder of the country, and especially for the regions that are trying hard to attract more industry. The questions are at last being raised which will lead on to the third stage of regional policy, the attempt to integrate the individual plans of each of the regions into a co-ordinated plan for the development of all the regions together. The machinery for this is being developed in the regional planning division of the DEA, and the Regional Economic Development Boards and Councils. And since the DEA also contains the economic planning division which draws up the national programme, the possibility of moving on to the fourth stage is clearly open.

The postwar policy for preventing regional or local unemployment in Britain was not entirely, though it was primarily, a policy of work-to-the-workers. Steps were also taken to encourage the movement of workers and their families permanently from areas of high unemployment to places where they would have a better chance of continuous employment. There were various measures, of which the most important was the Employment and Training Act of 1948. This chapter will, however, concentrate on the measures used to encourage the expansion of industry in areas of high unemployment.

This policy took three forms, which may be classified as deterrence, *accompagnement* and attraction. The first consists in measures to control the growth of industrial and other employment in rapidly expanding and sometimes congested areas, thereby not only relieving some of the problems of those areas, but also pushing industry out, with some chance that it might be persuaded to go to areas of high unemployment. The second is the policy of making areas more attractive to industry by improving local services and amenities, that has come to be called investment in infrastructure. The third is the granting of loans, subsidies or other aid to firms to persuade them to move.

The policy of deterrence was initiated in Britain under the Town and Country Planning Act of 1947. An Industrial Development Certificate was required to be obtained from the Board of Trade for all new factory buildings over a certain size. (This control had been included in the Distribution of Industry Bill in 1945, and seen as an accompaniment of the incentives provided to attract firms to the development areas. The clause had, however, been rejected, and between 1945 and 1947 the Government had relied on building licences to control the location of factory development.) Firms could not be forced to build a factory in a development area, but they could be prevented from building one in the location of their first preference, if it was a congested area, and then the various inducements under the 1945 Act might attract them to a development area.

In Britain as in France considerable emphasis has throughout been placed on a policy of *accompagnement* in addition to direct incentives. This policy of improving the basic structure of an area in order to make it more attractive to business has been essential in old industrial areas suffering from a structural decline in their basic industries. Here urban renewal has been a prerequisite of success in creating employment. Equally, however, it has been important to provide an infrastructure of services, such as housing and shops, road and rail services, power and water, in areas where industrial re-location was possible, but these services were either non-existent, as in the case of the British new towns, or inadequate.

Under the 1945 Act there was little direct financial assistance to firms, but in the late 1950s and 1960s it was gradually extended. The main provision of the Act was to allow the Board of Trade to acquire land, if necessary by compulsory purchase, and to erect industrial buildings. These were then let to firms at rents which were subsidized, but the actual provision of a building at a time when firms were finding the physical problems of expansion ex-tremely severe was probably a greater incentive to firms to move than was the financial help. The Board of Trade could also make loans to industrial estate companies for the same purpose. It could also acquire and restore derelict land, in order both to provide sites for factories and to improve the amenity of the areas. The Act also provided that the appropriate government department could make loans to local authorities and undertakings for the provision, where necessary, of transport, power, housing, etc. New Town Develop-ment Corporations carried out similar functions under the terms of the New Towns Act of 1946.

The chief financial incentive to firms in Britain to move to develop-ment areas after 1945 was a subsidy to the rents of the advance factories. There was a special reduction in rents over the first five years, and secondly, the rent after the first five years was based not on the cost of building, but on the commercial value of the factory, which reflected any locational disadvantages of the area. Thus, in principle, any excess of transport, or administrative, or labour costs over those in other, preferred, locations, would be offset in a lower commercial value, and hence a lower rent for the factory. Such studies as have been made of the effects on firms' costs of moving to development areas suggested that they certainly were not signi-ficantly worse off.[1]

Development areas
Section 4 of the 1945 Act gave power to the Treasury, acting on the

---

[1] See, for example, D. C. Hague and P. K. Newman, Costs in Alternative Locations: the Clothing Industry, NIESR, 1952; D. C. Hague and J. H. Dunning, Costs in Alternative Locations: the Radio Industry, Review of Economic Studies, Vol. XXII No. 3, 1955; and W. F. Luttrell, *The Costs of Industrial Movement*, NIESR, 1952.

advice of a Development Areas Treasury Advisory Committee (DATAC), to give grants or to make loans by way of general financial assistance to individual firms, where there were good prospects of eventual profitability. This requirement proved to be somewhat difficult to administer, and no grants and only a very few loans were given.[1] Apart from redefining the areas to which assistance was extended, the 1958 Distribution of Industry Act widened the scope of financial assistance to include commercial as well as industrial activity. Loans became, under this Act and the Local Employment Act of 1960, a much more active feature of the policy, reflecting the ending of the era of building shortages and consequent licensing, and the switch to a local, rather than a regional, approach. None the less, some major decisions with far-reaching effects on the distribution of industry, including the location of a steel strip mill in Scotland and of motor assembly plants in Scotland and on Merseyside, were made at this time by means of a combination of the negative control over industrial development and the positive incentive of a larger element of government financing. The Local Employment Act of 1960 extended a new building grant to firms wanting to build their own premises, amounting to 85 per cent of the difference between the notional[2] cost of construction of a building or factory, and its actual market value when completed. The Act therefore provided a direct capital subsidy covering the greater part of the capitalized extra costs of location in a relatively unfavourable district. The powers of the Board of Trade were also extended to building non-industrial premises for letting, thus bringing this aspect into line with the loans policy.

By the time of the first review of the operation of the 1945 Act,[3] it was evident that in the general postwar prosperity the problem of the development areas was nothing like so severe as before the war. Whereas in June 1939, 327,000 insured persons had still been unemployed in the areas, in June 1948 the number was only 102,000. The number of long-term unemployed, that is, unemployed for more than one year, was less than a fifth in June 1948 what it had

[1] See Select Committee on Estimates, Session 1955-6, Second Report, Development Areas, HMSO, 1955.

[2] A notional cost of building, rather than the actual cost, was used in order to prevent costs being inflated by the inclusion of unnecessary extras that would not contribute to the market value.

[3] HMSO, The Distribution of Industry, Cmnd. 7540, 1948.

been in June 1939. The war had created a keen demand for the products of the industries of the development areas. The Government put a quarter of the new war factories, some 130 factories covering 22 million square feet, in the areas, and in addition manufacturing firms from other parts of the country were dispersed to the areas. The demand for the products of other industries in the areas was very high, the restriction of output of the 'less essential' industries was less severe than in the rest of the country, the service industries were stimulated by the improvement in the other industries, and many people were of course taken into the armed services. In short, the development areas, having a much more plentiful supply of labour, were able to increase output more rapidly than the rest of the country. Immediately after the war the number of people looking for work increased as members of the forces were released, and even where factories could be converted to peacetime use some redundancy was inevitable during the transition, so unemployment increased for a while. But the capital goods of the development area industries were in keen demand at home and overseas, and the high level of employment elsewhere, together with the shortage of housing, led firms that wished to expand to look towards the areas as places where they could still get labour. This matched the Government's policy of publicizing the advantages of the areas and encouraging firms with positive inducements, and negative restrictions, to go there. The 1948 White Paper estimated that the increase in employment over the prewar figure was divided roughly equally among the capital goods, the building and consumer goods, and the service industries. Much of the improvement in the unemployment situation of the development area was then a result of the general change in economic conditions between the 1930s and the war and postwar periods. In these circumstances it is difficult to assess the impact of the policy of attracting industry to the areas after 1945. The table opposite sets out briefly the main comparisons between the development areas and Great Britain for the boom years 1951 and 1955, and for the years of recession, 1952 and 1958.

The general impression of these figures is that, while there was some improvement in the relative situation of the development areas between 1951 and 1955, this was associated with the difference between the national percentage of unemployed of $1 \cdot 4$ in 1951 and that of $1 \cdot 0$ in 1955. That this may have been the case is supported

	1951	1955	1952	1958
Percentages unemployed in Great Britain	1·4	1·0	1·9	2·4
Percentages unemployed in development areas	2·2–3·1	1·5–2·4	2·7–4·2	3·2–5·0
Differences between the percentages unemployed in the development areas and in Great Britain	0·8–1·8	0·5–1·4	0·8–2·3	0·8–2·6

Source: Ministry of Labour Gazette.

by the fact that the differential unemployment of the development areas expanded again in the recession of 1958, when it was greater than in the recession of 1952, in which national average unemployment did not reach such a high level. In years of expanding activity, when the labour force as a whole was very fully employed, the development areas attained virtually full employment, with unemployment percentages ranging between 1·5 and 2·4 per cent in 1955. Such low percentages gave the Government some justification for feeling that the policy was succeeding, and for not pressing it further. Indeed, we may say that the policy by 1955 had been as successful as it could possibly be, for in some of the areas labour was positively scarce and it was proving impossible to attract new firms for the excellent reason that they could not hope to obtain the labour they needed. In South Wales the National Coal Board was complaining that the new industries were attracting miners away from the pits. In the North-east Lancashire Development Area there were only 426 wholly unemployed on June 13, 1955. Of these 296 had been unemployed for less than eight weeks, 130 were registered as disabled, and 126 were aged 55 or over. In addition, there were at the same time 529 vacancies unfilled in North-east Lancashire.[1]

But the very success of the policy in finding jobs for the workers in the development areas in 1955 hampered the Board of Trade in their attempts to find a way of tackling two unsolved, though concealed, problems: the severe impact of cyclical unemployment in the development areas, and the prospect of secular declines in some of their basic industries. Both these problems were revealed by the

---

[1] *Economist Intelligence Unit, A Study of the Prospects for the Economic Development of North East Lancashire*, July 1959.

recession of 1958, which produced much greater unemployment in the areas than in other parts of the country, concentrated especially in coal and shipbuilding. In addition it was found to be difficult, even in 1955, to attract industry to the remoter and least economically and socially favourable districts where unemployment remained serious. It was suggested that future policy would have to emphasize the mobility of labour, rather than to try to bring factories to every pocket of unemployment.[1]

The retreat from regionalism in the late 1950s
The policy pursued under the Act of 1945 had been to bring industry only to substantial regions of high unemployment, Central Scotland, the North-east, West Cumberland, and South Wales, whose problems could be treated as those of building a healthy and diversified regional industrial structure. In a review of areas in 1948 the Board of Trade had refused to schedule isolated towns and districts which did not have a high absolute level of unemployment, as well as a high rate. Some of the areas added later to the four major regions that had already been special areas before 1939 appeared to contravene this principle. In 1946 South Lancashire and Wrexham were added, in 1949 Merseyside and the Scottish Highlands, and in 1953 North-east Lancashire. In the case of Wrexham, however, a Royal Ordnance factory existed, and financial help under the Act appeared to be a particularly economical method of providing employment for the men put out of work by its closing. In South Lancashire Section 5 of the Act was especially appropriate to deal with the problem of derelict land. The scheduling of the Scottish Highlands area around Inverness was surprising in view of the cogent arguments expressed in the 1948 White Paper against scheduling parts of North Wales whose unemployed were, and are, similarly scattered and small in aggregate number, and the policy had a doubtful success in the Highlands. The *Economist* Intelligence Unit, in its Report on the North-east Lancashire Development Area, concluded that the policy was not well adapted to such a small area.

In the light of this emphasis in past policy, the fears about the future prospects of the major development areas, and the difficulty of dealing with small pockets of unemployment within these areas, the subsequent development of policy for the location of industry presents some remarkable aspects.

[1] Evidence before the Select Committee on Estimates, op. cit., para. 86.

With rising unemployment in many parts of the country as industrial activity first stagnated in 1956 and 1957, and then declined into the recession of 1958, the Government decided to extend help to districts outside the development areas. They still did not deschedule any parts of the existing areas. Instead, the Distribution of Industry (Industrial Finance) Act of 1958 instituted a new kind of area to which the financial help for firms from the Treasury under Section 4 of the 1945 Act would be made available, and on less restricted terms. The existing development areas remained unchanged, but districts within them could in addition be designated for wider financial assistance to firms under the new Act.

The keynote of the new policy was to be flexibility. Localities could be added to or subtracted from the list of areas eligible for assistance by administrative action, without the need for a formal procedure of scheduling, and without consulting local authorities. The procedure was intended to allow help to be switched to new areas as new problems of local unemployment were revealed in different parts of the country. Grants and loans under the 1958 Act were to continue to be given on the advice of the Development Areas Treasury Advisory Committee, and the new areas came to be called 'DATAC' areas. Another aspect of the geographical flexibility of the new policy was that assistance could be given to enterprises *outside* the actual DATAC area, providing that this would be likely to reduce unemployment within the area. Grants and loans were also extended to commercial undertakings and not restricted to industry as under the 1945 Act. This reflected the switching of assistance to non-industrial, or not so exclusively industrial areas, but also enlarged the scope of loans in those parts of the development areas that could also get themselves on the new list of DATAC areas.

The Act of 1958 was superseded within two years by the Local Employment Act of 1960, and its short life was by no means successful. The Act may be criticized on a number of grounds, some concerning its practical application, and others more fundamental. The policy turned out to be much less flexible in operation than the legislators intended. The Act deliberately refrained from laying down a fixed percentage criterion for a 'high rate' of unemployment, since it was recognized that each area had its own local problems, and the gross percentage of unemployed did not necessarily mean the same thing in different places. But in putting areas on the list the President of the Board of Trade used a 4 per cent level of unemployment persisting over a period of one year. The period was used in the attempt to distinguish areas of persistent unemployment from those suffering temporarily in the recession. But its linking with a specific percentage could only bring a statistical and mechanistic approach to the administration of what was intended to be a highly flexible policy. It also left open the possibility of rapid changes in the areas listed for assistance as new areas crossed the 4-per-cent-for-one-year margin in an upward direction, and old DATAC areas sank below it. The Act did not operate long enough for this possibility of kaleidoscopic change to be realized, but the new list of unemployment districts under the Local Employment Act of 1960 showed bewildering changes from the DATAC areas. The new geographical flexibility also proved to be somewhat contradictory in practice. The use of a rigid unemployment criterion meant that in some cases, particularly in Norfolk, Lincolnshire and East Yorkshire, rural areas were listed but not the nearby market towns. The Act did indeed give permission for grants or loans to be made to enterprises situated outside the DATAC areas, if they were likely to contribute to reducing unemployment within the area, but this freedom was interpreted far too strictly, to include the direct employment of workers who would travel daily from the DATAC areas. The reduction of unemployment could well come about in other, more indirect ways; the undertaking might attract workers from other firms in the town, leaving vacancies elsewhere for workers from the DATAC areas, or workers might migrate the relatively short distance from the DATAC area to the town; or workers then employed in the DATAC area but living in the town might save the journey and leave their jobs open for some of the unemployed in the DATAC area. The policy of listing small areas was not applied flexibly enough to take account of the normal movement of workers, either commuting daily, or more permanently, within a small region. These practical difficulties in keeping the policy as flexible as it was intended to be raised the fundamental question of the validity of the small DATAC area concept as against the previous principle of securing full employment within major regions.

By superimposing a new structure of DATAC areas on to the old development areas the 1958 Act caused great confusion among firms and local authorities about what help could be extended to their areas. Under the 1945 legislation the country had been effectively divided into three kinds of areas: congested areas where Industrial

Development Certificates would normally be refused, non-congested areas where IDCs would normally be granted, and development areas where in addition to ease in getting an IDC, extra inducements were available. Later we might add the fourth category of those parts of the development areas where the 1945 powers were not exercised. After the 1958 Act matters were confused by the existence of no fewer than five different areas (or six if we include the administratively descheduled parts of the development areas). These were (a) areas that were both development and DATAC areas, (b) development areas only, (c) DATAC areas only, (d) non-congested areas where IDCs would normally be granted, (e) congested areas where IDCs would normally be refused. The Jay Report complained that: 'hardly a single industrialist or local authority representative . . . fully understands the application of all these powers to their own areas'.[1] The recession itself put many difficulties in the way of the effective use of the powers given in the Act. Inducements to industry to move to areas of high employment are more successful in times when businessmen are very keen to expand, and when they find labour scarce in the more prosperous areas. The Board of Trade had found development area inducements less successful in the recession of 1952 than in earlier postwar years. This did not matter greatly for a long-term policy based on reducing unemployment and introducing a more healthy diversification of industry in a major region, but it was a serious drawback to a policy expressly designed to be switched flexibly to new areas as high unemployment occurred in them. How could the method succeed if it was appropriate to conditions of general prosperity, whereas high unemployment showed itself most in time of recession? It is true that the emphasis had been moved from the building of advance factories to the more general financial inducements, but even these could not hope to result in more jobs except after the passage of some considerable time.

It has been suggested that the 4 per cent criterion served to distinguish unemployment resulting from the general state of business activity in the whole country, and a secular trend towards high unemployment in a given area.[2] But even if in prosperous years this could satisfactorily pick out areas needing help, in a

[1] Douglas Jay, *Unemployment*, 1959.
[2] A. J. Odber, Local Unemployment and the 1958 Act, *Scottish Journal of Political Economy*, November 1959.

recession all it could do was to add to the list many areas that would have to be removed again when business conditions improved. Many DATAC areas were so excluded from the new list of unemployment districts under the Act of 1960. Most of the Lancashire cotton towns were on the DATAC list, but not one was included in the new list.

Practical difficulties encountered in the recession, like those concerned with the flexibility of the new policy, again raised the question of its fundamental suitability. Could a policy designed originally to improve the regional structure of industry be extended to smaller pockets of unemployment, when these were primarily the result of a cyclical recession of trade. The Act of 1958 appears to have failed partly through the self-contradictory nature of its vaunted flexibility, and partly through its inappropriateness to the economic conditions in which it was introduced.

The Local Employment Act of 1960 carried further the revision of location-of-industry policy in the 1958 Act. It attempted to remove some of the difficulties encountered in operating the DATAC loans. Much of the confusion arising out of the overlap of development and DATAC areas was cleared away by abolishing both and putting in their place a single list of unemployment districts, which would be freely added to by the President of the Board of Trade. Equally districts could be removed by administrative action, without consulting local authorities, and without going through the order procedure in Parliament. As in the 1958 Act, the emphasis was on flexibility: on being able rapidly to switch aid from one part of the country to another.

The Board of Trade was allowed to take into account not only the existing level of unemployment (and the length of time it had persisted) but also the imminence of unemployment. In justifying the inclusion or exclusion of particular districts in the lists of unemployment districts future prospects both of redundancies and of the creation of new jobs that were already 'in the pipeline' were included in the calculations.

In England, the new list of development districts included parts of the old North-east development area, and the Merseyside area and West Cumberland. It excluded both the South Lancashire and North-east Lancashire development areas (the latter had also been a DATAC area) and all the cotton towns that had been designated as DATAC areas under the 1958 Act. The additions were mostly seaside resorts: Blackpool, Bridlington, Filey, most of Cornwall,

Ilfracombe, Margate and Ramsgate, Scarborough, Skegness, Mablethorpe and Whitby. As far as England was concerned the new Act had much the appearance of a measure for the relief of (seasonal?) unemployment in holiday towns. It is difficult to accept that a policy designed originally for major industrial areas was appropriate to these towns. In Scotland, much of the old development areas appeared on the new list, but several isolated towns were added. In Wales, parts of the development area were on the list, and other parts of Wales were added: Anglesey (which had been a DATAC area), Caernarvon, Bangor, Blaenau Ffestiniog, Portmadoc, Pwllheli, Milford Haven, Pembroke Dock and Rhyl.

Although the legislation of 1958 and 1960 contained many improvements in the forms of assistance to areas with high unemployment, it had one major fault, that it abandoned the regional approach. Even though large parts of the previous development areas were scheduled under the new Acts, there could be no proper approach to the problem of major regions, especially in Scotland and the North-east, while the chief object of the legislation was to relieve unemployment by districts.

Regional planning for national growth
The NEDC accepted their interpretation of previous regional policy in their second report, which came out strongly in favour of a growth policy for regions. 'Present policy, embodied in the Local Employment Act, is closely geared to the relief of high local unemployment in development districts designated by the Board of Trade, rather than to the formation of growth more generally in regions.'[1] They estimated that if the 1961 level of unemployment in the less prosperous regions (the Ministry of Labour's Northern, Wales, Scotland and Northern Ireland regions) could be reduced half-way towards the level of unemployment in the other more prosperous regions, and if the activity rates (the number of employees, employed and unemployed, as a percentage of the total population aged over 15) could similarly be raised half-way towards those of the more prosperous regions, 300,000 workers could be added to the national labour force, increasing it by 1·3 per cent. Taking a more cautious estimate of a 200,000 increase over five years, and allowing for the fact that many of the extra workers would be women on part-time, the NEDC concluded that the less prosperous areas could make a

[1] NEDC, *Conditions Favourable to Faster Growth*, HMSO, 1963, para. 94.

contribution of about 0·1 per cent per annum to national employment and hence to the national growth target.[1] Similarly, the DEA
estimated that the hoped-for increase in activity rates in the less
prosperous areas would result in a halving of the estimated 'manpower gap' of 400,000 between the number of additional workers
required in expanding, and the number released by the declining,
industries. So far as policy was concerned, the NEDC raised two main
arguments in favour of a regional method. First, the desirability of
developing industrial complexes in the natural growth points within
larger regions, with workers travelling reasonable distances daily to
and from their new jobs. Such 'growth points' were much more
likely to attract firms than were inducements to go to more isolated
localities. Secondly, they emphasized the need for investment in the
'social infrastructure' of areas that were trying to attract industry.
Such investment could not be effectively organized except on a
regional basis. The NEDC stand in favour of a return to a regional
policy was followed by White Papers on Scotland and the North-
east, both of which stressed growth points and investments in infrastructure, and a report on the South-east[2] which raised the issue of
the co-ordination of policy as between one region and another
because of the trend of migration into the region that contradicted
the hopes rested on the inducements to industry to move into, and
workers to stay in, the other regions. What the NEDC, and the movement for planning for growth in general, achieved by October 1964,
was merely to reverse the movement of policy in the Distribution
of Industry Act of 1958, and the Local Employment Act of 1960,
and to start people thinking once more in regional terms. They did
not produce any coherent and co-ordinated regional policy. The
DEA repeated in the National Plan the kind of analysis performed by
the NEDC, but without any significant advance.

Further progress has been made in the development of regional
institutions under the Labour Government. Scotland has long enjoyed a measure of regional autonomy under the Scottish Office, and
the Conservative Government made Mr Quintin Hogg, then Lord
Hailsham, Minister in charge of co-ordinating the policy of other

[1] NEDC, *Conditions Favourable to Faster Growth*, HMSO, 1963.
[2] HMSO, Central Scotland, A programme for Development and Growth,
Cmnd. 2188; HMSO, The North East, A Programme for Regional Development
and Growth, Cmnd. 2206; HMSO, South East Study, 1961–81; and South East
England, Cmnd. 2308.

government departments in the North-east. Further regional reports have now been published. The Labour Party promised in their 1964 election campaign a thorough-going regional policy with a regional administration to implement it. Under the Regional Division of the Department of Economic Affairs there are now Regional Economic Planning Boards run by a senior official of the Department, who is chairman and co-ordinator of regional officials from the main economic departments, Board of Trade, Transport, Power and Labour, and from social departments such as Housing and Health. These regional offices have research and statistical services, and work in close co-operation with local authorities, industry and the universities. Local advice is channelled through Regional Councils representing local authorities, firms and other interests. It seems clear that the next few years will see a new emphasis on regional planning, with the development of new machinery and policies, in order to solve the social problems of the regions with high unemployment and of the congested and still rapidly expanding regions, within the context of an overall growth policy that aims to extract the maximum possible output from the nation's resources.

As regards the institutional structure, the British system has tended much more towards the centralization characteristic of French regional policy than to the decentralization of Germany. Responsibility for overall regional policy has been moved from the Board of Trade to the Department of Economic Affairs, where it is closely associated with the national planners. The regional programmes published have not aimed at any greater decentralization of powers, but at encouraging greater co-ordination of the various arms of the central government with regard to the region in question, nor is it likely that the new regional administration will give greater responsibility to the local bodies in the regions. The regional Economic Planning Boards are Committees of civil servants, while the Regional Councils, which represent local interests, are purely advisory. Various local bodies which existed in the regions before the administrative changes of 1964–5 continue to operate, but still have no power.

REGIONAL PLANNING IN FRANCE

The problem of uneven regional development has also been recognized in France. It was dramatically outlined in 1948 by J. F.

Gravier.[1] There are two main aspects of the problem. First there is the extremely heavy and increasing concentration of population, industry and employment in the city of Paris and the surrounding *départements*. Secondly, there is the disparity in the population, employment and income levels between the regions north and east of a line from Le Havre to Marseille and those to the south and west. The latter regions, *le désert français*, are predominantly agricultural and since the war have suffered as a result of heavy migration from agriculture to industry, and from low levels of income per head due to the absence of industries with high productivity. This is the situation throughout the south-west; in Brittany there is the additional factor of high population densities and, in the absence of adequate industrial development, relatively heavy unemployment.

The population of the Paris region has grown by 29 per cent since 1945, while the increase in the total French population has been only 15 per cent. 60 per cent of the increase in the Paris region between 1954 and 1962 was the result of immigration from other regions and from abroad. The 1962 census showed that 18 per cent of the population and 29 per cent of the urban population lived in the Paris region. The importance of Paris is further magnified by the absence of other urban areas of comparable size. In 1962 the population of the city of Paris was 7·4 million. The next largest urban area was Lyon with 871,000 inhabitants.

Later studies[2] have indicated a lessening of the disparities in income per head between the various regions between 1951 and 1958. The differences, however, are still considerable. In the six regions of the south-west, income per head was only half that of the Paris region and 30 per cent below that of the relatively prosperous regions of Nord, Rhône-Alpes, Lorraine and Haute Normandie.

Estimates were made in the Fourth Plan (1962–5) of the manpower position in the various regions over the period of the Plan. After account had been taken of immigration both from abroad and from other regions the likely labour shortage in the Paris region was put at 175,000, nearly 5 per cent of the total labour force. In the regions of Brittany and the Loire on the other hand, probable un-

---

[1] J. F. Gravier, *Paris et le Désert Français*, Paris, Flammarion, 1947.

[2] Evolution Régionale des Revenus des Particuliers de 1955–6 à 1958, *Etudes et Conjuncture*, May 1961; and P. Bauchet, Regional Development Policies in France in *Area Development Policies in Britain and the Countries of the Common Market*, US Department of Commerce, 1965.

employment was put at 90,000. Unemployment was also likely in the Languedoc and the Massif Central to pose problems, while in the north-east, shortages, particularly of skilled labour, were predicted. The Fifth Plan underlined the need to develop industry in the west of France, and proposed that the ten regions of the west should receive 35–40 per cent of new industrial jobs to be created by 1970. Even then, this would only reduce the migration to the Paris and eastern regions by one-third.

The development of a regional policy to solve these problems dates from 1950 when a Plan National d'Aménagement du Territoire was drawn up by the Ministry for Reconstruction and Urban Development. This document provided a detailed inventory of the regional problems and emphasized the need to check the concentration of economic activity in certain areas and to develop regions where human and natural resources were under-utilized. To implement these proposals the Fonds National d'Aménagement du Territoire was set up in August 1950. But the first systematic legislative efforts did not come until June 1955 when, under the direction of M. Mendès-France and M. Faure, a package of twelve measures was introduced to stimulate the development of regions suffering from under-employment or inadequate development.[1] The control of industrial building in Paris was tightened and an arsenal of fiscal and financial incentives was established to aid decentralization into specified regions. The 'weapons' of regional policy were created at this time.

France has had a much longer history of national economic programmes, and therefore as might be supposed much more experience than Britain of the problems of fitting regional policy into a national plan. But the integration of regional plans into the national plan did not properly begin until the Fourth Plan and is still in its early stages. The First and Second Plans contained little analysis of the regional problem although the latter did include major irrigation projects administered by semi-public organizations, of which the Bas-Rhône, Languedoc and Durance valley schemes were the most important. The Third Plan was the first plan to have a regional chapter. The emphasis was mainly on the economic and social costs of the increasing concentration of economic activity in the Paris region. The promotion of development within the regions was much less closely analysed. The legislation of June 1955, however, marked

[1] *Journal Officiel*, July 2, 1955.

an important step forward, in ordering twenty-two regional action programmes (*programmes d'action régionale*) to be prepared under the guidance of the Commissariat du Plan in consultation with the Comité d'Expansion Economique of each *département* and other regional interests. So far only twelve of these have been published and only one, the plan for Brittany, really finalized.

The programmes had four main functions:

(a) A diagnosis of the problems of the region.

(b) The preparation of recommendations which would indicate the contribution the region could make to the expansion of the national economy and the action required to improve the situation in the region.

(c) To act as a framework within which a co-ordinated distribution of public investment by region could be developed.

(d) To act as a reference dossier for the regional authorities' and private industry's claims for State aid.

The programmes were scarcely satisfactory. They were intended to be co-ordinated with the national plan but the legislation did not specify how they should be drawn up and how the regional interests should participate. M. Bauchet is particularly critical. 'The preparation of the reports . . . was first done by Parisian civil servants who, in order to avoid collusion, were required not to visit the regions. But without power and without sufficient means of information in Paris, they gradually abandoned their task.'[1] In December 1958 the programmes of regional action were fused with the regional land-use plans and put under the authority of a new committee of the Commissariat du Plan, the Comité des Plans Régionaux.

The need for improvements in the organization of regional policy was recognized in the preparatory work on the Fourth Plan. In June 1960 France was divided into twenty-one programme regions (*régions de programme*), each grouping from 2 to 8 *départements* and with an average population of 1·5 million inhabitants.[2] These regions were to be the basic regional divisions of France for some thirty administrative agencies. This simplified greatly the previous situation of more than forty different administrative divisions of the

[1] P. Bauchet, *Economic Planning, The French Experience*, Heinemann, 1964, p. 106.
[2] *Journal Officiel*, June 3, 1960, p. 5007.

country. The delimitation of these regions took account of their economic and geographical nature but their boundaries coincided for political and administrative reasons with existing *département* boundaries. They also coincided roughly with the old French provinces which were the basic divisions of the country before 1789.

For each region an economic and social plan was to be drawn up, extending and revising the regional programmes of 1955. This task was given to *conférences interdépartementales*, originally established in 1959 and confirmed in 1961. These plans were to be reviewed by the Comité des Plans Régionaux of the Commissariat du Plan and were to be in effect regional sections of the national plan. The conferences were chaired by 'co-ordinating prefects' appointed in December 1961, and were to operate in consultation with the regional committees for economic expansion. The conference had an important and clearly defined role to perform in carrying out the regional objectives of the Fourth Plan.

One of the most significant innovations in the Plan were the '*tranches opératoires*'. These were the 'operational sections' of the Fourth Plan's regional policies and consisted of regional allocations of public investment projects for the period of the Plan. The time-tabling and financing of these projects were to be defined in detail, thus providing a definite basis for development in the regions. The interdepartmental conference was responsible for drawing up a programme of public investment projects, again in consultation with the regional expansion committees, outlining priorities and possible financial contributions from regional authorities. This document was then considered by the budgetary authorities, including the Commissariat du Plan, and '*tranches*' of investment for the various regions approved. The regional representative of the Ministry of Finance, the Trésorier Payeur Général, was represented on the conference and his views on the viability and financing of operations carried considerable weight.

Regional planning in the Fifth Plan continued along the same broad lines but with some important changes. There was first of all a strengthening of the regional organizations. In March 1964, the co-ordinating prefect was replaced by a regional prefect (*préfet de région*) whose function is to 'implement government policy on economic and regional development'.[1] He has much more authority

[1] Decree of March 14, 1964.

than his predecessor. He is more than simply a co-ordinator, being responsible for all matters affecting economic development in the *départements* within his programme region. He has a small 'mission' staffed by young civil servants, each covering a particular field of activity, who report directly to him. The interdepartmental conference was also reformed into a regional administrative conference (*conférence administrative régionale*). The members of the conference are the prefects of the *départements* in the region, the Tresorier Payeur Général and one other civil servant with relevant responsibilities, an *inspecteur général de l'économie nationale*. This body is consulted by the regional prefect in the preparation of the regional report and in addition has the right to make recommendations about the distribution of credits contained in the *tranches opératoires* among the different *départements*. The Paris region has been created as a special case. In 1961, the District of Paris was created, and now contains three *départements*: Seine, Seine-et-Oise and Seine-et-Marne. The development of this region is the responsibility of a delegate, M. Delouvrier, with an administrative council and a consultative economic and social council representing different interest groups.

The 1964 reforms sought also to formalize the process of consultation with regional interests. The privately organized committees for economic expansion were replaced by officially appointed Commissions de Développement Économique Régionale(CODER). These committees have a membership of fifty persons. The legislation requires that one quarter be locally elected office holders, the mayor of the regional capital, MPs, county councillors, etc. Half of the members must be representatives of industry and labour in the region and the remaining quarter personalities chosen for their competence. The CODERs act as the official channel through which regional interests can make their views known.

The greater integration of regional policy with the national plan posed the problem of co-ordination of effort at the national as well as the regional level and the need to treat regional development in the longer-term perspective of the national economic plan. The division of responsibility for economic and physical planning between the Commissariat du Plan and the Ministry of Construction had become quite illogical and there was an obvious need to expand and reorganize the work of research and synthesis on regional policies carried out in the Commissariat du Plan. To deal with this situation the responsibility for regional policy and planning at the national level was given to two new bodies. The conceptual analysis of the regional problem was entrusted to the Commission Nationale de l'Aménagement du Territoire (CNAT) which was established as a special commission of the Commissariat du Plan in February 1963.[1] Its members, fifty in number, are nominated by the Prime Minister on the grounds of their interests and expertise in regional matters. Representatives of government departments and the financial institutions are *ex officio* members. The Commission was responsible for working out the regional aspects of the Fifth Plan but it is also engaged on longer-term studies on regional and urban growth.[2]

Co-ordination and coherence were also required in the implementation of measures to promote regional development. In 1963, a second new institution, the Délégation à l'Aménagement du Territoire (DATAR) was established as the co-ordinating body for all aspects of regional development policy. DATAR is headed by a delegate, who is responsible to an interministerial committee on regional development and through it to the Prime Minister's Office. It is not a large organization (the total staff is thirty) and has roughly the same role in relation to regional development as the Commissariat du Plan has to national economic policy.

DATAR has three main functions. The first and most important is to ensure that the distribution of credits in the budget is consistent with the aims of regional policy and that the priorities of regional development are given due consideration. DATAR is therefore engaged in a dialogue with the Ministry of Finance and the 'spending' departments. This is the kind of influence which the French planners have exercised successfully at the national level, and with an able delegate and the direct backing of the Prime Minister, DATAR could have an important voice in regional policy. In addition it has at its disposal a special fund, the Fonds d'Intervention pour l'Aménagement du Territoire (FIAT), which it can use to aid public investment programmes which it considers important but which cannot be financed through the normal budgetary channels. This direct intervention is, however, strictly limited in scope. FIAT is voted only £12 million annually. Any aid given is short term, normally for one year, with assurances required that the project will be voted credits at the next

---

[1] *Journal Officiel*, February 15, 1963.
[2] See *Premier Rapport de la Commission Nationale de l'Aménagement du Territoire*, Paris, 1964.

budget. Finally, no project is taken on by FIAT unless the local authorities in the region are prepared to make a financial contribution of at least 30 or 40 per cent. There is, therefore, no question of FIAT acting as a large-scale subsidizing agency or of it being left responsible for doubtful or unfinished projects.

The second function of DATAR, which stems from the first, is the day-to-day liaison with government departments, the regional prefects and the CODERs about the implementation of the *tranches opératoires*.

The third function is the supervision and co-ordination of the numerous controls and incentives which have been introduced since 1955 to encourage industry and commerce to move to particular regions. DATAR is particularly concerned with simplifying and co-ordinating the complicated mass of legislation on regional aid and to this end a wide-ranging reform of procedures was introduced in May 1964.

The regionalization of the Fifth Plan was the first operation which the new and reformed institutions had to tackle and it involved a much fuller integration of regional planning into the national plan than in any previous plan. The first stage was to formulate the long-term aims of regional development up to 1985, and then outline priorities for the shorter period of the Fifth Plan. This task was the responsibility of CNAT. A particular effort was made to produce more and better information on population growth, internal migration and manpower requirements up to 1970. When these general sketches of regional development were completed the regional prefects were asked in the light of them to prepare detailed reports of the situation in their region. They were asked first to analyse the long-term prospects of the region, covering matters such as population trends, the consequences of a continued reduction in agricultural manpower, the problems and prospects of increased labour mobility, urban growth within the region and the concentration of population in certain cities and towns, education and training requirements and communications. This process of filling out an initial sketch with more detailed consultation was an extension of the methods used in French industrial planning. Together with the administrative reforms it indicated that regional development is now a permanent issue in France and that national and regional development must as a matter of course be dealt with in a co-ordinated way.

The second part of the regional prefect's report was an analysis of the economic development of the region during the period of the Plan. The absence of a system of regional accounting made a serious regional breakdown of industry forecasts impossible. There was, however, for the first time, close collaboration between the industrial Modernization Commissions and the regional authorities, which provided some indication of the changes in the industrial structure of the regions and the types of industry likely to be located in different regions. Even in its most rough and ready form, this kind of approach is in marked contrast to the general encouragement to decentralization which was the basis of earlier regional policy.

Finally, the regional prefect was required to make general recommendations about the public investment programmes necessary in the region over the period of the Plan. No detailed projects are put forward at this stage but the general needs of the region are argued and priorities both between and within different categories of expenditure are indicated.

When the regional reports are completed the familiar exercise in synthesis is performed by CNAT at the Commissariat du Plan. This gives the planners a further opportunity to consider together the industrial and regional aspects of the plan. The result of these deliberations appeared as the regional chapter of the Fifth Plan in which the *'grandes options'* of regional policy were set out.[1] The Plan was then presented to Parliament for approval. The task then became one of implementing the proposals and, in particular, the preparation of the *tranches opératoires* for each of the programme regions.

Implementation of regional planning
The integration of regional development into the national plan in the Fourth and Fifth Plans marks a clear shift in regional policy. Regional development is now regarded not simply as a social and political necessity but as an integral part of strategy for national economic growth. In 1955, when regional policy first got seriously under way, the aim of legislation was to limit the expansion of industry and commerce in the Paris region and by a system of loans, capital grants and tax concessions, to encourage development in areas where unemployment was serious and permanent. Twenty-six critical zones (*zones critiques*) were scheduled as falling into this

[1] Ve Plan de Développement Economique et Social (1966-70), Tome I, Paris, Imprimerie Nationale, November 1965, Chapter V.

L

category. In 1959 within the critical zones certain areas called special conversion zones (*zones spéciales de conversion*) were singled out for preferential treatment. These were regions where unemployment was particularly acute owing to the economic situation in the dominant industry in the region in the recession year of 1958. The coal mines at Béthune, shipbuilding at Nantes and St Nazaire, and the textile industry in Alsace and Lorraine, were among the worst hit areas.

In the special conversion zones capital grants were given at the maximum rate of 20 per cent as against an average over the critical zones of around 10 per cent. Administrative procedures were streamlined to ensure the minimum possible delay in examining requests for aid. In April 1960, these special conditions were extended to seven other areas: in Brittany, the St Nazaire district, Limoges, Montpelier and Bordeaux. The criteria of selection for the seven new areas was not, however, simply a high level of unemployment; they were all subsequently named in the Fourth Plan as growth areas. In the Fourth Plan, selective use of incentives to favour centres of growth had begun to replace the principle behind the earlier legislation which was the reduction of unemployment in areas where it seemed excessively high. It should be noted, however, that this is a very recent change. In 1959, capital grants were made available to firms moving to areas *outside* the original critical zones where the unemployment situation warranted it. Known as the 'case by case' policy (*'coup par coup'*) the aim of this measure was to spread aid even further and provide help to areas not previously scheduled where 'accidents' had caused unemployment to rise. It was brought into being as a result of the recession in 1958 and was not replaced until 1962 when the economy was again in a period of expansion, and unemployment in these areas had ceased to be an immediate problem (except in Brittany). The regional problem had by then become the longer-term one of dealing with the surplus of manpower and the consequent increase in migration that would emerge throughout western France as French agriculture became increasingly large scale and mechanized and the shortage of manpower in the Paris region and the other expanding regions of the north and east and the Lyon area.

The objective of regional policy in the Fourth Plan was 'not to guarantee every Frenchman a job in his own area. (This would be too rigid a recommendation for a growing economy.) It was to reduce to a reasonable level migration between regions that is due to the estimated gap between the demand for jobs, which are the result of population growth, immigration and the modernization of agriculture, and the supply of jobs resulting from the development of industry and commerce.'[1] The regional policy of the Fourth Plan thus had two basic aims. The first was to reduce the flow of immigration into the Paris region and avoid the economic and social costs which this involved. The second was to halt emigration from the poorer regions of the west, particularly Brittany. This required a deliberate policy of industrialization to absorb a growing population and the increasing numbers leaving agriculture. The problem was urgent, for the rate of migration threatened to leave certain areas of the west and south-west so severely depopulated as to make future development extremely difficult. To alleviate the labour shortage in the Paris region where so many of the fast growing industries are concentrated would require very heavy immigration which is unlikely to materialize quickly enough to prevent inflationary developments and the halting of expansion. The economic case for moving industry out of the Paris region was further strengthened by the fact that much of the surplus labour it was hoped it would employ would have previously been employed in agriculture. The substitution of employment in industries where productivity is higher would help to increase the level of income in the regions of the west and the nation as a whole.

As a result of this approach the regional problem is not confined to the more obviously less developed areas. Rather, it is defined in terms of the relationship between different regional economies and between them and the national economy. At the same time different regions require different measures. The Fourth Plan distinguished between regions where a policy of *accompagnement* is to be adopted and those where a policy of impulsion (*entraînement*) is required. 'In regions where agricultural, industrial and commercial expansion is spontaneous and sufficiently vigorous, the policy is one of accompaniment involving the development of public service investment, educational investment and the facilities for finance required for expansion without altering the natural growth of the economy, without massive aid and without spectacular projects aimed at altering natural development. . . . In less favoured regions government policy is different. It becomes one of impulsion involving

[1] IVe Plan, *Journal Officiel*, August 7, 1962, p. 16.

bolder anticipation of development and more significant amounts of aid.'[1]

Growth areas

The Plan also stated specifically that the decisions to present regional policy in terms of promoting growth rather than alleviating unemployment required a concentration of effort within the various regions on areas where self-sustaining growth was most likely to develop. The diffusion of aid over a large number of small areas was rejected as too costly and of doubtful efficacy. The Fourth Plan, therefore, embarked on a growth area strategy.

The Fifth Plan continued and developed it. Regional policy in the Fifth Plan must be seen in the context of the basic aim of the Plan: to make the French economy more competitive. The costs of promoting regional development have as a result been carefully weighed. Regional policy 'must, in a highly competitive situation, give every opportunity to the "strong" regions whose economic potential will benefit the whole economy. On the other hand, it must seek in the "weak" regions to promote development which will become self-sustaining so that these regions can play a part in the schemes for modernization and expansion. . . .'[2] This compromise approach means that regional development must be a highly selective operation and its effect on the national rate of growth must be taken into account. Emphasis on this point has had a significant influence on the Fifth Plan's regional policy. Up until the Fifth Plan the basic policy towards the Paris region had been one of restriction and since 1955 increasingly severe prohibitions had been put on industrial and commercial development in the capital. The Fifth Plan adopts a more subtle approach.

Its aim is to modernize the Paris region rather than halt its development. The Plan accepts the fact that the growth of the national economy must involve at least a moderate expansion of industry and employment in the Paris region. The task is to organize this expansion so that the economic and social costs which it creates are kept to a minimum. Accordingly there are plans for the creation of new and expanded towns within a radius of 150 kilometres of the city of Paris, which will anticipate and, it is hoped, prevent the outer 'ring' of the city of Paris expanding in an uncontrolled sprawl.

[1] IVe Plan, op. cit., p. 16.
[2] Ve Plan, op. cit., Tome I, p. 118.

During the Fifth Plan efforts will be concentrated on building up three new cities to the north and south of Paris, each with an eventual population of half a million. These cities will form part of a massive city region planned and administered as the District of Paris.

The economic and social costs of such an operation are naturally a major preoccupation of the planners. They have therefore laid emphasis on the need to make residents of the Paris region, both as producers and consumers, meet a larger part of the costs which they cause to be incurred by choosing to live in the region. Measures are to be introduced which will bring the price of city transport and the provision of water and sewage and car parking space more nearly into line with the real cost of providing these facilities. This policy of charging 'true costs' is to replace the previous system of physical controls on expansion. It is also regarded as a necessary preliminary to any rational policy of regional development. It will enable the planners to have a more accurate appreciation of 'the relationship between the policy adopted towards the location of industries in the Paris region, and the modifications made to it in the new cities, and the need to step up decentralization towards the regions which have to be industrialized'.[1] The Fifth Plan is therefore facing the problem of reconciling an active regional development policy with a costly effort to provide for continued, if controlled, growth of Paris. This underlines the importance of the Paris region as a natural area of growth in the French and indeed in the European economy. If producers and consumers are willing to meet the cost, the planners are prepared to let the Paris region expand.

The priority given to promoting national efficiency has also strengthened the case for organizing the development of regions other than the Paris region around a small number of predetermined growth areas. In the first place the concentration of activity in suitable locations which growth area policy demands is essential if industries in regions are to be given the opportunity to operate on a scale and in an environment which permits maximum efficiency to be achieved. Haphazard encouragement to firms to decentralize outside Paris to areas where local unemployment is above the national average, if it succeeded at all, would be much less likely to bring about these conditions. Secondly, the provision of an adequate modern infrastructure, which is essential to promote development, is extremely costly. The national economic interest requires that

[1] Ve Plan, op. cit., Tome I, p. 130.

economies of scale in setting up infrastructure should be obtained wherever possible in order to reduce the cost, that the assets when created should be fully utilized and that where infrastructure investment is designed not merely to meet the reasonable social needs of a region but to provide *in advance* the external economies which are required to attract industry, there should be a reasonable return in terms of increased production and productivity. The success of French regional policy will thus be determined by the efficiency of growth area policy.

Regional policy in the Fifth Plan adopts the growth area strategy at several levels. The most important example is the scheduling of eight 'balancing cities' (*métropoles d'équilibre*) which are to act as a counter-attraction to the pull of the Paris region and as the main urban and industrial growth centres in the country. The cities, or more exactly, city regions chosen are Lyon-Saint Etienne, Marseille, Lille-Roubaix-Tourcoing, Metz-Nancy, Bordeaux, Toulouse, Nantes-St Nazaire, and Strasbourg. The process of selection was far from arbitrary. Twenty different criteria were considered and a points system used to rank the main towns. One criterion was the distance of the town from the Paris region. Proximity to the capital ruled out otherwise suitable locations like Dijon, Rouen and Reims. The other two main factors taken into account were the size and nature of the area for which the town was an economic and social centre and the industrial structure of the area. The criteria chosen are significant in themselves, for they mark a definite departure from a policy based on the need to alleviate local unemployment. The towns chosen are those which have the potential for urban and industrial expansion, on a scale large enough to allow them to become the centres of large-scale industrial complexes. For example, the traditionally industrial area of Nantes-St Nazaire, and not Rennes, was named as the *métropole d'équilibre* in the north-west, although previously Rennes had been considered as the growth centre for Brittany. Nantes-St Nazaire was an established industrial centre whereas Rennes, despite the large Citroen plant, had not achieved the expansion which was expected. Thus the growth area which must play a large role in utilizing the surplus manpower in Brittany is not in fact situated within the region.

Already steps have been taken to organize the city regions for their new role. In June 1966 a bill was introduced proposing the creation of new 'urban communities' (*communautés urbaines*) in four of the city regions: Lille, Lyon, Bordeaux and Strasbourg.[1] The communities range in size from 330,000 persons in Strasbourg to almost a million persons in Lyon and Lille. The communities are to be administered by councils of forty or sixty members, depending on their size, elected by the local councils of the communes in the community. The number of representatives from each commune are proportional to the population of the commune. The councils will be responsible initially for industrial and town planning developments, housing, transport, and other services. The bill provides for a similar reorganization to be carried out if there is sufficient local backing in all towns with a population of more than 100,000 persons. The relations between this new second-tier authority, existing local authorities, and the regional prefects will clearly pose problems: the Lyon community, for instance, overlaps the boundaries of three *départements*. But the decision to create these new authorities establishes the *métropoles d'équilibre* as the focal points of regional and urban development.

The second application of growth area strategy concerns rural areas. The estimated reduction in the number of workers in agriculture from 20 per cent to less than 10 per cent of the total working population in 1980 will produce a considerable shift of people away from the countryside to the urban centres. At the same time the very inadequate facilities and services available in the villages in France must be modernized and expanded. There is, therefore, a strong case for concentrated development in certain areas which can be built up as the centres of agricultural population and as locations for the industries and services which agriculture requires. The planners in collaboration with the regional authorities have embarked on a study of possible 'rural centres'. The case for growth areas is therefore accepted for rural as well as urban development.

The reform in 1964 of the system of controls and incentives used to encourage regional development makes the system more selective in favour of growth areas. The most important financial aid given to firms establishing outside the Paris region has since 1955 been a capital grant or subsidy (*prime d'équipement*). The 1964 measures replaced this with two kinds of grant, the industrial development subsidy (*prime de développement industriel*) and the industrial adaptation subsidy (*prime d'adaptation industrielle*). The areas in which these new benefits are granted have been wholly redefined. Instead

[1] See *Le Monde*, June 10, 11, 12–13, 1966.

of a large number of specially scheduled areas France is now divided into five large zones. Zone five is a region of 100 to 150 kilometres around Paris where no incentives are granted. Zone four covers regions which are generally expanding where, again, no incentives are granted. Zone three covers regions where there is no serious problem on any substantial scale. Certain fiscal benefits, particularly reductions in local taxation and the tax on the sale of land, are granted but no subsidies. Zone two includes regions where the basic problem is redevelopment or adaptation. The areas concerned are few in number and almost entirely concentrated in the older industrial areas of north and east France. In such areas the industrial adaptation subsidy is available. This can be up to 20 per cent of total capital costs. This subsidy, however, may be withdrawn if activity in the areas improves. Finally, Zone one covers regions in the south and west where regional development is a long-term operation. These areas qualify for the industrial development subsidy which will remain available indefinitely.

The object of this reform was to remove the uncertainty caused by the multiplication of special areas scheduled under previous legislation and the reform was also intended to bring the system of incentives into conformity with the new broader based regional policy and to end the practice of providing aid to any area where local unemployment became a temporary problem. In Zone one the maximum subsidy, 20 per cent of the capital costs of expansion, is given in eight urban growth areas within the zone. The choice of these areas was based on their suitability for industrial development and their employment situation, but in general more weight was attached to the former. Only eight areas were selected since any larger number would have included areas with too small a population to support self-sustaining development.

Other forms of assistance are also being made more selective. The provision of advance factories is being given high priority in France and various agencies have been established to finance their construction. The planners are, however, concerned about the lack of co-ordination in this field. Some local authorities have been unsuccessful in attracting firms to occupy the factories which they have constructed and the costs have had to be met from local revenue, thus affecting the provision of other local services. In other cases factories have been constructed in areas where there is no pressing need for them. Advance factory construction is now to be undertaken only after consultation with the regional prefects. Similar controls are being put on the building of industrial estates. There is a considerable demand from local authorities in France for financial help for such projects, in order to attract industry and to house firms whose premises have been affected by urban re-development. The planners estimate that these demands greatly exceed the number of new jobs which will be created. They also wish to prevent too many estates being constructed which are too small to attract larger firms. They have, therefore, limited the number of areas which can be zoned as industrial estates and have restricted financial aid to the growth areas of the south and west.

CONCLUSIONS

Finally, it is still necessary to consider the economic case for the type of regional policy now being undertaken in Britain and France.

France has probably gone the furthest in the direction of a permanent and longer-term policy for all regions. The outstanding characteristic of French regional policy is undoubtedly its generality: 'it does not apply solely to critical or insufficiently developed areas; it covers the whole of the country and represents one of the means for assuring the balanced expansion of the national economy'.[1]

The twenty-one *régions de programme* are now firmly established as the framework of French regional policy. The new groupings mean that regional administration will now be co-ordinated at this level, and that those responsible for national planning will draft regional programmes on this geographical basis. In the first instance the co-ordinating machinery at the regional level took the form simply of the 'interdepartmental conference' under the chairmanship of the co-ordinating prefect assisted by an advisory 'committee for regional expansion'. But the Fifth Plan saw the introduction of the regional prefect with considerably greater powers. He has the authority to make decisions concerning the distribution of public investment and aid within the programme region and has, therefore, replaced the departmental prefect as the executive responsible for the economic and social development of the region. The reorganiza-tion has thus introduced an intermediate agency at a level between the national and departmental authorities. The point has clearly been taken that an effective and economically justifiable regional

[1] IVe Plan, op. cit., p. 42.

policy must be on a larger scale than the present administrative divisions. The recent proposals to set up urban communities is a further example of the new approach.

It is, however, important to note that despite the proliferation of new bodies at the regional level, regional policy in France is still essentially determined by the national authorities. The regional prefects are consulted before basic policy decisions are made but their main function is to ensure that once these have been decided they are implemented in an efficient and co-ordinated way. The regional prefect is therefore expected to spend much more time organizing the projects included in the *tranches opératoires* within the region than lobbying in Paris for alterations in the size and distribution of the credits allocated to his region. The centralist nature of French administration has been little altered by the emergence of regionalism and indeed its continued existence is the main reason why French regional policy has the appearance at least of being more organized and purposive than in any other west European country.

At the national level responsibility for regional policy is divided between the Commissariat du Plan and DATAR. The separation of the Commissariat's conceptual work and DATAR's task of implementing policy could lead to some confusion and overlapping. But both organizations are sufficiently small and flexible to prevent any serious problems arising. Moreover, both are advocates of regional policy. The really significant relationship is that between DATAR and the Ministry of Finance and other government departments. Regional policy in France is currently viewed with a very realistic eye and the pace at which it goes will depend on DATAR being able to present a strong case. DATAR must in fact build up in relation to regional development the kind of position which the Commissariat now enjoys in the formulation of national economic policy. If it succeeds in doing this regional development will become an issue which is automatically raised in all discussions of economic policy.

The reshaping of regional policy has not been without its critics. It has been argued that any increase in effectiveness which the new measures bring about will be at the expense of a proper consultation with regional interests. The replacement of the regional committees for economic expansion by the CODERs as the consultative body in the new system has been criticized as likely to submerge the views of regional representatives in an official and little-heeded sub-committee. There is some force in this argument and the planners are taking pains not to hinder progress by alienating the very interests whose participation is essential. Although public investment must inevitably continue to be organized from the centre, the provision of information, publicity and the attraction of private industry are all tasks for which the CODERS and other groups are well suited. The current regional development policies in France do, however, imply considerable changes and adaptation on the part of individuals, firms and institutions, and this must be kept in mind when regional complaints are being discussed.

Regional development in France has a long way to go. It is, however, probably more rationally thought out and formally organized than in most other economies. However vague some of the calculations may be, the integration of regional plans into a national growth plan enables a coherent view to be taken about the strategy required for different regions at different times. In particular it provides the framework for an assessment of the costs and benefits of dispersing economic activity away from the areas in which it would naturally concentrate. There are still severe statistical problems, but in developing the present planning arrangements considerable information about the regional economies and their relations to each other and the national economy must emerge. This situation is much more likely to lead to a rational debate about the regional policy and to compel vested interests both of regionalism and of centralism to take account of the facts.

The case for the type of regional policy now being undertaken in Britain and France has, however, still to be proved. The massive cost-benefit analysis needed to reach a firm conclusion has not been undertaken. In France the immense cost of regional development in terms of financial outlay and of its effects on national economic growth has resulted in an increasingly selective approach, and deliberate concentration on a small number of pre-determined growth areas whose expansion will benefit both the region and the nation. The sophisticated approach to the expansion of the Paris region in the Fifth Plan is an indication of the difficulties involved in harmonizing national and regional growth and the growing feeling in official circles that the real costs of regional development must be more accurately stated. The EEC, in their Medium-term Economic Policy Programme, also referred to the need to carry out cost-benefit studies. The Programme recognized that regional policy could not be based solely on helping to provide employment for previously unemployed or inactive workers in the medium term, but had to rest on appraisals of the long-term viability of industrial development in growth areas. The calculation of social costs is of course a major problem but another point of very great importance is the advantages and disadvantages of alternative locations for private industry. The liaison between industry and regional planning in France is likely to provide a lot of information on this question. It is important that it should. For unless more is known the costly process of building up growth areas may be unsuccessful in attracting industry because the private cost disadvantage of the area is too great for even a developed infrastructure and the external economies of proximity to other firms to overcome. The need becomes even greater if pressure is going to be put on private industry to locate in certain regions such as the west of France where the cost differentials may be assumed to be sizeable.

In Britain, similar recent developments in regional policy raise similar doubts. Unless thought is given to fundamental considerations, there is a danger that, as in 1958 and 1960, the policy will be a short-sighted one, swayed by the currently fashionable opinion, thereby endangering the future. In 1958 and 1960 the Government gave way to pressure to act quickly to alleviate patches of unemployment up and down the country. More recently the Department of Economic Affairs and the NEDC want action on regional problems to contribute to the fulfilment of their medium-term plans for the growth of the GNP. A regional policy designed primarily with this end in view will not necessarily be appropriate to the national interest over a longer period.

It is true that the new interest in the problem areas arises out of the contribution their labour reserves can make to national output; unemployment and underemployment are regarded not so much as social problems but rather as indications of the addition to the national labour force that could be obtained by the appropriate measures.

The case for giving incentives to firms to establish themselves in areas with high unemployment and low activity rates thus moves right away from the traditional economic analysis which stressed the efficiency of particular locations from the point of view of the individual firm, and assumed an infinitely long period in which adjustments of location would be made in response to changes in population, resources, and techniques. In their concern with maximizing output over a few years, the NEDC and the DEA rest their case on the impossibility, over a short period, of making all those perfect adjustments that are assumed to be made in the absence of intervention.

Such arguments, though perfectly valid in terms of the particular aim in view, a medium-term programme for growth, leave quite open the long-standing problem whether it is in the national interest in the long period, say, over twenty or thirty years, for special inducements to be given to firms to move to the less prosperous regions. The development of the economy over a longer period ought not be jeopardized in the effort to achieve an extra $0 \cdot 1$ per cent per annum in the current period. It is certainly naïve to suppose that if the location problem were left entirely to the operation of a free economy, industry would necessarily be attracted to such areas as would maximize output later this century; but equally it is uncertain that the correct solution is to be found by maximizing output from the less prosperous regions over a five- or six-year period. The NEDC supported their case for using the unemployed resources of the regions by reference to the kind of evidence that had previously been used to support the policy of inducements on social grounds. They referred to the fact that costs do not seem to differ very greatly between the more and the less prosperous regions, and that the main problem is the cost of moving and establishment, that is, initially higher costs. But these facts are quite partial and short-term. For example, one of the main reasons why cost comparisons work out favourably for the less prosperous regions is because hourly average earnings there are lower than the rest of the country. If the policy is successful, we should expect that earnings would rise gradually towards the national average, which raises the question, what then would be the economic position of firms that were attracted partly by the fact that earnings were lower? External economies gradually built up in growth areas would offset the rise in earnings, but the final total effect on costs would remain uncertain.

The above comments should not be taken to imply that the DEA has been wrong in advocating a regional policy that seeks to attract firms to areas where there is unemployment, or that it is better, taking a very long view, to let the less prosperous regions run down. All that is suggested is that there are questions about regional policy that, in the absence of adequate statistics and even of analytical apparatus, remain unanswered, and that a *caveat* should therefore be entered against allowing the fashion for growth planned over periods of four to six years to lead to difficulties in the more distant future.

If regional policy is to be henceforth considered as a constant and integral part of economic policy, it must also be decided whether it is preferable for the whole country concerned to be permanently divided into regions, each with its own centre for the co-ordination and promotion of regional policy, or whether it is better for the central authority to define regions and to re-draw boundaries as and when it thinks fit; and to what extent the regional bodies, whether they are set up on a permanent basis or not, should be primarily the agents of the central government, and how far they should represent local interests and authorities.

CHAPTER 11

THE BALANCE OF PAYMENTS

For a country in which international trade is significant the balance of payments is crucial for growth; the maintenance of an adequate growth rate requires that a country with an open economy should be competitive in foreign markets, while its industries must also be competitive in home markets for goods which can be imported, or demand at home will be directed to foreign goods.[1] In an uncompetitive country businessmen will not be willing to undertake expansion for two reasons. First, the relatively high prices of their exports will prevent them from gaining ground or even from maintaining their foothold in export markets (unless indeed the structure of their export trade is peculiarly favourable, and the OECD has shown that this is not the case for the majority of West European countries).[2] Secondly, businessmen will be reluctant to rely on the continued expansion of home demand because of the probability of its increasing diversion on to imported goods, and even more because they will expect that the deteriorating external payments position will eventually lead to restrictive policies at home which will curtail demand. Indeed, accelerated growth induced by expectations of rising home demand will, if it takes place, be self-frustrating since it will lead to increased imports which cannot be offset by increased exports. For the growth of an open economy to be rapid and sustained, then, it must be based on exports that are expanding at an appropriate rate. It follows that the situation of a slow-growing and uncompetitive economy, which is probably slow-growing because it is uncompetitive, and uncompetitive because slow-growing, is extremely difficult.

---

[1] This thesis is developed in an unpublished study by the OECD, *Growth and Economic Policy*, 1964; in the NIESR study by W. Beckerman, *The British Economy in 1975*, Cambridge University Press, 1965; and by A. Lamfalussy, *The United Kingdom and the Six*, Macmillan, 1963.

[2] OECD, op. cit.

To break out of this vicious circle it must make itself competitive, either by increasing its productivity faster than its rivals, or by increasing its prices less, or by a combination of the two. In this chapter an attempt is made to clarify the problem and to review the possible solutions with reference to the policies employed in Germany, France and Britain.

GERMANY

'After 1951–2 (Korean boom) and 1955, the year 1960 brought the fourth highest growth rate of real gross national product (8·8 per cent), and marked the high-point of the third wave of growth in the German economy since 1950. Since the autumn of 1963 our economy is experiencing its fourth cyclical upswing. An important propelling force in all these cases was clearly the growth of foreign demand.'[1] This excerpt from the First Report of the German Council of Economic Experts is itself a significant indicator that German experience bears out the OECD thesis regarding export-led growth. Even more convincing is the table opposite, published in the Third Report, indicating the impact of export demand on German investment.

The underlined figures for years in which each of the three components had a peak share in the annual growth give a clear indication that growth of exports preceded growth of investment, which in turn preceded growth of consumption. It need only be added that all Germany's main export industries—machine tools, motor vehicles, chemical and electrical products—have experienced very rapid rates of growth.

The Council of Economic Experts continued their account of the successful export performance of the German economy by reference to the stability of export-led growth:

' . . . export-oriented growth, in contrast to internally oriented growth, does not have to be checked for balance-of-payments reasons, . . . unchecked growth is faster growth, . . . faster growth, because it means greater productivity increases, favours one's competitive performance in export markets. The way this result is reached is as follows: experience shows that as real incomes rise industrial goods become cheaper in relation to services. For this reason, and because services are more important in the gross national

[1] *Sachverständigenrat: Jahresgutachten*, 1964, p. 13.

FINAL UTILIZATION OF GOODS AND SERVICES IN GERMANY,
1951–66

Year	Change in relation to the previous year in percentages	Shares in the annual growth in percentages		
		Exports	Investment	Private consumption
1951	23·1	29·1	16·6	40·6
1952	14·3	17·5	23·9	41·7
1953	7·5	27·8	22·7	66·3
1954	9·8	33·0	28·0	33·8
1955	16·0	19·9	36·3	37·7
1956	10·9	32·4	11·2	49·8
1957	10·0	35·3	12·5	43·9
1958	6·5	10·0	13·6	56·8
1959	9·5	24·5	30·8	33·5
1960	12·8	23·7	33·3	32·1
1961	9·3	8·9	22·6	51·2
1962	9·0	9·1	20·5	50·0
1963	6·6	21·8	13·5	42·9
1964*	9·9	19·2	36·9	38·1
1965*	9·9	15·6	22·7	45·0
1966*	6·6	29·5	6·2	52·0

Source: Sachverständigenrat: Jahresgutachten, 1966, p. 30.
* Provisional figures.

product than in exports, the internal price level rises in comparison with the export price level. Because of this "scissors movement", if the internal purchasing power of money is held steady, then the prices of industrial products and thus export prices (expressed in the home currency) sink in absolute terms. A country which achieves greater productivity increases than another will as a result of this, given fixed exchange rates, steadily improve its competitive position in international trade, so long as it does not allow its internal price level, because of the greater "scissors effect", to rise faster than that of its neighbours and partners. Countries with comparatively large productivity increases, but relatively small increases in the internal price level, will thus tend to accumulate export surpluses, if this trend is not countered by changes in the exchange rate.'[1]

[1] Sachverständigenrat, op. cit., p. 23.

Assessing the benefits and drawbacks of Germany's export-led growth, the experts calculated, on a purely arithmetical basis, that without the extra impulse from abroad Germany's real income per head would have been about one-tenth smaller in 1963, and that the internal price level would have been about $7\frac{1}{2}$ per cent lower. Recognizing that one of the drawbacks of export-led growth was the excessive liquidity entering the country from abroad, the experts nevertheless came to the conclusion that: ' . . . a comparison of German experience with that of Britain, where for balance-of-payments reasons a "stop-and-go" policy has to be used, shows clearly that a tendency towards excessive liquidity is less detrimental than the reverse.'[1]

This report was published in Germany in January 1965. The experience of that year and of the first half of 1966 led many observers to conclude that Germany's period of export-led growth was over, and that the German position was moving much closer to the British. Prices were rising and the balance of payments had gone into deficit. Germany, it seemed, had caught the 'English disease'. However, while it would be rash to pass final judgment on the German economic crisis of 1965–6, it seems misleading to compare it with the kind of difficulties which Britain was suffering in the same period. Throughout 1965 and the first half of 1966 the gold and foreign exchange reserves held by the Bundesbank remained enormous. Although the internal rise in prices was high by previous German standards, it was fairly modest by international standards. Finally, by the middle of 1966 prices had been stabilized, the trade balance was positive once more and, most important, the foreign orders received by German industry were increasing rapidly. It is true that in the latter part of 1966 and the first half of 1967 it seemed as though stabilization had worked too well and that there might be a severe internal recession in Germany. The foreign trade position was still strong, however, and by the end of 1967 an upswing seemed to be starting at home. The export-led growth cycle appeared to be beginning once more.

However, this general account and interpretation of the development of German exports in the period 1951–67 is merely a statement of what export-led growth looks like when once it has been attained. It is also very important, especially if one is seeking for pointers to guide British policy, to examine how Germany achieved the trans-

[1] *Sachverständigenrat,* op. cit., p. 25.

formation from her postwar crisis into this era of rapid export-led growth. The period of German postwar economic history which is most relevant to British problems is that around the time of the Korean War, when the Federal Republic experienced its most serious balance-of-payments crisis, and when it laid the foundations of its future surpluses and rapid economic growth.

The rapid transformation of Germany's balance-of-payments position in 1951 is probably the one point in the country's postwar economic experience which deserves the word 'miracle'. In the year 1950 Germany's external balance of goods and services showed a deficit of 2,500 million marks, a gap which not even foreign assistance amounting to 2,070 million marks could close. For 1951, during the first quarter of which Germany was still in an acute balance-of-payments crisis, the balance showed a surplus of 600 million marks. The following year there was a surplus of 2,340 million marks, and in 1953, 4,200 million marks. The period of massive surpluses had begun.

How did this transformation take place? An analysis requires a brief account of developments in Germany after the 1948 Currency Reform. The immediate effect of this Reform and of the simultaneous removal of a large number of price controls was to unleash long repressed consumer demand. This surge of demand, in the face of relatively inelastic supply, caused a rapid rise in prices. By the end of 1948 the Central Bank had, for the first time, to impose restrictive measures, and these, combined with a restrictive budgetary policy, and measures to liberalize trade, succeeded in stabilizing prices during 1949 and the first half of 1950. In 1949, however, the problem of unemployment, caused by both the unfreezing of markets and the flow of refugees from the East, began to make itself felt with increasing seriousness. Unemployment rose from 1·3 million in June 1949 to 2 million in February 1950, when it represented some 12 per cent of the working population. To counter this the Central Bank began to loosen its restrictive measures from the middle of 1949 onwards and began to take positive measures to promote investment. The Government was also preparing a 'public works' programme in the months before the Korean crisis broke out.

Finally, the balance-of-payments problem moved to the centre of the stage. During 1949 Germany's external balance of goods and services had showed a deficit but it was not a large one, and was more than compensated by Marshall Aid. In the second quarter of

1950 the balance actually showed a surplus. The outbreak of the Korean War in June 1950, however, changed the whole picture. The war provoked a new surge of internal demand, as well as an increase in the external demand for German goods—the former being caused largely by 'war nerves' and the latter by 'the almost insatiable hunger of numerous countries with stepped-up investment programmes for German capital goods.'[1] At the same time the prices of imported raw materials rose sharply as a result of increased world demand. The increase in home demand, together with the worsening of the terms of trade, caused the balance-of-payments position to deteriorate rapidly. At the same time prices went up at an alarming rate.

It should be explained here that certain circumstances placed Germany in a particularly exposed position when the Korean War broke out. In accordance with Dr Erhard's neo-liberal ideas, ambitious measures had been taken to liberalize trade in 1949 and 1950. As late as October 1950 a substantial reduction of barriers to imports from the OEEC area had taken place. Secondly, in comparison with the devaluation of sterling in 1949 (30·5 per cent), the devaluation of the Deutschemark in the same year was relatively modest (20·6 per cent). Lastly, the Government had cut income tax early in 1950. All these measures served to accentuate the trends started by the Korean War.

How did Germany surmount the crisis? There can be little doubt that the firm action of the authorities, based on a clear conception of the priorities of economic policy, contributed decisively to the outcome. From the start prime emphasis was placed on maintaining price stability. The Central Bank pursued a policy of vigorous deflation, using both orthodox and unorthodox means. Bank rate was raised sharply from 4 to 6 per cent in October 1950; minimum reserve requirements were raised by an average of 50 per cent; the Länder banks were instructed to follow a restrictive credit policy; and certain direct quantitative and qualitative controls were placed on the activities of the commercial banks. The Central Bank pursued this policy in virtual independence, on the 'basis of an exclusively economic diagnosis'.[2]

---

[1] Dr Otmar Emminger, *Währungspolitik im Wandel der Zeit*, Frankfurt, Fritz Knapp Verlag, 1966, p. 17.

[2] Cf. C. Mötteli, *Licht und Schatten der Sozialen Marktwirtschaft*, Erlenbach-Zürich, 1961, p. 128. Eucken's advocacy of an 'automatic' monetary policy should be recalled in this context (p. 40).

The policy of the Central Bank was of course accompanied by other measures. Import restrictions were imposed. At first these took the form of requiring importers to make a cash deposit of 50 per cent of the equivalent in marks of the foreign currency needed to pay for the imports concerned. Later, in February 1951, the liberalization measures taken within the framework of OEEC were rescinded. A special credit of 120 million dollars was obtained in December 1950 from the European Payments Union. The Government was given emergency powers in March 1951 by the *Wirtschaftssicherungsgesetz* to allocate certain raw materials, though this was rarely used. Finally, Finance Minister Schäffer pursued a strict policy of balancing the budget, even if it meant rescinding earlier tax concessions and, in 1951, raising the turnover tax by one-third.

By the second quarter of 1951 the German trade balance was out of deficit, and by the end of the year a significant surplus had appeared. The restrictive policy of the Central Bank, however, was relaxed only very slowly, and when it was quite clear that internal prices were falling. The credit squeeze was not loosened appreciably until October 1951, and it was not until May 1952 that minimum reserve requirements were lowered, and bank rate reduced from 6 to 5 per cent. In January 1952 the Government restarted its policy of import liberalization and in the course of that year most of the remaining direct controls on the economy were removed.

To what extent did Germany make use of special measures to foster exports during this period? Towards the end of the crisis certain tax inducements were introduced to favour incomes derived from exports; they were established by the *Exportförderungsgesetz* of June 1951, which lasted until 1956. The credit facilities granted to exporters during the early years of reconstruction were also probably more advantageous than in many other West European countries. One further factor which probably aided German exports in the years immediately following the payments crisis should also be mentioned, namely the large budgetary surpluses which were kept frozen at the Central Bank (the so-called 'Julius Tower', see p. 226 above). This freezing of internal demand probably served unintentionally as an incentive to German businessmen to look for markets abroad.

There are a number of other reasons why the German balance of payments moved so rapidly from a deficit to a surplus. The favourable structure of German exports has been mentioned in Chapter 2.

The concentration of German exports in those areas where world demand was increasing rapidly was undoubtedly the reason why German export prices were able to rise faster than the British during the Korean boom period. Dr Otmar Emminger suggests that the balance-of-payments position was also aided by the lower import-dependency of German industry as a result of over a decade of autarchy.[1] In 1952 the volume of raw materials and semi-finished goods imported into West Germany was only 7 per cent above that of 1936, while West German industrial production had increased by 45 per cent. This must of course be set against the country's increased dependence on food imports. Emminger also draws attention to the average German's low propensity to spend his money at that time on objects with a high import content; the Germans preferred to devote their higher incomes to housing, recreation, travel, and above all the building up of liquid reserves.

Viewed as a whole, the significant features of the 1950–2 period would seem to be:

1. The determination and vigour with which the primacy of price stability was maintained, a policy fully in keeping with neo-liberal principles. The fact that the Central Bank and other authorities did not relax their restrictive measures until internal prices were seen to be falling undoubtedly had repercussions in the international field. Recent analysis[2] has shown that although British export prices rose during the Korean boom rather more slowly than German, they did not remain stable or even fall, as the German prices did, when the boom was over, but continued a gradual upward movement. Undoubtedly this was one factor which gave German exports an edge over British exports in the years that followed: when the next cyclical upswing took place in Europe in 1955–6, German exporters were able to take full advantage of it.

2. Certain other factors also helped German exports during this early period, the most important of which would seem to be their favourable commodity structure.

3. During the period of crisis the German Government did not refrain from intervention of a very direct nature. There was no pretence of 'allowing market forces free play' when a severe dis-

[1] O. Emminger, op. cit., p. 25.
[2] S. J. Wells, *British Export Performance*, Cambridge University Press, 1964, pp. 62–3.

equilibrium occurred. Once equilibrium had been restored government controls and restrictions were dismantled with impressive speed though many incentives to exports as well as to investment and savings remained.

FRANCE

The interpretation of economic development in France in the light of the theory of export-induced growth is not quite so straightforward as in the case of Germany. French growth has been rapid, but has involved a considerable growth of imports, has been accompanied by a relatively high degree of inflation, and produced balance-of-payments crises in most years of the 1950s, when French exports grew markedly less than home demand, and certainly not fast enough to offset the increase in import demand which expansion based on home demand had induced. This problem was particularly acute in France, since it was necessary to import a high proportion of manufactured and semi-finished products. France was then an exception to the rule that rapid growth is based on international competitiveness and a strong export demand.

The explanation of this apparent paradox lies both in the nature of the French economy and in the economic policies pursued. The importance of export demand as a condition for growth depends on the size of imports relative to the national product. Until the late 1950s France was less dependent on international trade than the United Kingdom and most other West European countries, and as a result the import requirements of a faster rate of growth based on the expansion of home demand made fewer inroads into her foreign exchange reserves. Moreover, the franc is not a major international trading currency like the pound and devaluation has been viewed with far more equanimity than in Britain.

Foreign aid in various forms was also a considerable help well into the middle of the 1950s. In the immediate postwar years Marshall Aid funds enabled the programmes of the First Plan to go ahead in spite of rising imports, inflation and balance-of-payments deficits; and the 'counterpart fund', the equivalent in francs of the American aid, was used by the authorities to help to a considerable extent to finance the Plan's investment programmes. In Britain, these funds were held by the Treasury and not injected into the economy. When Marshall Aid ceased, the French economy continued to benefit from the expenditure of foreign governments in France and especially by 'offshore' purchases by NATO forces. This offset a large part of the deficit on current account during the first two years of the Second Plan and it was not until 1956 that the balance-of-payments constraint began really to influence economic policy.

The special circumstances of the French economy certainly permitted more audacious policies aimed at stepping up the rate of growth of the economy to be pursued, but it must be noted that every possible advantage was taken of them. The planners must take much of the credit for this. The First and Second Plans laid far greater emphasis on growth than stability and at no time, even in 1956–7, did they advocate a reduction in the level of demand as an effective counter to rising prices and an increasing trade deficit. With a propensity to import, particularly in the consumer goods industries, lower than that of most other European economies the deflation would have had to be severe and would have seriously affected investment. The balance-of-payments situation was dealt with first by the reimposition of import controls in 1957, after they had been reduced under the agreements within the OEEC, and then by devaluation in 1957 and 1958. Special incentives were also given to exporters holding the *carte d'exportateur* (see p. 198 above.)

These protective measures, added to an already naturally insulated economy, gave French industrialists an assurance that the economy would be to some degree shielded from international developments and prevented the unfavourable effect, otherwise to be expected, on the willingness to invest and to expand output.

The Third Plan, 1958–61, faced the French planners for the first time with the task of bringing external payments into balance as well as promoting faster growth. It also coincided with French entry into the European Economic Community, which opened the French economy to influences on which a system of indicative planning could have little direct effect. The investment programmes of the Plan were, however, aimed especially at developing import substitutes, and at improving France's previously poor performance in the export of manufactured goods.[1] This was considered an essential preparation for the increased foreign competition which the Common Market would bring. In the Fourth and Fifth Plans the problems of 'planning' an increased volume of international trade

[1] M. MacLennan, The Common Market and French Planning, *Journal of Common Market Studies*, Vol. I, No. 1, 1960.

have become one of the major preoccupations of the planners, who have also argued strongly for the adoption of planning methods similar to their own at the Community level. How far they succeeded in this is examined in Chapter 12.

In drawing up the Fourth Plan the planners gave considerable weight to the balance-of-payments constraint. Both their previous record and the logic of indicative planning might lead one to expect that a high output target would be set and a bold attempt made to achieve it even if this involved a limited period when imports were growing faster than exports. But this was not the approach. The planners deliberately outlined a 'policy of safeguards' which consisted of setting as a foreign trade target a surplus and not simply a balance on current account so that if exports failed steps could be taken to stimulate them before a deficit occurred. The surplus on current account forecast for 1965 was $800 million. But this was not achieved and despite an improvement in the trade balance in 1965 the current account at the end of the Fourth Plan showed a slight deficit.

Several factors were responsible. The price increases of 1963 and 1964 led to a switching of both industrial and consumer demand from home-produced to imported goods. The planners attribute the failure to meet the targets set for exports of manufactured goods to the 'weak' industrial structure of the French economy, that is, its lack of concentration and specialization. The measures required to amend this situation were seriously held back by the falling off in private investment as a result of the Stabilization Plan introduced in 1963. Despite these setbacks the overall balance of payments and thus the level of reserves remained reasonably satisfactory, though less so than in 1961 and 1962. This is attributable to the large inflow of long-term capital into France, particularly from the United States, since 1961. In the Fifth Plan, however, it is heavily emphasized that this offsetting factor cannot and indeed must not continue. The concentration of foreign investment in certain sectors of French industry, while conferring some benefits, has threatened to deprive the French Government of control over important industries. The Plan was, therefore, formulated on the assumption that much tighter controls would be exercised over foreign investment. It is indeed the aim of the Plan to make France a net exporter of private capital, so that French firms can establish commercial and industrial bases overseas as a means of furthering French exports and can afford the heavy expenditure likely to be required to exploit and explore sources of energy. A balance of current payments is thus more than ever desired.

The French planners accept that they cannot in any sense 'plan' exports or even imports, although it should be added that they have undertaken for the Fifth Plan a survey of prospects much more detailed and realistic than the exercise done in the British National Plan. They see their contribution as a qualitative one: to establish the preconditions for an increase in exports large enough to balance the rise in imports. Hence the priority that they give to raising productivity in French industry. This involves a whole series of measures on the side of production and supply, rather than the manipulation of demand through expectations influenced by an indicative plan.

BRITAIN

While France appears to have escaped the full rigours of the export-or-stagnate rule, Britain presents a fine case study of its operation, at the opposite pole from Germany. While this proposition could be documented, and has been, from the economic history of the 1950s in Britain,[1] it is more useful to refer to the situation in the mid-1960s and its development during the period in which a conscious effort has been made to secure an acceleration in the rate of growth.

The relationship of a growth programme to the balance of payments imposes two requirements: first, that the target for growth of the GDP should be consistent with the balance-of-payments constraint; and second, that if short-term restrictions become necessary, they should be devised in such a way as to do minimum damage to medium- and long-term growth prospects. The first requirement has, unfortunately, been largely ignored by the British planning bodies: the NEDC in 1963, and the DEA in 1965.

Briefly, the NEDC's plan required an annual rate of growth of exports of 5 per cent, to match the estimated growth of imports of 4 per cent and to achieve a modest balance-of-payments surplus. This was far above the previous trend of a 3 per cent per annum growth of exports, while the growth of imports proved to be seriously underestimated. Like the NEDC's export targets, the DEA's depended on

[1] See J. C. R. Dow, *The Management of the British Economy, 1945–50*, Cambridge University Press, 1965, especially Chapters XV and XVI.

hopes of a faster increase of productivity and on the still problematical success of the prices and incomes policy. They also depended on the developments in these fields in competitor countries, and were subject to such uncertainties that, while it would be unwise to say that exports could not have grown at the target rate, there was little ground for believing that they would. Since the target for imports was that they should be kept down to the same 4 per cent growth that the NEDC vainly hoped for, there was little reason for attaching greater credibility to the DEA's figures for the development of the balance of payments.

There were, however, several possibilities for continuing a faster rate of growth than had been achieved before 1963 even though the balance-of-payments developments remained disappointing in relation to the plan, and the policy of the British Government in the first half of 1964 was essentially one of using up all such possibilities before taking measures that would slow down growth. First the NEDC plan had budgeted for a surplus of £400 million a year by 1966, with a higher level of international lending, and some addition to the reserves. While these objectives were highly praiseworthy, the former on account of the needs of the underdeveloped nations, in particular, and the latter on account of the extremely slender reserves which had made earlier payments crises more acute and embarrassing, neither of them was essential to the fulfilment of the other objectives of the plan. By the spring of 1964 the projected addition to the reserves was abandoned, and the estimates for overseas lending were cut by £75 million. Some room for manoeuvre was thus allowed by the generosity of the expectations of the original plan.

Secondly, various possibilities were open to the British Government, as to other governments, for financing a temporary overseas deficit. Sterling has been supported by temporary credits from foreign central banks with the participation of the Bank for International Settlements and the United States Export-Import Bank and by drawings on the International Monetary Fund. The IMF exists for the purpose of enabling countries that incur temporary deficits to avoid having to deflate the home economy, and resort to IMF borrowings during a period of planned expansion is therefore perfectly proper. Similarly, assistance from other central banks has also become in recent years an established aspect of international economic co-operation, in the face of a crisis of confidence affecting an important world currency. However, such assistance can meet only temporary deficits on the current transactions and outflows of capital; there is pressure for repayment over a fairly short period; and for the deficit country to take other measures to correct the imbalance that gave rise to the necessity for borrowing.

There remain still other ways of allowing domestic expansion to continue even though the possibilities of international help have been exhausted, and internal action becomes essential. The Government can seek to operate directly on the balance of payments, while keeping effects on the level of demand at home to a minimum. Thus the British Government tried to avoid the curtailment of growth at home by imposing a 15 per cent surcharge on imports, coupled with tax concessions for exports estimated to amount to a subsidy of about $1\frac{1}{2}$ per cent on their prices, and favourable access to credit within the context of general restrictions. It also was a sign of the influence of the NEDC and the growth 'lobby' that both the main British parties were prepared to use a measure which had been more typical of the French, than of the British, approach to balance-of-payments difficulties in the previous decade. However, special import duties, like international borrowing, are only a temporary palliative. The Government had to promise to remove them as soon as possible, in order to obtain retrospective sanction from our partners in the GATT and in the EFTA. The surcharge was reduced to 10 per cent in April 1965, and the remaining 10 per cent was removed in October 1966, two years after its imposition.

While there may be some ways of avoiding the operation of the export constraint for a short time, and while Britain showed signs in 1964–6 of learning from the French example to use these devices in the interests of steady growth, all such efforts are futile if exports do not eventually benefit, and in time, from the period of expansion. The British Government spent the greater part of 1964 waiting for exports to turn up, and they stubbornly refused to do so. In 1965, exports did increase faster and with a low rate of increase of imports the balance of payments was considerably improved though not to the extent of moving into surplus. A further improvement in 1966 still did not entirely remove the deficit. It was therefore impossible to avoid the progressive imposition of more and more stringent restrictions, especially in the 'July packages' of 1965 and 1966. Although some attention was devoted, in devising these measures, to our second requirement that the harm done to longer-term growth prospects should be minimized, the shortfall on the first requirement that the growth target should be consistent with the balance-of-payments constraint was so substantial, and the measures therefore so tough, that considerable damage was undoubtedly done to growth prospects. Nor did the measures in the event improve the balance of payments enough to prevent the devaluation of November 1967.

The credibility of any plan for accelerating growth in Britain pivots upon the question of whether the balance of payments can be maintained at a satisfactory level at a higher rate of growth. Unless a happy outcome can be foreseen for the balance of payments before the end of any time that can be bought by the kind of temporary measures outlined above, either the credibility of the plan is affected and the economy does not act on the assumption that faster growth will be possible, or, if it does, an economic crisis ensues. The plan drawn up by the NEDC in 1963 must be faulted on this account. The target for exports was attainable only if the competitiveness of British industry could be significantly improved. This in turn was taken to require the holding down of British costs and prices by means of some form of incomes policy. But the NEDC was never able to suggest any good reason for thinking that an effective incomes policy could be in operation in time to help in implementing their programme for 1961 to 1966. The DEA made substantial progress in 1965 and 1966 in setting up the machinery for an incomes policy and in securing co-operation from business and trade union leaders, before the temporary freeze on all prices and incomes was imposed in July 1966. But it is essential that a whole growth programme should not be geared to some major effect on exports deriving from a hypothetical breakthrough in incomes policy. Chapter 9 has shown that incomes policies are very hard to establish, and even harder to make and keep effective. It was therefore very unfortunate that the National Plan's export and import targets were almost exact copies of the NEDC's.

Despite later changes, such as the developments in the operation of the prices and incomes policy and policies to improve the balance of payments on capital account, there are no grounds for altering the conclusion that the National Plan failed to show the feasibility of the planned rate of growth. On the contrary, the Plan showed that it was not feasible unless something drastic was done to the balance of payments, and should, therefore, have been the signal for either such drastic action or the abandonment of the target.

Acting, however, on the assumption that it could buy enough time by borrowing and temporary measures, and strenuously resisting devaluation, the Government adopted three broad lines of policy for improving the balance of payments. The first was to apply policies directly to the stimulation of exports or to restraining the growth of imports. Remissions of taxation or export subsidies can have speedy effect, although governments have hitherto felt their freedom of action to be limited by the GATT rules on fair trade. The budget of November 1964 remitted taxes amounting to a mere 1·5 per cent on export prices, though the removal of these remissions was announced after devaluation. If there were a shift in the general burden of taxation towards an added-value tax discussed above in Chapter 7, more substantial remissions could be provided. The Selective Employment Tax imposed in 1966 was intended to help manufacturers by means of the refunds to them together with premia, and thus to help, among others, those who export. But this tax in its initial form was not as relevantly discriminatory as other methods of encouraging exports, and any encouragement was diminished by the withdrawal of the premia for manufacturing after the devaluation. The added-value tax has the great advantage that it does not apply tax relief to broad categories of firms, many of which may either not be exporting at all or not in significant quantities, but specifically to goods actually exported. The replacement of present company taxation by an added-value tax might therefore be one of the most effective ways of providing a general incentive to exporters. The French system of *cartes d'exportateur* indicates another possibility in this direction (see p. 198 above), which has the merit of employing standard criteria for determining who should benefit, and of being restricted to those who do really well in increasing exports.

A second method of producing a long-term improvement in the balance of payments, and one which appeared to be popular with the Government in 1964-8, is to reduce imports by means of specific encouragement to the production at home of goods that have previously been imported. A simpler way of reducing imports is of course to take direct action by imposing higher tariffs or quotas, or by requiring advance payments for imports, as Italy and Japan have done, or restricting credit to importers. The British Government discriminated against importers in applying the credit restrictions in 1965 and 1966, as well as applying the import surcharges, but all these methods of curtailing imports suffer the major disadvantage that they do nothing to meet the demand for the goods previously imported. The policy of developing 'import-saving' or 'import-substitute' production meets this problem by reducing imports only in so far as they can be satisfactorily replaced by home production. This policy was followed by the Labour Government of 1945, the most significant examples of its operation being the establishment of oil refining in Britain, the support given to the coal industry and, above all, the system of agricultural support. The policy was put forward by both the Chancellor of the Exchequer[1] and the Leader of the Opposition[2] in 1964. It was also referred to in the NEDC Report on exports and has been pursued by the DEA and the Ministry of Technology.

As a solution that can be relied upon to help solve the balance-of-payments problem in the short or medium term, this policy has, however, one great disadvantage. Not much appears to be known about what the possibilities are, by what measures they might be exploited, what the quantitative effects might be, and how soon they would make a significant difference to the payments situation. The industries thought to be most likely candidates for extending import saving were those whose sponsorship was transferred to the Ministry of Technology when it was set up, namely machine tools, electronics and computers. These are modern growth industries in which imports have been rising rapidly. (A later addition to the list, in 1967, was the production of aluminium, for which the Government proposed to arrange a specially favourable electricity tariff. This plan, however, encountered opposition from some of Britain's EFTA partners, who regarded such a move as an unfair discrimination against their aluminium producers. For further references to inhibitions on internal planning arising out of international economic integration, see pp. 360–3.) Increasing international specialization may be part of the explanation for the higher imports but it can by no means be the whole explanation, since the exports of these industries have not risen at anything approaching the rate of increase of imports. If the reasons for this can be identified, then it seems sensible that measures to improve productivity and competitiveness might properly be concentrated on them first, in order to have the most direct and rapid effect on the balance of payments. This might be done through

[1] Mr Maudling in his Budget speech, House of Commons Debates, April 1964.
[2] Mr Wilson in a speech at Swansea, January 1964.

specific subsidies or tax incentives, or through government contracts which include conditions relating to the improvement of efficiency. Such an orientation of public spending would represent no more than a counterpart to the tariffs levied on private imports. Indeed, the use of a 'shadow tariff' for government purchases is a useful rule-of-thumb for determining where such a policy of 'infant-industry' protection is justified.[1]

While the effectiveness of efforts at import-saving is not certain enough for them to be regarded as a major element of balance-of-payments policy in the shorter run, then, some useful results might be obtained, especially if the resources used to develop the import-saving industries were previously unemployed, or if the measures used to expand their output are also at the same time measures that increase their efficiency and therefore raise the national product. In other words, the policy of developing import-saving industries may be valuable within the context of a plan for using the idle resources of the regions of high unemployment, or for improving productivity generally. To give priority to import-saving industries within these other areas of policy makes a good deal of sense in a predicament such as that of Britain in the 1960s. It could take effect on the balance of payments only after a considerable time, but this applies to a high proportion of measures to remove obstacles to growth.

A third specific policy for improving the balance of payments in the long term is to establish an incomes policy in an attempt to keep down the rise of prices and to ensure that they are in line with those of competing nations. Since the more particular interventions aimed directly at exports or imports, and subject to various contervailing effects, are limited, and slow to operate, then an incomes policy and devaluation (or export subsidies) appear to be the only general solutions that do not, like deflation, stand in the way of growth. Thus it was suggested that if the prices and incomes freeze imposed in July 1966 were maintained in fully effective operation for two years, it would have produced, on the assumption that other countries did not do likewise, a *de facto* devaluation of some 10 per cent. However, it is extremely doubtful whether a freeze could be so effective for such a period. A less draconian incomes policy would be less effective,

[1] An obvious candidate for a shadow tariff is military spending overseas. This was proposed in *The Times*, August 19, 1966.

and must be regarded as a longer-term policy: that is, it would by itself substantially improve international competitiveness only after several years, and not in the two or three years in which a complete freeze might make a substantial contribution.

These three types of policy did not prove capable of solving the balance-of-payments problem in time, and the pound was therefore devalued. Indeed, most of these special balance-of-payments measures, like most measures for accelerating the rate of growth of productivity and hence the growth of the economy in general, are by their nature such as to require a few years, and in some cases (such as industrial training and management training) many years, to bear fruit. The devaluation should give Britain the opportunity to secure a satisfactory balance of payments during the period in which the economy adapts itself to a higher rate of growth of productivity and exports. Examples of such an outcome were given earlier in this chapter where the way in which Germany and later France achieved export-led growth was described. The German 'miracle' followed the Currency Reform of 1948, the tough and persistent deflation of the early 1950s, and a series of reforms to stimulate investment and exports and to open up markets. The French 'miracle' proceeded for some time in the teeth of payments difficulties, but then accommodated them by a similar policy: devaluation accompanied by deflationary measures and the stimulus of competition provided by entry into the European Economic Community.

Devaluation gives Britain the opportunity to follow the example of Germany and France, but this opportunity will not be made use of unless, in the years following the devaluation, the rates of growth of exports and of productivity are in fact increased, and the rate of growth of imports remains within the limits imposed by the need for a satisfactory balance of payments, given the rate of growth of exports that is attained. This means that the price advantage gained by devaluation must not be lost, and there must therefore be disinflation to the extent required to release resources for the improvement in the trade balance that should follow the devaluation.

The Government accordingly announced, at the same time as the devaluation, a package of disinflationary measures, including higher taxes and bank rate, and cuts in public expenditure and tax allowances, to add to the measures that had already been applied. The danger remains, however, that cost-push inflation will eat away Britain's advantage, unless the relationship between the rate of

M

growth of productivity and that of incomes is at least as favourable as in the main countries that compete with Britain in world markets. This danger is increased by the rise in the domestic price level that follows inevitably from the rise in import prices, and which is bound to reinforce the pressures for higher incomes that were already building up, following the incomes freeze and during the period of 'severe restraint'. The deflationary measures therefore need to be supplemented by an effective incomes policy, if part and perhaps all of the cost advantage due to devaluation is not to be lost.

Given enough success in holding the price level by means of disinflationary measures and incomes policy, and the sufficient improvement in the balance of payments that should follow from this, it is still necessary to ensure that capacity grows fast enough to allow for a faster rate of growth of productivity. The measures to improve efficiency, described earlier, will contribute to this, but adequate investment in productive capacity will also be required. Here the measures that the Government announced when it devalued appeared less encouraging; the rise in corporation tax, and the ending of premia for manufacturers under the Selective Employment Tax, were not likely to encourage investment. If the devaluation is to succeed in providing a basis for faster growth together with balance-of-payments equilibrium, the encouragement of investment as well as of exports will have to be among the main objectives of economic policy.

The failure of Britain's first National Plan, due to the prolonged balance-of-payments crisis and followed by the devaluation, provide an excellent case study (albeit an expensive one) in the relationship between national programmes and economic policies. The targets of the programme are likely to be worse than useless unless existing trends in the economy combined with the economic policies adopted are sufficient to enable the economy to grow at more or less the intended rate. The existing trends in exports and imports, combined with the policies designed to improve the balance of payments, were not in the event sufficient to relax the external constraint enough to make possible the intended rate of growth, nor did it seem likely, even when the National Plan was published, that they would be. The many policies aimed at improving the rate of growth of productivity could be expected to bear fruit only in the longer term; and, until the devaluation, the policies that could have an effect in the shorter run, such as fiscal incentives for exports and controls on the export of capital, were clearly inadequate. The National Plan was therefore strangled by the external constraint.

The lesson is that, in preparing a national plan, a realistic view must be taken of the likely outcome of existing trends and economic policies with respect to the main constraints, of which the external constraint is, for Britain and the other two countries under review, one of the most important. If there is a gap between the targets and the likely outcome, then the gap must be eliminated either by reducing the targets, or by adopting more powerful policies that will be effective soon enough, or by a sufficient mixture of the two. If this is done, the programme can be a useful instrument of economic policy, and the broad fulfilment of its main targets a realistic objective. If not, the programme can hardly fail to be damaging. The British devaluation is a powerful instrument of economic policy that should bring results in the fairly short term. If it is followed through by means of policies that will prevent prices from rising too fast and provide enough encouragement to investment and, if any further encouragement is needed, to exports, it may enable Britain to break out of the vicious circle of slow growth of both productivity and exports, and to achieve a healthy balance of payments and a higher growth rate, to which a national programme and policies for growth would be able to make their full contribution.

CHAPTER 12

PLANNING IN THE EUROPEAN ECONOMIC COMMUNITY[1]

THE CO-ORDINATION OF ANTI-CYCLICAL POLICIES

The previous chapter has dealt with the conflict between the objective of economic growth and that of balance-of-payments equilibrium, and how this conflict may be resolved at national level. Undoubtedly the postwar trend towards the liberalization of trade and payments, coupled with a system of fixed exchange rates, has tended to make such conflict more rather than less likely. The greater a country's dependence on foreign trade, and the less its restrictions on money and capital movements, the greater the constraints on any process of planning for growth, except in so far as this consists of the deliberate sharpening of competition; and the more cyclical movements become international, the more each country has to take into account not only its own fluctuations but those of its neighbours as well. These facts have been brought home to Britain forcibly enough in recent years. Such conflicts tend to become still more accentuated, however, within an organization such as the European Economic Community, which demands not only the progressive dismantling of all restrictions on the movement of goods, services, labour and capital between its member States, but also, implicitly, the renunciation of any independent manipulation of exchange rates. In the early years of the Community when the members' economies were developing comparatively smoothly, and the removal of internal restrictions on trade had not progressed very far, the interdependence of each country's cyclical movements was not strikingly apparent.

---

[1] The substance of this chapter was published separately in Geoffrey Denton's *Planning in Europe: The Community's Medium-term Programme*, Chatham House/PEP European Series, No. 5, September 1967.

Since 1963, however, this interdependence has been clearly demonstrated. During 1963 it became clear that prices were rising much more rapidly in France and Italy, and to a lesser extent Holland, than in the other member States. This imbalance had an almost immediate effect on the other States. Germany, in particular, where prices were the most stable, became a magnet for foreign capital and its exports to its neighbours soared. While the German export surplus went up from 3,500 million marks in 1962 to over 6,000 million marks in 1963, the surplus in relation to Italy alone went up almost five-fold, by 1,800 million marks, and the balance in relation to France changed from a position of approximate equilibrium to a surplus of over 900 million marks. The massive inflow of capital into Germany soon raised fears of so-called 'imported inflation', that is, the danger that the excessive liquidity entering the country would spark off price increases there as well. In France and Italy on the other hand the balance-of-payments situation naturally became critical. The blame for the crisis tended to be placed by the German authorities on lack of monetary discipline by the deficit countries. The latter on the contrary tended to place the blame on those countries, like Germany, which pursued one-sidedly the objective of monetary stability and thus aggravated the problems of the deficit countries. What was important, however, was that, although they differed in this way over the causes, both sides agreed that, besides the national action that had to be taken—for example the 'stabilization plan' in France—some form of international action was also necessary.

This was the basic motive behind the EEC Council's Recommendation to member countries on measures to restore the internal and external economic equilibrium of the Community, which was issued in April 1964,[1] and which represents the most important plea for harmonious anti-cyclical policy so far taken by the EEC. The main emphasis of this Recommendation was on the restoration of price stability, to which it advised the member governments 'to accord priority in the coming months . . . over all other aims of economic policy or other political questions'. This objective was to be achieved in the main by a stricter control over public expenditure:

[1] The Recommendation was published in the *Journal Officiel des Communautés Européennes*, April 22, 1964, pp. 1029–64. The quotations following are from a PEP translation of this document, published in *Towards a Common Economic Policy for EEC*, 1964.

'Member States are recommended to limit the growth of Treasury expenditure of all sorts affecting the internal economy to a global rate which, as far as possible, does not exceed 5 per cent (comparing one calender year with another), irrespective of changes which might result from the method of financing the national debt. As far as it is constitutionally feasible they should induce regional and local authorities and public and semi-public enterprises to act in the same way. Where this is not possible governments are recommended to do all they can by means of negotiation to ensure that such authorities and enterprises will in fact act in this way. . . .

'If governments lack the legal or administrative powers to limit the growth of Treasury expenditure to an annual rate of 5 per cent, or if they cannot obtain the required decisions from their parliament sufficiently quickly, or if they themselves consider a greater rise of expenditure absolutely essential, they are recommended to supplement at once budgetary measures by fiscal measures so that current or newly imposed taxes can be temporarily increased up to a point at which the impact on nominal demand will be the same as that of the strict application of the rule outlined (above).' This was followed by certain details regarding non-inflationary methods of financing budgetary deficits. The recommendation also called on member States to try to persuade both sides of industry to accept an incomes policy for the remainder of 1964 and for 1965 based on keeping the nominal *per caput* incomes of all employed in line with the *per caput* growth of national production. It recommended measures to increase competition and to cut back excessive demand in the building sector, a strict policy towards credit, and greater co-operation over the financing of balance-of-payments deficits. Finally, Germany was specifically urged to increase its imports and to encourage the export of capital.

How far did the member States take note of this recommendation? It is of course very difficult to separate what countries would have done in any case from what they did as a result of recommendations by the EEC Council. Although the recommendation did not originate any completely new action, it gave an added urgency to certain programmes which were already being discussed. M. Marjolin, reporting on the implementation of the recommendation to the European Parliament in September 1964, concluded that the balance sheet was roughly as follows. Priority had been given to price stability by all member States; with some exceptions, monetary policy had followed the recommendation, as also had the methods used to finance public expenditure; one country, the Netherlands, had introduced further measures to increase competition; and Germany had carried through several measures to increase imports. On the other hand the evolution of public expenditure had not been entirely in line with the recommendation; its growth in nearly every country would exceed the 5 per cent rate in 1964. Scarcely any progress had been made towards defining and introducing an incomes policy and, with the exception of Italy, the situation in the building sector had not been remedied. M. Marjolin naturally took the opportunity of making further recommendations to the member States on how they could best continue their stabilization policies. Despite certain differences of view, therefore, a start had been made towards co-ordinating the six national anti-cyclical policies of the member countries.

The Community's moves towards the co-ordination of national anti-cyclical policies also have wider relevance. Recent developments in the Community have shown that in a world of free trade and fixed exchange rates, inflation and deflation are international processes requiring common action to contain them. If the provisions of the Rome Treaty have made this fact more transparent in the Common Market than elsewhere, it does not by any means imply that it is one that nations outside the Common Market can ignore. A country such as Britain, which is heavily engaged in trade with the outside world, need not have free trade with its neighbours to realize that both its anti-cyclical policy and theirs are of more than national importance. The methods that the Community has been evolving to co-ordinate cyclical policies may eventually prove to be of wider application, not only to other countries that may join the Community, but more generally in the relations between countries with similar economic systems.

THE EEC'S MEDIUM-TERM ECONOMIC POLICY PROGRAMME

An understanding of the nature and significance of the medium-term policy programme of the EEC requires some knowledge of the evolution of French and German economic policy in the new conditions of the 1960s in general, and in the new environment of the Common Market in particular. The following account draws on the earlier discussion of French and German policy. However, it also introduces three new elements. First, it relates economic policy changes to national attitudes to the development of the EEC institutions. Secondly, it considers the impact on the national economies of the liberalization of trade under the EEC. Thirdly, it describes the attitudes in France and Germany towards co-ordination of policies at the EEC level.

The genesis of the EEC Medium-term Policy Programme in French and German economic policy

The evolution of French planning, in response to changing pressures of events and advances in techniques of planning, may be divided into three phases, which have been described in some detail in Chapter 3. In the first phase, immediately after the Second World War, the stagnation of the economy in the 1930s plus the destruction and disruption of the war itself clearly required a programme of reconstruction whose main feature had to be heavy public investments in basic sectors such as energy and transport, which therefore formed the core of the First Plan. Even in the Second Plan, which moved on to a set of 'basic actions' in agriculture and manufacturing industry, there was neither the necessity, nor were the information or the techniques available, for a detailed indicative plan which could co-ordinate the activities of individual industries or provide the detailed framework to ensure that State interventions would stimulate the economy in desired directions. The second phase of French planning coincided roughly with the Third Plan, which ran from 1957 to 1961, but was drawn up in the years 1955 and 1956. By this time the foundations for rapid growth had been laid by the basic reconstruction programme in the First Plan and the hardly less fundamental investments of the Second; techniques of projection had begun to be used in a systematic way (an input-output table of the economy was available for the first time for 1954) and the planners had developed a theory of the operation of indicative planning.

This theory, and the Third Plan which derived from it, was based on certain assumptions regarding the nature both of the economy itself and of economic policy. The chief assumption was that the economy was largely protected from outside competition. This had indeed contributed to the restrictive attitude of French business which the planning in its second phase was designed to modify. Despite the degree of liberalization under the OEEC agreements, this was largely still the case before 1958. Secondly, it assumed a limited degree of dependence on foreign trade: not so limited as in the case of countries largely self-sufficient in raw materials, but small in relation to neighbouring European countries such as Britain and Germany, and even more so to Holland. Thirdly, the second-phase planning assumed, in practice if not in intention, that inflation would be tolerated, and that neither this nor any consequential balance-of-payments deficits would be met by restrictive measures of a kind that would slow down the rate of growth.[1] If these assumptions were to change, then the theoretical and practical dispositions of the planners would have to be adjusted.

The decision of the French Government to liberalize the economy, to sign the Treaty of Rome and to join in establishing the EEC in 1958 therefore implied a new strategy not only for external but also for internal economic policy. It implied that French planning would have to move on from the second phase almost before this had been properly established in the Third Plan. The changes in the basic assumptions of French policy are very important for the development of French and of EEC planning. There are four most significant changes:

1. As the level of tariffs between the member countries was progressively reduced, and as the common external tariff was established lower than the previous average level of French tariffs, and other liberalization measures proceeded, both exports and imports were expected to increase more rapidly.[2] It would therefore become necessary to reverse the previous reliance on protection and instead to take steps to make both exports and production for the home market more competitive, and to pay much more attention to the balance of payments in the plans. From being a difficulty that could be circumvented by import and exchange controls in the interests of faster growth, the balance of payments became a constraint to be respected by means of more orthodox measures (as has been the case in Britain during the past two decades).

2. The Community was designed not only to increase trade in

---

[1] See M. MacLennan, The Common Market and French Planning, *Journal of Common Market Studies*, Vol. III, No. 1.

[2] This did not, however, mean that it became more difficult to *forecast* trade developments. The planners found that market movements were easier to forecast than changes in the policies of governments, which had previously been more significant in this field.

goods but also to facilitate the movement of labour and capital within the Community. Foreign ownership of enterprises located in France was bound to disrupt the tight relationship built up between the planners and French industrialists, in two ways. First, in so far as the plans had relied on the *économie concertée* for their effectiveness, the foreign owners of capital would be outside the tight social network through which this aspect operated. Secondly, in so far as the plans had relied on real incentives to firms to comply with the targets, and especially on the central control over credit which the French planners could operate in the relatively under-developed state of the French capital market, these would not be effective against foreigners raising their capital outside France. In the event, American capital rather than capital from other EEC countries proved to be the main problem. American enterprises wished to establish themselves within the new customs union, and the structure of French industry facilitated to the process of buying their way in, even though the French Government on occasion might not have been amenable to it.

3. The EEC also had an immediate effect on the competitive position of French firms, as well as of firms throughout the Community.[1] Firms that had been monopolists in France found themselves only oligopolists or even less within the Community, and industries that had been cartelized within France faced a much more open competition from numerous firms within the Community. This factor also was not conducive to a continuance of planning on the model of the Third Plan.

4. Finally, it was feared that the rules of the Community governing internal policies affecting the fairness of trade operated against the very selective incentives, in monetary and in fiscal policy, that the French planners had previously used to considerable effect. Their influence on individual firms, even on firms raising their capital in France, would be gradually lessened by the progressive observance of these rules.

The EEC Programme refers specifically to the requirement that discriminations in favour of particular sectors should not distort competition, lest they be contrary to articles 92 to 94 of the Rome Treaty. This passage is perhaps worth quoting here, since it shows

[1] See D. Swann and D. L. McLachlan, *Concentration or Competition: A European Dilemma?* Chatham House/PEP European Series, No. 1, January 1967; see also p. 382.

that the French fears were not groundless: ' . . . Specific interventions arising out of policy for the structure of industry should always be temporary . . .' and 'with the disappearance of commercial barriers within the Community and the introduction of a common commercial policy . . . individual member States will no longer be free to use certain instruments of external trade policy that have previously played a prominent part in their policies for the structure of industry'.[1]

These considerable and inter-related difficulties arising out of the liberalization of the economy and made more urgent by joining the EEC were met by three major policy changes. First, the franc was devalued effectively in 1957 and officially in 1958 in order to produce an immediately favourable effect on the price competitiveness of French industry. But this measure would not solve the problem once and for all; it implied a new prominence for stabilization policy in order to consolidate and retain the immediate advantage won by devaluation. As a result, the economy lagged seriously behind the indications of the Third Plan in 1958 and 1959, and the Intermediate Plan of 1960 was needed to recover lost ground by speeding up growth in the final years of the Plan period. The Fourth Plan was interrupted by the Stabilization Plan of 1963. The planners had to pay far more attention to the reconciliation of their medium-term targets with the short-term movements of the economy. The planning system was therefore made much more 'sophisticated' with an emphasis on flexibility, and the insertion of *clignotants*, indicators of alert, which were to give early warning of potential conflicts between growth and price or balance-of-payments stability. In the Fifth Plan there also developed a new emphasis on 'value planning', that is, on planning the financial flows which are the counterpart of the 'real' developments, and whose equilibrium is essential to price stability and hence to success with the investment and production targets in the new atmosphere.

Secondly, the internal planning system was further amended in the light of the economic liberalization and various implications of the EEC: the capital movements, the effects on industrial structure of the wider market and the rules governing internal policies. The planning system reacted gradually to the changed conditions in the Fourth and Fifth Plans. Emphasis was removed from laying down specific targets for investment and output for industries, and in a

[1] Avant-projet de Premier Programme de Politique Economique à Moyen Terme, 1966–70, and Annexes, EEC, March 25, 1966, pp. III.13–4.

few cases even for individual firms, with whom the planners had close links, and on whom they could, if necessary, exert decisive pressure through their control over the sources of finance. The revised system that emerged in the 1960s stressed the broader structural objectives: the concentration of firms into larger groupings to gain economies of scale, to withstand the fiercer competition within the EEC, and to keep out the Americans, the encouragement of exports and of import saving to contribute to the balance of payments, and the achievement of regional balance. The importance of the quantitative targets, which had tended to be over-stated in previous expositions of the role of planning, was now played down.

Thirdly, the French planners made a determined effort to have planning adopted at the level of the EEC. As M. Hirsch put it: 'If planning is thus to be continued in France in spite—or rather because—of the Common Market, it would nevertheless be infinitely desirable to see effective planning begun also on the scale of the Common Market as a whole.'[1]

Once the importance of the exogenous factors had been so increased by the opening of the French economy to movements of goods and factors from the rest of the Community, the increase of competition and of capital investments from outside the Community, and the restrictions on the freedom of action of French economic policy, it was essential for the continuation of planning in France that some form of planning should be adopted for the Community as a whole.

M. Hirsch mentioned specifically the increasing co-operation within the EEC in the development of particular industries: electricity, railways, roads; in research; and through the associated communities, ECSC and Euratom, in steel and nuclear power. All these industries had quantitative programmes based on assumptions about the overall growth of the economy of the Six, yet there was no unified programme for the EEC as a whole. This case is perhaps not entirely convincing, since progress towards a real unification in these sectors has not been striking. But it is certainly logical, and could become more real if the Community overcomes present difficulties and moves forward in these areas. A better current example of the necessity of an EEC Programme from the French point of view is possibly

[1] E. Hirsch, French Planning and its European Application, *Journal of Common Market Studies*, Vol. I, No. 2. See also J. Bénard, Le Marché Commun et l'Avenir de la Planification Française, *Revue Economique*, No. 5, September 1964.

the fact that the freeing of trade under the Rome Treaty also requires the harmonization of taxes, especially indirect taxes. This implies some restraint on the power of French planners to manipulate taxes and has given them a great interest in the development of common and co-ordinated taxes that could be used to promote growth.

The same pressures that led to the attempt to have planning adopted by the EEC were modifying the nature of planning within France in directions favourable to attaining a satisfactory compromise with the EEC partners. Given the attitude of the German Government towards planning, the prospects for the adoption of a medium-term programme at the EEC level might none the less have been bleak had it not been that certain economic pressures were at the same time operating on the German Government to push them in the direction of a greater degree of planning, so that a reconciliation of French and German views could be achieved at Community level, a possibility that would have seemed very remote in the mid-1950s.

The German Government had been strongly opposed to any form of central planning, which was contrary to basic neo-liberal principles. Though it should be recognized that some of the German hostility to planning was more in word than in deed, there were many real divergences of view between Germany and France on aspects of economic policy of major importance, and the prospects for agreement on medium-term economic policy at the EEC level were not initially hopeful. Dr Erhard strongly voiced his disapproval of the original proposals of M. Marjolin contained in the 1962 Action Programme for the second stage of the development of the Community before the European Parliament in November 1963.[1] The leading points in Dr Erhard's speech may be paraphrased as follows:[2]

The centralization of economic decisions implied in the recommendations was contrary to a federal political system; there was no basis for this centralization in the Treaty of Rome; competition was a better regulator of the economic system than planning; belief in competition could not be reconciled with planning; medium-term forecasts were either useless or harmful.

Thus Dr Erhard condemned the proposals root and branch: as being at odds with the German constitution, with the EEC's

[1] European Parliament, *Débats*, Session 1962-3, sittings November 19-23, 1962, pp. 51-6.
[2] See PEP, op. cit., for fuller version.

constitution, with a central tenet of neo-liberal theory, and with practical experience of planning.[1]

Yet by 1966 the Germans and the French, with their partners, were able to reach a compromise at the EEC level. There were a number of reasons why this was possible. One was the changes in the internal French planning system. A second was the fact that the EEC institutions do not have the powers to operate a system of French planning at Community level or to force the other members of the Community to adopt it at national level. A third is that the French Government, while it would doubtless like to see the other members adopt a more 'French' economic system and policy, has strongly opposed any increase of supranational powers such as would enable the EEC institutions to play any part in French style planning. But a very significant fourth reason was that the Germans were themselves converted to acceptance of a degree of planning at the national level by 1966.

First, they were soon convinced, as were most West European countries in the early 1960s, that the pressures making for rapid growth in public investment and public spending in general required that some medium- or long-term programme of public finance be drawn up. This in turn required that there should be projections of the overall development of the economy, since the main problem was to reconcile an expanding public sector with the development of other sectors of the economy, though it was not until 1966 that this was finally accepted by the German Government.

Secondly, the large-scale immigration into Western Germany from the East ceased in the 1960s. Unemployment had also been eliminated, so the rapid expansion of the labour force that had contributed much to the rapid growth and stability of the 1950s had come to an end. Indeed, owing to demographic trends the future development of labour supply in Germany would be less favourable than in the rest of the Community or in Britain. (See pp. 384-5.) M. Hirsch thought that this trend was the main factor in the new German interest in economic policies of the French type.

Thirdly, while entry into the EEC was not so decisive for the reorientation of German as it had been for French policy, it is probable

---

[1] It should perhaps be noted that despite this seemingly comprehensive opposition to the proposals, Dr Erhard later accepted the necessity of a medium-term programme for the public finances in Germany.

that it emphasized the inflationary problem arising from export surpluses. The exclusive reliance on monetary regulation could no longer be maintained on account of the conflicting requirements of internal and external policy, and the German Government was finally led to propose in 1966 the constitutional amendment needed in order to control the finances of the individual Länder and to operate a more active budgetary policy. The problem of inflation, which was particularly severe in 1964 and 1965, and obviously a problem for the whole Community, led to agreement that the short-term economic policies of the member States should be co-ordinated. And via this conjunctural policy the Germans came round to accepting the need for a medium-term policy programme at the level of the Community, since the medium-term development of the economies determined the conditions which gave rise to the short-term disequilibria.

Fourthly, and we must here anticipate somewhat, the Community's medium-term policy discussions themselves influenced the German Government to abandon their previous policy of countenancing only private forecasts and projections made by independent institutes, and to set up their own official committee for the study of overall economic development. (See pp. 74–5.)

These developments of German economic policy are relatively recent, and a true assessment of their importance is difficult. That budgetary policy has been extremely important has been underlined by the fact that it played a decisive part in provoking the political crisis of 1966, which removed Dr Erhard, the architect of the social market economy, from the Chancellorship, brought the Social Democrats into the Government for the first time since 1945, and marked a certain shift in economic as in other policies. The changes have also certainly been in the direction of reducing the dichotomy between the German and the French economic regimes, and therefore contributing to the success of the Community's endeavours in the field of medium-term programming.

Members of the Medium-term Policy (MTP) Committee, all of whom, with the exception of the Commission's representatives, are drawn from and represent the individual member countries, found themselves, as the Commission expressed it in the Draft Programme, talking a 'common language' despite the well-known differences in national attitudes to planning.

In the 1950s the gradual application of neo-liberal principles in

Germany, and the extension and refinement of indicative planning in France, caused the two countries' economic managements to diverge. In the 1960s the changes in policy in the two countries have been convergent. Discussion on medium-term policy in the Community has both played a part in promoting this convergence, and benefited from it.

While changes within the national economies have thus been of the utmost importance in the development of the EEC's medium-term policy, it would be entirely misleading to talk of the acceptance of even a modified form of French-type planning at the level of the EEC. There was never any question of this happening, for the simple reason that the EEC does not have anything approaching the necessary powers. The question at issue was not whether to have a Community Plan, but whether to draw up an outline of economic policies, both national and Community, relevant to the medium- and long-term development of the members, and related to quantitative projections of the probable development of the economies, with a view to developing common policies, and harmonizing and co-ordinating national policies, in directions favourable to growth. There are in the EEC Programme no growth targets, or even indications, for individual industries; there is no system of industry committees to bring interest groups into the formation of the Community's Programme in detail; nor is there any acceptance that governmental intervention should be increased in the member States.

Moreover, it would be wrong to be over-impressed with the area of agreement shown within the documents, and to ignore the issues on which, though a nominally agreed policy is stated, this is so transparently made up of thesis and antithesis as to be little more than an agreement to differ. How much or how little such compromises may prove to mean in practice must await experience in implementing the principles laid down in the documents so far presented to the public.

Two elements of consensus were, then, reflected in the EEC Programme. One is the area of common thinking about the appropriate degree of programming for the individual national economy; the other is the range of agreement on the proper form and role of Community institutions in relation to the co-ordination of national policies and the formulation of common policies. These two elements are virtually inextricable, though in what follows an attempt has been made to separate them.

Common thinking about the extent to which national economies should be programmed is effectively limited to two areas:

(1) a 'highly forecast' market economy, in which four- or five-year projects for the economy as a whole and for major sectors and end-uses serve (a) to reduce the uncertainties of the private sector about possible future economic developments, (b) to guide the various governments' economic policies in directions conducive to growth, and (c) to give the private sector, therefore, some indications about the probable future orientation of government policies;

(2) the flexible programming of public expenditure, both capital and current within each national economy, primarily with a view to maintaining a reasonable relationship with the growth of the GDP, but also to ensure consistency and co-ordination in areas where official action may decisively affect the development of the national economy (such as regional policy, policy for aiding particular industries, infrastructure investments, education and vocational training, scientific and technical research, agriculture, energy and transport, housing and the general balance between public expenditure and income), and to give a guide to private industry as to the likely development of governmental and Community policies affecting them.

The Medium-term Programme of the EEC then reflects this narrow area of agreement about the role of national programmes, and in addition incorporates and relates to the national forecasts work already going on in the member States and in the European Communities in the areas where the Treaties of Rome (setting up the EEC) and of Paris (setting up the ECSC) were already fairly explicit, namely:

(3) the planning of regional development within each country and in the Community as a whole, in order to contribute to the growth of the economies, to secure balanced development of all areas, and to alleviate the social problems arising out of unbalanced development;

(4) the planning of industry, in the very limited sense of clarifying the implications for individual industries of the growth pattern revealed in the projections, so as to initiate and co-ordinate policies to ease the economic and social problems of readjustment of industrial structure, especially with regard to declining industries.

This last is the only area in which the EEC Programme can be said to have anything to do with the planning of industry, and it is of course very restricted in scope and objectives as compared with national planning as conceived in the French Modernization Commissions, or in the British Economic Development Committees.

Since the Programme is now available in published form, this section of the chapter concentrates on those aspects that appear of most interest in relation to the development of planning in Britain and in Western Europe in the late 1960s and early 1970s. Selection of the subjects for consideration is further limited by the fact that the MTP Committee has not so far been able to publish the results of its work on many issues of great interest, such as policy for research and development, and thus had little to say about them in the first Programme.

The nature of the quantitative indications

The quantitative projections were carried out separately from the work of the MTP Committee by the Study Group attached and reporting to the Commission.[1] This originally consisted entirely of independent experts, eminent economists and statisticians from universities and independent institutes throughout the member States, under the chairmanship of M. de Lettenhove, formerly Secretary General of the Belgian Programming Office. But the Study Group themselves recognized that, however strong the desire to separate projections from policy, they could never be based entirely on technical considerations, but also implied hypotheses as to policies which would affect economic development within the period; for example, the development of public expenditure, taxation, and social security transfers. This has now been recognized institutionally by the inclusion in the Study Group of officials from member States who are responsible for the work on medium-term forecasts in their own countries. But the insertion of the detailed policy implications of the projections was regarded as the task of the MTP Committee and not of the Study Group.

The projections followed in most cases the projections drawn up by national planners in each of the member States: for instance, the

[1] *Perspectives de Développement Economique de la CEE jusqu'en 1970*, April 1966.

projections of the Fifth Plan in France; for Italy, the preliminary projections for the new national plan; for Holland, the projections of the Central Planning Bureau, which had just begun to extend from short- to medium-term projections. Some of these national projections already included policy assumptions, and it was therefore impossible for the Study Group to pretend to the role of an independent forecasting institute for the Community. This is especially the case where the national forecasts had been prepared in considerable detail, and in accordance with a highly evolved planning procedure, as in France, since the choices among the various options had introduced a major prescriptive element. The extent to which this happened varied from country to country according to the nature of the 'projections' in each case.

The MTP Committee accepted the official national projections, for all members except Germany. The German Government submitted to the Committee a projection based on a growth rate of GDP of 3·5 per cent per annum for the period 1966–70. The Study Group, that is to say the German expert members of the Group, projected growth for Germany at a rate of 4·2 per cent. The Annexes to the Report of the Study Group contain the experts' projections for Germany, a memorandum from the Federal Economics Ministry and a comment by the experts on the Ministry's projections. The divergence of the official and the independent German views appears to have been based on the following considerations. The Ministry argued:

(a) that forecasting is very uncertain and it is possible only to indicate a range of possibilities for the development of the economy. Their range for the growth of GNP was from 2·5 to 4 per cent;

(b) that to adopt a single figure for growth of GNP near the top of the range as the basis for a Plan is to risk overstraining the economy and sacrifice of the primary objectives of full employment, price stability and balance of international payments;

(c) that a figure of 3·5 per cent was therefore the highest that should be adopted.

The experts took the view that there was, in addition to a fundamental divergence on the question of the potential rate of growth of productivity (which presumably accounts for the difference between the experts' 4·2 per cent and the German Ministry's maximum of 4 per cent), a difference as to the purpose of the projections:

'The projection of the Economics Ministry, in so far as it produces a rate of growth significantly below those experienced recently, implies a certain deliberate policy to check the growth of demand; that of the experts on the other hand is intended to define the perspectives of development which appear probable to them.'[1]

In other words, the Federal Economics Ministry was pursuing a cautious policy in the publication of projections in order to strengthen their hand in the struggle against inflation, while the German independent experts may have been concerned to insert a 'target' that would support a case for a faster growth of incomes. This was ironical, in that the Germans had for so long preached the separation of projections from policy and the avoidance of anything looking like an EEC central planning office, requirements that were institutionalized at EEC level in the creation of the Study Group separately from the MTP Committee. Yet it would be unfair to criticize the Germans for trying to incorporate their own objectives, based on their own priorities for economic policy, into the projections, when it was clear that owing to dependence on national plan figures other projections also incorporated governmental policy objectives. That the German case stands out merely suggests that the German experts were in greater sympathy with projections that incorporated an ambitious attitude to growth, than with one which incorporated a cautious attitude to stability. It is in fact probable, in the light of more recent developments, that the 3·5 per cent projection is the more realistic.

In the Draft Programme produced by the MTP Committee, the quantitative estimates were explained and interpreted in a cautious manner. The figures were described as providing only a general perspective to aid decisions in the private and public sectors. Their value to the private sector, even as mere general indications of future growth, was only touched on. They were evidently not officially expected to have any direct impact on private expectations and investment decisions. The possibilities in this direction were in any event limited by the fact that the estimates were not disaggregated to the level of individual industries. Indeed, even for the major sectoral analysis, figures for Germany were conspicuously absent.

The main emphasis then is on their value as a guide to public policy. The Committee underlined that: 'It is hardly possible . . . to conceive a medium-term economic and budgetary policy which did

[1] Perspectives de Développement Economique, op. cit., Annexe I, p. 46.

not rely on a quantitative appreciation of the possibilities for economic growth under certain conditions.'[1]

The essential purpose of the projections was described as being to: ' . . . indicate orders of magnitude and sound perspectives and to permit the responsible authorities to identify the limits of their actions; they open up the possibility, in foreseeing difficulties, to avoid having recourse to harsh measures which alone can be effective once the crisis is under way.'[2]

This statement clearly reflected French thinking about the inter-relation of medium-term plans and short-term policy described above on pp. 93–9. It was also apparently accepted by the German authorities as a proper function for the EEC Programme. But the emphasis was on flexibility, not on firm targets. The French Fifth Plan was referred to with approval, since: ' . . . the public authorities commit themselves to pursue the objectives, but do not guarantee their realization.'[3]

It was also stressed on repeated occasions that the projections were conditional. They were conditional on the realization of various 'real' requirements, such as the satisfactory development of the utilization of industry, and adequate progress in scientific and technological development. They were also conditional on a fundamental monetary requirement, that prices should remain stable. Any internal inflation of price levels would therefore disrupt the equilibrium of aggregate demand and supply; in particular, the growth of private consumption at a faster rate than allowed for in the Plan, which would be a consequence of increases in incomes exceeding the rate of growth of productivity, would prevent investment from growing at the projected rate, and therefore slow down the overall rate of growth. The projections were also recognized as being dependent on a condition of external payments equilibrium, which was partly a corollary of the internal monetary equilibrium, and partly at the mercy of economic forces in the world outside the Community. Excessive growth of incomes might lead to a faster rate of growth of imports than that allowed for, and thus to balance-of-payments difficulties, and consequent measures that would slow down growth. External events, such as a worsening of the Community's terms of trade, could have

[1] Avant-Projet, p. I.10.
[2] Projet de Programme de Politique Economique à Moyen Terme, 1966–70 (presenté par la Commission au Conseil), Com. (66) 170, April 29, 1966.
[3] Avant-Projet, op. cit., p. II.4.

a similar effect, and this underlined the need for flexibility in interpreting and applying the Programme.

This emphasizes that the Community's Programme did not merely follow developments that were thought to be inevitable or probable even in the absence of any planning interventions. The reconciliation of developments in different parts of the economy, in order to achieve the necessary equilibria, inevitably meant that the Programme contained a considerable prescriptive element. The projection for the whole Community was that the GDP would grow at 4·3 per cent per annum between 1966 and 1970 as compared with the actual growth of 4·9 per cent in the previous five-year period. But in order for growth to be at this rate, all productive investment would have to grow at 6·1 per cent, and public investment at twice the rate of GDP, namely at 8·5 per cent. The corollary was obvious: in order to leave adequate resources for these purposes, private consumption would have to be curtailed to a rate of growth of only 4·1 per cent per annum. Although this rate would still represent a growth of 3·3 per cent in consumption per head, doubling the standard of living in only twenty years, it also implied a fall in the rate of growth of private consumption from the 5·3 per cent of the earlier period. Budgetary policy would have to be made more rigorous, in order to curtail demand and prevent rising prices from diverting output to the consumer goods sector, and resulting in slowing down the rate of growth. Monetary policy was rejected for this purpose owing to its effects on investments. Thus the projections, while in no sense providing targets for individual industries, by forming a quantitative basis for public policy did set objectives for member governments. The Programme limited itself to stating that member governments had to consider the consequences of not achieving the necessary equilibria, and what specific measures to take in such a case,[1] but the implication was clear, and the greater part of the Programme was in fact a discussion of policies for keeping the economies as far as possible on the courses mapped out for them. By agreeing to the Programme, the member governments would 'express their intention to act in accordance with its main concepts' as the 1963 Recommendation laid down. It thus seemed clear that, for all the cautious language and diplomatic disclaimers, the Community's Programme did set broad objectives for its members, which, though expressly not to be treated as quantitative targets, were related to the quantitative

[1] Projet, op. cit., p. 5.

projections. Indeed, if the Programme had not set such objectives, there would have been little point in the Community publishing such a document. Moreover, the MTP Committee will investigate their progress in achieving the objectives.

A subject on which controversy still continued after publication of the first Community programme was the question whether to disaggregate the projections. German opposition is very strong since disaggregation to industry level is the key technical development which could decisively alter the nature of the EEC Programme from the compromise so far agreed on to something more akin to the detailed national 'indicative' planning of France (and Britain). Within the Commission the view was in favour of disaggregation, which was in any case required for the purpose of checking the consistency of the broader projections. There was a tendency to argue that the progress already achieved, as represented in the first Programme, has been the result of a process of 'educating' the Germans in the virtues of planning, and that this educative process would continue over some years. (Of course, the 'educative' process was two-way, and there were many examples in the Programme of German-type views having a strong influence.) Having accepted broad official projections, the Germans could well be induced to allow that in order for later EEC Programmes to be really helpful as a guide to governmental policy, industry-level projections should be published. However, in view of the keen opposition in Germany to anything smacking of targets for industry, and the removal of emphasis from the target element in the French Fifth Plan, it seemed unlikely that the EEC would employ any but the most cautious and conservative approach to the publication of industry-level projections. 'Disaggregation' by the planners need imply little more than the publication of some of the industry detail needed to check the consistency of the aggregates, and the drawing of conclusions for governmental policy from them. This would be a far cry from 'disaggregation' in the sense of the formation of industry commissions to draw interest groups into the preparation of the EEC Programme, as happens in France.

Interest groups, incomes policy and value planning
A great gulf exists between French and German attitudes to interest groups. In France, a notable feature of the machinery of indicative planning is the involvement of interest groups at industry level in

ECONOMIC PLANNING AND POLICIES

the preparation and implementation of the Plans. In Germany, on the contrary, there is an official doctrine that interest groups should so far as possible be kept out of the formation of policy. It was therefore to be expected that a particularly delicate compromise would need to be achieved in this field.

The attitude to interest groups in the Community's Programme seems to lie nearer to the German principle of exclusion than to the French concept of the *économie concertée*, and also reflects a difference in the attitude of the French Government towards the participation of interest groups at the Community as contrasted with the national level. It is also closely linked with the general nature of the projections, since they are not disaggregated to the level of the individual industry, there is no question of any industrial commissions representing firms and trade unions. But association of interest groups at the national level would be consistent with the nature of the work so far undertaken by the MTP Committee. Yet there is no provision for any association of interest groups at the national level in the detailed preparation of the Programme; and the MTP Committee is composed entirely of civil servants from the Governments and from the Community. The Draft Plan itself contains only a brief and unexplained mention of the need for close collaboration of Governments with social and professional groups in its implementation.[1] This seems to imply that active participation of interest groups in the preparation of programmes at EEC level is not felt to be desirable.

Interest groups at Community level were, however, *consulted* during the preparation of the Programme and after the draft Programme had been published. The latter form of consultation is required in accordance with paragraph 45 of the 1963 recommendation and paragraph 2 of the 1964 decision under which the Economic and Social Committee (ESC) is asked for its views before the Council of Ministers makes its decision on the adoption of the Plan. The ESC published their views in October 1966 in the form of a Report from a sub-committee on Medium-term Policy.[2] This Report is restricted to some fairly general observations on the limitations of the Programme: for example, that it rests on rather uncertain macroeconomic projections; that it needs to be more explicit on the means

[1] Avant-Projet, op. cit., p. I.6.
[2] Rapport du Sous-Comité 'Politique Economique à Moyen Terme' sur le 'Projet de Programme de Politique Economique à Moyen Terme, 1966–70,' Le Comité Economique et Social, CES 212/66, October 17, 1966.

of implementing the objectives; that it has relied on national projections without adequately studying the problems of their comparability at Community level; that this also implies that the effects
of economic integration are ignored; that the external payments
problems of the Community are only briefly touched on, whereas
they ought to have been regarded as one of the principal constraints
on growth; that a set of variants should have been presented to allow
informed political choice; that little work has been done on the
evolution of prices and the financing of investments; that the distinction is not always clear between working hypotheses and political
objectives; that the effects of the common agricultural policy have
not been studied. The Report recognizes, however, that the MTP
Committee could hardly have been expected to cope with all these
issues in its first exercise; these are recommendations for future
development rather than criticisms. The ESC sub-committee had
also been consulted during the work on the Programme, on matters
of particular interest to it, including the stability of employment,
regional policy, the redeployment of labour, and the eventual establishment of projections for industrial sectors.

This last subject on which they have been consulted suggests that
if future Programmes are indeed disaggregated to industry level, a
more formal and detailed consultation of interest groups might
possibly be developed. But it is too soon and too uncertain for
speculation on what form this might take to be useful. The EEC has
stimulated the formation of a number of trade associations at Community level and it is unlikely that these will refrain from seeking to
influence future Programmes, especially if these are disaggregated,
and some formal arrangements for consulting them may well develop,
though probably only in the longer term, since this would imply an
institutional change in the direction of supranationality.

The requirement that the growth of money incomes should be
contained within the level of the growth of productivity was clearly
recognized by the MTP Committee as one of the basic assumptions
of the Programme, which indeed sets out in some detail the economic
and social case for an incomes policy. In achieving this requirement
for the success of the Programme they felt that total reliance could
not be placed on governmental policies of restraining demand through
fiscal and monetary measures. Regular exchanges of view were also
recommended between the Governments and the 'social partners',
both on incomes and on prices, with a view to assigning: ' . . . limits

to the growth of different incomes within which the freedom of decision of the economic units may be exercised.'[1]

It is not surprising that the Community should subscribe to some kind of incomes policy; in one form or another this has become common practice in many Western economies. But agreement on a similar form of incomes policy for each of the member countries is likely to be inhibited by the great differences of attitude towards the forms of consultation and association with interest groups. The study of incomes policy is being carried further by the Working Group in the second phase of the MTP Committee's work, and the Second Programme, expected at the end of 1967, may reveal some progress towards co-ordinating policies in this area.

In any event, there has been little progress even in Holland towards the establishment of a permanent incomes policy, and harmonization of incomes policy in the Community must await developments in the member States.

It would also be unrealistic to think in the foreseeable future in terms of a single norm for incomes over the whole Community. A Community policy would presumably take the form of encouraging each member to devise a policy, appropriate to its own economic and institutional structure, to keep the growth of money incomes in line with the growth of the GDP. Since rates of growth of GDP vary (at present) so will the norms for incomes.

The MTP Committee also recognized the need for control over prices as being important both for psychological and for practical reasons in establishing an incomes policy. They declared that: '... prices should be kept under constant supervision and vigilance should be stepped up whenever there are signs of monopoly conditions occurring on the market.'[2]

There was no attempt positively to recommend any kind of actual price control; but merely a mention that price freezes could be used only in exceptional circumstances and for short periods, and that a flexible price policy would be needed, adapted to the varying circumstances of each industry, and requiring close contact between government and industry. The only solutions named specifically are market-oriented, namely: action against monopolies and restrictive agreements, and the opening of markets to improve supplies. In fact, competition is regarded as the best way to keep down prices.

[1] Avant-Projet, op. cit., p. III.21.
[2] Ibid.

(Competition policy in the EEC is discussed below on pp. 381–4.)

So far as value planning is concerned, the Study Group published a preliminary analysis of price movements.[1] The exercise consisted in projecting the movement of the average price level of the GDP on the assumption that prices of industrial output remain constant, with agricultural prices following a falling trend, and the prices of construction and services rising. The projections thus arrived at an estimate for the overall rise of prices over 1965–70 of 8–9 per cent for all members. This compares optimistically with rises in the price levels in 1960–5 of 20 per cent in Germany, 19 per cent in France, and 25 per cent in Italy. Thus the projection is conditional, and this is clearly recognized, on a major policy success in holding the prices of industrial goods stable. Its value is that it sets a norm for the evolution of prices which would represent a substantial improvement over that in 1960–65, while not aiming at complete stability of the overall price level, which would require the unrealistic assumption of falling prices for industrial output.

It therefore states a vital condition for the achievement of the growth of GDP indicated in the projections. However, while the objective is clear, the means of attaining it are still uncertain. Once more, this reflects the uncertain situation in the member States with regard to the practical possibilities of adequately regulating prices and incomes.

Regional and structural policy

Although an Annexe to the Draft Programme is devoted to regional policy,[2] there is little to say about this as yet in relation to the work of the MTP Committee. Regional policy is, of course, very important in other parts of the Commission. The Annexe is largely devoted to a review of the different kinds of regional problems within the Community and of the policies already applied by members and by the Community itself. The Committee recognized that policies for regional development were particularly valuable in relation to growth, in that they formed one wing of the policy for redeploying labour within the Community, on which growth prospects for the late 1960s depend very heavily. At the same time, the Programme recognizes that regional policy cannot be based solely on helping to provide employment for previously unemployed or inactive workers in the

[1] Perspectives, op. cit., Annexe IV, Evolution des Prix Relatifs.
[2] Avant-Projet, op. cit., Annexe III.

medium term, but must rest on appraisals of the long-term viability of industrial development in growth areas. Reference is made to the need for cost-benefit studies to inform decisions about developing backward areas, and the overall policy statement is another balanced and general compromise: the inducement of industry to move to areas of high unemployment or low activity rates is recommended, where this is economically justified. But, subject to this qualification in detail, the Commission regards inadequate regional policy as one of the three most lively threats to the implementation of the Programme.[1] (The other two are inflation and scientific and technological backwardness.)

The Programme approves of State intervention to aid the reconstruction and readaptation of declining industries, but insists that subsidies be openly shown, that they and other measures to aid declining industries must be temporary, and, indeed, that their demise must, so far as possible, be indicated from the outset.[2] The Commission specially emphasized the involvement of the Community in this area of planning by stressing that problem industries, equally with problem areas, required Community rather than purely national decisions.[3]

Common policies are required under the Treaty of Rome for industries such as agriculture and transport, and under the Treaty of Paris for coal and iron and steel.

The work of the Committee on structural policy is perhaps overshadowed by the failure of the European Communities to make the progress that had been hoped for in some of these industries. The common agricultural policy was agreed in 1966, but only after extremely difficult negotiations. Progress on a common transport policy has been exceedingly slow. On coal and steel progress has been negative: the rules for the common policy have not been observed, and when the ECSC is merged with the EEC, it is probable that much of the supranational power given to the High Authority in the Treaty of Paris will be removed. But the situation is not perhaps as bleak as these facts suggest. The ECSC was created for political rather than industrial or economic reasons, and the coal and steel industries may now take up a more normal position similar to that of other industries. Future progress in co-ordinated and com-

---

[1] Projet, op. cit., Annexe I, p. 13.
[2] Avant-Projet, op. cit., p. III.13.
[3] Projet, op. cit., pp. 3-4.

mon policies on industrial structure will be more soundly based on economic advantages. The MTP Committee can make a particular contribution by reconciling the estimates of output and employment in each industry with the projections for overall growth. The Working Group on structural policy is currently examining in detail the problems of three industries: agriculture, shipbuilding and electronics. The first two pose problems of major structural adaptation in difficult market conditions, while the third is regarded as an example of an expanding industry in which none the less structural problems are of great importance to future competitiveness especially with large American firms. One of the most urgent problems is to clarify what aids can be given for the adaptation of these industries consistently with the EEC rules against distortion of competition.

There is, strictly speaking, no Community policy for regional and industrial structural problems: only a co-ordination of the six national policies, plus an EEC Commission policy in so far as the Commission disposes of powers and funds. The main sources of finance for the Commission policy are the Social Fund, applied largely for regional purposes, and the FEOGA, the fund derived from the levies under the common agricultural policy. A substantial part of this fund is intended primarily for structural reform in agriculture; but discussions have been proceeding on using this money also for the attraction to such areas of other industries, and the retraining of surplus agricultural workers.

Funds controlled by the Commission are obviously allocated in accordance with Community criteria: that is, choices have to be made between regions in different member countries. In using their own national funds for regional policy, member States please themselves, though they are subject to the supervision of the Commission to ensure that by applying funds to aid a particular region they are not at the same time giving an unfair trading advantage to a particular industry, a policy which would require special permission.

Competition, economies of scale, and research and development
German and French attitudes to the concentration of firms to achieve economies of scale, and to the related question of the maintenance of competition, have differed widely. The French Government has shown relatively little interest in internal competition, but it has devoted a good deal of effort, especially since 1958, to rationalizing the previously excessively fragmented structure of many French

industries to enable them to compete in external markets. In Germany, the theory of the social market economy challenges the technological necessity of amalgamation to form larger units, and the 'medium-firm policy' is a practical attempt to maintain a competitive structure of industry. The German Government also fought a hard battle against strong opposition from industry to pass the Cartel Law in 1957. Though it is right to be sceptical of the practical outcome of this legislation, the hostile attitude of the German Government to concentration and monopoly must be recognized. Such an attitude was bound to be reflected in their approach to a Community policy in this area.

For both France and Germany it has been possible to redress the internal balance with regard to competition by calling into account the strong competition arising within the Community as tariff barriers were lowered between members. The problem of competition in a Community where the need for larger units is also recognized has been considered in a paper published by Chatham House and PEP, which concluded that: 'The process of merging national markets to form a common market makes a powerful contribution to the maintenance of competition. It is true that if the search for the optimum size of the firm (whether defined statically or dynamically) is pursued within a purely national context then the result could and probably would be a monopolistic or highly oligopolistic industrial structure. But when the process of concentration takes place within the context of a common market the threat to competition is automatically reduced, the monopolist in one State competes with the monopolist in another and oligopolies compete with oligopolies. In short, the degree of concentration at the Community level is less than the degree of concentration at the national level. With this in mind, it seems reasonable to say that, even if the merger movement proceeded apace for a number of years, conditions in most (but not, of course, all) Community industries would still be a good deal short of anything like monopoly of the larger market.'[1]

But in 1968 the Common Market will be complete and, while the final removal of the last few per cent of tariffs between members will not in itself end the process of opening up the whole Community market to all firms, it will in the 1970s become increasingly difficult in each country for any further erosion of competition to be shrugged off by reference to the growth of competition from other members.

[1] D. Swann and D. L. McLachlan, op. cit., p. 55.

Competition from outside the Community will still be important, and will be encouraged by any general tariff reductions such as those envisaged in the Kennedy round. But the completion of the customs union does seem to underline the need for the Community to put an adequate competition policy into effect.

The Chatham House/PEP study considered that such a Community policy would have to be directed less to forbidding mergers than to regulating their behaviour: ' . . . in order to achieve an efficient industrial structure, the classical model of competition has to be sacrificed.'[1]

But only the negative part of this prescription, that is, refraining from opposing, indeed encouraging, mergers has so far been adopted in France: 'The French probably still regard a policy for controlling mergers as an unnecessary luxury at the present time, since they are mesmerized by their particularly acute problem of small firms.'[2] There are certainly strong pressures for further concentration, especially with a view to being able to match the big American corporations in research and development. The EEC's Committee on Competition Policy reported in 1965 on the legal and other obstacles to desirable concentrations across national frontiers within the Community. As the study remarks, there must be some reluctance within the Competition Directorate in Brussels to accept that there is a real problem of erosion of competition arising out of the search for economies of scale.

The MTP Committee is particularly well placed to see both aspects of the problem in the perspective of the overall development of the Community. However, little progress has so far been made on this tremendously important subject. The Programme records another compromise: that concentration to take advantage of the economies of scale must be facilitated up to the point where it will no longer be certain that consumers and the economy as a whole will benefit.[3] Even this broad statement, however, cannot entirely contain the differences of view as to whether or not it is necessary or desirable to give positive encouragement to medium and small firms. A future confrontation of members' experiences in this respect is promised, the outcome of which should be most interesting.

The ability to finance research and development on an adequate

[1] D. Swann and D. L. McLachlan, op. cit., p. 57.
[2] Ibid., p. 58.
[3] Avant-Projet, op. cit., pp. III, 11–12.

scale is a key element in the move to a larger size of enterprises and is accepted by the MTP Committee as being, with inflation and regional imbalance, one of the most serious problems in the future development of the EEC economies. A Working Party is now studying the problem and a report on it is expected in the next version of the Programme. There is little in the present Programme other than a statement of the importance of the subject.

Manpower policy

That the EEC Programme shows a diminution in the prospective rate of growth of GDP for the Community as a whole in the period 1965–70 as compared with 1960–65 is attributable to the expectation that the supply of labour, measured in terms of man-hours per year, will decline. This deterioration of the labour supply also underlies two of the three major obstacles to achievement of the projected growth rates pinpointed in the Programme: inflation and regional imbalance. The slowing down in the growth of labour supply is attributed to the following factors. First, the annual growth of the total population is expected to slow down from 1·1 per cent in 1960–65 to 0·8 per cent in 1965–70. Secondly, the proportion of the total population included in the working population will diminish, especially on account of the extension of the years of full-time education. Thirdly, migration of workers within the Community and immigration from outside, though very hard to estimate, are expected to fall. For example, Germany is expected to benefit from only 350,000 immigrants (working and non-working) in 1965–70 against 835,000 in 1960–5, and France from only 740,000 as compared with 1,546,000. An important cause of this reduction of immigration into these countries is that Italian industry is expected to expand enough to reduce emigration from Italy, but the net immigration into the whole EEC will also be cut by more than half. Fourthly, despite reductions in the level of unemployment, notably in Italy, a decline in the number of hours worked will offset the annual increase in the total number employed (0·5 per cent for 1965–70 against 0·7 per cent for 1960–5). The conclusion is that the rise in the total number of hours worked will be very small in most of the members. The exceptions are Holland and Germany. In Holland, the increase in labour supply, already faster in 1960–5 than in the remainder of the Community, will continue to be faster in 1965–70; the total population will actually grow faster than in the earlier period. In Germany, the working population and the total employed are expected to be virtually unchanged from 1965–70. Given the decline in the number of hours worked, the total supply of labour in Germany is expected to fall. In alleviation of these problems, substantial movements of workers out of agriculture into industry and services are envisaged, especially in Italy and France.

Manpower policy is therefore examined in an Annexe to the Programme.[1] The policy solutions outlined there follow straight-forwardly from the review of the labour situation. They concern especially the speeding of the redeployment of labour. Regional policy is emphasized, and the necessity of programmes for the re-training of labour. Community policy is very important since some of the movements of labour needed to bring about redeployment must be across national boundaries; and the EEC Programme is important since members' estimates and policies for movements of labour across frontiers must be co-ordinated and related to the projections for growth of GNP. Manpower problems and policies in the EEC Programme therefore have many similarities with those outlined in the British National Plan, but the Six still enjoy greater possibilities for alleviating the labour supply situation by move-ment from agriculture and migration internationally within the Community.

PLANNING AND PROGRAMMING IN BRITAIN AND IN THE EEC

In assessing the influence of the Medium-term Programme within the present EEC, and its potential significance for Britain if Britain should enter the Community, it is essential to distinguish between the impact of the quantitative projections and the policy programme which is based on them, and the impact of the whole movement for economic integration within the EEC, of which the medium-term policy programme is only a small part. The Programme in itself represents only a very broad commitment by the member States to a certain general orientation of their national economic policies, and offers little or no restriction on their freedom to plan or not to plan their economies in any way they choose. But national planning is affected by other activities of the EEC, as has been shown above in relation to the French economy and the Programme becomes

[1] Projet, op. cit., Annexe II.

N

important as an element in the development of particular policies, whether common Community policies or co-ordinated national policies, which will have repercussions on the freedom to plan national economies. National planning may be further influenced as the MTP Committee proceeds to put flesh on the bare bones of its first Programme, in its annual reviews and reports on the situation in members' economies. The combined influence of the EEC in general and of the medium-term policy in particular is, then, to narrow the extreme limits of possible national approaches to economic planning; the anti-planning extreme is ruled out by the minimum commitment implied in the acceptance of the Programme, while the extreme interventionist position is precluded at national level by the existence of free trade between the member States and the rules that inhibit distortions of competition. Within the somewhat narrower band of permissible options, the member States are free to plan how they wish. To adopt the lapidary language of the MTP Committee (on incomes policy), the Programme may be said to set limits to the planning interventions of the member States, within which the freedom of 'decision of the sovereign economic units may be exercised'.

Apart from the question of British entry into the EEC and the possible implications of membership for British medium-term planning and policy, the EEC Programme may also be considered as a statement of common thinking in the Six about national economic planning, and especially as the outcome of the Franco-German dialogue, which may be used as a basis of comparison with the approach to planning in Britain. This is not meant to imply that the EEC Programme is in any sense a Plan for the Community, capable of being compared directly with the British National Plan. What it does is rather to summarize the national plans (where available) and projections of the members, and to indicate the problems they have, and the policies which, in the light of such common ground as exists between their different philosophies of economic management, they agree they should in principle follow in common, or at least co-ordinate. Comparisons between the Community's Programme, as representing the highest common factor of the thinking of the members of the Community, and planning in Britain are of intrinsic interest and value, if their limits are borne in mind. The first part of this Section, therefore, compares national planning in Britain and in the EEC countries, while the second part considers the questions relating to the EEC itself, and relevant to the British decision on membership.

National planning in Britain and in the EEC

The Community's Programme emphasizes factors on the demand side less than did the British National Plan. Demand was considered in a significant way in the Community's Programme only in relation to the need to restrain the growth of private consumption, leading to recommendations for fiscal policy and for incomes and prices policy. Though much of the British Plan was indeed devoted to an account of possible policies and developments on the side of the supply and utilization of labour and capital, there was also strong emphasis on the raising of demand expectations. The Plan was intended to create a general frame of mind in which the possibility of the GDP growing at 3·8 per cent per annum would be accepted and acted on. Expressions of determination and hortatory phrases designed to raise expectations played a large part. In contrast, the Community's Programme stated quite categorically that there is no likelihood that demand, rather than supply, could be the main constraint on growth in the period in 1970: ' . . . the medium-term growth prospects are unlikely to be adversely affected by the evolution of aggregate demand, but they are, on the contrary, susceptible to an insufficient elasticity of supply.'[1]

This difference of emphasis as between demand expectations and supply factors gives the Community's Programme an altogether different tone, and reflects, of course, the fact that it is a Programme for continuing so far as possible a growth that has already been rapid in most of the member countries. The problem is that the possibilities for growth in the late 1960s are not so favourable as in the previous period; expectations based on immediate past experience are therefore likely to exceed rather than to fall short of what is possible in view of the supply constraints.

It is especially with respect to Germany that the problem arises of maintaining a reasonable growth rate in the face of adverse developments on the supply side. The Committee accepted the projection prepared by the German Economics Ministry for 3·5 per cent per annum growth of GDP for 1765–70. This compares with 5·1 per cent per annum growth in Germany in 1960–5, and with a

---

[1] *Memorandum de la Commission sur la Programme d'action de la Communauté pendant la 2ème étape*, Com. (62) 300, October 24, 1962, p. III.2.

1965–70 average for the Community as a whole which is reduced to 4·3 per cent from the 1960–5 rate of 4·9 per cent almost entirely on account of the projected slowing down of German growth. The overall projections of 4·3 per cent in GDP, 3·8 per cent in GDP per occupied person, and 3·5 per cent in GDP per head for the Community may be compared with the 3·8 per cent, 3·4 per cent and 3 per cent respectively for the United Kingdom in the National Plan. There is, therefore, a difference of only about one half of one per cent between the Community's 'targets' (if we may so call them for a moment) and the British targets. The main distinction therefore concerned the prospect for the achievement of the rates of growth laid down. The global projections for the six member countries, for the Community as a whole and for the United Kingdom are given in the table on facing page.

If a league table for all seven countries is drawn up on the basis of these figures, Britain would rank about equal with Germany, and ahead of Luxembourg, but below Italy, France, Belgium and the Netherlands. However, there are two qualifications to be made to these comparisons. If the experts' view about growth possibilities in Germany were accepted in preference to those of the Federal Economics Ministry, the projected growth rate for Germany of 4·2 per cent would raise the Community average to 4·6 per cent. This would make the EEC rates for GDP, GDP per worker and GDP per head in 1965–70 almost identical with those for 1960–65. More important, whatever the view taken about the extent to which growth in the EEC will slow down, the British National Plan figures we are here comparing are not rates equal to or lower than those achieved in the earlier period, but aspirations that were already seriously discredited by July 1966, if not sooner. Comparison of the national performance in 1960–65 shows British growth rates about 1½ per cent per annum lower than the EEC average. The closing of the gap in growth rates depended mainly on the acceleration of growth in Britain in 1965–70 over the rate achieved in 1960–65. In the circumstances of the early months of 1967 this still did not seem possible.

The British approach to medium-term economic management probably lies somewhere on the spectrum that lay between the French and the German positions when the dialogue in the EEC began, and it is appropriate to ask how far the common ground delineated in the EEC Programme (that is, the four areas of planning outlined above, pp. 369–70) on which there appears to be broad

GROWTH OF THE NATIONAL PRODUCT—PROJECTIONS

Annual rates of growth in percentages at constant prices

	Gross domestic product		Gross domestic product per worker		Gross domestic product per head	
	1960–5	1965–70	1960–5	1965–70	1960–5	1965–70
Germany	5·1 (4·9)[1]	3·5 (4·2)	4·3 (4·2)	3·5 (4·2)	3·8 (3·6)	3·0 (3·4)
France	4·8	4·8	4·5	4·2	3·4	3·9
Italy	5·1	5·0	4·5	4·2	4·4	4·4
Netherlands	4·7	4·6	3·0	3·3	3·3	3·1
Belgium	4·5	4·1	3·4	3·4	3·8	3·5
Luxembourg	2·9	3·2	2·2	2·8	1·8	2·4
United Kingdom (1960–64, 1964–70)	4·9 (4·8)	4·3 (4·6)	4·3 (4·2)	3·8 (4·1)	3·8 (3·7)	3·5(3·7)
	3·4	3·8	2·7	3·4	2·6	3·0

Sources: For the Six and EEC, Memorandum de la Commission, op. cit., p. 119, Table 4.

For the UK, The National Plan, Chapter 2, p. 24, Table 2.1.

The UK estimates of GDP per head of the total population have been derived by subtracting the estimated growth of 0·8 per cent per annum in total population from the figures for growth of GDP.

[1] The figures in brackets are the growth rates for Germany and the EEC contained in the Report of the Study Group (*Recommandation de la Commission au Conseil sur la Politique à Moyen Terme de la Communauté*, July 25, 1963, Tables 2.11 and 2.12).

agreement within the EEC, could also provide a basis for the development of planning in Britain in the 1970s.

There would certainly be no disagreement with the second point in the EEC compromise: the flexible programming of public expenditure. This has now become common practice in Western Europe, and was the aspect of medium-term planning most readily adopted by the Germans.

Nor is there any difference of substance regarding regional policy, which is approved in the EEC Programme as being favourable to growth as well as important for social reasons, though in more cautious terms than have been employed in the British statements on this subject, as for example in the NEDC's *Conditions Favourable to Faster Growth* and the National Plan. The NEDC and the DEA have stressed the medium-term advantages of increasing the supply of labour, whereas the MTP Committee referred to the need for cost-benefit studies to ascertain how far aid to the development of backward regions was economically justified in the long term. The latter is certainly the correct approach. Of course, in Britain as in the EEC regional planning is currently centred on the concept of growth areas, which implies that development in such zones is expected to be justified in the long term, and not only in the sense of relief of social problems or immediate contribution to the active labour force. And while the EEC Programme stresses the need for cost-benefit studies as guides to regional policy decisions, there is no evidence that this has so far had a real impact on the policies of EEC members.

There is, however, a difference between the attitude of the EEC Committee to the uses of projections and that so far adopted in Britain. The compromise in favour of using projections largely as a guide to public policy, and only as a very general guide to private decisions, would seem sensible in view of the difficulties encountered in trying to use them more ambitiously in Britain in the NEDC's and the DEA's Plans. But the situation in the EEC is somewhat fluid in this respect, for the Germans are under strong pressure to accept the publication of projections disaggregated to industry level. Also, what is agreed at EEC level in this respect does not affect the freedom of individual countries to use industry projections within their own borders. Most important, the publication of 'target' projections for individual industries is only one aspect of planning in relation to industry, and, many would argue, by no means the most important. For Britain to adopt an attitude towards these projections similar to that of the EEC Programme would not mean the abandonment of the work of the DEA, the NEDC, the Economic Development Committees, the Prices and Incomes Board, the Ministry of Technology and the Industrial Reorganization Corporation in the adaptation of the structure of industry, and the promotion of efficiency and the growth of productivity. It certainly does not prevent, or imply any contradiction with, the detailed planning of industrial structure which continues in France. Some of these activities appear to come under the fourth point of the EEC compromise, which concerns financial aid for the structural readaptation of industry; and the MTP Committee already has a Working Group engaged in studies of the agricultural, shipbuilding and electronics industries. While the work of the MTP Committee is not and could not in the foreseeable future be centred on industrial planning, it by no means precludes such planning in the member States.

Another suggestive feature is the independence of the MTP Committee in relation to the institutional structure of the EEC and the separate publication of the EEC projections and their policy programme. The British practice in this respect has been to carry out both the quantitative programming and the policy investigations within the same organization, first in the National Economic Development Council which was in a semi-independent position and later in the Department of Economic Affairs. The strictly industrial aspect of planning has been separated, first in that the NEDC was divided between an economic and an industrial division, and later in that the industrial work was left with the NEDC when the economic work was moved to the DEA. Projections as well as policy orientations have been published together in the National Plan, though the NEDC published a separate review of policies. While it is essential that policy should be closely related to the projections, there is much to be said in favour of a separation of the establishment of projections from the specification of policy objectives. There is, of course, no exact parallel between what is appropriate for the EEC and what is appropriate for an individual country, and the separation of projections from policy in the EEC was a result of institutional problems rather than of deliberate intention, but the method of using a separate Study Group, even one which now has governmental representatives, nevertheless suggests consideration whether there could be advantages in allowing independent experts to prepare the quantitative part of future national plans. The debate about the German projections shows that policy cannot be entirely separated from projections, as the Study Group explained very clearly, but such a confrontation had the advantage of bringing the issues out into the open. It is open to question whether the benefits of access to official secrets outweigh those of independence. Preparation and publication of the quantitative part of a plan by an independent body would emphasize the scientific status of projections, and help to remove the stigma of association with politically inspired and instrumental targets, which have been discredited in Britain. The Government would not be committed to the projections as targets, but could concentrate on developing the policies, as the MTP Committee did in their rather different context.

Planning and British entry into the EEC
The acceptance by the Council of Ministers of the Six of the medium-term economic policy Programme in February 1967 raised many important questions for Britain at a time when economic planning was undergoing a reappraisal at home[1] and a second attempt to secure membership of the EEC was being prepared. If Britain does become a member this will have important implications for British economic planning and policy. If it does not, there are in any case some interesting points of comparison to be made between the EEC Programme and the British National Plan.

It has already been pointed out that the EEC sets certain limits on the power of planning in Britain since it would reduce the power of the member governments to plan their national economies in the way they wish. Britain would suffer restrictions on freedom of action similar to those faced by France in 1958. Most obviously, it would not be possible to attempt to get faster growth in Britain by any strategy centred on removing the balance-of-payments constraint by closely protecting the home market with tariffs and quotas, and encouraging exports by specific fiscal discriminations. So far, however, Britain has not gone very far along the protectionist road. In practice, therefore, a more far-reaching restriction on the freedom

---

[1] This was formally recognized by the DEA who stated in the December 1966 issue of their Progress Report that '. . . the crisis of July 1966 meant that many of the assumptions and figures in the National Plan were invalidated. . . . The First Secretary is to discuss further with [NEDC] and with other organizations concerned the kind of planning operation that will be most effective in achieving the objectives of growth.'

of action of the British Government would arise out of the common agricultural policy. Since the common prices are set each year in terms of unit values expressed in US dollars, unilateral devaluation of its currency by an individual member is made so complex an operation as to be very difficult; the currencies are now effectively linked. Thus in joining the EEC and accepting its common agricultural policy Britain would probably be giving up the freedom to vary the value of its currency. Any future devaluation would either have to be carried out in concert with the other members: or, individually, only if the British Government were prepared to raise the sterling price of farm products by the full amount of the devaluation in order to retain the dollar prices agreed under the common policy. Institutional arrangements for either of these courses of action have not yet been devised, and the latter would become less and less feasible as further common policies increased the magnitude and complexity of the consequential adjustments *vis-à-vis* the other members. This problem was avoided, so far as Britain is concerned, by the devaluation of November 1967, which may be regarded as an essential adjustment preceding entry into the Community. But the limitation on the freedom to adjust the value of the currency in future would have to be accepted.

With these vital exceptions of external commercial and monetary policy, it seems unlikely that the Community, which has already contained divergent economic regimes, in the German neo-liberal, the French *économie concertée*, and the Italian 'State capitalist' systems, would in its present stage of development much restrict the British Government in pursuing internal growth policies. Certainly the French have proved capable of adapting their policies and their planning. How far the Community might restrict national freedom of action in ten or twenty years' time is of course another question, on which only a very broad political judgment could be made.

The MTP Committee has been working on a wide range of economic problems and policies on which the Rome Treaty had little or nothing to say. The breadth of its work is at once its weakness and its strength: weakness, because there is a danger that its discussions will become bogged down in a morass of generalizations and compromises; strength, in that the inclusion of such a wide range of policies allows the Committee to balance the varying interests of the members, and thus gradually to make progress over the whole field of economic integration.

O

The wide scope of its work, together with the extremely short period from its formation to the date of the publication of its Draft Programme, mean that the first Programme is very incomplete, general, and in many areas superficial. The Committee has no powers and disposes of no funds that could enable it to press its views. It would, however, be mistaken to believe that effective work in the Community must await decisions on granting supranational powers to Community institutions.

The work of the Committee is not confined to drawing-up a medium-term policy programme every five years. The 1964 Decision[1] also gave the Committee important tasks ensuring the continuity of its influences:

'The Committee will examine the programme annually and make any necessary adaptations.

'The Committee shall study the medium-term economic policy of Member States and examine to what extent it can be reconciled with the programme adopted. . . .

'It shall analyse the course of economic development to ascertain the reasons for any divergence from the forecasts. . . .

'At the request of the Council or the Commission, *or on its own initiative* (our italics), the Committee shall be able to express opinions with a view to helping the competent institutions of the Community and Member States in the execution of the envisaged economic policy.'

These terms of reference for the continuing work of the Committee do not guarantee that it will exercise a strong influence on members' and Community policies, but they certainly give it every possibility of doing so. There would seem to be three major elements in the position of this Committee which will tend to give it a real influence. First its membership of the most senior officials, equivalent to the British Permanent Secretary level, and the direct representation of the Commission itself by three members, are bound to give it a strong position. The first Chairman was Dr Langer, State Secretary in the German Federal Ministry of Economic Affairs. After the change of Government in December 1966, Dr Arndt, the new State Secretary, was elected to succeed Dr Langer. Secondly, its central position in the structure of the Commission's economic

[1] *Decision du Conseil du 15 Avril 1964 Créant un Comité de Politique Economique à Moyen Terme.*

policy gives the potential to act as a co-ordinator of the work of other Committees, Groups, and Working Parties on the more detailed aspects of the economic development of the Community. The Committee is serviced by the Commission, though there is no separate programming office. Thirdly, its powers to examine the policies of member States in the light of the adopted programme, and to express opinions at the request of either the Commission or the Council or on its own initiative, put it in a position to bring considerable persuasive force to bear on the member governments to fulfil the programme once they have adopted it. The fact that the first Programme is not very explicit or detailed with respect to particular policies need not detract from the influence of the Committee, since it leaves them a relatively free hand to fill in the framework with further reports on particular problems. The first Programme was in any case drawn up in the short space of fifteen months, and had therefore to be limited to outlining very broad policy orientations in respect of most subjects. Three topics were treated in some detail in Annexes to the Programme: manpower policy, regional policy, and public finance. The Programme is to be revised annually, and future work is to contain three main features:

(a) a revision of the projections in so far as this is felt to be desirable in the light of another year's experience;

(b) a review of the policies and performance of the member States in the light of the broad objectives which in the first Programme they have undertaken to secure;

(c) more detailed reports on subjects that could not be treated fully in the first Programme.

The subjects on which the Committee has been working since the publication of the Draft Programme in March 1966 are revealed in the tasks of a number of Working Groups, whose terms of reference were published with the Draft Programme.[1] A Working Group on policy relating to industrial structure was set up to examine how far and by what policy instruments structural changes in the member States are influenced by government action; to ascertain how structural policy is linked with general growth policy, cyclical policy, and competition policy; and to study how structural policy is liable to affect economic development in the Community. A Working Group on 'incomes policy' was to report on the incomes policies being

[1] Avant-Projet, op. cit.

applied or attempted in the member States and in third countries, with particular reference to the United Kingdom. The Group was expected to rely heavily on work done by the OECD in this field. A third Group was to study 'scientific and technical research policy', and specifically 'the problems likely to arise from the formulation of a co-ordinated or common policy for scientific and technical research' and to 'make proposals for the introduction of such a policy, with due allowance for the possibility of co-operation with other countries'.

So far the Programme has been as much a confrontation of Members' national policies as a plan for the Community's collective policies; and it is in these confrontations that the Community's medium-term policy seems likely to impinge most directly and obviously on national economic policies. The British Government already faces such confrontations in the OECD, and there may be a tendency to disregard the significance of another confrontation in the EEC. The MTP Committee represents only a confrontation of national planners, who may themselves have difficulty in exercising influence over policy at home. Certainly the significance of more detailed confrontations in bodies dealing with specific subjects is more readily recognized. However, although it is far too early to assess how much influence the MTP Committee may achieve, there are reasons for thinking that it will not be correct to treat its future work as merely a discussion group at international level. So far the MTP Committee has been aiming to promote and co-ordinate policies for achieving each member's own national target, and in its first Programme confined itself to extremely general pronouncements about desirable policies for members to follow. For example, it suggested that fiscal rather than monetary policy should be used to maintain financial equilibrium since the use of monetary policy would adversely affect investment and thus prejudice the growth of output. This does not recommend any individual member to undertake any specific policy. But in reviewing progress in the individual countries on the basis of the Programme, it would be remarkable if the Committee did not eventually make fairly specific recommendations for desirable changes in fiscal policy to individual members. And the members, it must be recalled, have committed themselves to act in accordance with the policy programme approved by the Council of Ministers.

It would be foolish to over-estimate the significance of such a general undertaking; individual governments could easily delay implementing what the Committee recommends until it is no longer relevant. But the EEC Commission, through its representatives on the MTP Committee, and the other members through theirs, would be able to exert considerable pressure. This may well, therefore, become a rather powerful form of confrontation of economic policies. It would, moreover, apply in a new area. OECD, IMF and other existing confrontations concern short-term rather than medium- or long-term policy. If the pressures to conform were less urgent than in the case of the IMF, since the position of the currency would not be in question, the Commission would have more time to exert its influence, which would also be more fundamental and more permanent.

In discussing the prospects facing the British Government in the EEC in relation to planning, the debate between the Study Group and the German Government about the German projections is instructive. The EEC in effect provided a platform for the German expert members of the Study Group to challenge the Federal Ministry of Economics on its view of the prospects for the German economy. In this case the German experts were on the side of ambition in the projections, and opposed to the use of what they regarded as pessimistic objectives as an instrument of incomes policy, but the German Government was supported by the MTP Committee. If the United Kingdom had already been a member, the attitude of the Committee might have been different. They might well have argued that the 3·8 per cent per annum projection or target for growth of the GDP in the British National Plan was too high. But although the ensuing controversy might have its effect on British public opinion in relation to the target, it would not of course be open to the EEC institutions to compel the British Government to change its target.

In addition to the aspect of confrontation, there is also a more informal influence of the EEC institutions, and especially of the MTP Committee. This influence has been most marked in Germany, where official projections were established directly in response to the EEC activity, an inter-departmental group on science and research has been set up in connection with the EEC work in this field, and in October 1966 the German Government also initiated a new industrial structure policy, strongly influenced by the MTP Committee's Working Group on this subject. The German attitude to competition is also undergoing a metamorphosis, with a new emphasis on practical problems rather than theory. The MTP Committee has in addition inserted some economic considerations into the discussion of agricultural policy, which was in danger of being conducted almost entirely on financial criteria. Most of the influence of the Committee so far has been in the direction of more planning, since the major problem was to persuade the German Government in this direction. It would, however, be unwise to assume that it would always exert its influence in future in the same direction.

Looking into the future, it is possible to envisage a time when the maximization of the rate of growth of the Community as a whole could become an objective to be set alongside that of maximization of growth in each country. This would have considerable implications for matters such as regional policy, where the status of problem regions could come to be attached to whole national economies; and for incomes policy. But this, like most long-term predictions relating to the EEC, depends on the long-term political evolution of the Community.

CHAPTER 13

CONCLUSIONS

***

COMPARISONS BETWEEN THE THREE COUNTRIES

The distinction drawn in Chapter 1 between the neo-liberal and the neo-collectivist economic philosophies raised a number of complex questions which can now be re-examined in the light of the intervening chapters. Germany and France have pursued different policies in facing the problems of oligopolistic market structures, rapid technological progress and consequent uncertainty, and the growing influence of the State in economic life, and have each achieved rapid economic growth in the 1950s. Britain, combining elements of policies used in each of these neighbouring countries, has not. Is growth in Germany and in France attributable to their clearer choices in the 1950s about the general form of economic policy? Is it essential either to rely predominantly and systematically on State initiatives and national indicative planning, or else on a deliberately market-oriented system? If this choice must be made, which method is the better? Is it really essential, as Eucken has it, to draw a clear and unambiguous line between the co-ordination of individual economic decisions, and their subordination to State dictation? Can neo-liberal policies for making the market work more effectively be combined with neo-collectivist methods of supplementing and partly replacing it, in such a way as to take advantage of the best features of both the market and the centralist methods, or is this like 'trying to conduct two orchestras in one room'?[1]

The examination of policy, as opposed to theory, in earlier chapters has shown that the questions of whether a clear choice should be made between one system or the other, and, if so, which system should be chosen, cannot be answered merely by reference to French and German experience. The social market theory, faced with strong and persistent opposition from many interests in the

[1] *Grundsätze*, op. cit., p. 144.

German economy, has never been fully implemented, and further, some of the most recent actions taken by the German Government, notably the inauguration of a policy of 'concerted action' based on growth targets, seem to mark a departure from orthodox neo-liberalism. Nor were the French planners ever so powerful as to force the French economy in any detailed sense into the fulfilment of a rational and coherent set of industrial production targets, even before the successive changes in the direction of an open economy and more flexible planning that have taken place in recent years.

Thus while the best solution to the economic problems that were outlined in Chapter 1 is still a matter for lively controversy in France and Germany, as well as in Britain, the most notable differences among these three countries have been differences not of actual policy, but of the language in which the debate is conducted. In Germany, the starting point has been the impressive body of academic and official opinion in favour of the social market solution; in France, the initiative was seized soon after the war by M. Monnet and the planners; in Britain, opinion has fluctuated, and no one school of thought has predominated, though the balance tilted in the direction of a neo-collectivist method in the early 1960s. The debate has also been extended to the EEC, where the French have tried to gain acceptance for the grafting of some aspects of indicative planning on to the Community institutions, while the Germans have pressed for the adoption of a German type of competition policy within the Community.

But even if the divergences of economic philosophy have been greater than those of policy, there have still been very significant differences as well as some interesting similarities in the practice of the three countries. The evolution of the French Plans and of the British planning system was considered in Chapters 3 and 4, and Chapter 5 provided an analysis based largely on an examination of the two systems. The differences between the French and German systems of economic management, and the way in which these differences have tended to narrow in recent years, were outlined in Chapter 12. Here we confine ourselves to summarizing some of the points of similarity and difference as between policies in Germany and in Britain.

In Chapter 2 and in later chapters in which various aspects of German economic policy were examined, the reader may have been struck by the similarity of some leading features of German policy to British policy in the same period. German monetary policy may, given the constitutional independence of the Central Bank, have been more independent than the British, yet a similar problem arose as to the reconciliation of internal and external needs. The main difference was that after 1952 the Germans were trying to cope with the problems arising out of payments surpluses, whereas the British difficulty was usually the reverse. Again, Britain like Germany re-opened markets in the 1950s, and attempted to achieve the maximum possible degree of convertibility. Failure to enter the EEC did not prevent Britain from cutting tariffs, notably within EFTA. In respect of policy against restrictive practices, the German Law of 1957 and the British Act of 1956, with its prohibition of restrictive practices in general, coupled with an extensive set of 'gateways' through which they could be justified before the Restrictive Practices Court, are not dissimilar. So far as resale price maintenance is concerned, the 1964 Act appears to put Britain ahead of Germany in policy for making competition work. The *Mittelstandspolitik* is matched in Britain, and has been for many years, by the work of specialist Finance Houses, and the quantitative results of the German policy of providing special credits for small and medium-sized firms do not appear to be of a different order of magnitude.

Justification of the social market theory does not, however, rest on its practical results in these directions alone. The existence of this consistent theory for the guidance of economic policy has had other effects which suggest that its application in certain respects elsewhere, and especially in Britain, could eventually bring about substantial improvements in economic management. The reduction of tariffs went further in Germany than in Britain, even before German membership of the EEC brought the removal of tariff barriers against major industrial competitors within Europe. The policy against the concentration of economic power is not confined to the provision of finance for small and medium-sized firms but is expressed in a range of policies which have no counterpart in Britain (pp. 62–8). In other areas, too, the social market economy has also made substantial progress. It is probably in the reform of the tax system that German policy has most notably advanced on British in the direction of making the market work more efficiently. Although the proportion of GNP taken in taxes has risen in the past decade, and is now higher than the proportion in Britain, the form and structure of taxation are better adjusted to the maintenance of incentives, as discussed in

Chapter 7. The decision to adopt the added-value tax was likewise taken on the grounds that this tax would not distort market conditions and in particular would not encourage economically undesirable vertical integration, as the cascade turnover tax had done. In respect of savings and share-ownership, the Germans have created a wide range of effective incentives, while in Britain small savers have been deterred by rates of interest that barely enable them to retain the real value of savings in the face of inflation. The Germans, through the flexible policy of 'white areas', have largely succeeded in restoring a free market in housing, while in Britain blanket restrictions are still imposed. These examples suggest that the social market theory has had a pervasive influence for good on many aspects of German economic life.

The restriction of comparisons in this book to three countries is not intended to suggest that there is nothing to be learned from wider comparisons of economic policy and practice. Innovations of economic policy and the adoption of growth as an objective, associated with the formulation of programmes and plans, have now spread throughout most of Western Europe. These institutional and policy changes have provoked a keen interest in comparative studies of programmes and plans in Western Europe, and a considerable literature exists on the subject, notably on the French example. Economic planning of an imperative rather than an indicative type has meanwhile been employed in Eastern Europe over a longer period, and specialists in the Russian and Eastern European economies have studied the methods used in these socialist countries with the primary aim also of achieving faster growth. While, for many years, these studies have appeared to relate to economies whose management and social aims were so different as to present only very remote lessons, and these more by contrast than by comparison, for economic management in the West, more recently Eastern Europe has experienced problems and devised policies to meet them which appear significantly more relevant to the West. As Chapter 1 indicated, the distinction between indicative and imperative planning is not absolute, and East European countries that are beginning to use price indicators and profit incentives in a more widespread and flexible manner than hitherto are likely to encounter difficulties similar to those involved in trying to graft quantitative programming methods on to capitalist West European economies. The ideological bases of the societies may be different, and the directions from which the reconciliation of programming and competition must be attempted may be opposite, but it would be remarkable if there was not much to be learned on both sides from comparative studies of economic management in both Western and Eastern Europe. While studies of either Eastern or Western economic planning have frequently referred to interesting parallels from the other side, there has been little systematic comparison in detail, which might help towards solutions of some of the problems facing Western countries by reference to Eastern economies, and vice versa.

THE NEED FOR A STRATEGY OF GROWTH

The economic experiences of the three countries show that the adoption of any method of economic management cannot be said to be necessary in order to bring about rapid growth, for France and Germany have each achieved it with distinctly different methods. But both France and Germany, faced with the initial problem of breaking out of a vicious circle of slow growth into a virtuous circle of rapid growth, did adopt a consistent growth strategy. In Germany the breakthrough was achieved in the early 1950s by a considerable amount of selective intervention in favour of investment and exports and also by way of import controls, followed by a fairly thorough application of certain neo-liberal principles including a prolonged application of monetary restriction in the face of high unemployment. In France the breakthrough took the form of boosting public investment and guiding private investment with the help of indicative plans, and accepting the consequences, first of inflation accompanied by import controls and export subsidies, and later of the devaluation of the currency. In both Germany and France, a virtuous circle was thus established, of a high level of industrial investment, rapid growth of output, buoyant exports, and balance-of-payments surpluses. The methods were different, but in each country the policies, despite much internal dissension, were broadly consistent. That Britain meanwhile remained on the vicious circle of slow growth and balance-of-payments deficits may be attributed to a failure to accept that faster growth required powerful and consistent policies, such as an adjustment of the value of the currency or a really rigorous and persistent deflation, combined with a concentration of inducements for the increase of exports and of investments, in order to break the balance-of-payments constraint.

One reason for the British failure to devise and implement a satisfactory overall medium-term and long-term economic policy has been the concentration of effort and talent on the short-term problems. The examination of medium-term and long-term problems should, however, be accorded at least as much academic and intellectual recognition as work on short-term problems. The latter has far more prestige at present on account of the intellectual appeal and elegance of Keynesian and post-Keynesian economic analysis, and the relative ease with which quantitative techniques may be applied in short-term forecasting. In contrast, academic theories of growth are numerous and contradictory, and their application bedevilled by the difficulty of measuring many of the variables that the qualitative analysis suggests may be most important. But the French, without having any widely accepted body of theory (except after the event), pursued growth as their main objective to which short-term policy was subordinated in the 1950s. German neo-liberal economics has been regarded by those brought up in the Keynesian tradition as academically not respectable. Yet as Chapter 2 and later chapters have suggested, it would be foolish to dismiss the German example for a reason so far removed from the field of actual economic policies and achievements. The failure to adopt in Germany until very recently a short-term fiscal policy in the British sense was, indeed, partly attributable to the emphasis on medium-term and long-term policy. If, conversely, as much intellectual effort as went into short-term policy in Britain had been put into long-term, a British strategy for growth might have been devised much sooner.

It is sometimes suggested that, whatever the shortcomings of the 1950s, and the difficulties of 1964–7, Britain has been in the process of adopting a consistent strategy for growth, and one that is superior to either the German or the French models, which date back to the 1950s and are both showing signs of inadequacy as the fortuitous circumstances which undoubtedly played some part in allowing faster growth in those countries are disappearing. It is argued that by pressing ahead faster with a prices and incomes policy, and by using the DEA, the EDCs, the Ministry of Technology, the Industrial Reorganization Commission and the National Board for Prices and Incomes in a direct attempt to stimulate industrial productivity, exports and import-saving, Britain is now better equipped to face the problems of achieving faster growth in the late 1960s than either of her neighbours: although the quantitative programme of the

National Plan has been undermined by events, its associated institutions and policies represent a full and consistent policy for growth which requires neither deflation nor devaluation.

The examination of British policy in relation to prices and incomes in Chapter 9, and to the balance of payments in Chapter 11, do not support this suggestion. Apart from the element of quantitative programming, which has so far been unsuccessful but which, as concluded in Chapter 5, could be a useful though by no means decisive instrument, the British approach is best characterized as one of 'removing obstacles to growth'. The methods being applied are numerous, but of mixed validity and effectiveness. It is doubtful whether some of the most active lines of policy, on which considerable reliance has been placed, will have enough impact on growth. While regional policies can undoubtedly raise employment in the short term, there has been insufficient attempt, as was pointed out in Chapter 10, to establish whether the pursuit of 'balanced regional development' is in the best interests of raising investment, improving exports, and getting a faster growth rate in the longer run. The incomes policy has now been accorded widespread recognition in theory as a method of avoiding deflation or devaluation: but in practice it did not bring about a sufficient reduction in relative prices to make Britain internationally competitive enough to break the external constraint on growth in time to prevent devaluation. The specific measures to improve the balance of payments, before devaluation, likewise had inadequate practical effect. The same applies to the incentives to increase investment, which has in addition been discouraged by the effect on businessmen's confidence of the 1966-7 deflation.

The use of the EDCs to stimulate productivity in their industries is another element in Britain's current efforts to achieve faster growth. But the EDCs are as yet no more than small committees for each industry; and it will be some time before it can be known whether this method of stimulating productivity will have significant success. The measures for management and industrial training are certainly of great importance, but it will also be some years before they can have a substantial influence on the rate of growth, and probably decades before their impact is fully felt. A fuller use of market incentives of the neo-liberal type might have a quicker effect, but progress in applying such policies has been rather slow.

The strategy for growth must obviously differ from one country to another, depending on the institutional, historical and economic circumstances. But it is quite evident that, where a major constraint on growth exists, the correct strategy for growth must concentrate on breaking it. This means that a successful strategy for growth in Britain must centre on a substantial and sustained improvement in the balance of payments. In considering the contribution that can be made by different policies, it is important to be clear about the different time scales involved. In the long term everything is possible: the structure of industry can be altered, the level of skills of management and workers improved, and a permanent incomes policy can perhaps have substantial effect on the relative price levels. The new policies and institutions that have been developed in Britain in the 1960s in order to accelerate growth contain some valuable elements, although not all of these policies or institutions are justified either in theory or by evidence of practical effectiveness. But in almost all cases their effect on growth cannot be other than long term. With regard to the medium term, equivalent to the four or five years of a national programme, the armoury was lamentably bare, apart from the costly weapon of devaluation. Now that this has been used, and if inflation is prevented and the balance of payments responds sufficiently, the way seems open for faster growth in the 1970s.

ARE PLANNING AND MARKET SYSTEMS COMPATIBLE?

How far can the market forces that are the foundation of the neo-liberal system co-exist with institutions and policies such as those associated with the French plans or the British National Plan and incomes policy? Are the two irreconcilable? The functions and influence of national programmes were considered in Chapter 5, and those of incomes policies in Chapter 9. In industries which are not oligopolistic or monopolistic, there seems to be little justification for restricting the freedom of individual firms to take their own investment or output decisions, in order to force them collectively, as an industry, to hit the industrial target in a national programme. In these circumstances targets should be indicative in the sense of informative and should not be in conflict with competition between firms. Incentives or sanctions relating to classes of firms may alter the conditions of competition as between one industry and another, or as between one category of firms and another within each industry (e.g. large firms and small firms), but there is no reason why this should reduce the intensity of competition between firms; nor, as will be shown in the next section, can the selective use of policy instruments be said to destroy the market system, provided that such use is kept within certain limits. It should indeed be a basic aim of policy to make competition work in all such industries, and to keep the responsibility for investment and production decisions squarely with the individual firms.

It is in the case of monopolistic or oligopolistic industries that a really valid choice between a system based on targets and controls and a system based on the market appears to emerge. It must of course be recognized that the market in such industries is a very different thing from the market in an industry with many firms, none of them dominant. It must also be recognized that the mere existence of a national target does not necessarily imply that there has been any change in the competitive relationship between the firms in an oligopolistic industry; it is not likely that the British National Plan, for example, had any such effect. But it is nevertheless possible for neo-liberals to make a good case for strict non-interference in the decisions of oligopolistic firms relating to production, investment or prices, except in so far as it is necessary to intervene with the instruments of competition policy in order to maximize competition between them. Planners for their part can likewise make a good case for State intervention in the investment decisions of such firms, and for control of prices and incomes that are determined under conditions of monopoly or of oligopolistic competition.

The British steel industry before its renationalization provided an interesting example of a clash between a market-oriented restrictive practices policy and programme-oriented supervision by the Iron and Steel Board. The former sought to enforce price competition and thus rely on the profit motive to guide the development of the industry in meeting the demands on it from the rest of the economy; the Board, on the other hand, was given its powers on the assumption that oligopolistic behaviour, inevitable on technological grounds, would prevent the satisfactory development of the industry, and that it was therefore best to control the investment and pricing policies of steel firms in accordance with the output targets of a national programme. Steel is an outstanding case, but other industries are by no means entirely dissimilar. In such cases it can be argued that if the Government does not choose to plan at the level of the firm in accordance with national objectives, planning is likely to be effected through collusion between the firms. Such collusion might pursue private profit at the expense of the public good, so that the pretence that the market economy still operates effectively conceals a situation of what may be called irresponsible planning, which is less acceptable than responsible and democratic planning operating on investment decisions through the national programme and on prices through the control of prices and incomes.

The formulation within the EEC of the Medium-term Economic Policy Programme, described in Chapter 12, shows that the French and German Governments, together with the other member governments, have agreed on the principles that should guide the use of a wide range of long-term economic policies. The use of macro-economic forecasts as a background to policy-making has been accepted by the Germans, although without the publication of separate industry forecasts and with no question of quantitative target-planning for individual industries either at EEC level or in Germany itself. The need for flexible medium-term planning of public expenditure is also generally agreed, although the Germans had previously vigorously opposed the idea. The need for incomes policy is also accepted, though there would doubtless be disagreement as to whether price controls, used in France but abhorred by successive German governments, or controls over incomes may be a legitimate way of preventing inflation. There is no doubt that it would have been impossible until quite recently to obtain so much agreement between a plan-oriented French Government and a neo-liberal German Government on these and other elements of policy that figure in the Medium-term Programme, and that this reflects a substantial convergence between the two viewpoints, with the French returning to a measure of liberal orthodoxy and the Germans adopting certain elements of programming and of a 'planning' approach. This is partly because the facts of life press policy away from the pure milk of the neo-liberal or of the French 'planning' doctrine, although it may also indicate that German neo-liberals found it easier, at the level of economic policy, to come to terms with a government led by General de Gaulle than they would with a more left-wing French Government. But the convergence is still very limited in the crucial fields of 'industrial planning' and of providing prices and incomes policy with the teeth of government controls; and the agreement reached in the Medium-term Programme does little to indicate whether the EEC countries will eventually deal with the problem of monopolistic or oligopolistic industries by competition policy or by State intervention in those industries' decisions or investment, prices and incomes, or by some judicious combination of the two. As the size of firms continues to increase in relation to the size of the market, this problem seems destined to become the key issue of economic policy in the future. It must be admitted that in none of the three countries under study has policy really got to grips with it as yet, and that examination of their experience therefore enables one to conclude little about it, at least at the level of generalization. In so far as an element of State 'planning' does eventually prevail, we may see a 'dual economy' (not to be confused with a mixed economy or with 'dual economy' as applied to an under-developed economy) emerge, in which policy towards the monopolistic or oligopolistic industries draws more from the experience of French planning, while policy towards other industries is based more predominantly on neo-liberal principles.

But the type of market structure is not the only criterion for deciding with which section of such a 'dual' economy particular industries are to be classified. Another well-known criterion is the position of an industry in the system of inter-industry relationships. Industries that contribute to the economy producers' goods—materials and components for other industries—are certainly more amenable to forecasting techniques based on input-output relationships than those that sell the bulk of their output directly to consumers. Even if a consumer-goods industry should have a monopolistic structure, its sensitivity to the essentially exogenous and largely unplannable variations in consumers' tastes implies that flexible response to market forces will probably continue to be more relevant than participation in a national programme, as East European countries are now discovering.

TYPES OF INTERVENTION

There is a spectrum of methods whereby firms can be encouraged or obliged to comply with the objectives of economic policy or of a national programme, ranging from the psychological effect that may be hoped for purely as the result of publication of a national plan at one extreme, to commands having the force of law at the other. Between these extremes lie various methods of information, persuasion, influence, incentive, sanction and pressure, whose borders are difficult to demarcate. The arguments that indicative targets are something of a contradiction in terms, and that once a decision is made to attempt a certain policy the adoption of the means to bring about its implementation is implied, has already been mentioned. This would be true if to hit the quantitative targets were the sole or the overriding objective of economic policy. But this is far from having been the case in Britain, it is certainly not so in France at present, and it is doubtful how far it ever was the case in France. How detailed State intervention will be, and how far it will be persuasive or how far imperative, will depend on how detailed the objectives are and how much priority each objective has. The existence of industry targets will not necessarily lead to more detailed and more imperative intervention, unless they are regarded as objectives to be attained regardless of the effect on other objectives such as the preservation of responsibility for decision-taking within individual firms and the encouragement of competition between them. In determining how far to be guided by a programme, governments should from the start consider the methods of implementation that will be employed, and assess the importance of their effect in relation to the objectives.

A distinction may be made, following especially German neo-liberal thinking, between neutral and discriminatory measures for the achievement of economic policy objectives. Neutral interventions are those that do not distort the conditions of competition in the market, as opposed to discriminatory measures, which do distort them. It is important first to realize that a general and apparently non-discriminatory instrument, such as bank rate, may well not be neutral in its effects on different economic activities, as was pointed out in the Radcliffe Report, referred to on p. 158. The added-value tax, on the other hand, does seem to be competitively more neutral (although this depends on assumptions about how far the tax may be shifted from the firm that formally pays it), and this is its major attraction for German neo-liberals (see p. 192). Secondly, it is necessary to remember that there are many levels at which discrimination can take place, for example, firms versus individuals (corporation tax and income tax), service industries versus manufacturing industries (selective employment tax), less-developed versus more-developed regions (all kinds of regional policies), one industry versus other industries (subsidies for shipbuilding), one type of firm versus other types of firms within an industry (subsidies for hill farmers), or one firm versus others in its industry (a grant to develop a technologically advanced product). But although the distinction between neutral and discriminatory measures is, for these reasons, not easy to handle, it is nevertheless a useful one, because wherever the distinction can be made it implies the need to justify the discriminatory measures. This does *not* imply that such measures should not be taken, but only that, when the Government distorts the conditions under which consumers or producers make their choices about what to consume or what to produce and how to produce it, it should in each case have a good reason for doing so.

Nor does it follow that discriminatory measures should always cover as wide a front, i.e. be as nearly neutral, as possible. On the contrary, the French *carte d'exportateur*, which has given a substantial incentive to those firms that raise their exports to a certain percentage of their turnover, has a great deal to be said for it, from the point of view of stimulating exports, in comparison with the British Selective Employment Tax, which discriminates in favour of manufacturing industry and agriculture as a whole; and the German system of housing subsidies for those in need of them has many advantages over Britain's general housing subsidies. If an incentive or a sanction is neither more nor less specific than is required to achieve its objective, it is easier to calculate its benefits in relation to its costs, and thus to determine the effectiveness of the measure, and to determine when it is no longer needed. To favour more specific and discriminatory policies is, in fact, not the same thing as to favour more intervention by the State: if the measures are as specific as is appropriate to the objectives they are to serve, they will in fact imply less intervention than more general measures that are intended to fulfil the same objectives.

The idea of distinguishing between neutral and discriminatory measures is a useful one in assessing the nature of particular measures of State intervention in the economy. With further advances in econometrics, it might even become possible to measure the extent to which the whole range of government policy departs from competitive neutrality and thus how far it is supplementing or replacing the market system. Meanwhile, a very practical criterion to apply to selective interventions is whether they are permanent or temporary and, if the latter, the extent to which they are automatically degressive. Given that certain discriminatory measures are required, it is important that they should be continually reviewed with the object of abolishing them when they are no longer needed. More than this, the policies should, so far as possible, be designed to bring about structural changes which lead to the policies' eventual demise and, wherever appropriate, there should be a time-table for their gradual phasing out. Thus one should aim eventually to dispense with export incentives because the economy will, with their help, have become internationally competitive; and one would expect that subsidies to a particular industry, or region, would be necessary only in a period of readjustment, even if it might in some cases be a long period, and would promote the improvement in conditions that would make their continuation unnecessary. This is not to say, of course, that intervention in general would gradually wither away, for new problems or aims are likely to arise that will require new interventions.

The principle that each intervention should be temporary and degressive is one of the most fruitful ideas of the German neo-liberals, and one which the German Government has put into practice on a substantial scale. It intervened intensively in favour of invest-ment and exports during the period after the Currency Reform, until the basis for growth and stability has been achieved. In the following period, lasting till about 1962, many of those interventions were removed. Since 1962 there has been a renewal of interventions to meet the new situation created by the reduced supply of man-power and the growth of inflationary pressures.

There is not, however, much to be said for the view, which has been held particularly strongly in Germany, that monetary policy should be non-discriminatory and, partly for that reason, that it should have supremacy over all other types of policy. This view underestimates the extent to which monetary policy is in any case likely to have discriminatory effects; it leads to a failure to use fiscal and other instruments properly, which considerably reduces the effectiveness of economic policy; and it again reduces the power of economic policy if, while deliberately selective interventions with other instruments are held to be legitimate, monetary instruments alone are required to be used, for no apparent logical reason, in a global manner. The Germans have recently modified their former doctrine of the supremacy of monetary policy, for example by giving fiscal policy a much greater role than before.

Nor, if it is accepted, as in Britain, that monetary and fiscal policy are equally legitimate areas of economic policy, and should be used as discriminatorily as is necessary, does it seem sensible to rule out other instruments of policy such as physical controls. It is commonly held that the advantage lies in favour of monetary and fiscal policy, since they do not require such detailed administration or so great a degree of interference in individual behaviour. However, monetary policy and fiscal policy are sometimes used in a way that is just as detailed and specific as physical controls, as for example when a low-interest loan or a tax incentive is granted to a single firm; and physical controls can be more general, if for example, new building of offices is prohibited in the London area. Nor is it necessarily an advantage if administrative simplicity is achieved, so far as the central government is concerned, by passing the detailed control on to some non-official organization, for example, by instructing the banks to favour exporters during a credit squeeze and to leave the detailed implementation of this policy to the bank managers.

THE ROLE OF INTEREST GROUPS

Another major issue of economic policy, on which the French and the Germans have sharply divergent views, is the extent to which interest groups should be involved in the institutions where government policy is influenced or formed. The neo-liberal theory is that care should be taken to keep the influence of interest groups on policy at a minimum. Advisory committees in Germany, including the overall economic policy committees, are usually made up of independent experts, although the experts are often closely associated with interests, so that there is indirect or concealed representation. In France, the opposite view is taken, and interest groups are very closely and explicitly consulted in the planning process, especially through the Modernization Commissions. In Britain, although consultation with industry has not yet been so closely organized as in France, the habit has been to accept that interest groups have a right to be heard before the Government decides its policies, and planning under the NEDC and the DEA has been, in principle at least, tripartite. In the case of the NEDC the composition is formally tripartite, and in the case of the DEA recruitment from outside the civil service has served a similar purpose in a less formal way. This bringing together of the 'two sides' of industry, with the government representing the consumer and the general interest, is a point of particular sensitivity in the dialogue between neo-liberalism and indicative planning. The neo-liberals have seen the Government as an impartial authority, setting the conditions in which the competitive process takes place, while in Britain and France it is held that economic policy will be both more realistic and more acceptable if the interest groups concerned are involved in its formulation.

One of the neo-liberals' fears is that government policy will be contaminated by too much contact with interest groups, who will influence it unduly in favour of their private interests and against the public interest. It is hard to generalize about an argument which depends, as this does, on assumptions as to the behaviour of politicians, government officials and representatives of interest groups, which will clearly differ from country to country. What does seem clear, however, is that, while the arguments supporting the neo-liberal doctrine may, once again, carry some weight in relation to industries whose structure is not monopolistic or oligopolistic, it is hard to envisage a satisfactory economic policy in relation to basic industries dominated by big firms that does not depend on a dialogue, and perhaps a partnership, between the Government and the firms.

A second fear is that the representatives of interest groups will, if they are placed together in officially organized meetings, merely be encouraged to collude privately against the public interest. As far as the firms and trade associations are concerned, this argument was discussed earlier in this chapter; and many trade unions are already in a monopolistic position, as far as wage-bargaining goes, in their respective trades or industries. The possibilities of reducing the monopolistic element on both sides of the labour market and increasing the element of plant-by-plant bargaining were considered in Chapter 9.

A third aspect of consultation in the British and French planning systems is that it encourages co-operation between the representatives of employers and of labour, both at the national level in the preparation of the national plans, and at the industrial level in the Modernization Commissions and EDCs. This is paralleled at the level of the firm by joint consultation and other forms of co-operation in the productive process, of which the formal aspects at least are much more highly developed in Germany than in Britain or France. All these aspects and levels of co-operation between the suppliers of labour and of capital appear to be valuable, but it must be accepted that they do not imply important changes in the traditional free enterprise system. Some German neo-liberals have condemned the concept of co-determination on these grounds. But here again one must set any loss of independent action on the part of individual economic agents against any gain in productivity or social harmony, and weigh the chances of securing a truly competitive operation of the market against the possibility that co-operation will be fruitful. It does not seem wise to frustrate the will which undoubtedly exists, beneath the hostilities of industrial relations, for a new form of partnership between labour and capital; nor should one ignore the defects of the labour market left to itself, in present conditions of monopoly and without high unemployment, as a mechanism for securing a rapid rate of growth of productivity, while at the same time keeping increases of incomes within that rate of growth and thus making it possible to keep prices stable.

PLANNING AND DEMOCRACY

The main objective of economic policy in Britain in the 1970s will be to accelerate economic growth to a rate which is closer to what has been achieved in other West European countries, substantially faster than we have managed so far, and capable of meeting the aspirations of private individuals and of public authorities for higher material standards, without causing strain through excessive claims on resources. This is not a question of growth for its own sake, but of such an objective, set out in terms of growth of the GDP per man hour, being a useful general statement of the sum total of aspirations in particular fields, both private and public, such as urban redevelopment, more generous social services, aid to developing countries, more private motoring, shorter hours of work, etc.; and at the same time an indication of what the total addition to resources must be if these objectives are to be attained.

It has been argued that this objective is itself incompatible with an economy still based largely on the market, since for the Government to pursue growth in this way may lead to the restriction of individual freedom and responsibility; individuals in society may not accept all the implications of faster growth, and in attempting to force it on them the Government may be led into escalating intervention. But this view would seem to exaggerate the value of individual as against collective choices (that is choices made by individuals acting alone as against those made by individuals acting together in groups); it begs too many questions about the methods by which the objective will be pursued; and if accepted would doom governments to complete impotence and irrelevance on the most vital economic issues. For a growth objective merely reflects individual and social choices; and a collective decision, through elected representatives, in favour of a better health service or more roads, or even more of everything in the future at the cost of some restraint of consumption in the present, is at least as valid as the sum of individual choices of more leisure, more cars, more gambling or more books.

To say that the growth rate should be the outcome of individual decisions to save and invest, so that the correct social choice between consumption now and in the future is obtained through the market, is to ignore the many changes in the economy which have already made collective action decisive in determining its future development. There has been a rapid growth in the present century in the range and quantitative importance of social and public goods. A wide range of activities from the production of nuclear energy to social security have, in almost all countries, become part of public enterprise. Private enterprise has at the same time been transformed, especially as a consequence of the growing cost of research and development, and the consequential technological economies of scale, so that decisions in many (but by no means all) industries are increasingly centralized. Even so, some of the largest units in private industry find it necessary to turn to the State for help in financing their major investments. Such changes may not be welcomed, but they cannot be ignored. Unless methods can be devised of reversing these trends, consideration must be given to the problem of how they can be accommodated without too much damage to the kind of society we wish to create. Secondly, a more general intervention by the State in economic life has come about because of the aggregate results of economic decisions that are still left to individuals. If aggregate decisions to spend add up to more than the total of resources available, the real decisions are ultimately taken either by the workings of inflation or by the State when it determines what shall be curtailed in order to cure the resulting crisis. The market disciplines that in theory would prevent such an outcome have long been eroded, if they ever were effective. The only real choice, therefore, seems to be between hasty governmental decisions under pressure, and governmental decisions carefully arrived at after full consultation with the individuals who make up society.

In the face of these changes there is a natural tendency to polarize the discussion of economic policy. Some left-wing thinkers enthuse over these developments, interpret them as historically inevitable, and proceed to validate their interpretation, arguing on the assumption that the apparent necessity of some increase of State activity in the economic sphere must indicate the desirability of yet more State intervention. Problems which no one has yet been able to unravel, and on which the relevant information is possibly not available, will somehow be solved if the Government tells firms and individuals what to do. On the right, the freedom or supposed freedom of the individual tends to be defended on all fronts indiscriminately, including the condemnation of quantitative national programmes and their concomitant institutions and governmental policies as representing a major step towards socialism. At best, there is an attempt to restrict policy far too narrowly on the basis of a distinction between market-oriented and plan-oriented interventions. The blind application of such principles on either side is ill-suited to finding a rational solution to the problems of the real world.

It would be more helpful to recognize the principles both of collective action and of individual liberty and enterprise, and to seek to apply each of them in the proper proportions in relation to each problem. The issue is one of securing the optimum combination of two objectives which are to some degree contradictory. We have to apply market principles wherever they will be socially useful, and there is undoubtedly great scope for their reinforcement in the private sector as well as for their extension to areas in the public sector where they have not yet been used, for example, in the pricing of roads. At the same time, it must be recognized that to apply market principles in every situation may not be possible, or may not give as good a result as collective decisions. In many cases the best solution may well be a combination of market and collective principles, based on a clear view of what each can achieve.

The reconciliation of new institutions and methods of long-term economic policy with traditional democratic procedures presents a number of serious problems. Little thought has so far been given to devising appropriate procedures that will enable long-term planning to be effective while at the same time subject to democratic decision. From the point of view of the economic policy-makers, a number of separate problems are raised. First, it can be argued that the whole atmosphere in which current democratic politics are conducted is little suited to the emergence of a rational economic policy. The constant concern of the ruling party to preserve its current popularity and to win the next election may lead to a number of distortions: for example, the economically irrational favouring or protection of certain sectors of the economy which are considered to be politically important, or what is sometimes referred to as the 'political business cycle', where booms are artificially encouraged in certain politically critical situations and are punctured afterwards. Secondly, the fact that in a democratic system such as the British, Governments may suddenly change, makes constancy of economic policy a problem. Here, of course, the extent to which the main parties disagree about the fundamentals of economic policy will determine the degree of discontinuity; in Germany, where Christian Democrats and Social Democrats have been even less divided about economic policy than the parties in Britain, the dangers of a sudden break have not been so severe. Thirdly, the demands of parliamentary control frequently make it difficult for the executive to make the necessary short-term adjustments of economic policy. This is particularly the case in the budgetary field, where parliament's traditional control of the purse sometimes makes it difficult to use tax or public expenditure policy as a short-term cyclical weapon, though various expedients have now been devised in several countries to overcome this problem.

These factors certainly impede the establishment of a rational and consistent economic policy. On the other hand any attempt to withdraw economic policy from the undesirable ambience of democratic procedures leads to the danger of irresponsible power. Some people are more concerned with the converse of the issues raised in the previous paragraph, namely, how to reassert democratic control over an economic policy which is considered to be gradually slipping out of the hands of parliament. The British National Plan, which was intended to shape economic and social policy to the end of the 1960s, was produced within the DEA, submitted to the NEDC in advance of publication, and then published. It was debated in parliament only after publication, and since it presented, in detail, only one plan for the legislators either to accept or reject, the parliamentary debate can hardly be regarded as having played a significant part in the process. This situation is similar to that in France during the first three plans, when the part played by the Assembly was almost negligible, its role being essentially that of a rubber-stamp after the Commissariat, the Modernization Commissions and the Economic and Social Council had finished their work. Following considerable agitation for an increase in the participation of the Assembly, its approval for the basic priorities of the plans is now sought at an early stage, according to the procedures developed in the Fourth and Fifth Plans, described on pp. 90–3. But for Parliament to retain some control over technical decisions is not necessarily the most effective safeguard for democratic control over economic planning. In Germany, an alternative policy has been pursued in some instances, according to which segments of policy-making have been handed over to independent institutions which are made to operate as closely as possible in accordance with objective rules, so that it is clear if they break their trust. Another method is to supplement parliamentary participation in economic policy-making by the increased participation of interest groups. This corporatist view is apparent in both France and Britain, where the Modernization Commissions, the Economic and Social Council and the Economic Development Committees are seen sometimes as providing effective and informed participation by the people in economic decisions. Whether this view is justified must depend on the extent to which these bodies effectively represent all the main interests affected by the decisions and on the degree to which they can really influence the views of the national planners and policy-makers.

In deciding what kind of economy and society we wish to create, it will be necessary to maintain a balance between efficiency and responsibility; decisions cannot be left to be taken irresponsibly by technical experts, nor inefficiently by responsible representatives. Competition is itself a form of democracy; where and in so far as it is replaced or controlled by intervention, new forms of democratic supervision must be evolved.

INDEX